The Politics of Counter-Terror

Studies in Asian Security

Abiding Influence: Presidents, Nationalist Beliefs, and US Policy in the Asia Pacific, 1898–1972
Giuseppe Paparella, 2025

China's Rising Foreign Ministry: Practices and Representations of Assertive Diplomacy
Dylan M.H Loh, 2024

Enacting the Security Community: ASEAN's Never-ending Story
Stéphanie Martel, 2022

Overcoming Isolationism: Japan's Leadership in East Asian Security Multilateralism
Paul Midford, 2020

These Islands Are Ours: The Social Construction of Territorial Disputes in Northeast Asia
Alexander Bukh, 2020

Asia's Regional Architecture: Alliances and Institutions in the Pacific Century
Andrew Yeo, 2019

Rebranding China: Contested Status Signaling in the Changing Global Order
Xiaoyu Pu, 2019

The Reputational Imperative: Nehru's India in Territorial Conflict
Mahesh Shankar, 2018

The Indonesian Way: ASEAN, Europeanization, and Foreign Policy Debates in a New Democracy
Jürgen Rüland, 2018

Hard Target: Sanctions, Inducements, and the Case of North Korea
Stephan Haggard and Marcus Noland, 2017

The Supply Side of Security: A Market Theory of Military Alliances
Tongfi Kim, 2016

Protests Against U.S. Military Base Policy in Asia: Persuasion and Its Limits
Yuko Kawato, 2015

For a complete listing of titles in this series, visit the Stanford University Press website, www.sup.org.

The Politics of Counter-Terror

Islam and Security in the Postcolonial Muslim State

Nicholas Chan

STANFORD UNIVERSITY PRESS
Stanford, California

Stanford University Press
Stanford, California

Library of Congress Cataloging-in-Publication Data
Names: Chan, Nicholas, author
Title: The politics of counter-terror : Islam and security in the postcolonial Muslim state / Nicholas Chan.
Other titles: Studies in Asian security
Description: Stanford, California : Stanford University Press, 2026. | Series: Studies in Asian security | Includes bibliographical references and index.
Identifiers: LCCN 2025042777 (print) | LCCN 2025042778 (ebook) | ISBN 9781503644168 cloth | ISBN 9781503647046 ebook
Subjects: LCSH: Terrorism—Malaysia—Prevention | Terrorism—Religious aspects—Islam | National security—Malaysia | National security—Religious aspects—Islam | Islam and state—Malaysia | Malaysia—Politics and government
Classification: LCC HV6433.M3 C43 2026 (print) | LCC HV6433.M3 (ebook)
LC record available at https://lccn.loc.gov/2025042777
LC ebook record available at https://lccn.loc.gov/2025042778

Cover design: Daniel Benneworth-Gray
Cover art: CEphoto, Uwe Aranas, *Kuala Lumpur Courts Complex, Kuala Lumpur, Malaysia*
Typeset by Newgen in Garamond Premier Pro 10.25/13.5

The authorized representative in the EU for product safety and compliance is: Mare Nostrum Group B.V. | Doelen 72 | 4831 GR Breda | The Netherlands | Email address: gpsr@mare-nostrum.co.uk | KVK chamber of commerce number: 96249943

Printed and bound by CPI Group (UK) Ltd, Croydon, CR0 4YY

Contents

Acknowledgments

They say a book finds its author. This book about ontological (in)security found a hopelessly introverted and chronically insecure one. I could have thanked a lot more people for commenting on the draft to make it better, but my hermetic ways had prevented me from sharing drafts widely. The silver lining is that I can now credibly claim all omissions and weaknesses are truly mine. Yet even a solipsistic work such as this one has taken a village to nurture, and, therefore, accumulated many debts along the way. I can only do my best to list my thanks and apologize in advance for those I invariably missed.

As political science remains a male-dominated field, I am incredibly proud that the primary mentors of this book are all leading female scholars. At Cambridge, supervisors Iza Hussin and Ayşe Zarakol inducted me into academia with signature patience, warmth, and openness. Iza's work prompted me to go *deep* to see how Muslim state making is underpinned by hybridities rather than simply following fixed models or typologies. Ayşe was my way into (historical) international relations (IR), and her intellectual footprint can be found throughout this book. By developing intuitive frameworks that speak to how those of us from the non-West relate to the world, Ayşe's work encourages me to go *wide* and explore how the domestic and the minute are imbricated with the global, in both effect and affect. Following exposure to her books and papers, I went from intending to say something about Malaysian counter-terrorism to having a lot more to say about the War on Terror.

At the Australian National University, Evelyn Goh's inclusive leadership and genuine intellectual curiosity probably played a big role in how I have decided to plant my feet in IR even as my scholarly identity continues to shapeshift. At my insistence, Evelyn, hopefully not reluctantly, ended up as the shepherd and gatekeeper for this book project as it developed further during my postdoctoral years. It is safe to say this book would not have arrived at this point without Evelyn's exacting and generous mentorship. She was helpfully impatient with the earlier versions of my work that came with a diffuse framework and a self-indulgent way of writing, knowing that I was not ready and understood the book had to mature with me. At the same time, she was also unflinchingly patient when I wasn't patient with myself, seeing progress I couldn't recognize on my own. The fact that I felt the person drafting the first version was very different from the one drafting the final speaks to the personal growth I gained working with Evelyn. All my mentors are not sticklers to the political science or IR canon. I hope this book's explicitly multidisciplinary nature bears that legacy.

Other friends and colleagues in academia served as comrades and cushions on this journey. Farish Noor was like a cigarette with teacher, friend, and cheerleader all rolled into it, always smoldering with wisdom and humanity. John Sidel gave this project and my career more time than I could reasonably ask for; he was like the supervisor I never had. At the ANU, Evelyn Goh, Iain Henry, Amy King, and Stuti Bhatnagar anchored my arrival; Brendan Taylor, Andrew Carr, Greg Raymond, Meighan McCrae, Tommy Chai, and Kyungwon Suh provided much-needed camaraderie in the Strategic and Defence Studies Centre. Joseph MacKay, Deepak Nair, and Greg Fealy, together with Farish and Evelyn, sat through presentations and workshops for this book. Maria Tanyag, Yingxin Show, Rohan Mukherjee, Andrew Phillips, Sarah Logan, Quah Say Jye, and Dylan Loh were generous with advice and support as I was, in true "dogs chasing cars" fashion, always finding my bearings in academia.

Friends and colleagues in Cambridge, like Dan Smith, Alex Grigor, Lucas de Oliveira Paes, Surer Mohamed, Tobias Müller, David Talbot, Hayane Dahmen, and many others were great sources of joy, support, and memories in the BC (Before Covid) era. The unparalleled pastoral support I received from St. Catharine's College blessed this project with an ethos of care and empathy since its inception. I began my journey as a social science neophyte at the S. Rajaratnam School of International Studies, with Farish Noor, Leo Suryadinata, Daniel Chua, Wu Fengshi, and others paving my entry. The Malaysian studies space was a comfort zone of chatter and support, with Ahmad Fauzi, Azmil Tayeb, Aziff Azzudin, Danny Lim, Daniel Teoh, Dina Zaman, Helen Ting, Hew Wai Weng, Huda Ramli, Imran Rasid, Meredith Weiss, Ooi Kok Hin, Patricia Sloane-White, Sumit Mandal, Teoh Ann Siang, and Tricia Yeoh offering either playful banter or profound insights, sometimes both, along the way.

The Tunku Abdul Rahman Scholarship made my doctoral studies at Cambridge possible, ensuring that I evaded the "offer without scholarship" heartbreak that plagued many aspiring scholars who came without means. The Tunku Bursary Fund, the Santander Mobility Grant, and the APSA Asia Workshop Alumni Grant generously supported my fieldwork.

Despite the bleak subject matter, this is a project defined by Malaysian (and Singaporean) hospitality. I was regaled by interlocutors, informants, and interviewees in both countries who were willing to spend precious time with this socially aversive scholar who often walked in as a stranger with nothing to offer and no reputation to boot. I owe my thanks to following individuals, in no particular order: Ahmad El-Muhammady, Mohd Mizan Aslam, Dobby Chew, Amir Abd Hadi, Ayob Khan Mydin Pitchay, Saifuddin Abdullah, Liew Chin Tong, Mujahid Yusof Rawa, Dina Zaman, Ezra Zaid, Afiq Md Noor, Akil Yunus, Ahmad Fauzi Abdul Hamid, Azmil Tayeb, Ben Suffian, Badrul Hisham Ismail, Saari Sungib, Zairudin Hashim, Faisal Aziz, Jasminder Singh, Mohamed Imran Mohamed Taib, Mukhriz Mat Rus, Tan Sian Hoo, Adli Zakuan, Syahredzan Johan, Thomas Koruth Samuel, Ustaz Wan Ji Wan Hussin, Ustaz Zamihan Mat Zin al-Ghari, and Zan Azlee. Unfortunately, not every interviewee can be named for reasons of security and privacy. As an interpretive scholar, I should also say that I have taken reasonable interpretive license in processing these interviews; therefore, all misrepresentations and misunderstandings are strictly mine. *Minta maaf*, but above all, *terima kasih!*

The Studies in Asian Security Series at Stanford University Press is the best home this book could ever hope for. Amitav Acharya and David Leheny were my first ports-of-call, while Dan LoPreto was unbelievable in his patience, enthusiasm, and dedication. The two anonymous reviewers provided critical interventions, as well as injected much-needed confidence for this project. I was deeply grateful to be supported by the editorial team every step of the way. They saw a book when I was still working on one. Parts and versions of the argument developed in this book have appeared in the articles "In Moderation Of 'Strangers': Terrorism, Ontological (In)Security and Counter-Narratives In Malaysia," *Critical Studies of Security* 8, no. 1 (2020) and "Rethinking the Causes of Islamisation: Ontological (In)security, Postcoloniality, and Islam in Malaysia," *Journal of Southeast Asian Studies* 51, no. 3 (2023). I thank the journals and their publishers for the permission to revise and reuse those contents.

My family bookended everything I have done. I was fortunate to have parents who didn't demand that I explain my life choices—only that I demonstrate passion and ethics in all I do. My dad constructed a house of books before I started writing mine. As someone who could not afford a university education, Dad self-taught the ways of being a college-educated parent. He read persistently to his children, which was atypical for someone of his class background. My mom bore witness to my pathological single-mindedness since I was a kid, nurtured it into a strength, and loved me selflessly in spite of the absent-mindedness that came with it. She might not always understand my choices or ambition, but she knew I had to do it. My younger sisters, Yue and Ying, are like a reactor of joy, jokes, and jest. They held the fort of our parental home when this absent brother never quite lived up to the (admittedly very "Chinese") standards of being the "heir." Always formidable and wise, they were the "adults in the room" that I never grew into, and I am incredibly proud of them.

Lastly, Yih Shean, my partner who could effortlessly turn any journey into an adventure and any dwelling into a sweet home, deserves a standing ovation for putting up with a workaholic and the many tribulations of being an academic spouse in this brutal job market. Her indomitable strength, optimism, and kindness anchored me in the little things even as my work and intellectual horizons grew in scale and complexity. For being my blanket, my nucleus, and the source of my ontological security, I dedicate this book to her.

Nicholas Chan
August 2025, Canberra

The Politics of Counter-Terror

INTRODUCTION

"Islam Has Nothing to Do with Terrorism, Yet Counter-Terrorism Has Everything to Do with Islam"

> We are committed to fight Daesh, IS, Al-Qaeda, Abu Sayyaf—you name it. They are the enemy of the United States, they are also the enemy of Malaysia, and we will do our part to make sure that our part of the world is safe. We will also contribute in terms of the ideological warfare because you need to win the hearts and minds. And the key to it is to support moderate and progressive Muslim regimes and governments around the world, because that is the true face of Islam; that is the authentic face of Islam. The more you align with progressive and moderate regimes, the better it would be in terms of winning the hearts and minds of the Muslim world.
>
> —Najib Razak, Meeting at the White House, 2017[1]

Najib Razak, then prime minister of Malaysia, made the statement above when he met with then-President Donald Trump at the White House, a day after the sixteenth anniversary of the September 11 attacks. In the speech, Islam was couched in the language of "ideological warfare." "Moderate and progressive" Islam was treated as the ammunition needed to win the hearts and minds of Muslims against violent jihadism. Najib's speech also placed Malaysia discursively on two war fronts:

one where the terrorist is the enemy *external* to all of international society, and the other where the terrorist is a problem *internal* to Islam, making Malaysia's contribution as an insider ("the true face of Islam") an especially valuable one.[2] Such weaponization of "moderate Islam" is not uncommon among Muslim state elites.[3] For example, the Saudi crown prince spoke about ridding the world of Islamist terror and restoring "moderate Islam."[4] The Jordanian minister of religious affairs warned that clerics were "ground forces against extremists" and must preach "moderate Islam or else."[5] Through various initiatives, the Moroccan state positioned itself as a "model of moderate Islam" that served as a counterweight to jihadist violence in the Sahara.[6] These campaigns prompt the question, is promoting moderate Islam an actual counter-terror strategy? If so, how is "moderate Islam" operationalized? And if not, why does the idea of moderate Islam continue to gain social currency in international security debates?

Critics may dismiss this line of inquiry if they see the discourse of moderate Islam as nothing more than a red herring for the political agenda of Muslim elites, namely, a "PR campaign" for soft power pursuit and a smokescreen to "distract from the political reforms at home."[7] In Najib's case, it is arguable that his endearment to Trump was due to the need to deal with the Department of Justice's investigation of the 1MDB corruption scandal.[8] Be that as it may, my fieldwork reveals that *counter-terror in Malaysia has everything to do with Islam*. Even if religion's role in violence remains a contested issue,[9] Islamic institutions, actors, and expertise are deeply embedded in Malaysia's practices of counter-terror, not least informing the assumptions about what caused Muslim radicalization and how to remedy it. In other words, there appears to be a security logic that drives state elites and security practitioners to see Muslim radicalization as a problem in need of *religious* intervention. This logic undergirds a phenomenon I call the *Islamization of security*, whereby Islam becomes the optic through which the problem of "terrorism" is processed; the body of knowledge from which counter-terror "expertise" is constituted; and the object to be governed to secure the body politic.

This notion that security is "Islamized" invokes another term commonly found in critical security studies: the *securitization of Islam*. The securitization of Islam is a matter of considerable research that generally revolves around how conceptions of "Muslimness" are treated as both an existential threat and a site of intervention in Western societies after September 11.[10] However, Sarah Logan's findings that counterradicalization policies are linked to racialized notions of citizenship means that Muslim-majority states confront a different dynamic when contending with homegrown Islamist terrorism.[11] Yet, how Islam is interwoven into counter-terrorism in these settings where Islam occupies a central role in politics and governance (as in the case of Malaysia) remains underexplored. Given that Muslim states are critical to any effort to address the phenomenon of Muslim militancy and the threat of violent groups such as the Islamic State (IS) and Al-Qaeda, relying on Western cases to understand that the security logic in Muslim states is clearly not going to be productive for both theoretical and policy purposes.[12]

This book explores the origins of Malaysia's "Islamized" security logic but takes one step further to investigate how the logic affects counter-terrorism on a daily operational level. Arguing that the security logic employed in Malaysia's counter-terrorism is a combined product of status politics and governmental problem solving, this book challenges the idea that counter-terrorism is fundamentally about securing physical security for states. It does so by highlighting how ontological security concerns of status and identity infuse Malaysia's counter-terror discourses and practices, not least the worldviews of policymakers and practitioners. Indeed, the concept of ontological security serves as the thread that connects this book's multiscalar analysis of religion and security. Treating counter-terrorism as an ontological security seeking exercise means dealing with macro- and mesolevel questions of international hierarchies, religion, and state building, on the one hand; and microlevel observations of governmental practices that constitute the counter-terror regime, on the other.

Departing from instrumentalist readings that often view counter-terror politics as a domain where state actors seek to maximize realist interests of power seeking and profit making, this book charts a historical and constructivist account where neither materialist nor culturalist factors predetermine religion's incorporation into state security. On a theoretical level, it argues that the security logic behind Malaysia's counter-terrorism must be understood from its positionality as a postcolonial Muslim state that had to partake in a "war" that stigmatized Islam. This interrogation of the religion-security relationship as unfolding within a global security architecture necessitates an interdisciplinary view of counter-terrorism that connects theories from international relations (IR) and governance studies with insights from area studies scholarship on Islam and state building in Muslim societies. On an empirical level, my findings illustrate how counter-terrorism in a postcolonial Muslim state is entangled with larger questions of status, identity, and postcoloniality—entanglements that come with practical consequences as they trickle into practices of governance.

In tracing the origins of the "Islamized" security logic found in Malaysia's counter-terrorism, this book also sheds light on the relational and productive dimensions of security. In my case, counter-terrorism is *relational* as state epistemologies concerning Islam and violence are not a product of "scientific" inquisitions but rather of Muslim elite thinking as they grapple with Islam's marginality in prevailing global hierarchies—an issue tied to their status concerns. Counter-terrorism is productive because, as the security logic grounds Muslim radicalization in theological explanations, it *produces* the entity of the "terrorist" ontologically to render the problem of terrorism legible and manageable through a security framework that equates regulating Islam with regulating Muslim behavior. These fruitful explorations of religion and security are only possible if we adopt a different understanding of the *politics* of counter-terrorism, one that takes into account the institutional history of a postcolonial Muslim state and the international social geography it found itself in.

Finding the "Political" in Counter-Terror
A Distraction or a Front?

The literature on counter-terrorism can be broadly categorized into *institutionalist* and *legalist* accounts. The institutionalist literature explores an array of externalities, factors, and critical junctures that shape counter-terror responses of the state. They include normative contexts, institutional legacies, organizational dynamics, and even the emotional responses of leaders.[13] Conversely, legalist accounts scrutinize the legal frameworks of counter-terrorism and its legality, often measuring them against normative standards such as human rights or the rule of law.[14]

In these two bodies of work, the idea that we should think about the "politics" of counter-terrorism usually elicits two conclusions. First, in all its "irrationality," politics will drive counter-terror policies away from "rational" utilitarian goals, such as preventing radicalization or terrorist attacks. For example, McConaghy argues that the assassination of Louis Mountbatten had a significant impact on Margaret Thatcher. It led to an "increasingly muscular counter-terror campaign" that stoked the fire between the British state and the Irish Republican Army to burn "for another decade and a half."[15] In another study of the United Kingdom, Foley calls the period between 1995 and 2001 "Londonistan," arguing that a mild threat perception, an alleged "covenant of security," and a context that warranted "sensitive treatment of minority communities" culminated in "Britain's toleration of Islamist radicals" to its own detriment.[16]

The second viewpoint sees the politics of counter-terror as essentially *counter-terrorism politicized*, jettisoning any concerns for accountability and human rights in the process. In other words, counter-terrorism is merely a front to fulfill the interests of political actors. For example, scholars of law and legal ethnography have written about the "September 11 effect" as one that legitimized, normalized, and transmitted not just problematic legal norms and provisions but also extralegal and extrajudicial renditions of security governance.[17] Less-forgiving accounts accuse this security architecture as a (neo)imperialistic project, pinning it on a neoconservative agenda that turned Washington's Global War on Terror (GWOT) into "everybody else's."[18]

Unlike in Western states where the politics of counter-terror often meant Islam demonized, in Muslim states, counter-terror politicized usually meant *Islam politicized*. On this matter, the relatively thin literature about counter-terrorism in Muslim states still echoes the two interpretations of counter-terror politics above. Islam is understood as either a distraction to achieving "real" counter-terror objectives, or a "front" to conceal the fact that ostensibly counter-terror programs actually serve a separate set of realpolitik interests altogether—an accusation often leveled at campaigns that promote moderate Islam.[19] The "distraction" thesis can be seen in Henne's comparative study of counter-terrorism in forty-seven Muslim states.[20] He concludes that states facing strong influence from religion, such as Pakistan, will exhibit reduced cooperativeness with the US in counter-terrorism. Inversely, states characterized by weak state-religion ties, such as Türkiye and Egypt, tend to be more cooperative.[21] The implicit assumption here is that this reticence to cooperate with the US as a result of religion-state ties are departures from "effective" counter-terrorism.

Conversely, country studies that examine state religion as the theater of counter-terror usually lean toward the "political front" thesis. Wainscott attributes the bureaucratization of Islam and its institutionalized "reforms" in Morocco to "political opportunism" that capitalized on the GWOT to enable the state to take greater control of the religious domain to preserve its power and legitimacy.[22] Similarly, Feuer's work on the regulation of religious education in Morocco and Tunisia also characterizes these measures supposedly geared at counterradicalization as "authoritarian regimes' strategies of political survival."[23]

Two Gaps: The "Whos" and "Hows" of Counter-Terrorism

Important as the aforementioned perspectives are, their conception of counter-terror politics are ultimately self-limiting. The limitations stem from a lack of engagement with two questions the literature hinted at but did not address. The first concerns the *epistemologies* behind counter-terror practices. For example, both Wainscott's and Feuer's study of Tunisia and Morocco observes that terrorism is "viewed as a religious problem, rather than a political one" or as "fundamentally a problem of [religious] ignorance" (my addition).[24] Whereas one may argue that this obsession with regulating religion is about Muslim regimes consolidating power, it is also conceivable that they are expressions of a *security logic*: state actors approaching "counter-terrorism" based on their understanding of the problem. Bartolucci has highlighted that elite perceptions about terrorism have significant implications;

King Mohammed VI's distinction between "good" and "bad" Islam has led to efforts devoted to the teaching of the former in Moroccan schools.[25]

My point here is not to stress that a clean policy/politics binary exists. Rather, it is to recognize that if counter-terror is operationalized as a project of religious reform, regulation, and curation, there must be a political space in which such knowledge claims are made, contested, and reproduced. Considering that it is far from certain that correcting one's religiosity is the appropriate way to address the political phenomenon of Islamist extremism,[26] understanding the sociology of such knowledge is crucial, more so when scholars have shown that the habitus of terrorism studies is laden with significant prejudices, interests, and biases.[27]

Plausible explanations of where this "Islamized" understanding of terrorism originated have come from scholars theorizing the episteme of the GWOT. Those from the critical terrorism studies subfield attribute the global securitization of political Islam to a "hegemonic security narrative" that emerged from the US-led GWOT.[28] Critical scholars of religion such as Hurd and Mahmood locate this strategy of cultivating "moderate" Islam to defeat "radical" Islam within an "international political economy of good religion" (or, in Mahmood's reading, a cultural imperialist project) that operates under the belief that good governance has to "identify and nurture religion's transformative and benevolent powers while softening or disciplining its exclusionary edges."[29] The legacy of colonialism also features prominently in explorations of postcolonial security logics. Alzubairi argues that counter-terror laws in Arab states are merely "an extension of colonial policy under the new cloak of neo-colonialism," whereas Hussin sketches a "legal geography" that saw colonial legal frameworks and postcolonial law making sharing a legal logic that conflates "religious freedom, religious harmony, public order, and national security."[30]

Although Islam's securitization that resulted in a "moderate versus radical" binary is observed in Muslim states too, there is no evidence to suggest it came from uncritical adoptions of Western framings. To the contrary, through their own "moderate Islam" campaigns, Muslim states such as Malaysia have positioned themselves as veterans in managing "bad" religion, with the implicit message being that the West are latecomers to the game.[31] In my interviews, I did not find local counter-terror practitioners in Malaysia to be unthinkingly embedded in the Western-centric "international political economy of good religion" described by Hurd.[32] In fact, many of them have misgivings about the GWOT's anti-Muslim biases and the true intentions of its perpetrators. To be sure, I do not dispute that colonial legacies and neocolonial pressures are factors that drive many Muslim states to readjust toward the West's security agendas. Yet, considering the anxieties and ambiguities Muslim actors harbored toward the GWOT, we must dig deeper to understand how and why these analogical security logics got made and reproduced in a postcolonial Muslim state such as Malaysia in the first place. What are the political, institutional, and epistemic structures that sustain them?

The second gap in the literature concerns the issue of ontology. Here I refer to two conceptions: In a narrower sense, *ontology* refers to the intersubjective knowledge that "constitutes identities and interests."[33] In a broader sense, it encompasses visions of how the world is (and ought to be) that underpin social understandings of the agent-structure problem and, by extension, all social action.[34] If we conceptualize counter-terror as discursive practices undertaken by state actors qua state, then there is undoubtedly a social ontology that underlines these conducts. Unsurprisingly, constructivist accounts of counter-terror seem most interested in untangling this question of identity and meaning when "counter-terrorism" is conducted in the name of states. Löwenheim, for example, argues that the US's punitive campaign against Al-Qaeda is "in essence a *disciplinary* effort to reestablish and reproduce the relations of authority that existed in world politics prior to 9/11."[35] Mendelsohn claims that counter-terror is ultimately about international society defending the "sovereignty-based system" from the onslaught of terrorist groups acting as system-challenging actors.[36]

However, these accounts only address the issue from either the perspective of Great Powers, or from a universalist view of the "international." They say very little about counter-terrorism undertaken within, and in the name of, Muslim states. They also do not address what an epochal event such as the GWOT, with its popularization of Islamophobia, meant for Muslim state actors who had to perform counter-terrorism that, besides having a functional role, also manifested intersubjectively as a global security agenda.[37]

This lack of engagement with the social positionality of Muslim elites within the international order has implications for the research designs and conclusions drawn in studies about Muslim states and counter-terrorism. See, for example, Henne's study of Muslim states and counter-terrorism referenced above, which is one of the most comprehensive studies on the topic.[38] The research design takes Muslim states as the independent variable and their counter-terror cooperation with the US as the dependent variable. The latter is seemingly treated as a proxy to assess a state's commitment to counter-terrorism. Whereas I am not disputing the methodology of the study per se, the research design is rather illustrative of the political environment Muslim states found themselves post-GWOT. Despite diverse political, social, and historical associations with Islam, Muslim states still end up occupying a similar suspect position within international society, whereby any deviation from "Western" interest is automatically taken as a liability.

This Western-centricity is again replicated in this view that discourses of moderate Islam are instruments of "religious soft power," that is, Muslim states promote "moderate Islam" as "a way of appealing to Western nations and affirming their counter-terrorism credentials."[39] Even as they contain some grains of truth, these interpretations that focus on power and interest tend to fuel this stereotype of the "shrewd" Muslim autocrat.[40] They put little thought into analyzing how counter-terrorism in Muslim states (and by Muslim practitioners) are responding to a habitus that stigmatizes Islam and their Muslim identity, let alone the concrete ways in which these social factors influence the security logic that informs counter-terror practices.[41]

To simplify, the two gaps identified above primarily concern the "whos" and "hows" of counter-terrorism. These questions underpin the social, institutional, and contingent foundations of security logics, highlighting the inseparability between pursuits of physical security (threat elimination) and ontological security (recognition and identity stability). The "who" question is primarily about the social ontology of the "Muslim state" as a counter-terror actor. Addressing it requires us to consider seriously the historicity of the postcolonial label of the "Muslim state" and the social position of Islam within the cultural hierarchy of the modern international order. Approaching the issue from the ontology of the state also necessitates critical engagements with historical conceptions about religion, violence, modernity, and political order, all of which contribute directly to modern understandings of terrorism.[42] Lastly, dwelling in the "who" question also pushes us to recenter the GWOT within the perspectives of Muslim state actors without simplistic inferences about how their "Muslimness" is an asset or liability to counter-terror objectives.

Addressing the question of *how* one "wages" the GWOT in the name of a Muslim state is, in many ways, the harder question to tackle. It demands a rigorous empirical contribution from a field usually shrouded in secrecy. To open up this black box, this book adopts a historically informed and practice-oriented view of counter-terrorism that examines how institutionalized conceptions about religion and violence are translated into an array of governing discourses and technologies. Analytically, the former engenders placing state security within a broader history of state building, while the latter necessitates a "thick" description of how the subject of the "terrorist" is constructed and deconstructed in multiple counter-terror sites.

Central Argument and Contributions

Arguments

This book explores how Islam ended up so entrenched in Malaysia's counter-terrorism. The entrenchment is scrutinized via two phenomena: *the securitization of Islam* (a governmentality that takes guiding the interpretation of Islam as an imperative of security) and the *Islamization of security* (the embedding of Islamic actors, metaphors, and reasoning in daily practices of security). I argue, to understand these two phenomena, one must wrestle with Malaysia's positionality as a self-identified Muslim state in the post-GWOT international order, on the one hand, and the mechanisms of security governance that constitute "counter-terrorism," on the other. This constructivist anchor does not mean treating "terrorism" as a mere fiction of the powerful, but it does require us to shed the notion that counter-terrorism can ever be a neutral technical product resulting from straightforward "science-to-policy" translation, something anthropologists and sociologists have long debunked.

This book uses the Malaysian case to make two broader arguments about counter-terrorism and Islam. First, counter-terrorism is an enterprise deeply imbricated with the *status concerns* of Muslim state elites who found themselves immersed in a global civilizational discourse that casts the "Muslim terrorist" as the universal enemy.[43] As this book will demonstrate, the Malaysian establishment's concern with Islam's stigmatized status is not new. This long-standing concern, nevertheless, laid the institutional groundwork for Islam's securitization, leading to a governmentality that saw the best way to govern Muslims is through governing Islam. I chart this development by tracing a parallel process since the 1980s, whereby the more the Malaysian Muslim elites sought to counter Islam's stigmatization through statist institutionalization of "modernist" forms of Islam, the more (deviant) religiosity became the frame through which state elites narrated the cause of Muslim radicalism. Furthermore, I illustrate the resilience of such thinking by tracing its manifestation in the post-GWOT era, specifically between 2013 and 2019, when Malaysia had to deal with hundreds of IS-linked arrests. Through a close reading of counter-terror paperwork and interviews with security practitioners, policymakers, activists, and lawyers, I highlight how an "Islamized" security logic that concerns itself *with guiding and moderating interpretations of Islam* has infused all aspects of Malaysia's counter-terrorism, from public messaging to law enforcement, and from judicial discourses to rehabilitation programs.

The second argument is that counter-terrorism, when understood as governance, is not just a physical-security-seeking exercise. In counter-terrorism, the state governs as if it knows how radicalization happens, thus performing the ontological security-seeking function of making legible the "terrorist." In the case of Muslim-majority and institutionally Islamized Malaysia, which cannot "other" the Muslim terrorist, state narratives must delineate what distinguishes a Muslim radical from the "normal" pious Muslim who constitutes the core constituency of the body politic. Using primary sources that relate to daily operations of counter-terrorism, I uncover how the assumption that Muslim radicals are religiously "deviant" or "misguided" is central to the ways in which the Malaysian state demystifies the "terrorist" in biopolitical, judicial, and rehabilitative terms.

These two motives of ontological security seeking—one about securing recognition, the other about conjuring biopolitical clarity—are not incompatible. Rather, when understood together, they illustrate a politics of counter-terror in Muslim states that is as concerned with socionormative considerations of status and identity as it is with the *problématique* of governance. Tracking these processes provides an analytically eclectic and empirically rich account of how Islam's embedding in Malaysia's counter-terrorism is informed by a macrohistorical context that underpins Islam's stigmatization in the postcolonial international order, a mesoinstitutional history that witnesses Islam's institutionalization by the state, and microgovernmental practices that reflect the reasoning and worldview of elites and security practitioners in Malaysia. Such is the multiscalar view this book offers that separates it from the more conventional accounts of counter-terrorism found in IR and security studies.

Contributions

This book's ambition goes beyond providing a single-country, in-depth study of counter-terror. Rather, it engages with scholarship in historical IR, historical sociology, religion and politics, critical security studies, and governmentality to theorize how religion, identity, and postcoloniality feature in the security thinking and practices of Muslim states, as well as in Muslim state behavior in general. By conceptualizing security making in a Muslim state through the prisms of Muslim recognition seeking, developmentalist state building, and governance, this book makes three theoretical contributions.

The first contribution this book makes is to the War on Terror literature, which rarely interrogates what the GWOT meant socially for Muslim state elites and security practitioners who had to partake in it *as Muslims*, and how that affected the ways in which counter-terrorism is practiced as a form of governance. Not engaging with Muslim positionality is a glaring omission, given that the globalization of Islamophobia post-GWOT is well documented.[44] As much as it is difficult to believe that Muslim state actors are not affected by Islam's stigmatization as if they are some apathetic Machiavellis who care only about realpolitik interests, instrumentalist readings of Muslim state behavior still prevail. For example, Muslim state participation in the GWOT is often interpreted as acts of bandwagoning to curry favor with the West, if not as a front to silent local dissent. These depictions are not untrue, but my research problematizes them by showing that, despite being active collaborators in the GWOT, Muslim elites and security practitioners are profoundly affected by Islam's stigmatization. These sentiments can be found in foreign policy narratives and even in localized counter-terror discourses. Even if this study is about Malaysia specifically, its insights about status, stigma, and differentiated experiences of global governance projects that often run along the global North/South lines will be instructive for those working on areas such as climate change and pandemic management that, like the GWOT, is afflicted with the same issues of identities and hierarchies.[45]

This book's second contribution is that it offers a novel analytical framework to explore how religion matters in domestic and foreign policy without reducing it to either a set of theological beliefs and impasses, a sacred referent object, or an insuperable line dividing different communities of faith. Using an ontological security framework, the book highlights the relational processes that continually shape Islam's position in Malaysia's security governance. It shows that Islam's embedding in Malaysia's counter-terrorism is not a product of identity per se but rather tied to a sigma-correction agenda pursued by Malaysian Muslim elites that began long before the GWOT. I argue that the long-term preoccupation and insecurity of these elites with Islam's perceived incompatibility with "civilized" industrial modernity informed their thinking about the state-religion relationship and drove specific trajectories of statist Islamization. These developments, in turn, influenced how Muslim radicalism is articulated in domestic security discourses. By showing this duality where Islam is treated as both a source and solution to the felt stigmatization of these elites, this book also complicates identitarian views of ontological security that often take Islam as an identity stabilizer simply because it provides a sense of "Islamic collectiveness" to Muslims.[46]

The third contribution this book makes is to studies of Islam's securitization by offering a case study of a Muslim-majority state where Islam's intertwining with security is not, as in many Western settings, fraught with Islamophobic assumptions and prejudice.[47] Even as many Western states appear to have shared the same security logic with Malaysia that links religiosity to radicalization,[48] this book demonstrates that the construction of this security logic can take widely divergent paths. Whereas counter-terror efforts in the West are often associated with efforts to integrate the Muslim "other,"[49] I argue that the security thinking in Malaysia's counter-terrorism originated from a legacy of modernist state building that sees chaperoning and curating the masses' understanding of Islam as its mandate.

Moreover, I contend that treating these distinctive developments under the same rubric of the "securitization of Islam" conceals important differences. One overlooked dynamic found in Malaysia is the "Islamization of security," whereby security discourses are infused with theological stakes. Counter-terror practitioners in Malaysia not only think that security is about safeguarding the correct interpretation of Islam (and, by extension, Islam's good name); they also believe that the best way to govern Muslim political agency is through programs and policies that regulate the parameters of Muslim religiosity itself. This dynamic is clearly different from "secularized" forms of security thinking found in the West that saw overexpressions of Islamic piety as a potential risk factor. Thus, contrary to the popular opinion that counter-terrorism must always be undertaken at the expense of Islamic actors and movements (as in the case of Egypt and Saudi Arabia), this book brings to attention a case where counter-terror actually created more incentives to Islamize the state.[50]

To sustain its theoretical interventions, this book also makes a substantial empirical contribution through its granular tracing of *what states actually do when they claim to be "countering terror."* Through primary sources, I track Malaysia's counter-terrorism across a plurality of sites (e.g., in government offices, courts, mosques, policing, and prisons) and objectives (from law enforcement to counterradicalization and rehabilitation). For this purpose, I devise an original framework that maps Malaysia's counter-terror practices across three functional domains: prevention (state narratives about terrorism), preemption (judicial practices that ascertain "guilt"), and rehabilitation (practices commonly known as "deradicalization"). To my knowledge, this book is the first to offer comprehensive coverage of a counter-terror regime, differentiating it from the literature that usually only offers a segmental view, such as focusing only on counter-terror laws, deradicalization programs, counterradicalization messaging, and so on.[51]

This emphasis on comprehensiveness is not for its own sake. Rather, it helps us visualize how a security logic that treats terrorism as a product of religious deviancy or misguidance has permeated the counter-terror regime in Malaysia. Such a claim can only be made convincingly if one undertakes an interpretive study of the discourses of "terrorist making" within the mundane operational world of counter-terrorism, as opposed to moments-defining, elite-level speech acts favored by Copenhagen School approaches.[52] In other words, this book is as much an exercise in excavating the minutiae of security as it is about deciphering an overarching security logic.

Why Malaysia?

Three reasons underline why Malaysia is a promising case study to understand Islam's role in counter-terrorism. First, Malaysia enjoys the reputation of being a "bastion of moderate Islam" and is widely regarded as highly successful in its counter-terror efforts.[53] Even during a wave of IS-affiliated attacks across the globe in the mid-2010s, the only successful terrorist attack in Malaysia was a haphazard attack on a bar in 2016.[54] On the surface, this looks like a remarkable achievement when compared to the high-casualty attacks that happened in the region, such as in Bangkok (2015), Jakarta (2016), and Jolo (2019), or those in Europe, such as Paris (2015), Ankara (2015), Brussels (2016), and Manchester (2017).[55] Malaysia's ostensible counter-terror success was frequently attributed to its Islamic moderation, as illustrated by a US Congressional Report that asserts, "Malaysia is a moderate secular Islamic nation whose experience and cooperation could play a key role in coping with Islamic extremism, countering terrorism, and exerting a moderate influence on the Islamic community in Southeast Asia."[56]

At the same time, the reputation of moderate Islam is a product of the Malaysian government's active promotion.[57] Two prime ministers who came into power after September 11 had headlined their administration with some form of "moderation" slogan. They include the Islam Hadhari campaign by Abdullah Badawi, Malaysia's fifth prime minister (2003–2009), and the Global Movement of Moderates and the Wasatiyyah (Islamic Moderation) project by Najib Razak, the sixth prime minister (2009–2018). Thus, interrogating the Malaysian case allows for scrutiny of Islam's actual role in counter-terrorism (if any), and a rethinking of what these campaigns of moderate Islam meant *socially* for a Muslim state that found itself in the post-GWOT security order.

Second, Malaysia offers a more "pristine" view of our primary object of study: the security logic underlying counter-terror practices. The practice of counter-terrorism in Malaysia is unencumbered by counter-insurgency, messy geopolitics, and even mainstream politics. Unlike Indonesia, Thailand, or the Philippines, Malaysia does not face a separatist insurgency that has taken up an Islamist inflection.[58] Moreover, Malaysia's distance from conflict zones in the Middle East and North Africa region frees its counter-terrorism from the sectarian and geopolitical intrigues that have engulfed states such as Iran, Iraq, Türkiye, Syria, and Libya following the Iraq invasion and the Arab Spring. Thus, counter-terrorism in Malaysia is more comparable to domestic counter-terror policies in Western states than in many other Muslim states because the main priority is dealing with the specter of radicalization within the population rather than combatting a well-defined political foe conducting sustained armed resistance.

Mainstream politics in Malaysia also overlaps with counter-terrorism to a far smaller degree. Unlike in Egypt, Saudi Arabia, Tunisia, and Morocco, counter-terrorism has never been used as an excuse for the mass arrest of Islamists in Malaysia.[59] That is not to say Malaysia does not have its share of politically motivated crackdowns. Nevertheless, since the end of the Communist insurgency in the 1980s, counter-terror was never cited as the primary reason for sweeping political crackdowns, nor was the primary target of such crackdowns Malaysia's main Islamist party, the Pan-Malaysian Islamist Party (PAS).[60] Not only was it not forced underground or crippled by authoritarian repression, but PAS has also gained massive political ground throughout the years. It held the highest number of parliamentary seats since the general elections in 2022 and even enjoyed a short stint in government (2020–2022).[61] This tolerance of Islamization by a ruling ethnonationalist party is part of our puzzle, as we shall see in chapter 3.

Third, in recent years, Malaysia's counter-terrorism has an opening that offers the researcher a rare, if imperfect, glimpse into a world usually shrouded in secrecy. The period of this book's empirical focus is set in a so-called IS wave of terrorism (2013–2019), which coincides with a time when the Malaysian government was relatively open to providing information about its counter-terror operations. Malaysia's IS wave marks the beginning of a phase where terrorist offences were tried in court following the abolition of the Internal Security Act in 2012, which had enabled detention without trial in the past.[62] Vivid reporting by the media was possible as the police force was more open to sharing data. For example, counter-terror raids during this period were often followed by statements from the police that outlined the number of arrests made, the location of the arrests, and the age, sex, and even occupation of those arrested. Sometimes, the police even furnished photographs of the operations. Many Preventing/Countering Violent Extremism (P/CVE) materials were made accessible, including a manual detailing the deradicalization program.[63] This newfound transparency created a win-win situation. The authorities could capitalize on the fact that most terrorist suspects were tried in open courts to deflect criticism that counter-terrorism was just a front for political suppression. The researcher could interrogate the visibility of Malaysia's counter-terrorism as a form of politics itself, aligning with this book's interest in the intersection between counter-terror and status seeking in Muslim states.

Framework and Methodology

Tracking Counter-Terror Across Three Levels

From the outset, it should be noted that this book is not concerned with finding the correct definition for terrorism, nor is it about assessing counter-terrorism from a policy efficiency point of view.[64] My focus is on how state actors perform this discursive practice known as counter-terror, which, as an intersubjective policy endeavor, is necessarily political, hermeneutical, and entangled with operational concerns. Instead of joining the chorus of definitional debates,[65] I define counter-terror simply as forms of actions propagated by the state when it claims to be "countering terror." By *forms of actions* I refer to "the particular ways that security works in relation to its subjects, whether individuals or populations."[66] As this book is concerned with Islam's stigmatization, the only form of terrorism I will discuss is Islamist terrorism.

Counter-terrorism can also be understood as what David Scott calls a "problem space": "an ensemble of questions and answers around which a horizon of identifiable stakes (conceptual as well as ideological-political stakes) hangs."[67] For our purposes, it is the terrain on which the relationship between religion and security is articulated, contested, and translated into governance. But a meaningful understanding of the *politics* of counter-terrorism—one that covers its social and moral currency as an international security agenda, its political-ideological stakes, and its operational logics—requires a careful understanding of the two "worlds" it inhabits. On the one hand, there is a social world of states where status and identity matter. On the other hand, there is also a governmental world where assumptions of human behavior must be operationalized in problem-solving practices. These two terrains are interconnected yet operate on different rhythms and logics. For example, in the international social world, Malaysia is a Muslim state dragged into a counter-terror "war" not of their own making yet demanding of their strategic and normative allegiance, even as its religious identity is sometimes viewed suspiciously. In the governmental world, the Malaysian state has complete control of the operational machinery that translates the rhetoric of "war" into technologies of governance, rendering the problem of "terrorism" legible, logical, and amenable to the daily operations of the state.

To uncover the institutional origins and hermeneutical content of Malaysia's "Islamized" counter-terrorism in this complex setup, this book executes a three-level analysis. The first level is the *macrohistorical,* which situates the GWOT historically within an international hierarchical order that enables Islam's globalized stigmatization in the first place. Peering into this level of analysis involves looking at how postcolonial Malaysian Muslim elites wrestle with the judgment of history about Islam's supposed incompatibility with industrial modernity and how that conditioned their thinking about Islam's place in governance and modernization. The second level concerns the *mesoinstitutional,* where one examines how trajectories of state-led Islamization in Malaysia have created a security apparatus that habitually drew Islamic actors and injunctions into security practices and reasoning. For the third level of analysis, I track counter-terror on a *microgovernmental level,* that is, to the capillary sites of state power, and interrogate them as preventive, preemptive, and rehabilitative practices that constitute Malaysia's counter-terror regime.[68] These sites include courts, law enforcement, P/CVE campaigns, prisons, and mosques. My interest lies in how these practices are informed by—as well as themselves informing—specific conceptions of violence, radicalization, religion, and the Muslim body that ended up producing the "Islamized" security logic observed.

My goal here is not to establish definitive causal relations between the three levels. Rather, I embrace an epistemological position Sil and Katzenstein call "analytical eclecticism": an eschewing of parsimonious theory testing in favor of tracing "problem-specific interactions among a wide range of mechanisms operating within or across different domains and levels of social reality."[69] One observes this in how my three-level analysis navigates Islam's complex relationship with state security as historical, institutional, and hermeneutical. Instead of concrete variables, the framework corresponds with the social geographies that contextualize the Malaysian state's experience with the GWOT: one in which it must both seek and provide ontological security via discourses that counter Islam's stigmatization, on the one hand, and clarify the "problem" of Muslim radicalization to the populace, on the other. As will be illustrated in the next chapter, tracing religion and counter-terrorism across these interactions will entail a methodological suturing of a global-historical analysis of the international environment, a historical institutionalist dissection of Malaysia's state-religion relationship, and an interpretive analysis of governing narratives employed in the quotidian practices of counter-terror.

As Ditrych puts it, "there is no terrorism beyond the discourse of terrorism."[70] My focus on security logics, or, to use another term, the hermeneutics of counter-terrorism, necessarily elevates the importance of discourses. I define *discourse* broadly as "the space where intersubjective meaning is created, sustained, transformed and, accordingly, becomes constitutive of social reality."[71] However, discourses cannot be analyzed solely as a given set of texts within a vacuum. The intertextual and intersubjective nature of discourses necessitates my research design's historical, multiscalar, and multisite nature, so that "counter-terror" does not get boxed in as an ontological given. To be sure, my methodology does not hinge on an emancipatory ethos like that of the critical discourse analysis tradition.[72] As chapter 1 elaborates, it is grounded instead in an ontological security framework that approaches discourse as biographical narratives that are constitutive of the state's self-identity and as ordering narratives that translate counter-terror into performances of governance.

Methods and Sources

To illuminate the making of Malaysia's "Islamized" counter-terrorism across space and time, this book engages a multimethod research methodology. The method applied in each chapter is subjected to the site and level of analysis, as well as the theoretical lens taken. For example, while chapter 2 explores the relationship between state and religion in postcolonial Malaysia through a historical institutional analysis followed by a sociological study of early postcolonial elites, chapter 3 examines Islamization in Malaysia during the Mahathir era through a biographical analysis of Mahathir's political thinking, institutional analysis of Islamization, and discourse analysis of state narratives produced in response to incidents of Islamist militancy. Chapter 5 is a "thick" study of Malaysia's counter-terror regime that relies on detailed institutional mapping and discourse analysis of the narratives generated for Malaysia's P/CVE campaign. Consequently, chapter 6 follows Malaysia's counter-terrorism into the paperwork of courts, barracks, and prisons, while the concluding chapter draws from publicly available sources to construct an original biographical database of 130 individuals to assess the efficacy of Malaysia's "Islamized" counter-terror policies using a cursory sociological analysis of Malaysia's "IS problem."

If there is one guiding principle behind this book's eclectic approach, it is an ethnographic sensibility that is equal parts interpretive and excavatory.[73] My interpretive methodology is driven by a constructivist, "thick" understanding of the social that appreciates the interpellations between language, meaning, and context.[74] The excavatory nature of my research is made necessary by its heavy reliance on primary sources (e.g., practitioners and paperwork) to visualize counter-terrorism at the operational level. The clandestine nature of counter-terrorism also necessitates creative excavations to retrieve materials, as they are not found in centralized archives. It also compels intertextual readings to make sense of a trail of disparate findings illuminating Malaysia's counter-terror regime. Responding to the cliché that P/CVE needed a "whole-of-society" approach, my methodology also aims to capture Malaysia's counter-terror regime in a manner that covers its self-proclaimed comprehensiveness.[75] Nevertheless, it does so without losing sight of the interpretive value of these findings. That is, their ability to show how the relationship between Islam and security is directly influenced by local perceptions of international hierarchies as well as modern ideas of governance.

This book drew from three categories of sources. The first category consists of secondary sources in IR, international history, religion and colonialism, state sociology, and studies of contemporary Islam in Malaysia. These sources outline the historical, global, and domestic context leading up to the GWOT. The next category of sources are snapshots of Malaysia's counter-terrorism in action. They are mainly textual, albeit occasionally videographic, and are made up of state publications, PowerPoint slides, official statements, speeches, white papers, legislation, news reports, videos of seminars and interviews, and court documents. The third category consists of forty-nine semistructured interviews with a range of interlocutors involved in counter-terrorism in Malaysia and Singapore, including security officials, government bureaucrats, research officers, clerics, academics, public prosecutors, attorneys, family members of detainees, one former detainee, judges, ministers, human rights activists, and so on. Through snowballing, I tried to cover all the state institutions involved in Malaysia's counter-terrorism, from foreign affairs to policing, from religious institutions to the policymakers, and from the prosecution to the judiciary.[76] For reasons of security and access,[77] I decided not to pursue interviews with detainees and former detainees and opted to study detainee perspectives through proxy sources such as news reports, personal writings by detainees, court documents, activists, defendant lawyers, police officers, and family members.[78]

Despite this book's interest in understanding Malaysia's counter-terrorism from a structural and historical-institutional angle, it relies heavily on primary sources. Many of the sources I used are in Malay because they were explicitly aimed at a Malay-Muslim audience, such as an army guideline about identifying potentially radicalized soldiers, or *khutbahs* (Friday sermons) to be disseminated around mosques. These sources offer insights into the endogenous aspects of Malaysia's counter-terrorism, contrasting with the foreign policy narratives typically articulated in English, which often adopt a more cosmopolitan tone. To be sure, I do not rank sources by their audiences but rather seek to cover both elite discourses about counter-terror and Islam that are more rhetorical in nature and operational narratives generated for the purpose of "doing" counter-terrorism. I make no distinction between "talking shop" discourses and actual practices, acknowledging them as parts of a habitus in which counter-terrorism gains social meaning. Indeed, the most titillating discoveries come in the form of recurring themes that permeated the discourses (no matter their level or audience), such as the insistence that Islam is compatible with "rational" scientific modernity, or that Muslims got radicalized because they "misinterpreted" Islam. These findings reveal how postcolonial Muslim subjectivities are central to security thinking in Muslim states.

Fieldwork Notes

The fieldwork that contributed to this book was conducted in a nine-month period (January to September 2019) during the administration of the Pakatan Harapan (Alliance of Hope) government, which marks the first time a political transition at the federal level has happened in Malaysia.[79] Whereas that was an unexpected development for the researcher, the administration change facilitated the expanded access this research enjoyed. Having a new government enabled my informants to claim a degree of separation from past practices and, thus, be more critical in their opinions as civil servants. However, studying security, especially in an area such as counter-terror, puts me in a position where my work can have grave consequences for my informants. This is particularly true for civil servants who live with the wide-ranging powers of Malaysia's Official Secrets Act, and for family members whose loved ones were still in prison.[80] Having access to parties with competing interests—prosecution and law enforcement on one end, defense counsel and human rights activists on the other—also means that I have to tread carefully so that my access does not become a liability for my informants, more so for the nonstate actors.

Thus, I have taken the position to anonymize most of my informants even if they have not requested it, as long as my judgment is that exposure might adversely affect the individual. I also quote information from publicly available sources whenever possible instead of my interviews. This book's sparse citation of interviews does not diminish their role in the inductive research process. Interview data are instrumental in cross-checking information and gaining insights into the worldviews of security practitioners, including judges, public prosecutors, policymakers, police officers, government researchers, and rehabilitation experts. They also afford texture and context to the documents cited.

Book Overview

This book is organized in three parts: theory (chapter 1), history (chapters 2 and 3), and the GWOT-inflected present (chapters 4 to 6). They each cover different spatial and temporal dimensions of Malaysia's politics of counter-terror to trace the origins and workings of Malaysia's "Islamized" counter-terrorism. Chapter 1 lays out the conceptual framework that employs ontological security as the primary lens through which counter-terrorism's relationship with Islam in Malaysia is analyzed in this book. The framework brings the state's ontology back into our study of counter-terrorism, arguing that we can grapple with counter-terror meaningfully as a *social* practice only through understanding the state simultaneously as context, actor, and practice. In this understanding, the GWOT's nature as a moral exceptionalist discourse, Islam's position in the international order, and the identity of the state and the "terrorist" all matter in the formation of security logics.

Chapter 2 serves as the historical chapter that discusses how the question of Islam became a source of ontological insecurity for Malaysia's early indigenous elites. Through a sociological analysis of these elites' "insider-outsider" status, I show how they ended up in this situation where they felt insecure about being perceived as both too "Islamic" and not enough so. Chapter 3 dives into the tenure of Mahathir Mohamad, Malaysia's fourth and longest serving prime minister (1981–2003), to illustrate how his efforts to address this insecurity have led to state-building processes that ended up securitizing Islam. The first half of the chapter engages with Mahathir's writings about Islam and nation building as early as the 1970s and notes how the desire to correct Islam's stigmatization was translated into specific trajectories and forms of statist and modernist Islamization in the 1980s and 1990s. The second half of the chapter highlights how Mahathir's project to build an Islamic yet modern Muslim society has trickled into a security order that treats any kind of Muslim radicalism as a product of "deviant" religiosity.

Chapters 4, 5, and 6 wrestle with Malaysia's counter-terrorism in the post–September 11 milieu. Unlike later chapters, chapter 4 focuses on the foreign policy dimension. It chronicles Malaysia's entry into the post–September 11 era, demonstrating how countering Islam's stigmatization was on the minds of three successive administrations as they championed various permutations of the idea of "moderate Islam." These discourses also revealed how Malaysian Muslim elites struggled between speaking for the stigmatized Muslim world and claiming Malaysia's distinction from it. Chapter 5 turns to the workings of Malaysia's "Islamized" counter-terror regime, focusing on the years between 2013 and 2019 when Malaysia was dealing with hundreds of IS-linked arrests. The first half of the chapter highlights how religious authorities and experts have claimed and monopolized the authority to speak about IS in Malaysia. Such "claiming" happened through the release of legally binding fatwas, the increased role of Islamic agencies in counter-radicalization efforts, and an institutional preference for the ulamas (Islamic scholars) and the religiously learned to serve as counter-terror experts. The second part delves into the consequences of this "Islamized" habitus.

Chapter 6 retains chapter 5's focus on ground-level counter-terrorism but addresses a different set of questions. How does the state make "terrorism" governable? How are ideas such as counterradicalization or deradicalization operationalized, and what are the knowledge formations behind them? By analyzing the paperwork of counter-terrorism, the chapter demonstrates how biopolitical, judicial, and rehabilitative discourses made legible the "terrorist" in Malaysia's "Islamized" counter-terror regime. It captures how bureaucracies, courts, and prisons established the entity of the terrorist in a language of anatomical and behavioral certainty, and how efforts of prevention, preemption, and rehabilitation were operationalized based on cognitive-behavioral understandings of the radical as a religiously weak or misguided person. Finally, the conclusion summarizes the book's argument and reflects on its broader theoretical implications in studies of security and securitization, Muslim state behavior, and religion and ontological security in IR. I also made a policy intervention by highlighting the blind spots in the Malaysian government's diagnosis of the "IS problem" through a sociological survey of the Malaysian "radicals" based on original data.

ONE

On Stigma and Strangers

Ontological Security, the Muslim State, and Counter-Terror

This book argues that Malaysia's "Islamized" counter-terrorism is a product of a politics that transpired in three geographies: a macrohistorical context that situates the Global War on Terror (GWOT) within a discursive economy that intensified Islam's stigmatization, a mesoinstitutional history that structures the state-religion relationship, and microgovernmental practices that translate counter-terrorism into governance. As we shall see, these political processes are underpinned by the *ontological security needs* of postcolonial Muslim state building and security governance. To analyze how ontological security concerns fed into the institutional and discursive linkages between Islam and security in Malaysia, we will need a conceptual framework that performs three functions.

The first is to locate counter-terror in the three geographies noted above while recognizing the porosity between them. For example, the framework must be able to make sense of the relationship between Islam's stigmatization on the global level and Islam's securitization within the governance of Muslim states. Doing so means traversing multiple analytical domains: postcolonial Muslim elites' understanding of Islam's position in the modern international order, the state-building courses they charted as a result, and the governing narratives that address the problem of Muslim "radicalization" on a daily practical level. Second, the framework must contextualize the two security outcomes that are of particular interest to this book. They are: *Islam's securitization*, referring to Malaysia's increased institutional control over Islam and its active deployment of the idea of "moderate Islam" in security discourses; and *the Islamization of security*, where security governance is structured around a theological understanding of the "Muslim radical" as a religious deviant. Third, the framework must methodologically integrate the variety of empirical sources used—from secondary findings in the historical sociological literature to primary data and fieldwork findings—to shed light on the social and institutional origins of Malaysia's "Islamized" security logic, and the way it gets operationalized as governing practices.

This chapter unpacks my conceptual framework in three sections. The first section argues that approaching the state as simultaneously *context*, *actor*, and *practice* enables an understanding of counter-terror as relational to the macrohistorical context, as embodied by the state as the primary institutional actor, and as operational through an assemblage of governing technologies. Recognizing a statist ontology without internalizing its a priori assumptions grants us the analytical flexibility to understand Malaysia's politics of counter-terror beyond instrumentalist and technocratic framings that prioritize elite self-interest and problem solving. This nested conception of the state also treats religion as a variable that is not external to, but immanent within, a statist environment.

The second section unpacks the concepts of ontological security and stigmatization that are key to this book's theorization of counter-terrorism within Muslim states. It outlines how the GWOT functions as a moral exceptionalist discourse that exacerbates Islam's historically stigmatized status in the modern international order. I draw from and refine the ontological insecurity literature about the non-West in international relations (IR) to highlight the anxieties of the postcolonial Muslim body politic— an issue that is rarely addressed in the literature. This predicament is then applied on insights about state-religion relationships, showing how stigma correction has long been an elite motivation behind Islam's institutionalization and securitization in many Muslim states.

The third section establishes the postfoundationalist theory of governance to ground my fieldwork observation of Malaysia's "Islamized" counter-terrorism where Islamic actors, reasoning, and idioms pervade counter-terrorism on the microgovernmental level. I lay out the modern state's function as an ontological security provider and argue that counter-terror is best understood through an interpretive study of governing narratives. These narratives will have to grapple with the Malaysian Muslim terrorist's status as an ontological "stranger," as it is a hermeneutic problem for the Muslim state that cannot be easily externalized and expunged through identity "othering" discourses. Last, I present a case for understanding counter-terrorism as discourses of subject making within a security assemblage framework that both resolves the question of *where* to study counter-terror and sustains our interest in the uncovering of *security logics.*

The Counter-Terror State as Context, Actor, and Practices

To foster a relational view of counter-terror that can accommodate this book's multiscalar explorations, I propose a theory of the state that deconstructs it as three simultaneous "conditions of being":[1] the state as *context* (stateliness, or a system of states, as the prevailing ontological environment where counter-terrorism constitutes a meaningful activity), the state as an *actor* (referring to the state as the social agent performing counter-terrorism), and the state as *practices* (in that counter-terror is made up of diffused practices that reify the national security state).[2] Through this nested conception of the state, I make a case for studying counter-terrorism that, instead of surrendering truth claims about terrorism uncritically to statist epistemologies, asks the following question: When ontological claims of "terrorism" are made in the name of the modern state, what are the forms of knowledge and social relations (between states as well as between the governing and governed) they assume and engender? These questions link the social construct of the state to the security logic that manifests as counter-terrorism.

The Looming Image of the State: The State as Context and Actor

Migdal's conception of the state as a duality of image and practice best captures my approach that locates the politics of counter-terrorism within the productive tensions of the state as context, actor, and practices.[3] In Migdal's formulation, the state is an "image" because it exists as a homology that exists "from state to state," in the perceptions of "those inside and outside its claimed territory," and as an entity distinguishable and delineated from other states and the society it governs.[4] This image of the state points to the modern state both as a ubiquitous product of historical sociological developments and as distinct territorial entities. This image presides over the systemic environment in which "terrorism" gains intersubjective meaning. The context of stateliness, in that a system of sovereign states constitutes the international order, is the backdrop within which certain forms of terrorism can be, as Zarakol puts it, "purposefully threatening."[5] How threatening terrorism can be is inadvertently linked to a set of historically contingent ideas regarding sovereignty and legitimate violence; boundaries between state and nonstate, civil and military; and the position of religion in the international order as a "common social imaginary."[6]

The image of the state also looms over the frameworks and categories we use to understand terrorism. Foreign fighters of terrorist organizations are grouped by their national origins. Domestic and international terrorism are interpreted as distinct typologies in categorizing terrorism.[7] States are recognized as the sole counter-terror actor and are condemned harshly if they are found to have sponsored terrorism. The stigma placed on terrorism-sponsoring states does not just reflect a moral disdain toward terrorism; it also assumes an ontological and dialectical separation between the state and terrorism, wherein the modern state, through counter-terror, fulfils a moral purpose of its own (as we will see later).[8] Such moral claims often justify further monopolization and expansion of state violence, which, in its severe forms, can even take on the appearance of "well-intentioned" social engineering, as in the case of China's Xinjiang policy.[9]

Besides counter-terror actors, statist epistemologies also entrap those targeted by counter-terror actions. For instance, Li's study of the *mujahids* (combatants of jihad) in the Bosnian war revealed how, notwithstanding their rhetorical claim of independence, the "legal conditions of the sovereign order" continue to structure "contemporary jihads and the challenges they [the *mujahids*] faced."[10] In short, counter-terror politics is inherently about making, preserving, and reproducing political orders, with the state's image in performance and at stake. To think that there is a realm where counter-terror *actually occurs* and that the rest is just "politics" is to negate the fact that without the context of the international state system and the state as its key referent, *there is no counter-terrorism one can speak of.*[11]

In this book, the image of the Malaysian state exists in counter-terrorism not just as a security provider but also as a historical actor that claims a biographical existence through space and time.[12] My point here is not that states function as unitary actors. Rather, this image of the state as a temporally coherent social actor gave rise to a form of state personhood upon which biographical and ascriptive identities ("Muslim," "democratic," "Third World") and emotive qualities (such as national pride or shame) can be ascribed and invoked.[13] Ascriptive and affectional invocations obviously matter in structuring the international politics of counter-terror. For example, Malaysia's counter-terrorism necessarily concerns Malaysia's projected image as a responsible member of international society, as a postcolonial Muslim state that enjoys a reputation as a "moderate Islamic country,"[14] and as a role model of successful counter-terrorism.[15] Nonetheless, these images can only be understood in relation to the historicity and configuration of the international order that perpetuated Islam's stigmatization, which I will come back to in a later section.

The State as Practice: Knowledge, Governance, and the Disassembled State

Migdal's theorization of the state as practices dissolves the idea of a unitary state and argues that it is the "routine performance of state actors and agencies" that continuously reifies the image and presence of the state.[16] This conception supports our discussion in a later section on the need to disaggregate "counter-terrorism" and visualize it as an assemblage of institutions and practices. Disassembling the state into practices also releases our understanding of politics from the usual institutionalist focus on groups and interests. This practice-oriented view redirects our focus toward the security logic institutionalized and rationalized by these practices. In other words, the politics of counter-terror at the level of practices is mostly about the politics of *knowledge*, or, in Bourdieu's terms, "state forms of classification" that denominate the landscape of terrorism expertise.[17] Such knowledge practices can be seen in Preventing/Countering Violent Extremism (P/CVE) campaigns, judicial practices, and deradicalization programs that collectively compose the counter-terror regime.

James Scott's idea of "state simplifications" is undoubtedly most illustrative of a kind of high modernism that informs counter-terror practices.[18] The idea of P/CVE is, after all, about reducing "radicalization" into its governable bits, not least fueled by a penchant for social engineering that is best encapsulated by confident claims of being able to "deradicalize" a person. Yet, the epistemologies that emerged in counter-terror discourses and practices are not simply products of schematization or technical debates. They are inevitably bound to broader conceptions about religion, civility, and violence grounded within the ontology and epistemologies of the modern state. In other words, opting for a disassembled view of the state does not entail a poststructuralist view that abolishes the state's historical ontology that looms over counter-terror practices. Rather, as Lemke argues, "Political and sociological knowledge, operating with dualisms like individual and state, knowledge and power, and so on, plays a constitutive role in the emergence and reproduction of concrete forms of statehood."[19]

Acknowledging the looming *image* of the state in counter-terror *practices* means reconciling with the fact that the discursive relationship between counter-terrorism and Islam cannot be enacted without any reference to national interests, notions of good citizenship, or ideas of sovereignty.[20] As we will see in the empirical chapters, operational discourses of counter-terrorism in Malaysia, technical as they may appear, often ended up framing terrorism as harming the nation's (and Islam's) reputation, or as acts of disloyalty toward state leaders and symbols.

Managing Dualities: The Counter-Terror State as Performative and Practical

In recognizing the state as both image and practice, I disregard the binary between approaching the modern state as a unitary actor or disassembling it as governmentality. Instead, I propose that what gives meaning to counter-terrorism as a practice of state security revolves around a social ontology that relies on *stateliness* as the grounding principle of the international order; the state as an autonomous social *actor* vis-à-vis other states (and society); and the state as having a diffuse presence reified by an assemblage of *practices*.[21] In this nested conception of the state, my analysis of Islam and counter-terror does not rely on the two having an independent/dependent variable relationship. Rather, I argue that the intersection between Islam and counter-terrorism happens at two conjunctions for the postcolonial Muslim state. The first conjunction lies between the macrohistorical and mesoinstitutional, wherein statist concerns of identity and status drove the securitization of Islam institutionally and discursively. The second conjunction takes place between the mesoinstitutional and microgovernmental. Islam's integration into governance at the mesoinstitutional level sets the context for microgovernmental practices that manifest themselves as "Islamized" security, namely, the infusion of theological input and stakes into security reasoning. The next two sections will address these two conjunctions, respectively.

Given the nested conception, one might ask, is it possible to maintain these three levels of analysis as a coherent whole? Peter Jackson's discussion of the "regime of images" during the making of the modern Thai state provides an instructive example here.[22] By showing how the expansion of bureaucratic power advanced alongside an orchestration of "national performances of 'civilized' behaviour for foreign consumption" in nineteenth-century Siam, Jackson made a case for thinking about governmental practices (or indeed, performances) as naturally bifurcated into its "parallel local and international components."[23] As I will show in the later chapters, localized knowledge practices of counter-terror in Malaysia are similarly filled with obsessions about status, civility, and "good" religion that only matter if one considers the international social environment. The element of the audience—be it real or imagined, global or local—anchors the intersubjectivity of counter-terrorism as a discursive practice. State performativity, therefore, can tell us a lot of about counter-terrorism as a broader security milieu, and as a discursive vessel for elite and practitioner worldviews. This interest in performances also explains why my analysis of Malaysia's counter-terrorism departs from measuring it against any normative ideals and is largely unconcerned with the issue of state hypocrisy.[24] My interest is in the intersocial aspects of security, where questions of identity and status are pivotal to shaping security logics and practices.

Ontological Security, Stigmatization, and the Global War on Terror

This section establishes why counter-terrorism can be understood as an enterprise of ontological security seeking for the postcolonial Muslim state. It is ontological security seeking because counter-terrorism is intertwined with status concerns due to the intensified stigmatization of Islam felt by many Muslim elites (and indeed, the Muslim population writ large) post-GWOT. To begin understanding this sense of stigmatization, one must first address the GWOT's presence as a moral economy.

Wars on Uncivility: The Moral Exceptionalism of the Global War on Terror

The authoritarian norms instituted by the West post-GWOT, such as the Patriot Act and extraordinary rendition, are often blamed for the globalized erosion of civil liberties and human rights because they justified the controversial security laws and repression of dissidents in many non-Western states, including Muslim ones.[25] In this reading, the GWOT's expansion is depicted as a scenario of socialization. Perceptions of common interests, be they defined narrowly as regime security or broadly as the preservation of the Westphalian international order, are assumed to be behind the widespread adoption of the GWOT's security paradigm.[26] For example, Alzubairi characterizes the convergence between the West and Arab states in their increasingly militarist and exceptionalist counter-terror practices as happening under the cloak of "neo-colonialism."[27]

However, this view of the GWOT as a bandwagon that everyone hops on is complicated by the enterprise's *singular* focus on the Muslim terrorist, whose "Muslimness" is often treated as an essential part of the terrorist's pathology.[28] Thus, explaining the dynamics of Muslim states' participation in the GWOT as socialization is incomplete because it only accounts for identity differences in the international order without commenting on the nature of such differences. For example, we instinctively understood why the United States needed Muslim state partners in the GWOT (which means identity differences matter). However, given negative Muslim sentiments toward the GWOT, why would a Muslim state like Malaysia gladly play that part? That is the less-explored dimension.

The GWOT's impact on Islam's status in the international order should not be understated. According to anthropologist and legal scholar Darryl Li, the GWOT has been the "key organizing principle for the world order" for over a generation.[29] Nevertheless, that the GWOT has such staying power as a security paradigm is not because of the brute force of its chief perpetrator, the United States. The US has, in fact, suffered significant status loss due to the scandals and military adventurism conducted in the name of counter-terror.[30] Indeed, the (at least initial) global resonance with the GWOT is more likely due to its moral exceptionalist nature. That is, the campaign advanced as a discursive economy that carried with it a "modernizing" agenda of vanquishing incivility, unreason, and unimaginable evils— an agenda with both moral and political resonance.

Discourses in the early years of the GWOT are the most revealing of such a moral imperative. For example, in 2006, renowned IR scholar Barry Buzan described the GWOT as "international society against global uncivil society."[31] In this interpretation, the Islamist terrorist is implicitly portrayed as the "metaphysical" and "universal" enemy—an entity that "threatens humanity (civilization)" because it is "exceptionally prone to morally inferior and inhumane forms of enmity and violence."[32] In making Islam the qualifier to this universal enemy, the discourse fused readily with Huntington's Clash of Civilizations thesis. However, instead of Huntington's theory of civilizational incompatibility, the conventional understanding is that Islam's "bloody borders" mark the frontiers of civilizational decline.[33] This cultural indictment of Islam underpins the religion's stigmatization.

Scholars have long argued that terrorism is defined in dialectical opposition to the modern state that is imagined as this vehicle for social, moral, and material progress.[34] In this conception, terrorism is morally "evil" and "fanatical" because it tosses "the values and achievements of civilization to the wind."[35] Tracing discourses about terrorism from the 1930s to the 2000s, Ditrych identifies three "basic discourses"—"*civilization/barbarism*, *order/chaos*, and *political enemy/hostis humani generis*"—all of which assume conditions of *stateliness* and the organization of *statehood(s)* as a priori to notions of good and justice.[36] He argues that these discourses are integral to the constitution of "sovereign reason, which recognizes itself by excluding madness and chaos from the realm of 'civilization' and domesticates men in particular territorial sovereignties, where autonomy of reason can be established."[37]

However, states do not define terrorism from a position of epistemological assuredness. Zarakol made a vital intervention here by arguing that certain forms of terrorism fueled ontological insecurity within a statist order because they assault "the modern (state) project of reducing indeterminacy through classification and comparison."[38] "System-threatening" types of terrorism, such as the wave of anarchist terrorism in the early twentieth century and later transnational jihadism spearheaded by Al-Qaeda, are the most *ontologically threatening* to modern states because their claims of legitimacy cannot be "accommodated within the Westphalian order."[39] The ontologically threatening nature of groups like the anarchists and later Al-Qaeda explains how they ended up stoking a security discourse that depicts these actors as enemies of humanity.[40] This exceptional treatment of Al-Qaeda and IS contrasts with the less morally compromising label of "banditry" afforded to the Communist militants in Malaya, who arguably threatened the colonial government even more at their zenith but were seen as less threatening ontologically due to their nationalist goals.[41]

If (certain forms of) terrorism is understood as this threat to humanity, it is no surprise that counter-terrorism has historically underpinned the extraordinary expansion of state power and the institution of a global security architecture. The real and perceived threats of anarchist terrorism in the late nineteenth and early twentieth centuries and jihadist terrorism in the early twenty-first century led to a global counter-terror campaign that saw an ever-growing consortium of states coming together against a common "evil," which culminated in the establishment, diffusion, and integration of intelligence networks and security laws.[42] Whereas the International Anti-Anarchist Conference of 1898 witnessed the attendance of the "whole of Europe" and led to the eventual creation of the International Criminal Police Organisation (Interpol),[43] it was during the GWOT that the world finally witnessed a war on "terror" that enjoyed actual international participation via a truly global policing network.[44] The GWOT's rallying call of universal humanity led to its easy franchising. Even states that have long disputed US global hegemony, such as China and Russia, answered the call enthusiastically, with Xinjiang being the GWOT's more recent transplantation.[45] Put differently, the maxim of "We do not negotiate with terrorists" reached its apogee with the GWOT, for the discursive construction of "Muslim terrorist" as an incomprehensible and unspeakable evil precluded the issue from any political redress.[46]

Nevertheless, the low entry barrier to the GWOT unites international society as much as it divides it. Despite having rallied common purpose through the establishment and proliferation of counter-terror laws, agencies, and partnerships, the moral exceptionalist discourse of the GWOT also sharpened the *differences* in identities within international society, with the "civilized" and the "rest" separated along a line marked by Islam. This division does not breed conflict but rather the awareness of a status hierarchy: one where the Muslim identity is rendered ontologically distinct, politically suspect, and culturally inferior.[47] The proliferation of counter-terror discourses globally also led to the normalization and exacerbation of Islam's stigmatization, intensifying perceptions by Muslims and non-Muslims alike of Islam's suspect, or even pariah, status in the international order.

For Muslim states like Malaysia that have embraced Islam as part of their state identity following decades of Islamization, the stigmatization of Islam was felt particularly acutely.[48] It was not just a subjective experience, because accompanying the global hunt for "terrorists" was an audit regime that systematically scrutinized Muslim states in terms of their distance from "radical Islam" as well as their commitment to and capacity for counter-terror. For example, the US State Department's annual Country Reports on Terrorism covered a range of competencies, including "legislation, law enforcement, and border security," countering terrorist financing, "countering violent extremism," and "regional and international cooperation."[49] Individuals, charities, schools, companies, and organizations were screened against sanction lists with thousands of entries.[50]

Under the "with us or against us" mentality of the Bush Doctrine, Muslim states were placed under extra scrutiny for suspicions of sponsoring jihadist terrorism. Pakistan and Saudi Arabia, both key allies of the US in the Cold War, were named as prime suspects.[51] Despite Malaysia's well-regarded status as a "key partner" to

US counter-terrorism, it was also subjected to several humiliating instances.[52] Malaysian Muslim students in the US reportedly had their visas denied.[53] The deputy prime minister was forced to take off his shoes and belt at airport security, and the administration had to proactively counter reports of Malaysia being a "safe haven" for terrorists to shield it from economic repercussions.[54]

Muslim states have demonstrated awareness of the stigma in their active responses. One notable example is the formation of the Islamic Military Counter Terrorism Coalition (IMCTC) in 2015 to defeat the Islamic State (IS), which comprised forty Muslim states (including Palestine).[55] The coalition stated its goal as to "present a unified front against terrorist organisations" and to "reaffirm the moderate values of Islam and its principles of peace, tolerance and compassion."[56] Military involvement, however, was limited to just a few member nations. Interestingly, the coalition's host, Saudi Arabia, had claimed on the IMCTC website that it launched the second-highest number of airstrikes against IS after the US in Syria.[57] This need for rhetorical boasting suggests that the Saudi state was compensating for having to live with the ignominy of being the second-largest foreign fighter contributor to IS,[58] not to mention the constant comparisons made between its Wahhabi state and IS's self-declared caliphate.[59]

The fact that Muslim states need to display their resolve against IS despite there being a Global Coalition against Daesh (led by the US with participation from most of Europe and the Arab World) is rather telling.[60] It reveals a double logic in operation. On the one hand, like any other states, Muslim states perceived IS as the universal enemy whose reach, norms, and practice threatened a global order operating under Westphalian notions of territorial sovereignty, citizenship, and legitimate violence.[61] In other words, the threat was recognized on a *political* level. On the other hand, this need for Muslim states to combat IS separately under the banner of Islam also reinforces this idea that IS was an *internal enemy*: an enemy that could sully the reputation of all Muslim states by the very fact that Islamist terrorism was seen as "especially barbaric" by world leaders.[62] Notably, some of the writings in that period did not even try to distinguish between violent and nonviolent Islamists, let alone their internal differences, when making pronouncements like "Barbarism 2014."[63] IS's ability to position itself as out-of-bounds with civilization in global opinion made it threatening to the Muslim elites on an *ontological level*. It is to this problem of ontological insecurity that we will turn to next.

The Problem of Ontological Insecurity: Colonialism, Stigmatization, and the Muslim State

ONTOLOGICAL SECURITY IN INTERNATIONAL POLITICS

The experience of stigmatization disturbs our sense of ontological security. But what is ontological security? It is a concept first proposed by psychoanalyst R. D. Laing, who describes an ontologically secured person as someone confident of his "integral selfhood and personal identity."[64] This sense of self should be differentiated from ascriptive identities like race or religion, as "identity here still presumes continuity across time and space; but self-identity is such continuity as *interpreted reflexively* by the agent" (emphasis mine).[65]

According to Giddens, an agent's capacity to "keep a particular narrative going" is vital to maintaining ontological security.[66] However, this process of enacting a biographical continuity is anxiety ridden because "feelings of self-identity are both robust and fragile."[67] Giddens explains it as such: "Fragile, because the biography the individual reflexively holds in mind is only one 'story' among many other potential stories that could be told about her development as a self; robust, because a sense of self-identity is often securely enough held to weather major tensions or transitions in the social environments within which the person moves."[68]

This tension of maintaining the integrity of the self between the agent's reflexive monitoring and the constitutive influence of the social "other" is later adopted in IR to study state behavior from the ontological security perspective. Key to this shift is a seminal paper by Huysmans, which argues that security practices have an ontological function as they "order social life"; more importantly, they are cultural practices that establish "a meaningful life in the face of death."[69] This existential conception of security imbues state actions with a dimension of critical reflexivity and led to a burgeoning line of ontological security scholarship in IR, covering topics from foreign policy to nationalism and to the problem of race in state identity construction.[70]

One important contribution of the ontological security literature is that it interrogates the relationship between identity and state behavior not in terms of cultural determinism but rather in how identities are performed, renegotiated, and routinized in biographical narratives that construct and correspond to a historical self-identity of the state.[71] Narratives are important because "conceptually, the 'idea' of the state cannot exist without this narration to develop a sense of continuity. The reason states have an ontological security is because they have a historical account of themselves that has been 'built up' through the narrative of agents of the past, present, and the future."[72] Put differently, the state's existence is almost biographical, as narratives about interest, security, and governance are employed reflexively to continuously justify the existence of some form of state personhood.[73] This interpretation of the state enables us to understand why affective notions such as shame, anxiety, and guilt matter in international politics. Emotions, if we can call them that, are instrumental to the ontological security of state actors because they underwrite a "consistent sense of 'self'" in a state's actions.[74] Ontological insecurity arises when state actions are perceived to be "incongruent with its sense of self-identity," eliciting emotional responses such as guilt and shame.[75] As Steele demonstrates convincingly, living up to one's own standards to avoid ontological insecurity is a significant factor behind the "humanitarian, honor-driven, or moral action" of Western liberal states.[76] Nevertheless, identity-action inconsistency is not the only source of ontological insecurity for states.

Stigmatization, Colonization, and the Muslim State

If the problem for the "West" is not being able to live up to one's own standards, the problem for the "rest" is that they must live under the shadows of standards created by others. These concerns are part of an identity struggle, which saw many from the non-West struggling to become "authentically non-Western."[77] To understand this predicament, the concept of stigma in international politics is crucial. Theorized by IR scholar Ayşe Zarakol, who borrowed from Goffman's theory of stigma, the concept of stigmatization emerged as a challenge to the idea that socialization, understood as a largely consensual process of norm diffusion and internalization, is vital to holding the international order together.[78] More importantly, she illustrates how an uneven process of induction has led to an "established insider-outsider" divide in the international order, which left even former empires such as Türkiye, Japan, and Russia with an inferiority complex as they transitioned into their modern nation-state identities.[79]

In this divide, the non-West as the "outsider" suffers from a sense of inferiority because they are bound by a "relationship of unequals," a relationship that granted these newly formed states Westphalian sovereignty without recognizing their equality in status.[80] To make matters worse, this sense of stigmatization is extenuated by a double bind. On the one hand, the non-West joined this Eurocentric society of states of their own volition, often regarding it as a source of pride. After all, induction into the international society of states was understood as the ultimate goal of nationalist self-determination. On the other hand, in doing so, these states had committed themselves to an international order, "the rules of which they did not create, the norms of which were unfamiliar at best, the major players of which judged and explicitly labeled them as inferior, and the ontology of which convinced them that they indeed were lacking in some way."[81]

This process of fitting into a culturally specific hierarchy led national elites to internalize a "particular normative standard that defines one's own attributes as discreditable."[82] When this process of internalization is combined with an external environment that retains certain labels of difference reserved for non-Western states (such as "Muslim," "developing," "Global South"), a social dynamic of stigmatization is reinforced. While it may sound inane in writing, a stigma, when ingrained, is hard to escape due to a circular logic. The agent is stigmatized because they are aware that the difference in status is marked by a gap between the "superior" and the "inferior" (which means catching up is *necessary*). Yet, simultaneously, they also think that inherent differences themselves mark the gap (which implies catching up is *futile*). As Hobson and Sharman observe, these dynamics that generate perceptions of ranked differences are formative of the "social logic of hierarchy" that characterize governance in the modern world.[83] Alas, their work focuses solely on powerful actors: imperial states that could impose hierarchy and function without the stigma of being "outsiders" of the system.

Studies that grapple with this dynamic of stigmatization vis-à-vis formerly colonized states remain limited.[84] This lacuna in the scholarship is most felt when it comes to Muslim states. This is a significant category to omit, given that most Muslim states have experienced some form of European colonization, with their religio-cultural identity singled out as the reason for their defeat and inferiority.[85] Islam, notwithstanding its intersection with ideas of race,[86] is arguably the only stigmatized marker linked to a major religion that has also gained a truly global purchase, as witnessed in the global spread of Islamophobia.[87] Even anti-Semitism cannot claim such a globalized reach, as it is only confined to places with a Christian or Islamic heritage. The persistence of this sense of stigmatization can be seen in how a Malaysian academic writing in 2005 still invoked the category of the Muslim state in his lament about global hierarchies: "All said and done, it still remains so, and Muslim countries, whether of fundamentalist leaning or secular-modern inclination, are forced to operate by the same rules that emanated from Westphalia."[88]

"Muslimness" became such a salient marker of stigma because it is a label that is both externally imposed and internally embraced. Externally, the category of the "Muslim world" continues to occupy the global imagination. It remains a term repeatedly evoked as a pejorative shorthand for places where intellectual, social, and political reforms are needed. For example, a US State Department paper characterizes the Islamic world as this space where a "struggle of ideas" has to happen without any reference to the spatial or temporal context.[89] In international rankings, most Muslim states are assessed unfavorably, be it in terms of technological and cultural backwardness, institutional efficiency, or cultural and individual freedom. A recent academic study similarly considers it unproblematic to frame authoritarianism and socioeconomic underdevelopment of forty-nine Muslim states within a single narrative.[90] The "pathos" of the Muslim world becomes the scaffolding upon which, notwithstanding their gaping differences, countries like Indonesia, Iran, and Yemen are often placed on the same cognitive map in academic, political, and cultural discourses.

At the same time, the "Muslim state" (and its aggregate, the Muslim World) is also a category embraced enthusiastically by Muslim actors. The vast cultural, historical, geographical, and political variations among its members does not stop the Organisation of Islamic Cooperation from becoming the only religion-denominated international organization with a cross-continental membership.

"Muslimness" also functions as an identity marker with a historical, social, and political potency that intersects with but also transcends the nation-state. One witnesses this in long-standing transnational Muslim networks, expressions of solidary in the name of the *ummah* (Muslim faith community), and persistent, even if tenuous, calls for some form of Muslim collective governance, such as a caliphate.[91] As a confessional identity that is transcontinental in membership, "Muslimness" is arguably different from other stigmatized identity markers that are also embraced internally as a symbol of solidarity and empowerment. Notably, those markers are still defined by either some kind of territorial exclusivity (such as Pan-Africanism), or a nation-bound inclusivity (such as Black politics in the US that is often entangled with a broader and transracial vernacular of social justice).[92] The Muslim collective is ostensibly more "inclusive" in its international reach and membership, but that feature also makes its stigmatization more devastating to those who identify with it.

To be sure, the social construction of "Muslimness" as a collective identity of grievance and solidarity is not a natural byproduct of coreligionism. Rather, it originated in the voyages of high imperialism in the nineteenth century. Aydin summarizes this mutually reinforcing process succinctly in his argument that "*the idea of the Muslim world is inseparable from the claim that Muslims constitute a race.*"[93] On the one hand, colonial domination unfolded alongside the propagation, reproduction, and institutionalization of Orientalist ideas—ideas that racialized "Muslimness" as the marker of backwardness and incivility. Edward Said captures this process by arguing convincingly how the "Islamic Orient" came to denote "the Orientalists' power and not the Islamic people as humans nor their history as history."[94] Hurd also notes that "Western ideals of order, domesticity, and democratic governance were consolidated in part through opposition to an Islamic other," illustrating the power/knowledge implications of European colonization.[95] On the other hand, the "Muslim" aspect of the identities of the colonized people was also augmented by their shared experience of European colonization, with Islam gradually evolving into a discursive frame through which a sense of common suffering and destiny of the Muslim people was articulated.[96]

Intuitively, one might expect that the stigmatization of the Muslim identity would lead to Islam's renunciation in the political and cultural life of postcolonial Muslim societies. In their effort to "catch up" with the West, it is surmisable that nationalist Muslim elites would try to purge what they saw as the source of their weaknesses and humiliation. Indeed, that was the case in Türkiye. The Kemalist regime saw religion "as the biggest obstacle to joining 'Civilization,'" which led to the abolition of the caliphate and the banning of Islamic courts, lodges, and "attire" such as the fez and the hijab.[97]

Nevertheless, Kemalism is the exception rather than the norm. Unless one is referring to the former Communist regimes in Central Asia, most Muslim states have integrated Islam into their postcolonial statehood. This is evident in colonial protectorates-turned-monarchies such as Qatar, Jordan, Morocco, and Brunei that have adopted Islam as the central tenet of their absolutist or semiabsolutist kingships, as well as in secular militaristic regimes that have carried out some form of neoliberal nationalist Islamization at the latter phases of their administration, such as Egypt's Mubarak (1981–2011) and Indonesia's Suharto (1966–2008).[98] Rather than relegating Islam to the private sphere, as the Kemalist regime did, most postcolonial Muslim states, including contemporary Türkiye, have embraced their Islamic identity in a more overt fashion, exposing them further to Islam's stigmatization in the post-GWOT context.

Embracing Stigma or Correcting Stigma? Islam and Ontological Security Seeking

If stigmatization does not necessarily lead to the renunciation of Islam, the Islamization that transpired in Muslim states when they were not ruled by Islamist governments (such as Malaysia and Egypt) must be seen in a different light.[99] By *Islamization* I do not mean a single-minded, highly coercive process of building an Islamic state (as that of postrevolution Iran or the Taliban), but rather a statist project that approaches the state's Islamic-ness as something always "in-the-making."[100] Granted, Islamization is a complicated phenomenon driven by an array of political and socioeconomic factors operating both globally and locally.[101] But the fact that it occurs primarily as a state-driven process for many Muslim societies also suggests that stigmatization does not foreclose the possibility of state elites adopting the heavily stigmatized marker.[102] While observers often like to highlight Islamization's "creeping" nature, Islamization very much hinges on a politics of optics since it is about making a statement about the state's identity.[103] For example, as chapter 3 will show, Malaysia's extensive state-led Islamization project was not only geared at effecting sociopolitical change; it also buttressed a foreign policy where the state's "overt Muslim character" was projected outward.[104] These historical dynamics must be comprehended to understand how Malaysian state elites dealt with Islam's stigmatization during the GWOT.

The IR literature on stigma management speaks very little to the Malaysian experience. For example, the three stigma management strategies proposed by Adler-Nissen—stigma recognition, stigma rejection, and counter-stigmatization—do not appear to capture the identity struggle of many postcolonial Muslim states.[105] In these settings, elites often prevaricate between integrating Islam into the state identity and distancing from it. Counter-stigmatization, which refers to the agent turning its stigmatization into "an emblem of pride, identifying with the group of stigmatised," comes closest.[106] One observes this in postrevolution Iran, where, much like Cuba, the regime employed "counterdiplomacy" tactics to invert its pariah status.

However, notwithstanding the efforts of leaders such as Malaysia's Mahathir to cultivate their "third world iconoclast" image, most postcolonial Muslim elites do not deal with their stigma by inverting the moral plane.[107] Malaysia's Cold War positioning and its active embrace of foreign investment-friendly developmentalist economics also stymied any grounds for claiming a truly revolutionary image.[108]

The strategy chosen by most Muslim elites appears to be that of *stigma correction*. This strategy contains elements of stigma recognition, which entails the stigmatized "internalising the value judgment made by the 'audience of normals,'" but they do so in hopes of reversing the pejorative connotations associated with the stigmatized marker they cannot abandon (in this case, Islam).[109] As I will show in chapter 3, this strategy can be seen in how Mahathir's state-led Islamization was advanced along what anthropologist Michael Peletz calls "modernity's holy trinity—urbanization, industrialization, and bureaucratization."[110] Mahathir's Islamization in the 1980s–1990s used Islam as a symbolic resource to stabilize Malaysia's nascent postcolonial state identity as well as to satisfy the status-seeking imperatives of Muslim elites and the new Muslim middle class who sought to prove they could harmonize Islam with totems of modernity such as finance, science, and technology.[111] In other words, even as these Muslim elites internalized the West's "teleological view of human development and progress centred on the concept of modernity,"[112] they still strove to demonstrate that modernization can be achieved in one's own terms—terms that can undermine the chain of signification behind Islam's supposed incompatibility with modernity.

Understanding the dynamics between Islamization and stigmatization is vital to our discussion of the politics of counter-terror for two reasons. First, it uncovers the linkage between the international and local dynamic through which Malaysia's secular ethnonationalist regime gradually adopted an "Islamic" identity. Second, understanding Islamization as a strategy of stigma correction underscores the fact that Muslim states such as Malaysia have long started this governmental project of curating Islam against its "worse" impulses. State discourses about Islam post–September 11 have to be read within this institutional history and not seen as mere reaction toward the GWOT. The historical awareness should apply especially to understanding the moderate Islam campaigns that Putrajaya pursued as it entered the GWOT. It is to this idea of moderate Islam that we will turn to next.

Moderate Islam as Stigma Correction: The Securitization of Islam

> Moderate (verb): To exercise a controlling influence over; to regulate, restrain, control, rule.
>
> —Oxford English Dictionary[113]

Discussions about moderate Islam are incredibly fraught because the term has shifting meanings and purposes. Often, it is a qualifier within a spectrum—"liberal," "moderate," and "radical"—to discern and classify different Muslim actors and versions of Islam, even though these categories are contentious themselves.[114] For the Islamic law scholar Mohammad Hashim Kamali, the concept refers to the Quranic teaching of *wasatiyyah* (moderation) that undergirds the "self-identity and worldview of the Muslim community."[115] Whereas the concept is now increasingly inflected by the GWOT security paradigm, it is important to note that the term's politicization extends far back. Interestingly, the idea of "moderate Islam" does not originate in the Muslim world, nor is there evidence that it is a coherent theological concept. Rather, the idea first emerged in the West. Hicks traces the term's genealogy back to the Cold War period when the idealization of "Indo-Persian Sufism" by US-based scholars such as Wilfred Cantwell Smith, Fazlur Rahman, and Hossain Nasr turned it into an epistemic category: a more "moderate" and "mystical" form of Islam compared to the rigid, dogmatic Islam of the Arabs.[116] The legacy of such thinking can be seen in the "tolerant Sufi/violent Salafi" dichotomy still embraced by many security analysts today.[117] Saddled by an imperial history and racialization dynamics, this binary view of Islam is widely deployed in security paradigms in Europe, where Islam is seen as "*the problem and the solution at the same time*" (emphasis in original).[118]

After September 11, ideas about moderate Islam were no longer confined to the West as Muslim governments began their own investments in the concept "through international declarations, religious training centres or interfaith initiatives."[119] These projects were usually dismissed as lip service geared at boosting "the international reputations" of these regimes and "to reassure non-Muslim allies of these regimes' commitment to the overarching international counter-terror security agenda" with little to no commitment to policy reforms.[120] Their existence also speaks to a cartography of the world marred by the Bush doctrine, as Muslim states were eager to get on the "good" side of an imagined moderate/radical Muslim divide. In this understanding, the moderate Islam discourse functions as a signaling device, or "soft power," to facilitate trust between Muslim states and the West (especially the US) in a security climate where a perceived lack of buy-in of the GWOT, especially from Muslims, is treated with deep suspicion.[121]

Viewing moderate Islam as a normative ideal or strategic rhetoric still does not explain why it gained meaningful traction among Muslim elites in the post-GWOT security milieu. I call it meaningful employment because elite understandings of "moderate Islam" have influenced security thinking in counter-terrorism, as we shall see in the empirical chapters. I argue that this situation can only be fully grasped within the broader problem of ontological insecurity faced by these postcolonial Muslim elites. That is, as a result of the experience of colonization, postcolonial Muslim societies have internalized a sense of inferiority—a perceived "modernity deficit" that made these societies particularly vulnerable to the indictment of GWOT's moral-culturalist discourses.[122] The championing of moderate Islam by Muslim political actors is tied to how significant Islam's stigmatization in world politics is.

The stigmatization meant that, unlike other normative goods such as democracy that have no need for cultural specificity or qualitative gradations (think "moderate" or "European" democracy), moderate Islam's selling point lies in its specificity: it is a *specific* form of Islam only found in *limited* settings.[123] Indeed, discourses of moderate Islam propounded by states such as Jordan, Morocco, and Indonesia all tried to graft Islam's "moderation" onto some reductive and often invented categories of national or regional traditions, mythologies, and cultures.[124]

If the discourse of moderate Islam is about Muslims responding to Islam's stigmatization, that explains the *performative* nature of moderate Islam campaigns and the concept's indivisibility from Islam's *securitization* in the Muslim states that were most active in promoting it.[125] Counter-terrorism offers an outlet for Muslim elites and security practitioners who wish to distance themselves from the judged (i.e., the Muslim "terrorists" deemed bestial, barbaric, and backward), as well as to correct said judgment (i.e., the view that Islam is inherently violent and "irrational"). For these actors, successful counter-terrorism is not only about securing public order; it also signals their success in *moderating* Islam, an achievement tied to their status insecurity.[126]

Counter-Terrorism, Governance, and the Stranger's Dilemma

I have thus far surveyed the macrohistorical and mesoinstitutional factors that establish the institutional and discursive context for Islam's securitization in Malaysia. Such securitization is underscored by a discourse that frames the promotion and protection of "moderate" Islam as a security and status imperative for Muslim state elites. In this section, we will move into the discussion of the governance framework this book uses to examine the *microgovernmental* observations of the "Islamization of security": the phenomenon that Islamic actors, expertise, and reasoning feature prominently in daily counter-terror practices. Making the case that security is "Islamized" necessitates an analytical framework that focuses on the hermeneutics of security. To operationalize counter-terrorism, the state must be able to identify, explain, and rehabilitate the "radical" Muslim subject. This need to claim knowledge of bodies and their radical possibilities is necessarily an objective of *governance*. Put differently, if our previous focus on the securitization of Islam highlights the historical institutional trajectory that looms over the making of a security logic, this turn to the Islamization of security sheds light on how this security logic is translated into governance.

This section discusses the interpretive framework that enables our conceptualization of Malaysia's "Islamized" counter-terrorism as governance. My framework also supports the theoretical and empirical shift for the analyses in chapters 5 and 6, which bring attention to the micropolitics of Malaysia's "Islamized" counter-terror regime via institutional mapping and discourse analysis of its security logics. This shift encompasses two analytical moves. First, counter-terrorism is disassembled empirically into different sites of governance, such as Preventing/Countering Violent Extremism (P/CVE) campaigns, mosques, courts, and prisons. Second, the analysis adopts a "thick" understanding of security that highlights the embeddedness of Islam in Malaysia's counter-terrorism and asks what the concrete outcomes are when security is organized as such. These two moves guide my enquiry toward a more primary source-reliant methodology. They enable me to argue that the permeation of Islamic actors and vocabularies in counter-terror practices is not just a case of the state instrumentalizing religion for security. Counter-terrorism in Malaysia is directly implicated in the discursive construction of the Muslim body as a governable site for ontological security needs.

Counter-Terror as Governance: Narratives and Order-Making

In his seminal essay "Revolutionary War and Counter-Insurgency," Eqbal Ahmad wrote that an insurgency's "major task is to outadminister the established authority."[127] The inverse is true as well. In facing terrorism, especially where insurgencies are absent, the government's job is to outgovern the "terrorist" group. They must prevent radicalization and recruitment, identify potential militants, delegitimize the ideology, freeze funding, secure against attacks, and prosecute offenders, all of which are mechanisms of *governance*. In other words, notwithstanding the martial rhetoric of the GWOT, counter-terror involves a "whole series of practices that do not fall under the description of war."[128] Nonetheless, to argue that counter-terror constitutes a form of governance, we must first define governance and explore how it can be studied.

For our purpose, a generic definition of governance would suffice, in that it refers to acts to regulate human conduct through a set of norms, institutions, and practices. As mentioned in an earlier section, the jurisdiction of counter-terror lies solely with the state. Thus, our view of governance is reasonably state-centric, even if the ideas and praxis of governance are unlikely to demonstrate a neat state-society divide.[129] What this book is most interested in is not the question of who governs but rather the *order-making* properties of governance. In conceptualizing terrorists as "predators" that intend to "destroy the normative order and replace it with their own political vision," Löwenheim alluded to the relationship between governance, counter-terror, and order: "Predators, on the other hand, are an issue of *governance*. Governance . . . deals with broader political aspects of the preservation and reproduction of a social system" (emphasis added).[130]

By linking governance to order making, I borrow from political theorist Mark Bevir's postfoundationalist framework that emphasizes the function of narratives as the primary object of study to understand governance. By his definition, governance relies on narratives inherited as "historical traditions" that are "then revised in response to dilemmas" by political actors.[131] To approach governance as historical narratives does not imply a complete negation of institutions and human interests. Rather, it is to ground institutions and individuals within discursive structures that frame governing activities as historically contingent and socially meaningful.[132] Thus, narratives play a dual role here. First, narratives structure governance as a social practice, thereby allowing the cultural reification of the state to take place (where the "governors" fashion themselves as agents of government). Second, narratives establish governance as a social reality for the governed through discourses that outline the logic, legitimacy, and language of governance. In other words, narratives of governance—laws, guidelines, memos, speeches, circulars, blueprints, and reports—provide structures of legibility for governing actors to think about how to govern and why so, and for the governed to understand governance as rules and ostensible "rational" facts of life. The component of narratives and paperwork is, therefore, indispensable in understanding counter-terrorism as a facet of governance.[133]

Bevir's approach is also helpful to this book's multilevel analysis because of its emphasis on "situated agency," which implies that a social agent can transform an "inherited language, discourse, or tradition" but not always transcend it.[134] It avoids the trappings of radical autonomy found in poststructuralist approaches, thus allowing the researcher to critically engage with questions of history, state identity, and international society—all of which are instrumental to our theorization of the relationship between religion, status, and state security. Like any other social actors, counter-terror practitioners are inevitably immersed in discourses of history, memory, and identity that socialize them into specific conceptions of the nation and world politics.[135] For example, terms like *Islam*, *jihad*, or *the caliphate* can never be understood as value-neutral and ahistorical signifiers in counter-terror discourses in Muslim states as they are crucial to articulating the "Muslimness" of the state. Narratives of governance, therefore, not only structure the reasoning of governmental action but also frame them reflexively in reference to the polity or other forms of collective identity (e.g., the *ummah*, or international society). As we shall see in chapters 5 and 6, discourses of securing religion, the Muslim population, and the body politic populate Malaysia's counter-terror practices, without which knowledge practices performed in the name of counter-terror will have no ontological grounding.

Locating governance in narratives also pushes us to take seriously the hermeneutic environments in which it transpires. This conceptualization gives credence to the metahistorical idea that the modern state is expected to function as a central narrator in contemporary politics. Referring to the rhetorical power of political actors, Marlow highlights the "storied character" of modern governmentality: "Political-cultural identity is, to a lesser or greater extent, informed by what politicians (amongst many others) do and say. The 'stories' that politicians tell (among a whole multitude of other 'stories') play a social role as to the way in which people come to understand themselves in the wider scheme of things—ontological and existential narratives and understandings underlie much of the "storytelling.'"[136] What this means is that the modern state now plays the role of a modern ontological security provider (OSP), "in an environment where increasingly 'disembedded' individuals needed to be told which strangers were enemies and which were friends, and which experts were to be trusted and which were just quacks."[137]

*

Granted, it is only since the seventeenth century that "people look to the structures of political authority [the modern state] as their main institutional source of ontological security" (addition mine).[138] However, acknowledging the state's status as an OSP also signifies a need to shift from the securitization theory paradigm. The classic definition of securitization is offered by the Copenhagen School, which defines securitization as a kind of speech act employed by a securitizing actor to present a "certain problem as an existential threat" to the referent object, precipitating "emergency measures and justifying actions outside the normal bounds of political procedure" as a result.[139] In this understanding, the "terrorist" is usually whomever the state declares as such.

However, if the state plays the role of the OSP, the state must demonstrate knowledge of the "terrorist" to make "its management practicable."[140] This is more so the case when we consider the fact that counter-terror's operationalization in Malaysia—with its investigation, arrest, and prosecution of hundreds of suspects in the post-IS era—is closer to routine techniques of "administering uncertainty and 'mapping' dangers" instead of moments of rupture where elite actors carve out zones for exceptional actions by invoking a vague yet omnipotent enemy.[141] This understanding of the GWOT as waged by "mundane technologies and mostly relatively unspectacular actions" reinforces Huysmans's appeal that the crux of security lies not in fiery speeches but rather in the "little security nothings."[142]

Counter-Terror as Ontological Security Seeking: Confronting the Stranger's Dilemma

Securitization theory's portrayal of the counter-terror state as exercising total epistemic control over the issue of "terrorism" is also complicated by the terrorist's status as the ontological "stranger," who reveals the limits of statist categories.[143] This concept of the ontological "stranger" is first introduced by sociologist Zygmunt Bauman, who argues that the nation-state's obsession with "state-enforced homogeneity" amplifies the political salience of the category of the "stranger."[144] He went as far as to argue that the "*national state is designed primarily to deal with the problem of strangers, not enemies.*"[145] As the embodiment of this ambivalence between the "natives, who are friends, and the foreigners, who are current or potential enemies," the "stranger" disrupts the modern state's penchant for homogeneity.[146] Therefore, as Huysmans puts it, the stranger is fundamentally a "hermeneutic problem."[147] It is the *undecidable* that transcends the vital insider/outsider boundaries enforced by the nation-state, disrupting the state's capability to maintain us/them distinctions that are key to its functioning. Zarakol brought such insights into her theorization of the "strangeness" of terrorism, arguing that terrorist activity aims "to confuse and collapse existing categories of civilian/official, stranger/enemy, citizen/threat. It is for this reason that 'terrorism' is so difficult to define and categorise: the activity itself is an assault on the modern (state) project of reducing indeterminacy through classification and comparison."[148]

This "stranger's dilemma" is the most pronounced when it concerns the relational dynamics between the Muslim state and IS as a transnational phenomenon of Muslim militancy and migration. The IS-linked "citizen-terrorist" straddles all the legible categories most familiar to the nation-state: insider/outsider, civilian/combatant, friend/enemy. As Muslim citizens in a Muslim-majority nation, these individuals can exert a claim of indigeneity. Hence, they are very much *insiders*. However, their swearing of allegiance to a foreign, state-like entity that declared war against the (self-identified) Muslim state places them firmly on "*outsider*" territory. To complicate matters, the variegated pathways of participation—including nonviolent ones such as merely swearing the *ba'iah* (pledge of allegiance) toward IS, making financial contributions, or moving to the so-called caliphate as settlers and not combatants—also "removes violence as an essence from which the 'terrorist' can be depicted as a perilous entity in security discourses."[149] These arguably nonterrorist attributes scramble stable categories of civilian/combatant, or friend/enemy.

By conceptually treating the Muslim terrorist as a "stranger" to the Muslim state, my formulation of the stranger differs from Bauman's. Bauman's idea of strangeness is rooted in the ethnoreligious and cultural undecidability of a member within a nation-state, in which stigmatization serves as "the convenient weapon in the defence against the unwelcome ambiguity of the stranger."[150] My formulation of the stranger instead focuses on *subject liminality*. By this I mean, at least from the Muslim state's perspective, that the "strangeness" of the Muslim subject revolves around their radical contingency that can render the stable and familiar categories of race, religion, and citizenship inapplicable when demarcating friend/enemy boundaries. As Combes puts it succinctly in her study of the liminality of the Boston Marathon bombers as White, homegrown terrorists, confronting strangeness in terrorism discourses is about confronting "bodies that are at once like us yet not like us."[151] In other words, whereas Bauman's stranger exudes as much familiarity as unfamiliarity, my conception of the stranger is someone who can easily flip from the terrain of the familiar to the unfamiliar, a process that may see a "terroristic" mode of being bursting into the open.

One sees this difficulty with liminality played out in the Malaysian case. For obvious reasons, the "othering" mechanism used to securitize Muslims in Muslim-minority societies is impossible to replicate in Muslim-majority Malaysia.[152] Identity markers of marginality such as race, religion, language, and appearances that can be used to define a "suspect" community are inapplicable to the Malay-Muslim majority Malaysian state "searching" for the Malay-Muslim terrorist.[153] There was also no geographical fixity to the threat, as exposed "cells" consisted of members from all over the country.[154] Nor were these individuals organized enough to be considered a movement, unlike in the cases of Muslim militancy in Indonesia, Southern Thailand, or Mindanao, which operated, to some extent, as insurgencies.[155] Even the legal category of the "terrorist" offers no comfort. As we will see in chapter 6, the legal definition encompasses everything from someone who has caused physical harm to someone who merely expressed perhaps a positive opinion for a terrorist movement in a chat group. This makes it impossible for the state to convincingly articulate the levels of danger associated with a terrorist, especially in a social context where "Muslimness" is the marker of in-group boundaries and not out-group ones.

If one must deal with this dormant "strangeness" within the population, its ambivalence must be *demystified* before it can be governed. Eliminating the stranger's ambiguity is not a surprising turn for modern governance. Indeed, speaking historically and sociologically, what distinguishes the modern state from the premodern ones is its *subject-making* ambition. Aided by the "unprecedented technological resources and managerial capacities offered by the modern State," the modern "gardening" state operates under the optimism that it can cultivate "humans as one does bananas and pineapples."[156] As detestable as the agricultural analogy may sound, favorable views toward eugenics expressed by Asian modernizers during the 1970s and 1980s suggest that this idea of the state as a gardener is not as alien or unpalatable to the governing elites as one may think.[157] As we will see in the empirical chapters later, the social-engineering ambition of the Malaysian state to create modern, "moderate," and "worldly" Muslims long preceded the GWOT. In fact, the GWOT's cultural indictment of Islam merely exacerbated the anxieties of these gardening elites because the emergence of the "terrorist" in the image of the religious fanatic reminded them of their failures in human cultivation.

If counter-terror is about demystifying strangeness, then the performative element of it is vital. Such performances of knowing help the state regain epistemic control over a situation of perceived radical unknowability. Being able to dispense "counter-terror knowledge" also sits well with Muslim elites who sought to position themselves as valuable counter-terror partners with something to offer. This can be seen in how Muslim states enthusiastically shared their deradicalization programs that usually had a "religious" component with the West, even as they were otherwise reticent about any scrutiny on their security apparatus.[158] In Malaysia's case, the performativity was channeled through a more public counter-terror campaign post-2013, with the state sharing more information on the hundreds of terrorism-related arrests it made. The government also executed a P/CVE campaign to mitigate public panic when news of a significant number of Malaysians getting involved with IS surfaced. This performance of "knowing" the pathology of radicalization is very much the security logic this book is most interested in, and it is readily observable in the *subject-making* discourses of counter-terrorism.

Counter-Terror as Subject Making: A Biopolitical Security Assemblage

The concept of "subject making" has two functions: heuristical and analytical. It is a heuristic device because it describes a governmentality that revolves around an imagined anatomy of the "terrorist."[159] Across different domains of counter-terrorism, this "body" of a terrorist is treated as deconstructible into legible parts to enable enterprises of surveillance, punishment, and correction. These enterprises inform specific assumptions and understandings about what indicators, pathways, and actions make a person a terrorist and how to "unmake" a terrorist for deradicalization purposes. Put differently, subject-making discourses show how counter-terrorism is geared toward addressing biopolitical risks. Its narratives and practices are primarily about claiming control over "both the disciplinary order of the body and the aleatory events that occur in the biological multiplicity."[160]

My conception of subject making necessarily brings in comparisons with Foucault. I borrow substantially from Foucault's theorization of biopower, pastoral governmentality, and how governance operates as discursive economies of truth making.[161] Yet, I do not adopt Foucault's triangular notion of power (sovereign, disciplinary, and biopower) in the vein of other studies of counter-terrorism.[162] Instead, I center my analysis specifically on the anatomies of the Muslim terrorist that is propagated and reproduced in governmental discourses—discourses that are too often taken for granted as utterances of "terrorism expertise." As we will see in the empirical chapters, the discursive clarity proffered by the Malaysian state on why radicalization occurred among Muslims is rooted in a specific state-building history rather than being an apolitical outcome of "scientific" inquiry.

Analytically, this interest in "subject making" also anchors the security assemblage approach I used to tackle the methodological question of where to study counter-terror. The concept of the assemblage is borrowed from the literature of anthropology and of science and technology studies that refer to "the sociotechnical chains of material-semiotic relations and agents that are aligned and stabilised to produce particular forms of organisation and knowledge across different fields of practice."[163]

As an anthropological concept, the security assemblage approach is analytically useful because it interrogates how "forms of action work and what types of security they produce"—questions my interpretive framework is meant to address.[164] Methodologically, the approach enables the researcher to study counter-terror discourses and practices without confining the inquiry to specific institutions, actors, or localities. This freedom allows us to trace and visualize the security logics within a wider array of counter-terror discourse and practices.

To exercise this understanding of counter-terrorism as a security assemblage (an assembly of forms of security actions), I mapped Malaysia's counter-terror regime in chapter 6 via three functional areas—preventive, preemptive, and rehabilitative (see Table 1). By *prevention*, I refer to practices behind P/CVE campaigns targeted at informing, monitoring, and alerting the public of the threat of terrorism. By *preemption*, I refer to operations that led to arrests and prosecutions of suspects deemed to have committed a terrorism crime.[165] By *rehabilitation*, I refer to "deradicalization" programs conducted for terrorism detainees. In each functional area, counter-terrorism manifests as subject-making discourses that render the terrorist as a biopolitical, judicial, and redemptive subject, respectively, each justifying a set of social, legal, and penal interventions. As chapter 6 will illustrate, these discourses function to delineate the terrorist "body" with surprising clarity by indexing behavioral traits, religiosity, and psychometric profiles to enable governmental interventions.

TABLE 1 The Functional Domains of a Counter-Terror Regime

Prevention	Pre-emption	Rehabilitation
Public awareness campaigns	Law enforcement	"Deradicalization"
Monitoring	Prosecution	Post-release integration
Mass-targeting "Counter-radicalization" Practices	Surveillance	
Research		

This twin focus on security assemblages and subject-making discourses grounds my fieldwork observation of what I theorized as the "Islamization of security." The assemblage framework visualizes *where* said Islamization occurs, whereas the analysis of "subject-making" discourses denotes *how* it occurs. This conceptual grounding allows me to depart from scholarly accounts that frame the intertwining of religion and security as the state exercising symbolic power,[166] or as a natural outcome of authoritarian control.[167] Identifying counter-terrorism as operating through "subject-making" narratives, I take a largely hermeneutical approach to interrogating the relationship between security and religion. Hence, my analytical and empirical focus is on how the Muslim state narrates the Muslim "terrorist"—their pathology, transgression, and redeemability—within governing technologies that operationalize counter-terrorism on a day-to-day basis.

By observing how state power works through religiously inflected discourses, this book also reaffirms the Asadian logic that religion is "produced discursively rather than objectively found."[168] Islam's integration into governance does not presuppose any outcomes. Rather, the outcome depends on what elites and practitioners think governance is supposed to deliver and what its limits are. Put simply, a security logic not only functions as a pronouncement of the "problem" but also prescribes a role for the state, something that can only be understood if we unpack the historical sociological and institutional foundations of state power. For example, Malaysia's counter-terrorism contains a form of pastoral governmentality that imagines itself as benevolent and aims to provide "comprehensive guidance" to its subjects.[169] Beneath the constant denunciation of the Muslim terrorist as religious "deviants" is also an understanding among Malaysian security practitioners that the terrorist is an object for salvation rather than elimination.[170]

An Eclectic Framework

As a recap, Figure 1 provides a graphical representation of the multilayered framework this book employs to study Malaysia's "Islamized" counter-terrorism: its *origins, logics,* and *workings*. The framework relies on three components: a nested

FIGURE 1 Three-Level Islam and Security-Making Framework

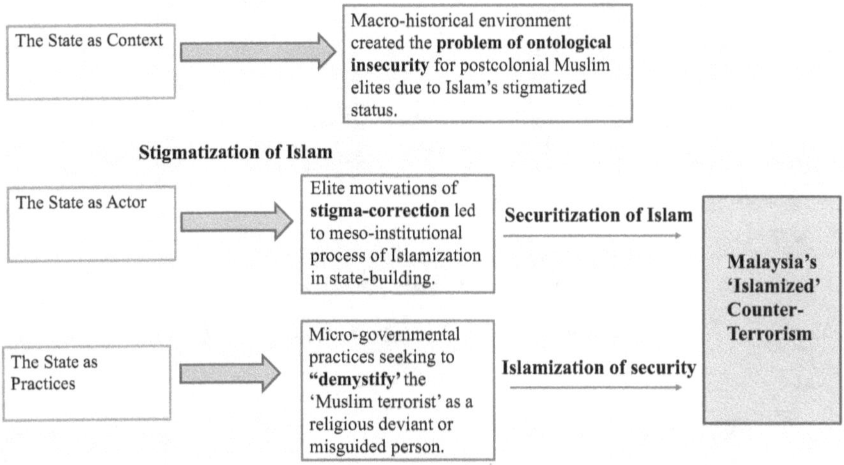

concept of the state, a weaving of ontological security concerns into institutionalized security formations, and a granular focus on the intersections between Islam, postcolonial Muslim elite status seeking, and security governance. My eclectic approach bridges theories that normally do not converse with one another, such as ontological security in IR, studies of state-religion relationships, and security assemblages, offering a sophisticated tracing of Malaysia's politics of counter-terror as embedded in both epistemological constructs and operational minutiae. These rich findings also go beyond the narrow field of counter-terrorism to provide fresh insights into how Islam fits into the foreign policy, elite worldviews, and security governance of Muslim states.

I will end this chapter with a caveat. Even as the book traverses three levels of analysis, I do not privilege any level or the theoretical apparatus associated with them. Rather, by suturing concepts such as stigmatization, Islamization, and securitization together, I aim to provide an interpretive analysis that sheds light on both the social and operational aspects of counter-terrorism within Muslim states, which is rarely addressed in the literature. Indeed, when applied on the Malaysian case, this eclectic framework reveals the duality of counter-terrorism as a security enterprise, whereby the Muslim state is imbricated within a social struggle to counter Islam's stigmatization, on the one hand, and having to operationalize counter-terrorism practically, on the other. The anxieties and uncertainties embedded in the enterprise also denote the centrality of ontological (in)security in Muslim state behavior and the formation of their governmental logics. In the next chapter, we will explore how this problem of ontological insecurity arose among the postcolonial indigenous elites in the first place.

TWO

The Roots of Ontological Insecurity

Islam and Postcolonial Nation Building in Malaysia

To understand Islam's relationship with state security, one must first follow the evolution of Islam's institutional and discursive role in politics and governance. This chapter explores how the institutional context and sociopolitical meaning of Islam changed from the precolonial period to the early years of Malaysia's independence, with the colonial encounter serving as a pivotal moment of transformation as the architecture of the colonial state rendered, reconfigured, and reified Islam's relationship with politics and governance. To be sure, my aim here is not to offer a definitive history but rather to illustrate how Islam became a source of ontological insecurity for the Westernized postcolonial Malay-Muslim elites who inherited a structurally colonial state in the name of indigenous representation.

Through a historical institutionalist and sociological analysis, this chapter demonstrates that a sense of stigmatization was present with the postcolonial Muslim elites from the very beginning. This sense was sharpened as these elites sought to address the self-identity needs of the nascent postcolonial state vis-à-vis the countervailing demands of external recognition and indigenous authenticity. I argue that, in trying to pursue both performance and representative legitimacy, the early Malay political and administrative elites were torn, at least in their minds, between two divergent but ostensibly "Western" measures of progress. On the one hand, there was the commitment, even if only formalistically, toward a democratic ideal of popular representation. This commitment exposed them to "bottom-up" challenges that were articulated in the idioms and demands for some form of Islamic governance. On the other hand, the elites were driven by a sense of urgency to achieve material progress for Malaysia through a schema of modernization that saw little need for indigenous knowledge, practices, and culture—elements that were often slotted under the category of "religion" within the colonial epistemology they inherited.[1] I contend that as these postcolonial Westernized elites jostled with the question of Islam in considerations of state identity and governing ideology, they were also trying to reconcile with their own positionality as simultaneously "insiders" and "outsiders" of both international and domestic society.

The rest of the chapter proceeds as follows. First, I provide the institutional backdrop by outlining how colonial intervention profoundly altered Islam's relationship with state power. During colonial rule, the metaphysically defined relationship between Islam and conceptions of Malay kingship was replaced by an institutionalized tension marked by Islam's institutional marginality and its symbolic centrality in articulating (post)colonial Malay statehood. Second, I unpack this tension in relation to the social positionality of the Westernized elites of the political and administrative class as simultaneously insiders and outsiders of the postcolonial global order. I argue that this dualism of being Westernized traditional elites conditioned their thinking about modernization and popular legitimacy, with methods and trajectories to achieve the former often seen as irrelevant to, or even at odds with, securing the latter. Last, I discuss how the ambiguity associated with Islam's constitutional role as the religion of the federation has contributed to a sense of ontological insecurity among the Malaysian Muslim elites as they presided and prevaricated over contestations about state identity and ideology on one end, and practical concerns of governance vis-à-vis their visions about modernization and economic development on the other.

Islam and the State in Precolonial and Colonial Malaya: Synergies and Tension

Any articulation of the state-religion relationship is bound to confront Talal Asad's problematization of the secular bias that informs the scholarship.[2] Those who followed Asad's critique have contended that a Eurocentric view of the state-religion relationship has resulted in understandings of state and religion as mutually exclusive and predatory entities, producing understandings of the relationship that lean toward outlining typologies of separation.[3] These typologies often pit the state's assumed secularity against the infringement of religion (and vice versa), at the expense of interrogating ideas about statehood and religion within historically contingent and mutually constitutive discursive relations. For example, the Islamic state is often defined as the exact opposite of the secular state: a polity whose presence can only be articulated in the absence of any secularity. These binary conceptions of state forms have now made their way into revisionist historiographies that frame colonialism's real impact on Muslim-majority societies as its usurping of some form of ideal Islamic state.[4] Needless to say, these ahistorical narratives oversimplify how the experience of colonialism fundamentally altered Islam's social and political meaning, including making it more prominent as a source of "indigenous" power. Examining these changes critically is pivotal to understanding how the idea of the Islamic state has become a source of ontological insecurity for the postcolonial Muslim elites.

Islam in the Cosmologies of Precolonial Malaya

Contrary to the revisionist claims above, historians have long demonstrated that it is futile to try to locate a timeless version of Islam in the political praxis of precolonial Southeast Asia.[5] Their works depict a fluid and organic process of change and adaptation since Islam began to take root within Indianized polities such as Pasai, Aceh, and Melaka at the end of the thirteenth century.[6] In the case of precolonial Malaya, states (or rather, polities) and religion were interwoven in ways that elude the bureaucratic and legalistic framework through which they operate today. While there were indeed written laws modeled after Islamic jurisprudence, such as the Hukum Kanun Melaka,[7] the induction of Islam into Hindu-Buddhist Malay kingdoms in archipelagic Southeast Asia also fostered a recasting of "Islamic idioms" onto preexisting "semifeudalistic" ideas about statecraft and kingship.[8] For example, the idea of Malay kingship had its metaphysical origins in the Hindu-Buddhist concept of the *devaraja* (divine kingship). With the coming of Islam, the Arabic term *daulat* gradually came to signify the concept.[9] To be sure, what transpired was not merely a semantical change but a reinvention of the cosmos of Malay political culture, as "god-kings" were refashioned into kings who drew their legitimacy as "the protector and patron of Islam."[10]

The evolution of ideas surrounding Malay kingship brought upon by the rulers' adoption of Islam occurred within a setting where the sovereign resided not with any state in the modern sense, but rather centralized and personified by the "condition of having a *raja* [ruler]," that is, the *kerajaan,* which remains the contemporary Malay term for government.[11] Historian Anthony Milner, for example, interpreted the courtly texts and legal digest as "products not of the discourse of *syariah,* but of that of the *kerajaan.*"[12] In other words, both religion and state (the state as a kingly sovereign, that is) conditioned the parameters of one another, leading to cascading formations of court culture, rituals, and norms. Expectations of the ruled, the *rakyat* (the masses), were also articulated in reference to the *kerajaan*. For example, treason was denounced through the concept of *derhaka*, a Sanskrit term that had retained its contemporary usage despite the coming of Islam. Acts of disloyalty to the king were depicted as "tantamount to challenging the universal order," further cementing the sacrosanct status of Malay kingship.[13] The syncretic and synergistic nature of state, religion, and governance in precolonial Malaya would be the canvas upon which the transformative and traumatic changes of British colonialism were introduced.

Islam and the Colonial State in Malaya

British colonialism initially reached the shores of the Malay Peninsula as ad-hoc trading agreements and territorial grabs to establish trading posts, as was the case with Penang and Singapore. Nevertheless, by the end of the nineteenth century, the entire Malay peninsula was absorbed into colonial rule and organized as an administrative unit consisting of three blocs: the Straits Settlements (1826), the Federated Malay States (1895), and the rest as the Unfederated Malay States. To borrow from James Scott, colonialism was disruptive to Southeast Asia because of the way it brought "nonstate spaces and people to heel," which meant the idea of governance itself was radically changed.[14] The colonial state turned out to be institutionally and ontologically different from the precolonial state that was institutionally fragmented, limited in material power, and legitimized symbolically by ruler-subject ties understood in religio-cosmological terms.[15] Although haphazardly and unevenly built, the colonial state was schematic and penetrative in governmentality, bureaucratic and centralized in apparatus, text bound and impersonal in rules, and industrial and capitalistic in goals.[16] It was a "governmental state" that tasked itself with the *problématique* of population management, giving rise to population control technologies such as census taking and communal zoning.[17] The basis for such infrastructural and political-epistemological developments in the late nineteenth century stemmed from an "ideology of good government" introduced "first as a discourse and then in actual practice," underwritten by the ideals of the Scottish Enlightenment and racialized views of the civilizing mission.[18] Nevertheless, as Farish Noor reminds us, colonial state building "was driven from the outset by the logic of an imperial political economy."[19] Conceptions of good governance and the power-knowledge complex the project drew from were never divorced from the politico-economic calculations of the metropole.

The British mission to provide "good government" was confounded by the question of Islam. Unlike in areas such as mineral extraction and cash-crop agriculture that primarily unfolded at the unpopulated frontiers of the Malay Peninsula, the colonial administrators were not given a de novo situation to start with for issues of religion. They struggled to define, categorize, and comprehend Islam because its symbolic, functional, and legal roles in the precolonial state did not conform to models of state-church relations in Europe. As discussed above, Islam was part and parcel of the political, cultural, and moral economy of Malay society, and was symbolically tied to the Malay rulers as organizing figures of the cosmos of the *kerajaan*. As a result, the colonial operatives and bureaucrats often found themselves coming into conflicts and contestations with local elites who saw encroachments into domains related to Islam as infringements on their influence and interests.[20]

Nevertheless, unlike in Burma and many parts of the South Asian subcontinent where British colonial rule was direct and oppressive,[21] the British consistently maintained—except for in the Straits Settlements—that they were merely advisers (even if hardly so in practice) in the Malay Peninsula. That is, they were vicegerents to Malay rulers who remained as the designated head of states. To "disguise the highly interventionist nature of indirect rule," the colonial government and the Malay royalty embraced a form of outwardly Malay political culture Amoroso calls "traditionalism." The political culture was, in reality, a set of invented traditions that created "new rituals" out of colonial appropriation and refashioned Malay court culture to glamorize the "British-defined ruling class."[22]

Amoroso's observation of traditionalism also explains a paradox of prejudice and sentimentality that underscored the colonial administration of Islam. While eager to foster growth and returns on their investments, the colonial government also imagined itself as the "civilized" and benevolent guiding hand of the natives and had developed a penchant for preserving "a political culture condemned as unviable in the modern world."[23] The "unviability" of Islam was noted in Stephens's observation of British colonial governance in South Asia, where the religion was deemed a source of irrationality and very much an obstacle to secular governance and the market economy.[24] In Malaya, where the British ruled with a softer touch, the result was a political arrangement that saw Islam's legal role reduced to that of personal status law, on the one hand, and its sympathetic preservation within a Malay cultural package that was placed in the control of the Malay rulers, on the other. Along with Malay customs, Islamic affairs—defined in terms of "private" religion, such as in matters of matrimony, family, and worship and rituals—was the only domain where the Malay rulers could be said to have enjoyed any practical autonomy, an institutional peculiarity that was not found in colonies such as British India or the Dutch Indies.[25]

This contradictory mandate of conservation and change embraced by the colonial authorities had resulted in another paradox. As argued by political scientist Iza Hussin, Islam's codification and institutional marginalization as Islamic law (or rather, as Anglo-Muslim law) were accompanied by an increase in the significance of Islam and Islamic law as a source of symbolic authority and as an arena for political contest for Muslim elites.[26] This feature continued well into postcolonial Malaysia and has been addressed by scholars in different analytical frames, such as the "judicialization of religion," the "shariaization of the Malay-Muslim identity," and the politics of "majority making."[27] Suffice to say, the concentration and elevation of the Muslim elite's institutional and symbolic power within the domains of Muslim worship, family matters, and personal status ushered in profound alterations in the discursive interpellations between state, religion, and (Muslim) bodies within the sociopolitical consciousness of Malay-Muslims.[28] A bridging of sorts occurred. Muslim *subjects* were linked to the "forms and powers of the colonial state," the Muslim *state* drew its identity and legitimacy through claims of representation and control over Islam, and the Muslim *religion* was structured by state power exercised in law, bureaucracy, and governance.[29] What was being transformed by the colonial intervention was the political sociology of Islam itself, as seen in the elite hierarchies created, the administrative rationalization of Islamic affairs, and the narrowing of hermeneutical possibilities as state orthodoxies were formed and codified.[30]

The centralization of "Muslimness" in Malay political discourse also meant that Islam gradually became a site for articulating indigenous claims vis-à-vis a colonial political economy perceived as foreign and too welcoming of sojourners from China and India.[31] By the early twentieth century, Islamic reformist ideas from the Dutch Indies and the Arab world had begun fueling debates in periodicals, newspapers, and books on how the Muslim world could tap into the teachings of Islam for rejuvenation from its current state of political, economic, and societal malaise.[32] For our purposes, there were four noteworthy features in the emergence of Islam as an intellectual and political resource of reform and resistance in Malaya. First, despite the British apprehensions about a fanatical Wahhabi conspiracy (the label applied to many of the modernist reformists active in the Straits Settlements at the time),[33] violence was rarely part of the strategy. Instead, the discourse was mainly about social reform and religious purification.[34] Historically, anticolonial violence in Malaya, such as the Pahang uprising (1891–1895) and the Kelantan Rebellion (1915), were not overtly "religious" campaigns but manifestations of local grievances intertwined with complex court politics, even as some of them took on "anti-colonial, millenarian features" later.[35] Prominent Islamist leaders of the early twentieth century such as Burhanuddin Al-Helmy, who was once the president of the Pan-Malayan (and later Malaysian) Islamic Party (PAS), never condoned violence as a method for anticolonial struggle, despite having close ties with militant radical nationalists and Communists.[36]

Second, whereas strands of Muslim reformist thought were propagated in anticolonial rhetoric, a significant portion of the critique by the reformist *kaum muda* (young faction), especially in the prewar years, was directed inward at Malay society.[37] One key recipient of their diatribe was the religio-political elites, also known as the *kaum tua* (old faction), who benefited from the traditionalist forms of power and privilege as abetted by the colonial rulers. In his close reading of *Al-Imam* (a short-lived publication edited by the *kaum muda*), Milner outlined how the magazine posed a profound critique against "the philosophical underpinnings of the *kerajaan* political culture," questioning not only the self-indulgent conduct of the royals but also their legitimacy as the "focus of loyalty" of the Malays.[38] The magazine was also unsparing in its attack against "established religion," claiming that it was laden with "un-Islamic" rituals and customs. Its writers preached against uncritical deference toward the traditional religious elites—referring mainly to the ulamas—and called for urgent reforms in Islamic education and practice.[39]

Third, transnational Muslim solidarity in the name of the *ummah* (the Muslim collective) became a key signifier of anticolonial discourse; a development that benefited from print capitalism, circuitries of Muslim travel and education, and a rising consciousness about the Muslim world's shared experience of European imperialism.[40] Even so, this did not signify a clear-cut abandonment of local commitments. As Muhamad Ali noted: "In the Indonesian-Malay world of the first half of the twentieth century, Muslim scholars viewed Islam as a new path to progress, allowing them to adopt and adapt the concept of *jam'iyyah* (organisation) and Western political parties and administration, rejecting the Islamic political order of caliphate (*khilafah*) without rejecting the sense of a global *ummah* and, in Malay cases, the sultanate."[41]

Fourth, debates about Muslim empowerment, ethics, and emancipation were infused with more references to the sharia (Islamic law).[42] Understood as "more than a compendium of rules," the sharia's status as divine law anchored debates and diagnoses about Muslim decline and subjugation, with its realization deemed the true path forward amid a "web of custom and superstition which can confuse Muslim thinking."[43] However, such discourses of Muslim revivalism also decentered the Malay rulers and the *kerajaan* as the ontological grounding of Malay politics in its privileging of *ijtihad* (independent reasoning) as the key to progress, social justice, and Muslim revival in the face of imperial power and alien immigration.

Vibrant as their intellectual causes may be, the "Islamic reformists were the most unfortunate losers" in this episode of Malaya's preindependence history, as their project of anticolonialism was hijacked by the conservative aristocracy.[44] Nevertheless, amid the turmoil, Islam ended up playing an important role in developing an "assertive political consciousness" among the Malays.[45] The four features of the Islamist challenge—nonviolence, social critique, pan-Muslim consciousness, and sharia-mindedness—would continue to shape the contours, debates, and imaginations of Malaysia's political landscape, demonstrating the extent to which the lexicon of Islam had permeated Malay political consciousness and collective imaginaries. These pressures would become a major source of ontological insecurity for those who won the custodianship to the Malayan (and later Malaysian) state: the Westernized Malay elite from the United Malays National Organisation (UMNO). which served as Malaysia's hegemonic ruling party from 1957 to 2018.[46]

Between Inheritance and Independence: Islam and the Ontological Insecurity of Malaysia's Early Elites (1957–1981)

The previous section laid out the context in which Islam was embedded, transformed, and contested in state, society, and politics in colonial Malaya. Malaya's independence in 1957, and later Malaysia's formation in 1963, ushered in the question of whether self-rule made any difference to Islam's position in Malaysian politics.[47] To approach this question, we must first unpack what Malaysia's attainment of modern nation-statehood meant. In his theorization of modern nation-states as imagined communities, Ben Anderson argues that these states are ontologically grounded in "homogenous, empty time," which he also calls "horizontal, secular time."[48] This understanding entails a particular spatial-temporal conception of the global geography. On a temporal level, the idea of living in "horizontal, secular" time enables the germinating nationalist consciousness to embrace a linear view of history and conjure "national" histories that extend to a past without nation-states. On the spatial level, imagining the world as suspended calendrically within "homogenous, empty" time situates nations as parallel communities within the same space-time continuum.[49] The result is that nation-states are reified within a cosmology, or, alternatively, a kind of "chronopolitics" that posits that "nations imagine themselves among each other horizontally, across one clock moment existing simultaneously and evenly, symmetrically."[50]

Anderson's reading of state symmetry is problematized by Kelly, who argues that, in skipping its colonial foundations, what Anderson did was "really reproducing the story of modernization."[51] By pushing the question of coloniality aside, differences between states were not taken as varietals with history, but rather as stratifications delineated by a "method of comparison" that conceptualized states as comparable and rankable within the modernization framework consisting of developmental categories like "stages" or "worlds."[52] Despite having emerged from European experiences of state building "characterized by industrialization, rationality, bureaucracy, and efficiency in war-making," these nomenclatures emerging from regionally and culturally specific experience had taken on universalist pretensions.[53] Not only that, the modernization framework that presumed a kind of state symmetry revolved around an understanding that development (or lack thereof) was an "individual state problem."[54] This statist worldview, thus, energized a sense of agency within state elites as they could now fashion themselves as autonomous modernizers striving to attain progress and recognition for their respective nations. However, it also locked the non-West within an asymmetrical epistemological relationship whereby the imagined West remained the sole referent for ideas about progress and development.[55]

Thus, as they achieved independence, postcolonial state elites faced an exogenous environment where there was the expectation to "catch up" and ascend the modernization ladder. At the same time, they were subjected to endogenous pressures from the societies they governed to articulate and express a national identity that was premised on some ideals of non-Western authenticity.[56] Put differently, postcolonial leaders were torn between the need to achieve ontological *sameness* (modernizing like everybody else) and *difference* (a self-identity of the postcolonial state distinct from others, especially their former colonial masters) at the same time. The former was driven by the normative standards and material exigencies ingrained within the Eurocentric international hierarchy, while promises of self-determination in nationalist politics fueled the latter.[57] Indeed, for many living in these decolonized states, being rid of colonial overlordship (at least nominally) meant that the goal of indigenous actualization had no reason to be delayed. Calls to reconcile identity (statehood) and practice (statecraft) were now pressing and legitimate, and the task fell on the shoulders of state elites who had to both define and "actualize the presentation of the state."[58]

In Malaysia, among such calls for decolonial and indigenous authenticity was an appeal for more Islamization that had made its way into the Malay political mainstream. However, as I argued in the previous chapter, the international order the postcolonial elites found themselves in remained a racialized one, where religio-cultural differences were treated as markers of superiority and inferiority, with Islam often cast out as the "other" of industrial modernity. The internalization of this stigma also meant that the position of Islam had become a source of ontological insecurity for the postcolonial Malay elites. To further outline this dynamic, I will first discuss the sociological background of these elites, followed by an analysis of Islam's salience in Malaysia's constitutional and identity politics.

The Elites

Malaya's independence in 1957 was precipitated by the formation of the Alliance Party, a consociationalist coalition consisting of UMNO, the Malayan Chinese Association, and the Malayan Indian Congress that represented the three major ethnic groups in Peninsula Malaya.[59] Led by pro-aristocrat, pro-capitalist Malayan

Anglophone elites (with the whiskey-drinking, race-horse-owning Tunku Abdul Rahman as their leader) and having secured British endorsement, the Alliance Party managed to secure tremendous victories in the local and national elections. Gaining fifty-one out of fifty-two seats in the federal legislative council election in 1955, the Alliance Party negotiated for Malaya's independence in 1957. It went on to become the hegemonic ruling coalition of Malaysia for the next sixty-one years until its successor, the Barisan Nasional (National Front), was defeated electorally in 2018.[60]

The early political elites in Malaysia are best typologized by what Benda calls "modernizing traditional elites." A few features characterized these elites. First, they were recruited on an "ascriptive basis" from established "social classes, strata or groups"; second, they derived their "social preeminence" from Western education and outlook; and third, they comprised "a fairly distinct minority within the traditional classes of their origin."[61] By virtue of their class positions in lineages, commerce, civil service, and communal organizations, these communal elites claimed representation of their respective ethnic groups and worked with the British to counter threats "from below" in the form of labor movements; anticolonial, radical Malay nationalists; and a militant Communist movement with an overwhelmingly ethnic Chinese membership.[62] The suppression of these political challenges, in turn, consolidated their status as future leaders of a gestating nation. In this section, my discussion of the elites, however, pertains only to the Malay-Muslim aristocratic, political, and administrative elites who held immense power during Malaysia's formative moments following the significant expansion of state capacity due to the colonial state's extensive counterinsurgency campaign against the Communist militants in the mid-twentieth century.[63] As the designated political heirs of the British, these Malay elites held the most senior political positions in the country[64] and were most represented in the civil service.[65] Therefore, they were most consequential in setting the agenda for questions of state identity, including that of Islam's position in postcolonial Malaysia.

The profiles of UMNO's first four presidents best illustrate Benda's typology of the modernizing traditional elites.[66] Onn Jaafar, the founding president of UMNO, came from a lineage of *Menteri Besars* (chief ministers) in the southern state of Johor and was once the sultan's advisor and a *Menteri Besar* himself.[67] His successor Tunku Abdul Rahman (henceforth the Tunku), Malaysia's first prime minister (1957–1970), was a prince from the Malay state of Kedah and once served as a district officer and later in the Legal Department of the Federation. Malaysia's second prime minister (1970–1976), Abdul Razak, was of Pahang nobility and served in various capacities as a member of the elite Malay Administrative Service, including as state secretary at the mere age of twenty-eight in 1950, the highest rank available in the bureaucracy of the Pahang state. Hussein Onn, son of Onn Jaafar, was once a member of the Johor military and the police force before serving in both the Johor and Malayan civil service. He became Malaysia's third prime minister (1976–1981) after Abdul Razak's untimely demise. All four were educated in elite schools set up by the British in Malaya and had traveled to the UK for their education (with all three prime ministers earning a law degree).

Interestingly, John Funston's record of UMNO's Executive Committee members before 1969 shows a similar social makeup, in that most of these leaders were graduates of English education (though not necessarily at the tertiary level), with many being senior members of the civil service.[68] As heirs of a traditionalist power hierarchy, these elites enjoyed a working relationship with the British, which, in turn, exposed them to Western education and administrative experience within the colonial state apparatus. Their social position as Anglophones with close ties to royalty also meant that they were well suited to managing relations between the trifecta that sustained the colonial political economy: the British colonial authorities, the non-Malay communal and business elites, and the palaces.[69]

While the traditional aspect of these modernizing traditional elites is evident from our discussion of traditionalism above, Benda does not elucidate the modernizing aspect. How did the Malay political and administrative elites approach the question of modernization? What were their views about it vis-à-vis questions of Westernization, democracy, and the local context? Where did Islam fit in the grander scheme of things? Very little research has been done on the subject. A notable exception is James Scott's study about the political ideology of the early administrative elites in Malaysia, based on his dissertation research on the Malayan Civil Service in the early 1960s. Scott argues that, despite Malaysia's continuity in institutional arrangement from colonial to postcolonial rule, there was a "discontinuity in political ideologies" as the nation's stewardship was passed to the postcolonial elites.[70] The discontinuity was due to a cultural dualism among the elites marked by a "coexistence of Western values at the peripheral level, together with more traditional notions in the central region."[71] For Scott, what gave birth to this dualism was the elites' socialization that combined an upbringing entrenched in traditional culture (an engineered traditionalism, as noted above) followed by prolonged exposure to Western values and education. Their lack of in-depth commitment toward democracy was the product of a gap between these two worldviews, with Western ideas about liberal democracy forming only the periphery but not the core of their belief system.[72] In any case, I argue that this "central-periphery" metaphor is less illustrative of the dynamic and that the amalgamation of Western values and local beliefs by these elites can be better understood if interpreted through Zarakol's theorization of the "established-outsider" dynamic in international politics and the stigmatization effects it created.[73] Commitments by postcolonial indigenous elites toward Western norms of democracy and individual rights cannot be analyzed without first interrogating the self-reflexivity of these elites in terms of their historically situated positionality in the global order, which, in turn, influenced their understanding of what Westernization could bring to their nations.

On the question of social positionality, two features separated the postcolonial Malaysian elites from those in Indonesia, Burma, Thailand, Pakistan, or even Türkiye. They were neither participants in a revolutionary war (many were arguably counterrevolutionaries against the anticolonial nationalists and Communists) nor a class of militarized elites who arose from coups and countercoups due to a perceived need to confront existential invasive or disintegrative threats.[74] A relatively stable transition from colonial to postcolonial rule meant that the traditional modernizing elites of Malaysia benefited significantly from the "opportunities for education, status, and pay" the status quo afforded them.[75] Yet, to label them "Westernized"—a category defined in opposition to the anticolonial, revolutionary, intelligentsia class in Vietnam and Indonesia—risks oversimplifying their global positionality based on the bipolar logic of the Cold War.[76] Given the experience of the Japanese Occupation and the rise of anticolonial discourse among the educated class, the fact that they were colonized subjects of a foreign imperial force was not lost to these elites. After all, UMNO's birth in 1946 was precipitated by Malay aristocratic elites leading a Malay mass protest movement against the Malayan Union project that was perceived as a threat toward Malay political dominance.[77]

The positionality of the early Malay political and administrative elites is better understood as a *contradiction*. They were "outsiders" of an imperial order that excluded the colonized periphery, often on the implicit basis of race.[78] Yet, at the same time, they were also "insiders" by virtue of ascending a social hierarchy instituted and erected by British colonialism. In this context, being the indigenous insider was not a meritocratic outcome but rather qualified by specific exposure, outlooks, and knowledge associated with the West.[79] As Scott observed, they were "self-conscious local modernizers who may vilify the West but are nonetheless the bearers of much of its heritage."[80] However, given the disproportionate concentration of elite educational institutions, capital, and technology in the West, the Westernized elites remained outsiders in this global hierarchy of merit as non-White, non-Europeans.[81] Thus, I argue Scott's observation of a central-periphery duality among the early postcolonial elites is not so much a product of cognitive dissonance after the socialization of contrasting values, but rather a self-understanding of these elites of their global and local positionality. Their domestic centrality as political and administrative elites was legitimized by their position as political insiders associated with the former colonial administration. However, their ascendance of the domestic hierarchy was always underscored by a conscious realization of their outsider status marked by a global color line that relegated Malaysia to the margins.[82] This experience of marginality within a stratified global hierarchy sharpened the appeal of nationalism among the elites, as having control over the "nation" gave them a sovereign space to formulate a state identity that was, by definition, exceptional.

The experience of colonization and the racialized global order also fostered an "existential dilemma par excellence" among the state elites, in that differences in "material capability" with the West had "become a moral, social, and cultural issue."[83] For some, this led to the pursuits of modernization that were ridden with cultural angst, as witnessed in how projects aiming to build a capitalist industrial society were often accompanied by an active embrace of European attire, lifestyle, and mannerisms in place of local customs and traditions, as if they were markers of progress.[84] Yet, this penchant for creative destruction shown by the Kemalist nationalists in Türkiye and the reformists of Meiji Japan was not observed in postcolonial Malaysia.[85] Despite having internalized the colonial image of the Malays as "tradition-bound, fatalistic and indolent people," as noted in Maaruf's documentation of the Tunku's writings, the Malay administrative and political elites never embarked on a frantic Westernization project to overhaul the status quo, even as they fashioned themselves to be the chaperones of modernity.[86]

To be sure, the idea of being "modern" in their own terms and turf was not new to the Malayan elites. Hussin wrote about a politics of representation in the photographic depictions of the sultan of Johor in the late nineteenth century, whereby the signaling of his "amenability to Western ideas" was always balanced by a demonstration of "continued allegiance to existing hierarchies, practices, and religious mores."[87] Amoroso's description of how the UMNO aristocrats "appropriated the role of protecting the rulers, and the Malay tradition, from British efforts to destroy them" indicated not only political deftness but also a deep desire to preserve indigenous identity and its prestige markers.[88] Thus, in addressing how postcolonial elites dealt with the question of Westernization and modernization, it is important to identify which image of the West the postcolonial Malay elites were referencing and which image of modernity they wanted to show the world.

The two images of modernity these elites had to contend with were that of a democracy and an industrialized nation. According to Scott, for the early administrative elites, "the civic culture of a stable democracy is perceived to be every bit as *modern* as the steel mills or armies of technicians and engineers that characterize industrial states" (emphasis mine).[89] Thus, it is perhaps unsurprising that the ruling elites saw greater value in cultivating technocratic competence via the administrative state, considering that many of them were the highly valued technicians and engineers themselves (or upper management who sought out such expertise). Scott's survey found these elites to be paternalistic, indifferent toward ideology, disdainful of politics (partially due to their perception of how the politicians lacked finesse and education), and fearful of the "retrograde masses," all suggesting an obsession in attaining secular, material progress instead of committing to a broader democratization agenda.[90] Historian Anthony Milner even wrote that the Tunku was known to be an admirer of the Turkish revolution, to the extent he was called a "Kemal-Ataturk type" by his Islamist critics.[91] In retrospect, Scott's detection of only a "formalistic" belief in democracy among the Malayan elites is unsurprising, given that their contact with Western superiority came in the form of its coercive, material power instead of democratic liberation.[92]

Yet, as paternalistic and self-assured as they were, the Malay elites could not escape the gaze of both international society and their own. In Scott's account, the administrative elites had a "feeling that the West is watching," which made them acutely aware of not only their nation's socioeconomic status but also its democratic status.[93] This status awareness can be seen in how the elites acknowledged that having elections "was an absolute requirement for any state that aspires to international respectability."[94] Unlike neighboring Suharto's military rule that spanned decades, the fact that parliamentary rule was reinstated in Malaysia after only two years of emergency rule following the May 13, 1969, racial riots also illustrates the elites' concern about their democratic standing.[95] Without the structural conditions that led to the rise of an autonomous militaristic, bureaucratic elite who saw total control of power as instrumental to achieving growth and stability, such as in Thailand, Türkiye, Pakistan, and Burma, both performance and representative legitimacy remained equally important to the political and administrative elites in Malaysia.[96] Having earned their right to rule within a colonial-endorsed electoral regime instead of a revolutionary one, the elites were particularly susceptible to bottom-up challenges, especially when it was articulated in a language such as Islam that stood outside the technocratic realm they monopolized.

Religion of the Federation: Identity or Ideology?

Having covered the sociological and ideological makeup of the ruling elites, we will now move on to the institutional and political context in which the position of Islam within the federation of Malaysia was contested during its early years in the 1960s and 1970s. One key arena of contention was the constitution itself, an area where Islam's judicialization was pursued.[97] Historians have shown that in the process of drafting Malaya's constitution, the Malay sultans, the aristocrats, and the communal elites from the Alliance Party were unanimous in their opinion that the federation would, by all intentions and means, be a secular state.[98] However, a clause was introduced in the Constitution: Article 3(1) that stipulates that "Islam is the religion of the Federation; but other religions may be practised in peace and harmony in any part of the Federation." Pressured even by its own members to include the clause, UMNO leadership managed to extract an agreement from its less enthusiastic partners, the Malayan Chinese Association and Malayan Indian Congress.[99] Interestingly, the Malay rulers objected to it, fearing that the federal government would usurp their control over Islam at the state level.[100]

The recognition of Islam as the official religion was not an acquiescence toward theocratic rule. Rather, it underscored the precarious intercommunal balance of power at a time when the Malay population had only a slight edge over the non-Malay population following decades of in-migration of workers from China and the Indian subcontinent to support the labor-intensive colonial economy.[101] Given that the legal definition of a Malay was inextricably tied to the Muslim faith, the confessional identity of the state—couched in the language of "official religion"—had served as a marker of Malay (and by extension UMNO's) supremacy within a multicultural social landscape.[102] The product of this balancing is a constitution that establishes the special position of the Malays, such as in their categorization as *bumiputeras* (sons of the soil; Article 153);[103] the designation of the Malay ruler as the constitutional head of state and of Islam (Article 3[2–3]); the prohibition against proselytizing Muslims (Article 11[4]);[104] and at the same time, the maintenance of provisions that safeguard more secular, liberal, and egalitarian notions of citizenship, freedom, and basic rights.[105]

For the many Muslim activists motivated by anticolonial Islamist ideologies, the constitution represented a dissonance because they viewed building a Muslim nation on top of a structurally secular colonial state as an inherently problematic undertaking.[106] In the nascent years of the postcolonial era, agitations against this dissonance were largely taken up by PAS. Founded in 1951, PAS was invested in turning Malaysia into an Islamic state—the contours of which were left amorphous, apart from that it would be "the means of an end" to implement Islamic law.[107] Whereas this vision of the Islamic state was not immune to influences from foreign Islamist revivalist movements, local contingencies also impacted PAS's political trajectory significantly. For instance, Marican argues that it was UMNO's liberal accommodation of non-Malay interests, especially the jus soli conferment of citizenship, that precipitated PAS's "sudden change from an Islamic welfare association to a political party committed to defend Malay rights," with many of its members coming from UMNO.[108]

Under close inspection, PAS's championing of Islamic sovereignty and pro-Malay social welfare, education, and language policies in the early decades after independence can be understood as tactics to outflank UMNO's position as the legitimate protector of Malay-Muslim interests instead of gearing toward an abject overturning of the political system.[109] Indeed, perceived elite distance from the grassroots in matters such as language, culture, and religion, as embodied by the Tunku's aloof personality and leadership, compounded religion's saliency in debates about state identity as it was interwoven with broader issues of class, interests, and ethics.[110] Nasr, for example, aptly described the nature of Islamism as an "ideological challenge from below."[111] PAS's rise as a formidable foe of UMNO was felt almost immediately after the bliss of independence. In the first general election of Malaya in 1959, PAS won 21.4 percent of the votes, as well as two state assemblies. The Alliance Party's share of the popular vote dropped precipitously from 81 percent in 1955 to 51.8 percent in 1959, although it retained control of parliament thanks to the first-past-the-post electoral system.[112]

Malaysia's ethnoreligiously diverse demography further complicated matters around Islam and state identity. With the non-Malay, non-Muslim population composing close to 40 percent of the population in the early decades of independence, any fundamental change that required a constitutional amendment was almost impossible under normal circumstances. However, Islam as an oppositional discourse of reform and resistance continued to gain traction among the Malays as the sense of socioeconomic alienation experienced during colonial, "secular" rule persisted during the first decade of Alliance rule.[113] Intercommunal inequality was felt most starkly when the Malays compared themselves to the Chinese community. Even by 1969, the share capital ownership of the *bumiputeras* (most of them Malays) was only a meager 1.5 percent, as compared to the 22.8 percent of the Chinese.[114] According to 1963 figures, the Malays were also overrepresented in the nation's poverty population (74 percent), while underrepresented in university enrolment (11 percent).[115] Yet, the Tunku's infamous remark that "unless we are prepared to drown every non-Malay, we can never think of an Islamic Administration" also illustrates how calls to restore Islam's centrality in Malaysia were denied by the UMNO elites using a pragmatic reasoning of preserving intercommunal peace.[116] This blockade further frustrated the proponents of Islamization, many of whom had taken the introduction of Islamic laws such as Hudud (the Islamic Penal Code) to be the keystone of an Islamic state since the 1970s.[117]

The Tunku's rhetorical resort to demographic pragmatism also revealed the Malay elites' reluctance to publicly commit to an ideological dissociation from Islam despite their private indifference. Indeed, there were no signs that the Malay elites, despite their Westernized outlook and subscription to a secular model of development, wanted a wholesale rejection of Islam in Malaysia's social and political life. On the contrary, religion and tradition remained central to the cultural worldview of the UMNO elites. Party leaders often expressed concerns that the perceived moral decline in the West would find its way to the Malay youth.[118] Socialized into an (invented) traditionalist worldview that conferred a symbolic position to Islam but had little use for it in governance, the Malay political and administrative elites were content in keeping the status quo where the administration of Islam was left with the Malay rulers as the titular heads of religion.[119] Unlike their Islamist opponents, they made a conscious break between Islam as an identity marker and ideological resource, however unstable that break may have been.

However, Islam's potential as both identity and ideology still created a liminal space that became a source of ontological insecurity for the ruling Muslim elites. Questions about Islam could breach the technocratic assuredness of the administrative Malay-Muslim elites because it challenged their insider status in social hierarchies both global and local. Being seen as more "Muslim" sharpened their outsider status within a Eurocentric global order they were otherwise comfortable with, while being accused as insufficiently Islamic by domestic stakeholders also casted them as outsiders in Malaysia's Malay-Muslim-centric ethnocracy.[120] Believing that "aspects of Islamic belief" were "retarding Malay economic development,"[121] these elites struggled with the dual promises of decolonization: to both "catch up" and be autonomous. On the one hand, there was the goal of material prosperity and economic development, which underpinned their international recognition as modernizers; on the other hand, there was the goal of Muslim identity actualization that could usher in structural and spiritual emancipation from the colonial masters, which buttressed the elites' claim to indigenous legitimacy and moral supremacy.

In other words, because UMNO's secular-leaning ethnonationalist elites never chose to expel or elevate Islam aggressively to reshape their state identities (unlike the case of Kemalism or Khomeini's revolutionary Iran), they were unable to reconcile their modernizing ambition (and their desire to be recognized as "modern" by the West) with Islam's centrality in the traditionalist social structures from which they ascended and drew claims of popular legitimacy.[122] This need to secure both performance and representative legitimacy would continue to produce ambiguities and tensions as Westernized Malay-Muslim ruling elites struggled with where and how Islam fit within the modern Malaysian state, even as experimentations with religion and politics were flourishing across the globe in the fluid geography of the Cold War.[123]

Conclusion

The Global War on Terror (GWOT)'s stigmatizing effects on Muslim states is not a predetermined outcome that originates from so-called incompatible, civilizational differences between the "secular" West and "nonsecular" Muslim world. Rather, the stigmatization stems from how Muslim state actors think about the stigmatized marker (in this case, Islam), their relationship with it, and the broader episteme that defines questions of status and success. The extent of elite internalization of the judgment of inferiority and perceptions of distance between state identity and the stigmatized marker are equally important in terms of how stigmatized actors react to the sociocultural hierarchy. A genealogical tracing of how Islam was conceived of by Malay-Muslim elites in relation to Malaysian statehood and governance is, therefore, necessary to understand this dynamic before we move into the post-GWOT world.

This chapter forms the first part of that tracing. It covers Islam's changing institutional, sociopolitical, and symbolic role in Malaya from the precolonial era to the period before Mahathir Mohamad became the prime minister of Malaysia in 1981. I show that the roots of Islam as a source of ontological insecurity for the postcolonial elites were laid from the very beginning as a result of a state architecture inherited from the colonial administration; the global social positionality of the early cohorts of Malay political and administrative elites; and the symbolic importance of Islam as a marker of indigenous identity and anticolonial resistance. The Westernized Malay political and administrative elites faced a dilemma as they saw a limited role for Islam in governance and their modernization project, yet their claim to indigeneity continued to depend on invocations of Islam. It was not until Mahathir's takeover that there was a serious effort to resolve these tensions, from which serious efforts to define "modern" and "moderate" Islam began.

THREE

Mahathir and the Making of Malaysia's "Islamic" Leviathan

Modernizing Islam, Moderating Islam (1981–2001)

> Islam is perhaps the most misunderstood religion in the world today and indeed throughout history. It is not only misunderstood by non-Muslims, but it is also misunderstood by Muslims themselves. How else can there be so many Muslim sects with beliefs and teachings which are so different and contradictory? Some must be wrong, the result of not understanding or misunderstanding Islam.
>
> —Mahathir Mohamad, speech at Oxford University, 1996[1]

In the previous chapter, I argued that the question of Islam had become a source of ontological insecurity for the postcolonial Malay-Muslim elites. Their simultaneous pursuit of performance and representative legitimacy had put them in a bind as they adjudicated Islam's position in governance. As the ideological and political heirs of British colonial rule, these Westernized, Anglophone elites did not see much role for Islam in Malaysia's modernization. Yet their social legitimacy as indigenous elites of a modern nation-state drew heavily from their ascriptive and constitutional identity as Malay-Muslims, which helped separate them from the non-Malay, non-Muslim minorities in Malaysia's fractious communal landscape.[2]

The question of Islam was thus sandwiched between these elites' (self-regarded) status as modernizers and their political standing as communal elites. Being seen as too attached to Islam would increase their stigmatization within a Eurocentric global hierarchy. However, being perceived as too detached from Islam would open up challenges to their legitimacy to rule. Given this dilemma, the early generations of Malay elites were content to maintain the status quo of a relatively distant state-Islam relationship.

A critical turn happened with the ascendency of Mahathir Mohamad (henceforth Mahathir) as the fourth prime minister of Malaysia (1981–2003). Mahathir represented a change in elite strategy in addressing the "problem" of Islam as a source of ontological insecurity. He strove to implement a governing vision in which Islam is recognized as compatible, if not central, to Malaysia's attainment of industrial modernity. Unlike his predecessors, Mahathir actively confronted Islam's stigmatization in his articulation and actualization of a vision of "Islamic" modernity for Malaysia. He found the problem in the misunderstanding of Islam as noted in the opening quote. This vision led to specific trajectories and forms of Islamization, all geared at addressing the perception that Islam was unamenable and anachronistic to modern living. The discursive construction of the Muslim "radical" as someone driven by religious deviancy proceeded in tandem with the state's project to nurture Muslims into modern, entrepreneurial subjects. One effect of Islamization is what I call the *Islamization of security*, in which perceived Muslim unorthodoxy or even radicalization was increasingly dealt with as religious deviancy *discursively*, and by authorities with theological expertise *institutionally*.

This chapter is divided into three sections. Collectively, they address how the motive of ontological security seeking animated changes in Malaysia's state-Islam relationship and how a seemingly modernist Islamization framework led to Islam's deepening role in Malaysia's security governance. The first section explores Mahathir the person, to discuss a shift in the Malay elite mindset that heralded a slew of Islamization programs that drastically transformed Malaysia's political, institutional, and social landscape. Whereas his then deputy, the renowned Muslim youth activist Anwar Ibrahim (henceforth Anwar), is often credited as the major force behind the state-led Islamization during the Mahathir years,[3] I argue that Mahathir himself had made a case for Islam's wider incorporation in governance well before he became prime minister, through an analysis of his early writings.

The second section explores Mahathir's Islamization as a project that took on specific trajectory and forms. The trajectory taken was one of Islam's governmentalization, whereas its forms were bureaucratization, professionalization, corporatization, and the Islamization of the sciences. I argue that these modalities reflected state efforts to increase the visibility and accessibility of a "modern" and "moderate" form of Islam to improve Islam's stigmatized image. The third section addresses the implications of these state-building pathways in the security realm. Parallel to the state's cultivation of moderate Islam was the development of a securitized language of Islamic deviancy. I illustrate this by carefully examining state discourses surrounding two "deviant" movements: Darul Arqam, a commune-living, neo-Sufi movement, and Al-Ma'unah, an esoteric, Malay martial arts group that turned into a heist-staging militia. State explication of Muslim militancy had turned toward the theological, with these movements portrayed as regressions toward backward, unsophisticated, and fanatical Islam. These developments prefigured the contours of the moderate Islam discourse that populated the post–September 11 security milieu, setting the path for a politics of counter-terror that equate the state's ability to moderate "deviant" or "aberrant" Islam as a measure of its ability to stem Muslim radicalization.

Mahathir's "Islamic" Modernity: Materializing Islam in a Materialistic World

> A common source of confusion is the relationship between spirituality and an individual's economic status. Poverty does not mean spiritual strength and wealth does not mean spiritual weakness.
>
> —Mahathir Mohamad, *The Challenge*[4]

Scholars have generally agreed that Malaysia's Islamization occurred most pervasively during Mahathir's twenty-two-year rule in Malaysia, which led to profound changes in social mores, institutional culture, and political norms.[5] By *Islamization*, I refer to a sociopolitical phenomenon that saw calls, convictions, and causes to safeguard, elevate, and entrench Islamic values and teachings increasingly pervading political, social, and economic life. This chapter's handling of Malaysia's Islamization will be somewhat different from two prominent theories proposed by anthropologists, historians, and political scientists to explain Malaysia's Islamization. The first is the revivalist theory that favors a bottom-up and transnational explanation, focusing on social changes and religious mobilization in Malaysia that intensified following the Iranian Revolution of 1979.[6] The second is the "Islamization race" theory that opts for a top-down explanation, pointing to the heated contest between the two major Malay-Muslim parties in Malaysia, the ruling ethnonationalist United Malays National Organisation (UMNO) and the Islamist Pan-Malaysian Islamic Party (PAS), as the catalyst that augmented Islam's social and institutional role in Malaysia.[7]

This chapter leans toward a top-down explanation, but argues that the *trajectory* and *forms* of Malaysia's state-led Islamization are better understood as stigma correction strategies that address the state elites' insecurities about Islam's position, the origins of which I have discussed in chapter 2.[8] As his thinking about Islam's role in Malaysia's modernization was markedly different from his predecessors, Mahathir's leadership was a crucial turning point. As we shall see, his ideas informed the overarching vision under which specific forms of Islamization were pursued and later resulted in the formation of an "Islamized" security habitus.

Mahathir's background best characterizes the break he represented. The youngest son of a headmaster of a government English school who was trained as a medical doctor, Mahathir was not roped into politics by social connections or wealth. Instead, he crafted his fortune as a "self-made man"—an experience that percolated deeply into his anti-aristocratic, Malay nationalist political philosophy.[9] A result of a strange mix of fortune and fortitude, Mahathir's ascendency resembled the internal changes within UMNO and was certainly a radical break from UMNO's preference for blue-blooded aristocrats.[10] In the words of Mauzy and Milne, Mahathir was "the first prime minister not to have been educated in Britain, the first not of aristocratic birth, the first not trained as a lawyer, and the first who does not play golf."[11] Politically, however, Mahathir was not an outlier. The impatience and pushback against Tunku Abdul Rahman's (henceforth the Tunku) perceived accommodation of Chinese demands and his laissez-faire economic policies by the Malay ultras within UMNO preceded and even buoyed Mahathir's political career.[12] After the racial riots of Malaysia in 1969, the government took on a more interventionist role in socioeconomic policies via the New Economic Policy (NEP). The NEP was broadly aimed at poverty eradication, but it had a more specific target of reducing interethnic inequality through a plethora of preferential and affirmative action policies that favored the Malays in government contracts, scholarships, housing, and civil service employment.[13]

When Mahathir rose to power, he enjoyed both the advantage of leading an UMNO whose control by the Anglophone elites was waning and the increased infrastructural power of the state that was expanded by the NEP's social engineering ambitions.[14] Mahathir made the most out of the situation, eventually securing for himself a form of personalized authoritarian rule with considerable power concentrated in the Prime Minister's Office, which Slater calls "an iron fist in an iron cage."[15] But the question remains, how did someone like Mahathir, who was derogatorily called a *murtad* (apostate) and liberal by his Islamist opponents, preside over an Islamization project that was arguably the most transformative of any Malaysian prime minister?[16] For this, we must turn to the writings of the man himself.

Making Islam Work: The Challenge According to Mahathir Mohamad

If the previous cohorts of Anglophone UMNO elites could only prevaricate between settling for more Westernization for modernization's sake or more indigenization through enacting some "Islamic" policies to better reflect the (Malay-centric) demos, Mahathir was determined to escape this binary and chart his own course. Refusing to resort to both Western apologia and anti-West rejectionism, Mahathir subverted the dilemma by arguing explicitly that economic development, in its accumulation of material wealth as well as the advancement of science and technology, would be a lost cause without the spiritual guidance of religion, which, in the case of Muslims, is Islam. These ideas were laid out most concretely in his third book, *The Challenge*, a book written in the 1970s with the Malay edition published in 1976 (and the English translation in 1986).[17] As someone known for his remarkably coherent and resilient worldview, and who does not delegate his writing, we can be reasonably confident that Mahathir's writings reflect his thinking.[18] Notably, *The Challenge* was written before Malaysia achieved considerable success in its development and industrialization programs in the late 1980s and early 1990s. This signals that Mahathir's firm belief in Islam's positive role in attaining industrial modernity for Malaysia was not a post-hoc formulation.

The Challenge is similar to Mahathir's most famous book, *The Malay Dilemma* (discussed below), in that it took the form of a thesis instead of propaganda and was written in a paternalistic, unsentimental, and prescriptive tone that was fashionably Mahathir's. Interestingly, as a career politician climbing the ranks of UMNO when the book was written, Mahathir only dedicated five pages to matters related to PAS and UMNO. The rest of the book was devoted to its namesake: the challenge of changing the "misinterpretation of Islam" by the Malays.[19] Mahathir's call for Islam's reinterpretation stemmed from what he saw as the relative backwardness of the Muslim world, which he attributed to a false binary in the minds of many Muslims that separated the profane from the sacred, leading to an overemphasis on spiritual gains instead of worldly ones. He found these preoccupations to be "rigid and doctrinaire," not to mention impractical and unpracticable, and saw no utility in differentiating between "Islamic" and "secular" knowledge.[20] Largely self-taught in his understanding of Islam, Mahathir had little patience for abstract academic debates and for the religious authorities he deemed to have failed the Muslims. For him, hanging in the balance for the Malays was "survival itself."[21] This is how he articulated the stakes: "If a Muslim society, because of its wish to be known as a staunchly Islamic one, became weak in the so-called 'worldly' knowledge necessary for its survival, and was finally destroyed by enemies, leaving not a single person alive, then as far as that society was concerned, Islam would no longer exist."[22]

In Mahathir's opinion, when properly understood, Islam is a "theology of progress" that is progressive and rational, and does not confuse accumulating material gains with materialism.[23] Known for his disdain of the ascetic, he argued that renouncing the world would only lead to weaknesses in the faith. Mahathir's Islam necessitated worldly success because, for him, reality must "strengthen" the faith instead of testing its limits.[24] The reality for Mahathir was that Muslims were victimized, marginalized, and superseded by others in the global order; the only way for them to regain their place and dignity was through hard work. In fact, in *The Challenge* he made it explicit that "there is no reason why Muslims should not work hard."[25] Unsurprisingly, both Schottmann and Khoo have noted a certain Protestant ethic in Mahathir's exegesis, as seen in his emphasis on "industriousness, honesty, self-denial, discipline, thrift, diligence, and individual piety."[26]

The way Mahathir made his case for reinterpreting Islam, in that it was framed in a language of pragmatic urgency, matches a pattern found in Zarakol's study of Turkish, Russian, and Japanese elites.[27] In these cases, memories of punishing encounters with the West resulted in national elites developing a sense of anxiety over their perceived and "demonstrable" inferiority (in the standards of the West), thereby eliciting a "catching up" drive that was often articulated within the same standards set up by the West.[28] Clearly, Mahathir had his sights set on the goal of catching up with the West on the same economic, social, cultural, and military grounds upon which the West proclaimed its superiority. After all, Mahathir's "theology of progress" relied on Muslims recognizing that the "rational" pursuit of economic growth is Islamic.[29] In *The Challenge*, he wrote about how despite having enjoyed abundant oil wealth, the Gulf states "continue to lack 'worldly' ability and efficiency (as a result of the insufficient pursuit of 'worldly' knowledge)."[30] Even as recent as 2019, Mahathir still lamented the fact that none of the fifty-two Muslim countries was considered a "developed nation" and that they had "no desire to compete" with the rest of the world.[31]

Mahathir's concerns about Muslim decline were not just rooted in material observations. Rather, his internalization of the judgment of inferiority of his community was so deep that it stood almost on cultural/epigenetic grounds. This is best seen in Mahathir's first book and arguably his magnum opus, *The Malay Dilemma*, published in 1970. The book was written from the political wilderness during Mahathir's exile from UMNO (1969–1972); he thought his political career was practically over. Interestingly, instead of centering the book on his personal spat with the Tunku who expelled him from UMNO, Mahathir went on to produce a quasi-sociological study of Malay "backwardness" with him, staying true to his medical training, offering "therapeutic diagnosis."[32] He was unapologetic in wanting "no less than to remake the Malays"[33] through pinpointing "the basic faults which must be corrected or adjusted in order that other measures to help the progress of the Malays may stand a better chance of succeeding."[34]

Though not out of bounds from the ideas of his contemporaries such as Lee Kuan Yew,[35] Mahathir's diagnosis of Malay weaknesses was undoubtedly contentious as it threaded on social Darwinist grounds, with Malay inferiority attributed to "environmental," "intrinsic," and "hereditary" factors.[36] For example, in *The Malay Dilemma*, he argued that, compared to the Chinese community that had strict rules against inbreeding (11), marital inbreeding was common among Malay families, which, in turn, retained "debilitating" hereditary and environmental traits within the Malay community (39). He derogatorily called the rural Malay community "purebred" (40), problematizing their deep religiosity and "animist beliefs" as a product of their social and genetic isolation (41). His negative portrayal of the Malays was contrasted with his reluctant, albeit racialized, admiration of the Chinese, whom he called "inherently good businessmen" (111). However, this focus on one's acumen and strength in commerce was also reflective of Mahathir's internalization of the colonial judgment, which similarly assessed its subjects based on pseudoscientific ideas of racial differences and each race's compatibility with the needs of the colonial market economy.[37]

Mahathir's ideas were certainly not unique among his peers. In his seminal work, *The Myth of the Lazy Native*, sociologist Syed Hussein Alatas bemoaned that myths about native indolence, once perpetuated to justify colonial rule, became the worldview of local elites as well.[38] Referencing a book published in 1970 by UMNO-linked intellectuals entitled *Revolusi Mental* (Mental revolution), which also called for the Malays to change their "old" ways, Alatas criticized these elites for being "under the spell of the colonial image of the Malays" in their scapegoating of indigenous culture instead of critically examining the effects of the racialized and exploitative nature of colonial capitalism.[39] According to Alatas, in perpetuating essentialist ideas of Malay indolence, these elites fashioned themselves as "modernised and progressive" and thus well poised to transform the "Malay character."[40] Mahathir adopted this stance unapologetically in his clinical attitudes toward the Malays.

What marked Mahathir apart from the writers of *Revolusi Mental* was that his critique of the Malay community was more pointed, while his call to reconcile the Islamic faith with material development was also more explicit. Even as Mahathir internalized the judgment of Malay inferiority, he could not accept Islam's stigmatization. Rather, his narrative splits race from religion, shifting the stigma to the Malay character that he claimed needed "rehabilitation" while positing Islam as a transcendental, albeit indigenous, resource for reform.[41] This line of thinking marked a significant shift from the earlier UMNO elites who were, at best, ambivalent about Islam's centrality in the modernization project. To be sure, these ideas were not original to Mahathir. Schottmann has demonstrated how Mahathir's upbringing and intellectual predilections had exposed him, directly and indirectly, to sources of modernist Islamic thinking that stretch from the *kaum muda* in the 1920s to reformist figures like Fazlur Rahman and Seyyed Hossain Nasr in the 1980s.[42] What made Mahathir's case special is that, as someone who rose to the pinnacle of power, he could put his unique blend of nationalist and Islamic modernist thinking into practice. As we shall see, Mahathir's penchant for "ratiocination" in Islamic reasoning and his distaste for any *khurafat* (superstition) was well reflected in the forms of Islamization his administration pursued.[43]

To make his case for Islam's (re)incorporation into the modern political order, Mahathir also turned his gaze back on the West in *The Challenge*. He did so not to proclaim a different set of standards but simply to measure the West against their own criteria of success and progress. In his social Darwinist outlook, Mahathir had accepted the global hierarchy and its power differentials, as seen from his tacit recognition of the qualities that enabled the West to hold onto its colonies. He saw no reason why the East "should reject the values and norms developed during their colonisation by the West" (47). In fact, Mahathir barely concealed his admiration for what he considered "old" Western values, especially "good discipline" that, in his mind, gave the West their competitive edge over the colonized.[44] The "Western" values Mahathir rejected were not those associated with the colonizing West but rather the postmodern West, which, for him, was the product of "a radical change in the Western psyche" after losing the colonies (46). For Mahathir, postmodernism exemplified a West in disillusionment and decline: a West in which, he lamented, old values such as "orderliness, discipline and firm social organisation" had given way to materialism's untrammeled greed, moral relativism, and hedonism (46).[45] He even criticized the UK Labour government for the compromises it made with striking workers because, to Mahathir, the protesters represented the "unrest and oppression" that stemmed from the insatiable desires of materialism (60–61).

To address the nihilistic and unsatisfying nature of human greed, which he believed permeated all levels of society, from king to commoner, Mahathir stressed the indispensability of religious teachings and principles as the foundation of human ethics and spiritual fulfillment—neither of which, he argued, could be provided by capitalism or communism. He argued that religion was needed *because of*, not despite, the modern capitalist order. As Mahathir noted, "Clearly, if capitalists can be controlled or brought back to the right path, their activities can benefit society" (57).

Put differently, Mahathir's interpretation of Islam was a response to the perceived excesses of Western materialism and the ascetic retreatism he saw in Muslim societies. His understanding of Islam as a guiding compass and empowering ethos charted a course for Malaysia to achieve "Western" success without wholesale

Westernization. There was no need for Malaysia to follow Western notions of human rights, which, according to Mahathir, "recognize no limits" (72). Safe to say, Mahathir harbored no intentions to follow the footsteps of Revolutionary Iran or the Taliban, whose claim of Islamic legitimacy was often articulated in repudiation of the norms and hierarchies of the international order. The last thing Mahathir wanted was for Malaysia to be seen as a pariah in the eyes of the West. His emphasis that Islam was compatible and even conducive to industrial modernity was about securing Malaysia's place within the prevailing order, while enabling Malaysian Muslims to hold their religious values and identity close and proud.

What I have shown thus far is that there was an ontological security-seeking element to Mahathir's thinking. The man was grappling with Malaysia's status as a postcolonial Muslim state and Islam's baggage as a stigmatized cultural marker simultaneously, thereby locking the goals of seeking recognition for one with another. But in claiming that the *challenge* was about harnessing the "true" teaching of Islam so that Muslims could gain control of "material wealth and modern knowledge" while preserving their spirituality, the task laid ahead for Mahathir was, therefore, to show that *Islam works*.[46] This stigma correction motive lay at the heart of Mahathir's Islamization projects.

Islamization as Ontological Security Seeking: Governing while Modernizing Islam

Mahathir's thinking found its way into the trajectory and forms through which Islamization occurred in Malaysia. By *trajectory*, I refer to the sequence in which Islamization transpired in Malaysia, which began with promoting Islamic values and culminating in the extensive institutionalization of Islam within the state bureaucracy. The trajectory was also one that witnessed a significant degree of governmental direction, involvement, and control. By *forms*, I refer to the four processes that integrated Islam into Malaysia's social and political life in its recognizably "modern" form: bureaucratization, professionalization, corporatization, and integration with the sciences.

These developments were guided by an elite mindset that modernity could be nurtured "Islamically," and that the venture necessarily needed constant *moderation* from the state. They also furthered what scholars such as Eickelman, Piscatori, and Starrett call the objectification and functionalization of Islam, which resulted in both Islam's separation as a self-contained and practicable field of knowledge and its merger with "strategic and utilitarian ends of the modern and secular discourse of policy," including security, as we shall see.[47] As an enterprise of stigma correction, the Islamization project was also paired with a recognition-seeking motive that aimed to feature Malaysia as a role model of how Islam could coexist with, and even usher in, modernity, civility, and economic prosperity. These developments would, in turn, shape the institutional and discursive context of Islam's securitization, not to mention foreshadowing the securitized moderate Islam discourse that would be popularized and propagated in the post–Global War on Terror (GWOT) landscape.

I must start with a caveat here. My emphasis on Mahathir's thinking in the previous section does not signify that he is solely responsible for Malaysia's Islamization. The process is necessarily a complex one, given the confluence of international and local factors, not to mention the complex state-society interactions that underpinned it.[48] What I am stressing here is that Mahathir's framing of Islam as necessarily compatible with industry modernity was instrumental to his administration's receptivity toward *specific* forms of Islamization in Malaysia, even if he failed to control that process eventually.[49] In refusing to treat Mahathir's Islamization as merely a "cynical manipulation of popular sentiment" in response to an Islamist opposition, I address one peculiarity of Mahathir's rule.[50] That is, despite his propensity for ruthless authoritarian rule,[51] Mahathir did not, as in the case of Suharto and the many secularist authoritarian regimes in the Arab world, orchestrate a severe crushing of his Islamist opponents. Unlike the Tunku (who enjoyed a more "liberal" reputation relative to Mahathir's strongman's persona) whose detention of PAS President Dr. Burhanuddin el-Helmy using security laws during Konfrontasi (1963–1966) practically ended the man's political career,[52] Mahathir never ordered the detention of PAS presidents or any of its senior figures, even though it was during Mahathir's rule that PAS hostility toward UMNO was at its peak. Even Ustaz Abdul Hadi Awang, who wrote a controversial edict excommunicating UMNO members as heretics in 1982, was never subjected to security laws such as the Sedition Act and the Internal Security Act (ISA).[53] The same cannot be said for the Chinese-dominated Democratic Action Party. During a politically motivated crackdown known as Operasi Lalang in 1987, its leader Lim Kit Siang and several of its senior figures were all detained under the ISA.

Governmentalizing Islam: From Islamic Values to "Islamic Leviathan"

Mahathir's first Islamization policy is the Dasar Penerapan Nilai-Nilai Islam Dalam Pentadbiran Negara (Assimilation of Islamic values in the administration of the country). Introduced in 1985, it remains active today.[54] The program sought to nurture selected "Islamic" values within the civil service, such as accountability, responsibility, honesty, dedication, toleration, diligence, and cleanliness. Starting with values was unsurprising for Mahathir, as it dovetailed with his worldview that Islam's unique contribution to secular modernity was to provide a moral correction to its hedonist, individualist, and immoral trappings. The values selected also reflected Mahathir's desire to cultivate a work ethic among the Malay-Muslims, the lack thereof, for him, stemming from a gross misunderstanding of Islam.[55] The written rationale of this policy cited below echoed the overlapping themes of identity, recognition, and survival that preoccupied Mahathir's writings: "In this context, the most important element in the shaping of the Malaysian identity are values. Values enable the formation of a *respected* society. A people that does not have certain life values will always become the *victims* of those who pursued said values. As an extension, those who developed good values will come to *control* those who did not cultivate good command of said values" (emphasis mine).[56]

State interventions to steer Islam in the "correct" way grew progressively under the Mahathir government. This led to the building of what Nasr calls the "Islamic leviathan."[57] I agree with Nasr's terminology but not his instrumentalist reading of the process. Nasr argues that the Islamic leviathan was built under a "conscious strategy" to expand "state power, capacity and reach" for economic growth, while simultaneously repackaging the postcolonial state as Islamic for ideological control.[58] I contend that it was actually the concern to cultivate "modern" Islam, undergirded by a paternalistic view that most of the masses got Islam wrong, that led to Malaysia's Islamic leviathan being built in the top-down, modernist way it was. As Hamayotsu noted, the construction of Malaysia's Islamic leviathan took place against the backdrop of a "competition between the federal and state Malay authorities."[59] Since the administration of Islam in Malaysia is constitutionally defined as a state-level affair under the control of the Malay rulers, the governmentalization of Islam, therefore, involved creating additional bureaucratic structures and circumventions to centralize control of Islam at the federal level, allowing Mahathir and other like-minded reformist elites to exercise their influence over Islam.

The proximity of the Islamization project to Mahathir himself can be seen from the fact that the most important institutions for the project were all parked under the prime minister's portfolio. The first is the Jabatan Kemajuan Islam Malaysia (JAKIM, Department of Islamic Development in Malaysia), which began as a unit in 1974, was upgraded to a section in 1984, and eventually became a minister-headed department under the Prime Minister's Department. JAKIM played a critical role in Mahathir's Islamization drive. Not only is it the secretariat of the National Fatwa Council, which is the highest Islamic authority in the country, but JAKIM also manages many aspects of Muslim life in Malaysia.[60] Domains such as halal certification, the hajj pilgrimage, religious education in national schools, and the monitoring and inspection of Islam-related films and publications are currently all centralized within JAKIM.[61] As it is armed with resources that far surpassed the state-level religious authorities,[62] political scientist Maznah Mohamad's characterization of the department as the "face of statist Islam" best describes JAKIM's prominence in Muslim governance in Malaysia.[63]

If JAKIM provided the institutional muscle to guide Malaysia's Islamization, another agency established by Mahathir, the Institute of Islamic Understanding (IKIM), supplied the intellectual foundations. Established in 1992, IKIM is a think-tank-esque outfit formed to buttress Mahathir's attempt to situate Islam within a corporatist regime that combined neoliberal economic prescriptions with state clientelism to nurture a Malay capitalist and professional class.[64] As Nasr argues: "IKIM was to portray capitalist development as compatible with Islamic values. . . . IKIM seeks to justify the pursuit of wealth, the administrative values and practices that are needed for managing it, and to rationalize globalization, consumerism, foreign investment, limited labor rights, income inequality, and the like in terms of Islam. It seeks to develop Islamic values of capitalism and articulate the notion of an 'Islamic developmental state.'"[65]

Whereas it is uncertain as to how successful JAKIM and IKIM were in shaping "Malaysian Islam" to Mahathir's satisfaction, what is clear is that these developments—all concentrated within the Prime Minister's Department—reflected a form of paternalism that is somewhat characteristic of ontological security-seeking elites described by Zarakol in her comparative study of Thailand and Türkiye.[66] For statespersons like Mahathir, in order to catch up with the West, their mandate to modernize must extend to Islam as well. However, Islamization was not just about projecting Malaysia's Islamic identity; it was also about ensuring that a particular image of Islam would prevail in Malaysia. What image then?

Modernizing Islam: The Four Forms of Islamization

Malaysia's state-engineered portraiture of modernized Islam has four images: bureaucratic, professional, corporate friendly, and inclusive of the sciences. These images were meant to showcase Islam's compatibility with a vision of civil, capitalist, and industrial modernity. They were the products of four forms of (statist) Islamization pursued extensively during the Mahathir years. To be sure, my observations of these forms are by no means a definitive or novel account of Malaysia's Islamization.[67] They dovetail with anthropological findings on how visions of Islamic modernity and civil society were negotiated, structured, and performed in "strategic loci" such as courts, bureaucracies, markets, and schools in Malaysia.[68] However, my analysis here draws from these findings to show that the Islamization project led by Mahathir's administration had an image-building element as it sought to increase the *visibility* and *accessibility* of modernized Islam. These projects, in turn, fostered the mesoinstitutional changes that further ingrained Islam's centrality in governance, perpetuating a governmentality that saw regulating and reforming Islam as key to guiding and modernizing Muslim lives.

Whereas Mahathir is by no means the sole architect of Malaysia's Islamization, his imprint is undoubtedly there, as seen in how early these projects were launched during his tenure as prime minister. For example, the International Islamic University of Malaysia (IIUM) and the Bank Islam (see below) were both started in 1983, just two years into Mahathir's premiership. This means that our prior analysis of Mahathir's thinking about Islam and modernization is directly relevant to understanding the forms of Islamization pursued by his administration. These insights also complicate theories that claim Malaysia's Islamization was primarily driven by state capture by Islamic actors, such as the ulamas (Islamic scholars), bureaucrats, and ideologues who were sympathetic to the Islamist agenda.[69] Although credible on their own, I argue that these observations of state capture and ideological hegemony in the institutionalist literature are secondary effects of an ontological security-seeking enterprise that harnessed state power into actualizing particular forms of Islam. The underlying motive of the enterprise was about combatting the stigma of Islam as unamenable to modernization and development.

The first form of Islamization pursued by the Mahathir government is bureaucratization, the product of which is described by Maznah Mohamad as Malaysia's "Divine Bureaucracy."[70] Understood by Weber as the foundation of the modern rational-legal order, it goes without saying that Malaysia's Divine Bureaucracy, informed by its business suit aesthetics and managerialist philosophy, has increased the visibility and accessibility of a "modern" form of Islam.[71] Take, for example, Malaysia's halal business industry, which is regarded as a global pioneer.[72] The Islamic bureaucracy operationalized halal certification through "evidence-based standardisation, certification and auditing procedure," transforming an activity that was initially based on the individual and social ethical judgment of Muslims into rules- and procedural-based mechanisms that defined most aspects of modern living.[73] Bureaucratization also increased the visibility of a modernized Islam in halal logos and professional certificates. The rationalization, regulation, and routinization of halal certification also facilitated entry for a variety of players, including non-Muslim entrepreneurs who intended to cater to the Muslim market, thus inadvertently increasing the accessibility of modernized Islam.[74] No doubt, bureaucratization through its disenchantment and operationalization of Islam has had far-reaching and profound impacts on the social and religious lives of Malaysians.[75] Yet, in the mind of its purveyors, bureaucratized Islam was also about making Islam central to modern living too.[76]

The second form of modernist Islamization took shape as professionalization. As Islam's bureaucratization heralded the influx of professionals such as accountants, managers, and technicians into what was supposed to be the religious domain, the rituals and practices of Islam were also subjected to the pressures of professionalization. For example, one of the key reform areas in Malaysia's Islamic governance was the professionalization of sharia court judges and lawyers, many of whom had undergone training in law schools and were taught by law professors.[77] The position of the mufti[78] is now increasingly held by office bearers who earned their PhDs in universities as opposed to individuals trained "informally" through systems of discipleship or traditional Islamic learning centers such as the *pondoks* and madrasahs.[79] In fact, even the curriculum of Islamic education in Malaysia was standardized and systematized considerably, making it a subject just like any other, enabling even non-Muslims to take it in examinations without having to profess the faith.[80] Put simply, professionalization created the structures of legibility that enabled the accessibility of modernized Islam by both nonexperts and non-Muslims. As Mohamad puts it, most of the faceless bureaucrats that staffed the Divine Bureaucracy were not individuals qualified by their religious training but professional civil servants who "could be transferred to any government department."[81] But through the active incorporation of professionals, the Islamization project increased the visibility and accessibility of Islam among the professional managerial class, thus assimilating the religion into bourgeois lifestyles.

The third form is corporatization, which is the integration of Islam within the corporate domain as well as active efforts to portray Islam as conducive and complementary to commercial and corporate activities.[82] For reasons of brevity, I will only elaborate on the latter here through the example of Malaysia's Islamic finance industry, a signature area in Mahathir's effort to corporatize Islam. As early as the late 1980s, Mahathir had argued at length that nonusurious forms of *riba* (interest) were halal. He lamented that a "form over substance" interpretation of Islam had prevented Muslims from becoming "strong through a financial system that enables commerce and social life to sustain a fair and just society."[83] Arguably, Mahathir's exhortations bore fruit. Since the institution of Malaysia's first Islamic bank in 1983, the nation's Islamic finance industry went on to achieve considerable success that, by 2019, it accounted for "over 20% of global Islamic finance assets."[84] This fervent push for Islamic finance also aligns with the goal to increase the visibility and accessibility of modernized Islam, as banking is a visible pillar of modern living, and Islamic finance is accessible to the global financial market.

The last form of Islamization entails efforts to "Islamize" the sciences. Whereas this idea of "Islamizing" the sciences was linked to the "Islamization of knowledge" project championed by Mahathir's then-protégé Anwar and his intellectual mentor Syed Naquib al-Attas, I will not dwell on the intellectual content of the project here.[85] What is pertinent to our discussion is how the agenda has driven the Islamization of the sciences in the tertiary education sector. For example, in IIUM where the Islamization of knowledge project is based, most of the subjects taught are in the science, technology, engineering, and mathematics (STEM) fields, with English and Arabic as the medium of instruction to fulfill the university's proclaimed "international" character. In 1998, the Malaysian government established the Islamic University College of Malaysia, which was later upgraded to the Islamic Science University of Malaysia (USIM) in 2007. According to USIM's website, its objective is to unite the "revelational sciences (Naqli knowledge) and the rational sciences (Aqli knowledge)."[86] The ethos reflects its status as one of the progenies of the Islamization of the sciences project. Like IIUM, USIM offers Islamic studies alongside subjects like medicine, dentistry, accounting, and tourism. Revealingly, its top management were all largely chosen for their STEM and not Islamic expertise.[87] Whatever the critique of such amalgamations is,[88] having STEM subjects "harmonized" with Islam within these Islamic universities has increased the visibility and accessibility of a science-compatible Islam, more so via the sizable number of graduates they fed into the workforce.

Considering the complexity and scale of the Islamization enterprise, it is difficult, if not impossible, to tell whether this motive of status seeking was consciously shared by all the participating actors. Many would have approached it as a job, some would be driven by profit and power, and others would hold ideas about Islamization that did not align with Mahathir's modernist and developmentalist version. Nevertheless, Hamayotsu's documentation of how sharia court officials found it important to "show to the Western world that Islam—and sharia—works in Malaysia" is telling of this dialectical process of chasing both internal reform and external recognition.[89] Given its ontological security-seeking motive, seeking external recognition is undoubtedly central to the project. Notably, Mahathir's Islamization drive transpired within a period of rapid economic growth in Malaysia. Malaysia's GDP grew at an annual nearly 9 percent rate from the late 1980s until the Asian Financial Crisis in 1997, earning it the moniker of one of the "new Asian tigers."[90] In this period, the nation launched its national car, built the world's tallest building, and gradually pivoted into heavy industries such as shipbuilding and steelmaking. These achievements generated a sense of confidence within the Mahathir administration that it had gotten Islam "right" as a "balanced, moderate and modernising force that would not impede foreign investment, that was accepting of certain secular Western forms and that has taken account of current political realities in the Muslim and outside world."[91] They also fueled an "Islamic extraversion" in Malaysian foreign policy whereby Malaysia's social stability and economic progress were celebrated as an achievement of "true" Islam, one worthy of international recognition and emulation by the Muslim world.[92]

The actualizing of Islam in the many totems of modernity (bureaucracy, finance, corporations, science, and technocracy) also signifies a stigma correction agenda that took Islam's representation in Orientalist images of Arab despotism seriously and sought distance from it. This mindset, and how it was tinged with a sense of Malaysian exceptionalism, is best seen in how a prominent Malaysian political analyst has likened Malaysia to "an oasis in a desert of turmoil" in a book entitled *Malaysia and the Islamic World*.[93] Given Mahathir's known antipathy toward the Arab states for their inability to stand up for the Muslim world due to their "fratricidal wars, civil wars, failed Governments and many other catastrophes," it is unsurprising that he saw the need for Malaysia to step up and claim the mantle of Islam for itself.[94] Indeed, displacing Islam from its association with the Middle Eastern heartland was a long-standing ambition of Mahathir's.[95] Even as it was pursued with less zeal, such stigma-correcting efforts were continued by his successors, as seen in the publication of a guideline for the practice of Islam in space after the first Malaysian astronaut was launched into outer space in 2007.[96]

Securitizing "Deviant" Islam: Deviants, Heretics, and Repents

As the Malaysian state sought to increase the visibility and accessibility of "modernized" Islam, it treated any expressions of Muslim subjectivities that were inaccessible in the rational-legal form as "unmodern," deviant, and threatening, and, therefore, whose visibility in the public sphere had to be eliminated to preserve Islam's image. Muslim elites viewed these forms of religiosity as the reverse image of their bureaucratic, professionalized, corporation-friendly, science-compatible Islam: "deviant" Islam that is inimical or incompatible with state visions of modernity and industrial growth. To be sure, the label of deviancy has been a prevailing feature in intra-Muslim debates since the colonial period when the palace-linked religious establishment had to fend off challenges from the modernist *kaum muda* group.[97] However, contextualizing Malaysian elite framings of modern and deviant Islam within the framework of ontological security seeking enables us to understand how the state got into the business of actively regulating and rehabilitating expressions of Islam in the first place. Going against instrumentalist readings, I argue that such ambition to control practices and interpretations of Islam was not so much about securing hegemonic control as it was about instituting a form of biopolitical governance to modernize the Malay character.

This imperative to modernize the Malays can be traced back to Mahathir's own concern about the phenomenon of amok, which he described in *The Malay Dilemma* as "yet another fact of the Malay character."[98] According to him, someone who went amok was to have achieved a "final and complete escape from reason and training"—the antithesis to his understanding of "true" Islam as a rational and modernist religion.[99] Mahathir's reading of amok underlines his racialized thinking that anyone who governs the Malays has to be constantly vigilant: "Civilization has subdued the Malay. He still harbours his resentment, but he is better able to control it. He is a better man for it. But it remains an essential part of his make-up, a basic part of his character."[100]

Thus, unsurprisingly, it was during Mahathir's tenure that one witnessed two overlapping transformations in governance. First, the federal government became the main actor in regulating religious deviancy. Second, purportedly unorthodox and fringe Muslim groups were dealt with as if they were national security threats.[101] The process began in 1985 with the establishment of the Pusat Islam (Islamic Center), which hosted the Unit Akidah dan Ajaran Sesat (Unit for Faith and Deviant Teachings). The unit was expanded and inherited by Pusat Islam's successor, JAKIM. In 1996, JAKIM was reportedly monitoring 47 deviant Islamic movements, but by the early 2000s, that number had grown to 125.[102] Tracking deviant teachings through research, monitoring, and the coordination of fatwas constituted one of the largest expenditures in JAKIM's budget.[103] During the 2013 general elections, the manifesto of the ruling coalition, the Barisan Nasional (National Front, BN), even claimed the reduction of the number of *ajaran sesat* (deviant Islamic movements) from 95 to 8 between the years 2009 to 2014 as one of the achievements of the government.[104]

This preoccupation with eradicating and rehabilitating deviant Islam resulted in not just the securitization of Islam, whereby the state saw as its duty the protection of the sanctity of religion. It also heralded the Islamization of security, as Islamic idioms, parables, and reasoning were adopted to explain Muslim radicalism as theological deviancies, foreshadowing the Islamized counter-terror discourses and practices observed post–September 11. In the upcoming subsections, I will highlight this logic of Islamized security-at-work through two cases of deviant groups: the neo-Sufi movement Darul Arqam and a *silat* (Malay martial arts) militant movement known as al-Ma'unah. Particular attention is given to how state discourses explained their radicalism to the public, often resorting to accusations of religious misguidance or deviancy.

The Case of Darul Arqam

Established in 1968 by Ustaz Ashaari Muhammad, the Darul Arqam (hereafter Arqam) movement was a neo-Sufi *tariqa* (Sufi order) that populated the *dakwah* (proselytization) landscape in Malaysia in the 1970s.[105] Like the other Islamist revivalist movements, Arqam's expansion occurred in conjunction with the Malaysian state's proactive implementation of the NEP as an ethnocentric corporatist project, which engendered a new generation of Malays experiencing social uplifting and dislocation in the form of urbanization, (overseas) education, migration, and middle-class formation.[106] As a close-knit Sufi order led by a charismatic leader who claimed to be restoring a utopian socioreligious order, Arqam appealed to "youths caught in the tension between their identity as Muslims, as idealistic social experimenters and future career technocrats, without other clear role models available."[107]

Arqam's appeal was distinct from the other Islamist movements in two major ways. First, unlike most other *dakwah* movements that operated as mass movements, Arqam maintained a high degree of social isolation, with its ten thousand members (1994 estimates) living in forty-four self-sufficient communes across Malaysia.[108] Anthropologist Sharifah Zaleha Syed Hassan wrote about the self-sufficient and Spartan nature of the communes:

> The inhabitants of Madinah Al Arqam consisted of families as well as unmarried men and women. Unlike the residents in the other sub-villages of Sungai Pencala, those in the commune led a Spartan lifestyle. Houses were generally small and barely furnished. There was a noticeable absence of television and radio sets, chairs, tables and other paraphernalia which normally decorate Malay homes. Members of the commune undertook various activities such as selling sundry goods, making clothes and producing foodstuff for public consumption, working on the vegetable plots, training choirboys, recording religious songs on cassettes and videotapes, writing and publishing books. The proceeds that they got from the sale of their products and the gains acquired from their business undertakings were used to refinance the various projects or channelled into the village or the jihad fund. The commune also created a common pool of food items and clothing from which members drew to satisfy their daily needs.[109]

Second, whereas mainstream Malay politics was framed around capturing or contesting the largesse and patronage presided over by the NEP clientelist state,[110] the Arqam community built up its economic strength largely without state support. By 1994, it owned a multinational conglomerate with twenty-two business sections and accumulated assets up to MYR 300 million.[111] This economic independence buttressed Arqam's political independence, as it forsook the path of "conventional electoral and pressure group politics" taken by Islamist groups such as the Angkatan Belia Islam Malaysia (Malaysian Islamic Youth Movement, ABIM)[112] and practiced only the "politics of *dakwah* and *tarbiyyah*."[113]

Tensions with the government escalated as the group's membership grew. This was exacerbated by its popularity reaching the upper echelons of Malay society (including that of politicians and senior civil servants), not to mention Ashaari's alleged involvement in intra-UMNO politics by challenging Mahathir's leadership.[114] Arqam was eventually banned in 1994. During Arqam's banning, one witnessed the Islamization of security in action as highly technical arguments of religious deviancy were used to denounce the group, while the national security law, the ISA, was deployed in a wave of detentions under as-yet-unproven claims of Arqam owning a "suicide army" that would be used to overthrow the government.[115] The banning began following a fatwa from the National Fatwa Council that ruled that Arqam had deviated from the true teachings of Islam. The fatwa dismissed the theological validity of the Aurad Muhammadiyah that was foundational to the *tariqah* (Sufi order) and the movement's belief that Sheikh Muhammad As-Suhaimi, the founder of the *tariqah*, would reemerge as the Iman Mahdi (the Muslim savior).[116] The fatwa called for the total prohibition of Arqam's "practices, materials and activities"; the closure of its schools and for its students be put in "special class"; and action against civil servants found to be its members.[117] The fatwa also stated that the ISA could be used to enforce the ban.[118]

Whether Arqam's banning was for religious or political reasons is a matter of considerable debate.[119] Mahathir's later warming to Arqam's successor, Global Ikhwan Services and Business Holdings (GISB), and his remark that a crackdown against GISB in 2024 was "excessive" also added a dose of poignancy to the intrigue.[120] Whatever Mahathir's opinion of it is now, the distinction is irrelevant if we understand Malaysia's state-led Islamization in the 1980s and 1990s as an effort to cultivate its version of Islamic modernity. As Nagata argues correctly, the main issue with Arqam was that it "was beyond the control of the normal political process or politicians."[121] The enigmatic nature of Arqam was buttressed by how it appeared as a mélange of contradictions. The movement was globalist in its entrepreneurial expansion but isolationist in its commune lifestyle. It appealed to "highly skilled, middle-class, cosmopolitan youth" but embraced mystic beliefs and an anticonsumerist, Spartan lifestyle.[122] It was nonpolitical in that it was not pursuing the Islamic state ideal through state capture, such as that of PAS. Yet Arqam was proactive in instituting its vision of an "Islamic social order" through proselytization, commune building, and its business empire.[123]

Simply put, Arqam was the countervision to the state's "commitment to a western/capitalist pattern of modernization" as it revealed the possibility of a political economy whereby Islam, economic development, and Muslim subjectivity could develop in ways that were unrestrained by the developmentalist parameters set by the Malaysian state.[124] Moreover, it appealed to the same crowd the state's modernization ambition depended on: young, highly educated, and middle-class Malay-Muslims who would form the technocratic and administrative base of the industrializing economy. Insecurities about Arqam's challenge toward the state's vision of being both "Islamic" and "modern" were also laced with a concern about how "unmodern" the group seemed. After all, fanaticism was "singled out" as the reason for Arqam's banning, with Mahathir personally criticizing the group as a "personality cult."[125] The Unit for Faith and Deviant Teachings of the Islamic Center claimed that Arqam's deviant teachings and false doctrines were instilling *taksub* (extreme fealty) and "fanaticism" among its followers.[126] Schools of Arqam were also closed for "allegedly neglecting the modern sciences and emphasising, instead, creating a cult figure out of Ustaz Ashaari."[127] Arqam's characterization as neglecting science and fanatical meant that curbing its influence was central to the Malaysian state's efforts to reverse Islam's stigmatization as an irrational and anti-science religion.

The Arqam case also demonstrated one aspect of the Islamization of security: its emphasis on expressions of *taubat* (repentance) and on rehabilitation. After his arrest under the ISA, Ashaari was made to go on national television and confess his heresy.[128] Similarly, members of Arqam had to announce their repentance and their intention to "return to mainstream life" publicly and participate in a strict rehabilitation regime.[129] These performative acts of repentance and redemption reflect a pastoral governmentality ingrained in Malaysia's "Islamized" security practices, belying a high modernist confidence that the "gardening" state could reengineer Muslim minds and deliver their salvation.[130] This ruling mindset that viewed governing the hermeneutics of Islam as vital to managing Muslim thoughts and behavior would find its way into the design of terrorist rehabilitation programs in the 2000s, as chapter 6 will show. Perhaps not coincidentally, mechanisms of faith control expanded after the Arqam affair. Most of the state-level Syariah Criminal Offenses Enactments instituted after the mid-1990s, such as in the Federal Territories (1997), Johor (1997), Selangor (1995), Pahang (2013), Penang (1996), Sarawak (2001), and Terengganu (2001), contained a section dedicated to the control of *akidah*, with "wrongful worship" and "false doctrines" criminalized as sharia offenses.[131]

The Case of Al-Ma'unah

The Al-Ma'unah affair refers to a standoff between the Malaysian government and a group of militants organized under the banner of Al-Ma'unah, led by Mohd Amin Mohd Razali (henceforth Amin).[132] Amin was an ex-army officer who also happened to be a *silat* practitioner, mystic, and traditional healer, and was only twenty-nine years old when he led the coup. On July 2, 2000, Amin and more than twenty of his followers successfully executed a heist at two military bases in Grik, Perak, taking over hundreds of firearms and thousands of rounds of ammunition. Intending to start a rebellion to overthrow the government, the group set up base in Gunung Jenalik, Sauk, in the state of Perak to launch attacks, but were rounded up by security forces after a siege a few days later. Three casualties were recorded, including two hostages taken by the group. Most of the men involved in the case were charged with the offence of waging war against the Yang Di-Pertuan Agong (king of Malaysia), the first time the statute was ever used in Malaysia. Amin and three of his lieutenants were hanged, while fifteen of his accomplices were sentenced to life imprisonment.[133] The incident shocked the nation, given its bizarre nature, the reported involvement of army personnel,[134] and the fact that armed conflicts as such were practically unheard of in Malaysia after the Second Communist Insurgency ended in 1989.[135]

On a broader historical level, however, Al-Ma'unah marked a continuation of Malaysia's history of localized, rural-based, and somewhat eccentric millenarian Islamist militancy. Back in 1984, a government white paper entitled *Threat to Muslim Unity and National Security* was dedicated to the issue, listing six deviant groups with names ranging from CRYPTO to Tentera Sabilulllah (Army of God).[136] These groups were accused of violent plots, practicing "black magic," and wanting to establish "the Government of Jesus" (4–6). The white paper marked the first time religious deviancy was labeled a national security threat for "deliberately misinterpreting the teachings of Islam" (2). As the early 1980s was also a period where UMNO and PAS's rhetoric had intensified to a point where both parties were calling each other *kafirs* (infidels), the white paper accused PAS of causing "confusion and generated hatred, anger, and enmity among members of the Malay/Muslim community" (21).[137] The Memali incident in 1985 that witnessed a violent standoff between a fiery PAS leader by the name of Ibrahim Mahmood (aka Ibrahim Libya), his supporters, and the government was the crescendo of this confrontation.

Whereas checking PAS's influence by associating it with radicalism was undeniably part of the government's objective, the white paper about the Memali incident also revealed a genuine concern with Muslim confusion about Islam and their amenability to "religious passions."[138] Indeed, Mahathir himself expressed his worry that "Muslims themselves are frequently confused and interpret Islam for their own purpose."[139] The Mahathir administration saw this confusion as a problem, as their Islamization project was about getting Islam "right" in its modernity-compatible form and not regressing into the realms of mysticism and the occult, or worse, violent fanaticism. The 1984 white paper also belied a status-seeking concern in its claim that these deviant movements had "*no intention to enhance the status of Islam* in this country" (emphasis mine).[140] These developments ushered in the top-down Islamization I discussed above; centralization was seen as necessary, as state elites perceived the stakes of failure in faith control as potentially disruptive to their modernization project that would, in time, secure recognition for Malaysia as a simultaneously modern and Islamic country.

By the time the Al-Ma'unah affair occurred, the federal Islamic bureaucracy was well established to explicate the theological underpinnings of a security threat. Nevertheless, a white paper was never released for the Al-Ma'unah affair (despite pledges to do so), which also means there is no official account of the event.[141] Instead, the Ministry of Information published a booklet entitled *Al-Ma'unah Sesat di Sauk* (Al-Ma'unah: The deviants at Sauk) containing interviews with the prime minister, the inspector general of police, and two Islamic bureaucrats: the minister in charge of Islamic affairs, Abdul Hamid Othman, and the deputy director of the IKIM, Abdul Munir Yaaacob.[142] In the typical fashion of government publications then, the publication painted PAS as culpable for cultivating hatred against the government. They were even called the *khawarij* (exiters)—a concept we will come back to in chapter 5—for their extreme teachings, self-righteousness, and penchant for calling others *kafirs* (66).

Considerable use of Islamic concepts and hermeneutics is noted in the booklet, especially in the chapter containing the interview of the minister in charge of Islamic affairs and the deputy director of IKIM.[143] Instead of discussing the event, the priority of the two appeared to be about reasserting the legitimacy of Malaysia as an Islamic state. Multiple reasons were given for that conclusion. The interviewees paraphrased the jurist Muhammad ibn al-Hasan Shaybani's claim that "wherever there are Muslims and wherever there is peace, that is enough for recognition of an Islamic state" (67); outlined broad features such as Muslim leadership and the principles of justice, harmony, freedom, and equality (68, 70); and made the rather trivial point that fifty-four countries from the Organisation of Islamic Cooperation had recognized Malaysia as an Islamic state (69). Concepts such as jihad and *daulah Islamiyah* (Islamic state) were also discussed in rather technical terms to denounce the cause of the militants (66–70, 76–79). This resort to technical debates of Islamic concepts in discussing Muslim militancy marks a significant feature of "Islamized" security that we will see in Malaysia's counter-terror discourses post–September 11. Nevertheless, in actively contesting Al-Ma'unah's claim about how "un-Islamic" the Malaysian state was, the two interlocutors also inadvertently affirmed a security logic that Muslim radicalism was grounded in their religiosity. This understanding of violent extremism as a product of deviant Islam can be seen from the fact that the interviewees even claimed that the Al-Ma'unah members could be healed in a "faith rehabilitation center" (84).[144] In news reports, Al-Ma'unah was also lumped together with other nonviolent deviant groups as if religious deviancy was the common denominator of political violence.[145]

Mahathir was even less charitable in his interview, which is unsurprising, given that his modernist leanings were based on a conviction that "true" Islam could free "the Malays from the shackles of superstitions, fairy tales, myths and all kinds of nonsensical beliefs."[146] He attributed the militants' actions to their *kepercayaan karut* (superstitious belief) in *ilmu kebal* (invulnerability). He denounced their attitude toward knowledge as irrational and naive, saying that "real courageous people will plan ahead of danger" instead of behaving like cowards who "had to borrow strength from the supernatural" (14). Mahathir chided the *kebodohan* (stupidity) of their militants, claiming that they were defeated with relative ease because they set up their base at a place that "could be easily surrounded," and that their whole strategy was based on "a delusion that they possessed supernatural powers nobody else had" (16). Mahathir's exasperation and condescension are characteristic of his blunt personality, but also reveal an almost paternalistic disappointment from someone who considered his life's work the removal of superstitions and irrational beliefs from Malay society. The status-conscious aspect of this enterprise can be seen in a speech he made in April 2001 in Dubai, just a few months after the Al-Ma'unah incident. In the speech, he urged Muslim states that they "must correct their [non-Muslims'] wrong impressions of Islam as being an anachronism given to violent and irrational behaviours. It is the duty of Muslims to give Islam a good image even if it gains us nothing."[147]

Mahathir's assumption of a binary between the rational, scientific, and pragmatic and the superstitious, affective, and unrealistic ("right" versus "wrong" Islam) was shared by many others too. For example, writing about the incident, a journalist posed a question in disbelief: "Why do better-educated Malays join fringe groups that mix mainstream Islam with a brand of mysticism that borders on the ridiculous?" He then answered the question himself by saying such behaviors would remain "as long as Muslims seek a short cut to heaven."[148] Whereas there was certainly a religious dimension to the incident, interpretations that assumed religious deviancy and devotion as the underlying factors also papered over some of the more outstanding features of the insurgency. For example, it was led by a thirty-year-old who came from a modest family, with close to half of the group being much older than him in their late thirties and forties, which is atypical for a cult or most deviant religious movements.[149] There was also the oddity—if we take the movement as one organized around theological authority—that while the leader, Amin, was not religiously trained, one of his followers was an Islamic studies graduate from Al-Azhar University in Egypt. As a center of modernist Islamic learning, what an Al-Azhar education provided and what Amin professed in his charismatic leadership could not be more different. However, as I will discuss in the final chapter, these idiosyncrasies are not alien to Muslim militancy in Malaysia, including in the so-called Salafi jihadist movements that will populate the landscape in the following decades. They were simply overlooked by the "Islamized" lens through which Muslim radicalism was interpreted.

Mahathir's Islamization: Outcomes in Status and Security

In this chapter, I approach Mahathir's tenure as the period when the integration of Islam and Malaysia's national security apparatus occurred most intensively. However, even as Malaysia made the most reputational gains for being a "moderate" and modernized Muslim state during the Mahathir years, what actually transpired was the state's moderation of Islamic orthodoxy and orthopraxy through institutional and (extra)legal mechanisms of faith control. I attribute this development to the state-led Islamization that proceeded under Mahathir's tacit support (albeit increasingly begrudgingly so in his later years), arguing that an ontological security-seeking motive geared at reversing Islam's stigmatization within the Eurocentric international order was central to the state's control and securitization of Islam. As outlined by my discussion of the four forms of Islamization pursued by the Mahathir administration, this impetus to get Islam "right" in its modernized form stemmed from a mindset that deviant Islam was pervasive in Malay society and incendiary in nature. Hence, for these elites, Islam's practice in Malaysia needed intensive state guidance and control. These mesoinstitutional developments are consequential, as they have led to Islam's disenchantment and a conservative and exclusivist "turn" in its sociopolitical expressions in Malaysia.[150] Ironically, these outcomes went against Mahathir's goal of grounding Muslim religiosity in *akal* (rationality) and *ijtihad* (independent reasoning) and not in a "police state."[151]

In approaching Malaysia's Islamization as an enterprise of ontological security seeking, I address deviant Islam not only as a discursive construction of the state but also as a source of insecurity for the modernizing elites who were keen to rid Islam of its stigma as an obscurantist, irrational, and fanatical religion. This can be seen from the fact that the forms of Islam subjected to the most severe forms of state repression mostly belonged to groups with more "enchanted" ways of being in their mysticism, reliance on charismatic leaders, and millenarian beliefs, as opposed to the formidable Islamist opposition that posed a real threat to the government. My argument here is not to dispute state claims of violent extremism (although the claim can sometimes be spurious). Rather, by analyzing the security logic underneath, I illustrate and problematize a form of security governance that fostered the discursive and institutional integration of the security apparatus and the religious bureaucracy, on the one hand, and the emergence of a security logic that viewed governing the limits of Islam's interpretation as equivalent to governing the limits of Muslim political subjectivity, on the other. This development of an "Islamized" vernacular of security, as seen in the increasing deployment of Islamic idioms, parables, and *tafsir* (Quranic exegesis) in state security discourses, would continue into the post–September 11 security landscape.

Finally, it's worth reflecting on whether these efforts to guide, curate, and reform Islam actually lived up to their recognition-seeking goal. Whereas efforts to portray Malaysia as an authentic and progressive Islamic state were empowering for many Malaysian Muslims, the underlying ontological security-seeking motive also sustained a psychological dependence on the West. As stigmatized actors, such dependence meant that these Muslim elites who saw themselves as nation builders craved recognition from their Western counterparts, which they seldom received. This sense of disappointment about Malaysia's lack of recognition as the embodiment of "true" Islam can be seen in this excerpt of a speech Mahathir gave at Oxford University: "One would have thought that Muslims and non-Muslims would look to Malaysia as an example of the practice of Islam. But the West and their media refuse to recognize that the Muslims of Malaysia actually exemplify the teachings of Islam. They prefer to regard Malaysian Muslims and their behaviour as aberrations. They keep on asking about fundamentalism in Malaysia and, when told that there are really no Islamic fundamentalists of the kind they describe, they reject the claim. The prejudice against Islam and Muslims remains even with Malaysia."[152]

Ironically enough, it was during the GWOT that Malaysia finally received the recognition it craved. Malaysia's capitalizing on that recognition while navigating a situation where Islam's stigmatization could not have been more severe will be the subject of the next chapter.

FOUR

The Bastion of Moderate Islam?

Malaysia's Response to the Global War on Terror

The onset of the Global War on Terror (GWOT) in 2001 saw counter-terrorism propelled to the forefront of the security agenda of many Muslim states, Malaysia included. The ease at which the vocabulary of security changed from addressing local threats of Muslim militancy to countering global terror has led to scholars framing Malaysia's participation in the GWOT as a case of bandwagoning. In this version of events, Muslim elites were using counter-terrorism as a front to suppress political dissidents, and therefore their promotion of "moderate Islam" was nothing more than lip service paid to be in the good books of Washington.[1] However, what we have learned in the preceding chapters should convince us these perspectives are incomplete for two reasons. First, they neglect the GWOT's intensification of Islam's stigmatization that rendered the Muslim identity suspect in international society, something I have covered in the theoretical chapter. Second, by picturing Muslim state elites as mere opportunists, such realist interpretations of the global social environment overlook the fact that Muslim political actors have long attempted to reverse Islam's stigmatization, as chapter 3 has shown. For Malaysia's Muslim elites, responding to the GWOT was not just about maximizing material gains. Amid a wave of suspicion trained at Muslims and Muslim states, the calculus also involved securing status gains to preserve their nation's status as a respectable, "civilized" member of international society.

This chapter takes a turn to the foreign policy dimension to locate counter-terrorism within a domain of politics defined not just by geopolitical or realpolitik interests but also by social concerns of status and identity. Through discourse analysis of policy documents and speeches, it highlights how three successive administrations in Malaysia have fostered and promoted a discourse of moderate Islam in state narratives as an attempt to reverse Islam's stigmatization while positioning Malaysia as a proactive and uniquely successful counter-terror partner to the United States. This empirical focus on speeches and policy statements is meant to capture the status preoccupations of postcolonial Muslim state elites in Malaysia as they navigated the post-GWOT security landscape that treated their religious identity as both liability and asset. Their meditations about what moderate Islam is supposed to achieve and how it fits with specific security imperatives provide us with a glimpse of how Muslim elite status-seeking furthered the securitization of Islam in the post-GWOT world. These foreign-policy narratives also underpinned two discursive strategies of ontological security seeking. The first is about asserting Malaysia's position as a responsible global partner that contributed to the GWOT operationally and intellectually. The second is to portray Malaysian (moderate) Islam as exceptional and superior to that practiced in the Arab World.

What follows are four sections. The first problematizes Malaysia's reputation as a moderate Muslim state. It argues that the label is a product of Islam's stigmatization in the international order, wherein a Muslim state's apparent successes were taken as evidence of Islam *moderated.* The second discusses the many facets of Mahathir's idiosyncratic response toward the GWOT, which included positioning Malaysia as a key ally of the US in counter-terror, making a controversial declaration that Malaysia is an Islamic state, and channeling the discussion of terrorism toward "root cause" debates. I argue that these maneuverings are best understood as discourses of stigma correction. Collectively, they sought to distance Malaysia from the stigma of terrorism and to protect Islam's reputation from its association with extremism and violence.

The third section turns to Mahathir's successor, Abdullah Ahmad Badawi's idea of "Civilizational Islam," or Islam Hadhari. I show that the discourse contains the trappings of the "civilizational" paradigm that underlined Mahathir's long-standing quest to prove Islam's capacity for economic progress. Alas, it also reproduces this idea that terrorism is a product of civilizational deficit. The fourth section traces the Najib Razak administration's capitalization of the concept of moderation (and moderate Islam) as the world recoiled from the televised horrors of the Islamic State (IS) that had claimed a so-called caliphate for itself. Unlike his predecessors, Najib's moderation campaign pivoted directly into the Preventing and Countering

Violent Extremism (P/CVE) paradigm. I argue that this development signified not so much Najib's personal convictions, but rather the global popularization of this idea that moderate Islam could be the antidote to jihadist extremism.

Malaysia as the "Moderate" Muslim Partner: Success or Stigma?

Scholars such as Saba Mahmood and Mahmood Mamdani have argued convincingly that beneath the coercive wars of the GWOT lies a culturalist imperial vision that bifurcated Islam into its "good" and "bad" halves, with the cultivation of moderate Islam understood to be "an antidote and prophylactic to fundamentalist interpretations of Islam."[2] Indeed, when the GWOT began, Washington was interested in seeking partners for "moderate network building" in the Muslim world.[3] Malaysia fitted the bill in two ways. First, while it was not a major theater of operation for the US counter-terror campaign, Malaysia has enjoyed a solid reputation of being a moderate Muslim state, a topic we will return to later.[4] Second, as Washington sought to open up a "second front" for the GWOT in Southeast Asia, Malaysia's relative stability as a Muslim-majority country gave the impression that it was a bastion against radical Islam surrounded by hotspots of Muslim militancy in Aceh, Southern Thailand, and Mindanao in the Philippines. To be sure, Malaysia's placing on such a pedestal was based on wildly alarmist writings about the threat of radical Islam in Southeast Asia in the early 2000s.[5]

Malaysia's reputation for moderation is worth a closer look here. After all, the label only gained wide purchase in the post–September 11 environment. For instance, a search on Factiva with the terms "Malaysia" and "moderate Islam" yielded less than 10 hits before 2001, while the hits climbed to 25 in 2001, 75 in 2002, and reached 143 in 2004.[6] Undeniably, the nation did enjoy nominal successes on several fronts. Economically, it presided over a sufficiently diversified and export-led industrial economy with a per capita GDP that was the highest among Muslim states, barring the Gulf petrostates and Brunei.[7] Its political system was that of a relatively competitive parliamentary democracy punctuated only by a two-year emergency rule following the ethnic riots in 1969.[8] This put Malaysia, at least within the parameters of democratization, ahead of many Middle Eastern states, where military, theocratic, or monarchy rule continued to reinforce stereotypes of these societies as hotbeds of "patrimonialism, orientalist despotism, and totalizing faith."[9] The relative sociopolitical stability of Malaysia was considered a standout when compared to the sectarian warfare in Lebanon, the revolutionary fervor of mullah-ruled Iran, Egypt's recurring political violence, Türkiye's military coups, and the major riots that preceded the fall of Suharto's New Order regime in 1998 in neighboring Indonesia. Malaysia's exceptional achievements saw it bestowed the "honor" of being the "voice of reason" by the US government.[10] Within the "with us or against us" worldview of the Bush doctrine, Malaysia was presumably a moderate Muslim partner that could stand with the US amid a wave of "Muslim rage" against Western norms and freedoms.[11]

This case of Malaysian exceptionalism was itself a product of a broader episteme that normalized Islam's stigmatized status. Two assumptions informed Malaysia's "crowning" as a model of moderate Islam: that its success was predicated on the state successfully modulating Islam's influence, and that Islam's integration with modernity only happened as an exception and not the norm. These assumptions discursively sutured Malaysia's (neoliberally defined) socioeconomic successes with its supposedly Islamic moderation, creating the almost tautological claim that Malaysia is successful because it is moderate. Such reasoning can be seen in the language of news reports that came out in the Western media's frantic search for moderate Islam post–September 11. For example, see this excerpt from the *Business Times* in 2002: "'GO TO Malaysia if you want to see moderate Islam at work,' a French scholar was told in Egypt and Morocco. . . . He was not disappointed and was pleasantly surprised, like many others, to see progress and development in Islamic Malaysia. 'I did not expect it to be such a modern country,' he admitted when met in Kuala Lumpur recently."[12] Or this prologue of an interview with Mahathir in November 2001 published in a French magazine: "Malaysia is the only country with a Muslim majority which has managed to steer itself away from destitution, and has experienced economic success (apart for royalties from petroleum resources). And what a success!"[13]

As popular as these claims were, there was hardly any explication of the relationship between Malaysia's so-called moderation and its socioeconomic success in their content. Even as Malaysia's successes could be qualified, its claim to moderation never was. This speaks to Islam's stigmatization, in that a Muslim state's achievements were automatically understood as a rare instance where the influence of Islam was contained. Malaysia's success was celebrated as exceptional precisely because it was regarded as part of the "Islamic" world where such outcomes were de facto ruled out. As Malaysian elites also internalized this worldview, the label of "moderate Islam" would soon become a discursive vehicle through which they sought to regain their ontological security when they felt Malaysia's Islamic connection was pushing it to the edge of "civilization."

Searching for Root Causes: Mahathir's Scalpel to the Problem (2001–2003)

When the September 11 attacks occurred, Mahathir was in the final years of his premiership after dealing with the fallout of the 1997 Asian Financial Crisis and the acrimonious break with his protégé and heir apparent Anwar Ibrahim.[14] The international criticism that followed Mahathir's unceremonious sacking of Anwar, not to mention the latter's prosecution based on what many believed to be spurious charges of corruption and sodomy, led to observers claiming that September 11 was a "godsend" for Mahathir for two reasons.[15] First, Malaysia's successful positioning as a key US ally in the GWOT helped divert US-Malaysia relations away from the Anwar issue as the hunt for terrorists became the number one priority for the US.[16] Second, global consternation about radical Islam also facilitated Mahathir's effort to portray the Pan-Malaysian Islamic Party (PAS), which strongly protested Anwar's treatment by the government, as peddlers of a militant, fanatical, and extremist version of Islam. These realist views aside, Mahathir's joining of the GWOT bandwagon, despite his anti-West rhetoric, was also unsurprising when seen from the English School's point of view.[17] Al-Qaeda's claim of pan-national Muslim solidarity in the name of the *ummah* and its refusal to acknowledge state sovereignty surely did not bode well for the legitimacy of Muslim leaders operating within the Westphalian nationalist framework.[18]

Whereas critics may have found Mahathir's astute turning of the GWOT to his political advantage opportunistic, in Mahathir's mind, "The 11 September attack on New York and Washington is an unmitigated disaster for Muslims all over the world. Our image, which had not been good, has been made worse."[19] Mahathir's sentiment was understandable when one considers that reversing Islam's stigmatization was his life's work, as chapter 3 has illustrated. But the GWOT's operationalization within a moral exceptionalist discourse and its singular focus on the "Muslim terrorist" meant that Islam's stigmatization was intensified. The GWOT also shifted the parameters upon which Islam was judged. If Islam's stigmatization before September 11 was predominantly about its perceived incompatibility with the demands of industrial modernity (thereby making it the "pariah"), after September 11 its perceived connection to global terrorism would have made it into the "universal enemy" of the international order.[20]

Despite the nation's well-regarded moderate standing, Malaysia was still tarnished by the GWOT's broad brush, especially during its early days. For example, Malaysian Muslim students were denied visas in the US.[21] In 2002, the administration had to proactively counter reports of the nation being "safe haven" for terrorists to shelter it from potential economic damage when it was revealed by a *Newsweek* report that some of the Al-Qaeda operatives met in Kuala Lumpur in 2000.[22] This is notwithstanding the fact that the Malaysian authorities had acquiesced to the CIA's request to maintain surveillance of the meeting. In contrast, Germany did not have to defend itself against similar accusations, despite being the hosting grounds of the "Hamburg contingent," which included Mohamad Atta, one of the masterminds of the September 11 attacks.[23]

Mahathir's response to the GWOT can be understood as ontological security-seeking strategies aiming to achieve two goals: to distance Malaysia from the stigma of Islamist terrorism, and to address Islam's stigmatization itself. To achieve the former, the Mahathir government was quick to position itself as a key Muslim ally and partner to the US counter-terror efforts. Mahathir condemned the September 11 attacks strongly and even wrote a letter to President Bush "on ways to fight terrorism."[24] Notable efforts at rapprochement had transpired between the two countries too. Bush and Mahathir met face-to-face at the sidelines of the Asia-Pacific Economic Cooperation meeting on October 20, 2001, followed by Mahathir's visit to Washington in May 2002, with counter-terrorism high on the agenda. With US funding, the Southeast Asia Regional Centre for Counter-Terrorism was set up in Kuala Lumpur in 2003, further strengthening the close security ties between the two countries.[25]

The Malaysian government was also quick to prove its counter-terror credentials on the operational front. Between 2001 and 2002, the security apparatus had successfully cracked down on militants from the Jemaah Islamiyah (JI) and its affiliate, the Kumpulan Mujahidin Malaysia (Malaysian Mujahidin Movement), officially retracting the tacit refuge given to JI members since the 1980s.[26] In May 2002, Najib Razak, then defense minister of Malaysia, proudly claimed in a speech to the US Heritage Foundation that the government had detained "62 terrorists and militias with global and regional links."[27] The success of Mahathir's status-seeking efforts can be seen from the compliments received. For example, US Trade Representative Robert Zoellick stressed that "the US views Malaysia as an Islamic country which could serve the others as a role model for leadership and economic development."[28] James Kelly, the US assistant secretary for East Asia and the Pacific, also told Mahathir that the US viewed him "as a moderate Muslim leader of a progressive and modern Muslim state" and that Malaysia was a "beacon of stability."[29] The Malaysians' yearning to be taken as a serious and capable counter-terror partner contrasted with the attitudes of their Indonesian counterparts. According to security analyst Sidney Jones, Indonesian President Megawati Sukarnoputri (2001–2004) and her cabinet did not think the country "had a problem" until the Bali Bombing in October 2002.[30] Mahathir's long-standing concern with how Muslim states should correct Islam's stigmatization proactively is useful in explaining such differences in perceptions of the "terrorism" problem.

Mahathir's effort to correct Islam's stigmatization following the GWOT was characterized by a sophisticated, if idiosyncratic, narrative. As chapter 3 illustrated, Mahathir's overarching strategy had always been about redeeming Islam's image by projecting Malaysia as a role model where Islam could coexist with scientific progress and industrial modernity. Although Mahathir's efforts in the 1990s to position

Malaysia as a model of "true" Islam was met with limited success, the onset of the GWOT turbocharged his pursuit of such recognition. I argue that this clamor for recognition underlined his contentious declaration that Malaysia "was already an Islamic state" on September 29, 2001.[31] The timing of the landmark announcement is rather telling.[32] Given that it was barely two weeks from the September 11 attacks, Mahathir's announcement was likely an illustration of his eagerness to reclaim Islam from its stigmatization by blending it with Malaysia's moderate, progressive image. Indeed, when asked to clarify his controversial statement, Mahathir rhetorically doubled down on by claiming that Malaysia was not moderate but a "fundamentalist Islamic country" for the simple reason that it practiced the "fundamentals of Islam."[33]

Instrumentalist readings attribute Mahathir's "Islamic state" announcement to yet another move to "out-Islamize" the Islamist opposition, PAS.[34] But as Liow noted, this Islamic state of Mahathir's "is essentially a construction of his own administration."[35] There are reasons to believe that Mahathir, as well as many within his administration, genuinely believed Malaysia reflected a model Islamic state. Skepticism about the authenticity of Malaysia's Islamic state status often hinged on the fact that Malaysia did not implement *hudud* laws, a fact capitalized on by PAS to challenge the government's Islamic credentials.[36] Ironically, such skepticism also came from Western interlocutors who seemed eager to see harsh versions of Islamic laws as authentically Islamic, while paying little attention to Malaysia's two-decades-long Islamization project that attempted to represent a more modern, corporate- and science-friendly Islam, whatever the flaws and fallout of such a brand of Islam may be.[37] It is not my intention here to adjudicate the highly contested debates about what constitutes an authentic Islamic state, or if such an entity is possible.[38] Rather, the point here is just to show how the image of an Islamic state defined by brutal laws and chastened societies often converged in the imaginations of both the ultraconservative Islamists and Western commentators, to the frustrations of recognition-seeking, modernist Muslim elites such as Mahathir.

Mahathir's stigma correction strategy also saw him leading initiatives that strove to change the fixation on the Muslim terrorist by driving the discourse toward terrorism's *root causes*. These efforts relied on his growing critique of the anti-Islam bias of the GWOT. In a conference on terrorism held in November 2001, Mahathir lamented that "despite protests that the war against terrorists is not a war against Islam, what cannot be denied is that only Muslim terrorists are being targeted."[39] In his speeches, Mahathir attempted to make a case that resolving terrorism's root causes was the only way to combat terrorism. He staked his diagnosis on Malaysia's success in tackling the Communist Emergency (1948–1960), claiming that offering citizenship to "over a million non-Malays" was key to why the counterinsurgency campaign succeeded.[40] The root cause for Islamist terrorism, for Mahathir, was the Palestinian issue: "In the Muslim world there is a great deal of anger which the West cannot understand. But the Muslim world, weak and unable to be of any help to the Palestinians, see in the unwillingness of the West to stop the Israelis as a sign that the West is anti-Palestine, anti-Arab and anti-Muslim. Most Muslims will only feel anger, will talk but will do nothing. *But among the billion Muslims there must be those whose anger cannot be contained. These are the people who will resort to terror tactics*" (emphasis mine).[41]

Eager to decouple Muslims from the stigma of terrorism, Mahathir also offered a broad definition for terrorism in an Organisation of Islamic Cooperation gathering in April 2002: "I would like to suggest here that armed attacks or other forms of attack against civilians must be regarded as acts of terror and the perpetrators regarded as terrorists. Whether the attackers are acting on their own or on the orders of their Governments, whether they are regulars or irregulars, if the attack is against civilians, then they must be considered as terrorists. Groups or Governments, which support attacks on civilians, must be regarded as terrorists, irrespective of the justification of the operations carried out, irrespective of the nobility of the struggle."[42] Mahathir's drive to reclaim the definition of terrorism can be traced to his long-standing criticism of US "hypocrisy and double standards" in backing Israel's occupation of Palestine.[43] His discursive strategy had two prongs: changing the parameters of the stigma (by widening terrorism's definition so that it was not limited to Muslims), and challenging the stigmatizing actor (by raising the US's double standards).

Yet Mahathir's aggressive efforts for stigma correction also showed signs of a stigmatized actor, in that he was as concerned about the GWOT's discrediting of Islam as he was about how Muslims would exhibit "discreditable" attributes themselves. His speeches about the Muslim world's right to righteous indignation because of how the West discriminated against the Muslim world often conflicted, perhaps unknowingly, with his tacit acceptance of the label of inferiority that was foisted on Muslim states. For example, the fact that Mahathir tried to define terrorism first in an Organisation of Islamic Cooperation meeting signals his internalization of the association made between the Muslim world and terrorism. Islam's "poor image" was not lost to Mahathir, nor was the need for Muslims and Muslim states to proactively gain "the respect of the world."[44] Mahathir located the roots of terrorism within Muslim grievance and powerlessness; both, for him, were a direct product of the backwardness of the Muslim world. When speaking at a dialogue session with Islamic intellectuals in Rabat, Morocco, he claimed in his characteristic bluntness that "Muslims everywhere are *backward, badly educated and are incapable of applying modern knowledge* in the administration and development of Muslim countries, in their defence and the protection of the *ummah*" (emphasis added).[45]

Mahathir's implied solution to the problem of terrorism was couched in a realist outlook—Muslim states simply had to rise to the challenge and regain their stature in the international order.[46] For him, to enhance Islam's image, the Muslim world must reconcile their understanding of religion with the needs of industrial, scientific modernity as they had "missed the industrial revolution because [they] were suspicious of the products of industry."[47] In Mahathir's mind, missing out on industrialization and its attendant "rational" mindset was why Muslims resorted to the "irrationality" of terrorism. This idea of a modernity deficit can be seen in his almost culturalist characterization of "Muslim rage": "Our only reaction is to become more and more angry. Angry people cannot think properly. And so we find some of our people reacting irrationally. They launch their own attacks, killing just about anybody including fellow Muslims to vent their anger and frustration."[48]

Put differently, Mahathir's politics of counter-terror was not just about making strategic gains but was also a continuation of his persistent effort to articulate the stakes of what would happen if Muslims did not catch up with the "developed" world. Seen in this light, it is perhaps understandable that Mahathir stressed the futility of Muslim anger almost in a "Don't get angry, get even" fashion. However, in so doing, he ended up surrendering the right to set the parameters of said "evenness" back to the West.

Moderate Islam as Civilizational Islam: Badawi's Islam Hadhari (2003–2009)

Mahathir's abrupt resignation in June 2002 paved the way for his deputy, Abdullah Ahmad Badawi (henceforth Badawi), to assume leadership of a regime that had only recently weathered both the Asian Financial Crisis and the political turmoil following Anwar Ibrahim's dismissal. Born in a prominent religious family and known for his more affable personality, Badawi was considered a breath of fresh air for many Malaysians after years of experiencing Mahathir's more combative ways.[49] Mahathir's unpopularity in the final years of his tenure led to the rise of the Mahazalim discourse that conflated the man with "all that is wrong in Malaysia."[50] Leveraging his religious credentials, Badawi chose the slogan of "Islam Hadhari" (which loosely translates to Civilizational Islam) to headline his administration. Riding off on Mahathir's "Islamic state" declaration, Islam Hadhari was meant to signify the government's commitment to an "alternative model to the Islamic state articulated by PAS" that was fit for Malaysia's plural society.[51] At the same time, it also served as a rallying call for Malay empowerment within the government's developmentalist framework.

Even though it did not introduce substantial changes, Islam Hadhari was a significant milestone in Malaysian politics as it was the first time the Barisan Nasional

(National Front) government opted for an Islamic slogan as its governing philosophy. Whereas state-led Islamization projects were pursued proactively during the Mahathir's years, Mahathir never proposed a coherent policy for, or based overtly on, Islam, with the notable exception of the Assimilation of Islamic Values in Governance Policy adopted early in his tenure (see chapter 3). Mahathir's most well-known slogan, Vision 2020, was primarily geared at Malaysia achieving "developed nation" status by 2020. While it called for the establishment of "a fully moral and ethical society, whose citizens are strong in religions and spiritual values," the working paper that introduced Vision 2020 does not even contain one mention of Islam.[52] Instead, it promoted the ethnicity-transcending idea of Bangsa Malaysia (the Malaysian people),[53] an idea that was more amenable to Malaysia's plural society. By comparison, Islam Hadhari effectively "narrows the national discourse to an Islamic one."[54]

To be sure, the ideals of Islam Hadhari hardly deviated from the Islam championed by Mahathir: a moderate, developmentalist, and capitalist-friendly Islam.[55] Its call for social justice, economic development, and Malay competitiveness spelled a continuation of the policy status quo—perhaps with less clientelism and corruption, something Badawi promised to deliver as he leveraged on his "Mr. Clean" reputation. According to sociologist Terence Chong, Islam Hadhari's idea of the model moderate Muslim was the Malay capitalist who would be the "engine of national modernisation."[56] Nevertheless, despite Badawi's initial popularity and his command of one of the largest parliamentary majorities in Malaysian history,[57] the Islam Hadhari project is largely considered a failure. The project did not lead to a more Islamic government, nor did it gain any meaningful results to match the "lofty civilizational ideals" marked by its ten encompassing principles.[58]

As expected of any political slogan that claimed to be the guiding philosophy for the entire government, Islam Hadhari's eclectic framing meant it suffered from significant ambiguity in terms of scope, normative commitments, practicability, and intended audience.[59] During its implementation, the project was met with major obstacles, including the conservative backlash against Islam Hadhari's perceived liberal leanings, the insurmountable gap between theory and practice exacerbated by the project's vacuous intellectual content, and the fact that the religious bureaucracy was unable to provide both the "intellectual sophistication" and "fortitude" to ensure its holistic application.[60] Besides, Badawi's weak leadership also meant that he was on the losing side when faced with the expanded and empowered religious bureaucracy Mahathir built. As Saat noted, "The ulama overpowered his administration and Abdullah lost control. The ulama Abdullah placed in positions of power were interpreting Islam Hadhari that contradicted the way the leader had hoped. Instead of improving multiracial ties, the religious elites during his administration pushed their conservative and exclusive fatwas."[61]

Be that as it may, Islam Hadhari remains useful for this book as it illustrates the enduring nature of the sense of ontological insecurity that anchored Mahathir's worldview. Discursively speaking, Islam Hadhari was framed in both the lexicon of Malay-Muslim insecurity and the security paradigm of the GWOT. The policy speech that introduced the idea was laden with calls for the Malays "to change their *tasawwur* (worldview)" and to harness Islam's "true" teaching to "improve Malay competitiveness" through "the pursuit of knowledge, the mastery of science and technology and economic activity."[62] In other words, the discourse of Islam Hadhari inherited Mahathir's preoccupations with the survival of the Malay-Muslims in the modern world, even as it dropped the epigenetic overtones of his diagnosis of Malay weakness. In stressing that there was no divide "between so-called secular knowledge and religious knowledge" and in its call for changing "negative values and traits," the challenges articulated in Badawi's Islam Hadhari project were not very different from those outlined in Mahathir's *The Challenge* three decades ago.[63]

The campaign's adoption of the English translation of Civilizational Islam is revealing too. Islam Hadhari was supposed to be Badawi's response toward the "Clash of Civilization" paradigm, which, for him, was a "self-fulfilling prophecy" that could only be dispelled through meaningful "inter-religious, intercultural, and inter-civilisational" dialogues.[64] Nevertheless, the inability of the discourse of Islam Hadhari to escape Islam's stigmatization weakened its appeal and objectives. Undertones of self-stigmatization can be seen in a speech Badawi gave in front of an Australian audience: "[Islam Hadhari] is not an approach to pacify the West. It is neither an approach to apologise for the perceived Islamic threat, *nor an approach to seek approval from the non-Muslims* for a more friendly and gentle image of Islam. It is an approach that seeks to *make Muslims understand that progress is enjoined by Islam*. It is an approach that is *compatible with modernity* and yet firmly rooted in the noble values and injunctions of Islam. It is an approach that values substance and not form" (emphasis mine).[65] This quote is illustrative because, while the first half claims that "what Islam represents" is not beholden to Western eyes, the second half goes on the defensive by stressing that Islam is receptive to "progress" and "modernity." Both terms were invoked as if they were self-explanatory, reflecting the assumed universality of those terms even if their genesis was rooted in the historical and cultural particularity of the Enlightenment tradition.[66] Despite vowing to resist apologia, Badawi still had to assert to a Western audience that Islam Hadhari was "entirely consistent with democracy" in the same speech.[67] The discourse of Islam Hadhari might have been targeted at correcting Western misperceptions of Islam, but it carried with it the implicit idea that even Muslims had forgotten that Islam could be driven "towards good, towards progress, towards development."[68] Instead of claiming that Muslims were occupying the middle ground as some kind of "silent majority," Badawi's Islam Hadhari evacuated the middle by stressing that the Muslim world had to earn their place there too, "The non-Muslim world, especially the West, must be prepared to discard their prejudices against Islam and be willing to engage in genuine dialogue. At the same time, Muslims too must be prepared to begin a process of reform and renewal in their respective Muslim countries."[69]

Even as Badawi elevated Malaysia's status by claiming that "Malaysia offers a modest working model of renewal, reform, and perhaps a renaissance in the Muslim world," the discourse of Islam Hadhari exposed the difficulties Muslim actors faced in escaping Islam's stigmatization, more so in the post-GWOT world.[70] Malaysia's quest for recognition as a moderate (read: successful) Muslim state was often bound with a tacit acceptance of the inferiority of the Muslim world, which even the self-celebratory tones of the Islam Hadhari discourse could not dissociate from. This silent logic that social backwardness was a result of Muslims misunderstanding Islam continued to reproduce the pathologization of Muslim-majority societies as generally explicable by—and uniquely beholden to—their religiosity.

Moderate Islam Going Global: Najib's *Wasatiyyah* and the Global Movement of Moderates (2009–2018)

Badawi's successor Najib Razak (henceforth Najib) came to power in the aftermath of the ruling government suffering one of its greatest electoral setbacks since 1969.[71] Najib began his premiership on the centrist, inclusive platform of 1Malaysia. He pursued neoliberal-minded reforms by instilling deregulation and technocratic changes in areas such as public administration, the economy, and education.[72] While dealing with the fallout of the financial crisis of 2008 was an important factor, Najib's reform agenda, executed under the Government Transformation Programme and Economic Transformation Programme, was also in response to Badawi's failures to tackle the long-standing issues of bureaucratic inefficiency, economic stagnation, and brain drain.[73] In other words, they were the kind of policies that largely conformed with the ideals of modern, developmental, moderately Islamic Malaysia, which is why it did not take long for Najib to announce a moderate Islam campaign of his own. After launching the idea in the UN General Assembly in 2010, he went on to set up the Global Movement of Moderates Foundation (GMMF) as a government-linked entity and the Wasatiyyah Institute of Malaysia (IWM) under the Prime Minister's Department in 2012.[74]

In terms of discursive content and modus operandi, little had changed from Islam Hadhari. Najib's moderate Islam campaign was largely centered on sloganeering, seminars, and discussions of abstract ideas, with little institutional heft and political will afforded to produce substantive changes. Themes from the past persisted, such as naming the Palestinian issue as the root cause of terrorism.[75] Such continuity is not unexpected, given that the chief theologian behind the Islam Hadhari and *wasatiyyah* campaigns is the same person: Abdullah Md Zin (henceforth Dr. Abdullah).[76] A two-term member of parliament for Besut, Terengganu, with a master's degree in sharia from Al-Azhar University and a doctorate in Islamic studies from the University of Kent, Dr. Abdullah was not a politician who enjoyed particular clout in UMNO. He was drawn into these projects for his religious expertise. He acted as Najib's religious adviser during his tenure too. Interestingly, back in an interview in 2004, Dr Abdullah explained that *wasatiyyah*, which meant "the balanced approach of life," was the "preferable" term to define Islam Hadhari compared to "progressive" or "moderate" Islam, considering the Western connotations of those terms.[77] The gap between how local Muslim elites understood the idea of moderate Islam and how national leaders conveyed it abroad helps explain why Najib split his campaign for moderation between the IWM and the GMMF.

Whereas the IWM's focus was directed at a local audience, the GMMF took on a more international outlook. Conceived as an alliance "from all faiths who are committed to work together to combat and marginalise extremists who have held the world hostage with their bigotry and bias," the GMMF was a state-funded foundation led by an UMNO politician with a "liberal" reputation, Saifuddin Abdullah (henceforth Saifuddin).[78] The choice of Saifuddin signaled the image Najib wanted for GMMF, at least on the international front and during its early years.[79] The GMMF's foreign-policy-focused nature was seen in two of its key initiatives: the Langkawi Declaration signed by the members of the Association of Southeast Asian Nations recognizing moderation as "a core value in the pursuit of long-lasting peace and a tool to defuse tensions, negate radicalism and counter-extremism in all its forms and manifestations"; and the passing of a resolution at the United Nations proclaiming the year 2019 as the Year of Moderation.[80] Neither measures carried any meaningful impact,[81] but the fact that Najib's promotion of GMMF caught the attention of Secretary of State Hillary Clinton and President Barack Obama showed that they served the purpose of cementing Malaysia's reputation as the moderate Muslim ally to the US.[82]

The social currency enjoyed by GMMF's moderation campaign was sparked by the rise of IS, which started as an insurgent group in Iraq and Syria but eventually made sufficient territorial gains and declared itself to be a global caliphate on June 29, 2014.[83] The group captivated global attention, first through its swift territorial expansion, military victories, and influx of foreign fighters; and second, through visual spectacles of violence—including beheadings, immolation, and the enslavement of Yazidis—publicized by a savvy media campaign.[84] IS's notoriety consigned Islam to unprecedented levels of scrutiny. Not only were the choreographed imageries of graphic violence reaffirming prejudices about Islam's supposed fanaticism (Obama called IS "especially barbaric"),[85] the fact that they served as "visual manifestations" of an "alternative political order"—one made under the claim of Islamic authenticity—once again raised consternation about Islam's status as a source of antimodern insurgency against the international order.[86] Reminiscent of the alarmist discourses that emerged after the September 11 attacks, IS's rise to fame was accompanied by a slew of articles and analyses that debated Islam's relationship to violence and extremism.[87] The resurfacing of these tropes, not to mention the overwhelming tendency from scholars and the media alike to read IS's appeal from the movement's doctrine sans the geopolitical chaos from which it emerged,[88] reflects the latent suspicion international society held against Islam, that it was somehow responsible for producing the "terrorist" horrible enough to be regarded as *hostis humani generis*.

In chapter 1, I elaborated that the GWOT's moral exceptionalist framing explains why the risk of being seen as part of the "uncivil" and "barbaric" would have exacerbated the sense of ontological insecurity among the Muslim elites.[89] Indeed, Muslim states had responded in greater magnitude to the IS problem compared to the early post–September 11 years. Examples of such measures included joining the US-led Global Coalition against IS;[90] organizing the Islamic Military Counter-Terrorism Coalition (IMCTC) under Saudi leadership; and launching countermessaging centers such as the Hedayah Centre in the United Arab Emirates and the Global Centre for Combating Extremist Ideology (Etidal) in Saudi Arabia. The countering of Islam's stigmatization following the rise of IS was not only confined to state actors. In 2014, 126 Muslim scholars and theologians wrote a letter in rebuke of IS's self-proclaimed caliph, Abu Bakr al-Baghdadi.[91] However, as Wasserstein muses, "It is cast as a letter but we have no way of knowing if it might have been delivered. . . . Nor it is clear that al-Baghdadi is in fact the intended audience for the Letter. An open letter is generally intended for public consumption."[92] The fact that the letter was presented as an open letter and hosted on an English-language website illustrates the public performative nature of the endeavor. The detailed arguments about scripture in the letter were as much about convincing a Muslim audience as they were about convincing a non-Muslim one. In other words, the important issue here is not about from whom Islam was reclaimed but rather *for whom* this act of reclaiming was performed.

Malaysia was similarly proactive in demonstrating its counter-terror credentials. It was a member of two aforementioned military alliances against IS (the IMCTC and the US-led global coalition),[93] although its military involvement was minimal. Najib's "moderation" campaign also quickly adapted to the situation. At one point, his administration made plans to host up to three separate countermessaging centers.[94] The GMMF also pivoted toward creating counternarratives for P/CVE projects,[95] while the IWM published a booklet outlining Malaysia's *wasatiyyah* approach to tackle extremism.[96] Tellingly, the booklet credited Mahathir's initiative of integrating Islamic values into governance for "playing an important role in weakening the tendencies of certain parties in the Malay-Muslim community to establish extremist groups to oppose the government."[97] It even claimed that Malaysia had done a better job in Islamizing its political life than the Arab states, further advancing the idea that Malaysia was the moderate Islamic state par excellence.[98] This sense of self-assuredness was bolstered by Malaysia's relative security from the wave of IS-affiliated or -inspired attacks in Europe, the Middle East, and Southeast Asia between 2014 and 2018 when the group was at its peak strength.[99] Thus, Najib could not miss the opportunity to demonstrate how Malaysia's moderate Islam was the ideal formula that could combat extremism and achieve economic success simultaneously: "Malaysia stands ready to share its experience; of upholding Islam and marginalising extremism; of implementing the objectives of Shariah while practising democracy; of maintaining a multi-ethnic society where different faiths coexist and prosper; and showing that *Islam can not only succeed, but drive progress and successful economic development*" (emphasis mine).[100]

Impassioned and self-assured as the rhetoric may sound, they were nevertheless discursively bound to the problem of ontological insecurity that undergirded Malaysia's long-running quest for recognition as a model and moderate Islamic state. Ironically, just like the Amman Message in 2004, or the Marrakesh Declaration in 2016, Malaysia's call for moderation only gained purchase in international society because of the GWOT's stigmatizing effects on Islam.[101] The GMMF's rhetorical positioning as "a coalition of moderates" versus "extremists of all religions" was premised on the need to cancel the discursive equivalence between Islam and extremism.[102] Nevertheless, Muslim proponents of the moderation discourse often found their calls for moderation interpreted as referring *specifically* to Islam, regardless of their actual intentions. Tellingly, when Najib appointed a conservative Islamist figure, Nasharuddin Mat Isa,[103] to head the GMMF following the departure of Saifuddin in 2015, the latter ended up turning its mission to combating Islamophobia.[104] At one point, he even claimed that terrorist groups were "invented" to tarnish the reputation of Islam.[105] This shift in tone and priority but not its stigma correction agenda of the GMMF only reinforces one observation: no matter the leaning of its leadership, the discourse of moderation remains captive by the exigencies of the GWOT.

Whose Middle Ground? The Dilemmas of Moderate Islam

Considering that the Malaysian government had long strived to seek recognition as the exemplary Islamic state, the post-GWOT deluge of negative publicity surrounding Islam only meant that status-seeking elites such as Mahathir were experiencing greater stigmatization at the same time that their country had achieved an ostensibly higher standard of development. Mahathir's sudden declaration that Malaysia is an Islamic state following the September 11 attacks in 2001 and, later, Najib's convening of an "international group of Sunni and Shia scholars" to "define an Islamic State" following IS's emergence in 2015[106] illustrate performative attempts to wrestle back the signifier of Islam that is increasingly integral to the Malaysian state identity. Whereas it is difficult to know what Najib and Badawi personally thought about the GWOT as they did not produce highly personal writings such as did Mahathir, it is quite telling that, as administrations that came into power in the post-GWOT era, both have chosen to headline their governments with some form of moderate Islam branding. These maneuverings, when read in the context of the *status needs* of the Muslim elites who had to navigate the GWOT's stigmatizing effects, highlight a social element of state behavior that is not covered by either instrumentalist readings that only focus on political survival of the elites or constructivist accounts that presume a "states versus terrorism" unity grounded in the survival of the order.

To be sure, status concerns were not confined to state elites well socialized in the international diplomatic circuit. Even an Islamist party like PAS, which was famous for its anti-West rhetoric and vocal support of the Taliban during the US invasion of Afghanistan in 2001, eventually dissociated itself from the group, stressing that they were "nothing like the Taliban."[107] In other words, the motive of ontological security seeking is not only present in elite discourses and state behaviors; it also provides a crucial linkage between the international environment and domestic politics, structuring motivations and strategic calculations for a variety of actors.[108]

Malaysia's deployment of the moderate Islam discourse to seek ontological security also has its challenges. First, without a history where national elites dabbled in alternative forms of internationalism without fear of ostracization by the West (such as Sukarno's hosting of the Bandung Conference and Iran's exporting of the revolution),[109] Malaysia's search for ontological security has always been confined to a tradition of crowd-pleasing "middle" positioning.[110] Having neither the gumption nor substance to articulate a truly "third-way" position that addressed the roots of its ontological insecurity, Malaysia's call for moderation in the post-GWOT world was arguably as mild as its advocacy of nonalignment during the Cold War.[111] Second, Malaysia's claim to the mantle of moderate Islam was often articulated within a discourse that subtly positioned it as exceptional among the other Muslim states. The messaging conflicted with the goal of reversing Islam's stigmatization, as depicting Malaysia's success as a rarity in the Muslim world only reinforced prejudices that took peace, toleration, and economic success in Muslim societies as *anomalies* instead of norms. And last, as much as the discourse of moderate Islam served the purpose of ontological security seeking by claiming that "we are not like them" (the terrorists), it also reinforced a taxonomy of Islam that divided the religion into its "moderate" and "radical" variants to align with international security imperatives.[112] But how would this abstract idea of moderate Islam fulfill the expectation that it could both prevent and counter Muslim radicalism? That question can only be addressed if we examine how counter-terrorism is operationalized in Malaysia, which will be the subject of the next chapter.

FIVE

"Islamized" Security

Defining and Defending (Theological) Authority in Counter-Terrorism

In the upcoming two chapters, we will take a methodological and empirical turn to examine counter-terror's interpellation with Islam at the microgovernmental level. This shift helps us understand how ideas about "moderate" Islam, something we touched on in the previous chapter, are operationalized in daily practices of counter-terrorism. Chapter 5 surveys the institutional contours of Malaysia's "Islamized" counter-terror regime, while chapter 6 analyzes governing narratives that construct the figure of the "Muslim terrorist" to justify state and social interventions. To visualize Malaysia's counter-terror regime and its security logic, I rely on a combination of discourse analysis of primary materials, institutional mapping, actor tracing, and fieldwork interviews with security practitioners and those who experienced Malaysia's counter-terror regime firsthand, such as attorneys, activists, and family members of detainees.

Together, these two chapters offer a multisite, practice-oriented view of Malaysia's counter-terrorism that focuses on the years between 2013 and 2018.[1] This period is chosen because it is a time when Malaysia witnessed a significant spike in terrorism-related operations due to the emergence of the Islamic State (IS) and its so-called caliphate in an area spanning both Syria and Iraq. The period also coincided with a highly public counter-terror campaign waged by the Malaysian government, which led to the prosecution of hundreds of individuals under terrorism offences in open courts for the first time in Malaysian history. Despite the enormity of this enterprise (in Malaysia and elsewhere),[2] scant research has been done to interrogate how states perform counter-terror, especially not in a way that covers the counter-terror regime as a whole—encompassing sites such as the bureaucracy, the courtroom, the security apparatus, the mosques, and the penitentiary. My multisite approach is arguably the first of its kind in the study of counter-terrorism. Such a broad scope helps trace and illuminate the pervasiveness of the security logic this book is most interested in: one that treats the Muslim "radical" as a religious deviant. My "thick" reading of counter-terrorism borrows from the security assemblage framework employed in anthropological studies of security that seeks to capture "*how these forms of action work and what types of security they produce*" (emphasis mine).[3] This approach also denaturalizes claims of knowledge and expertise within counter-terrorism and insists on identifying the contingent nature under which notions of authority are formed. As we shall see, this question of "authority" is a crucial one in the composition of security logics.

Chapter 5 engages with this question of *authority* by tracing the prevalence of Islamic actors, reasoning, and expertise within Malaysia's counter-terrorism, and by highlighting a discursive economy in Malaysia that "Islamizes" security via its habitual deference to religious authorities and expertise. In doing so, I illustrate how knowledge practices of counter-terror are constituted within a setting where the Muslim state's presence loomed large over a field whose nature and claim to scientific rigor are often contested.[4] Unlike in many Western states, there is no concrete division between terrorism studies as a field of academic study and counter-terrorism as a field of practice in Malaysia. This proximity of terrorism expertise to the religious bureaucracy fueled two outcomes: the institutional conflation of theological expertise with terrorism expertise, and the discursive construction of terrorism as a product of individuals "misunderstanding" Islam. They dovetailed with an institutional history that has long sought to stamp out "wrong" Islam, as well as with global aspirations about "moderate Islam" and its functionality in Preventing/Countering Violent Extremism (P/CVE) projects. To be sure, notwithstanding its frequent invocation of moderation, "Islamized" counter-terror in Malaysia did not become the vessel to promote a more "liberal" version of Islam many Western observers had hoped for.[5]

This chapter proceeds in two parts. The first part sheds light on how religious authorities were roped into different functional areas in Malaysia's counter-terror regime, such as publication control, issuing fatwas, and public communication, and as experts who adjudicated questions surrounding Muslim radicalization and oversaw the "deradicalization" programs. The second part reviews the consequences of having a security assemblage whereby theological expertise is institutionalized as counter-terror expertise. Specifically, I draw attention to how counter-terrorism has become a domain in which exegetical authority was fought over between the religious establishment and the terrorists as their imagined foe, on the one hand, and between scholars from different schools of theology, on the other. As the enterprise was depicted as defending the sacred authority of the religious establishment instead of addressing forms of radical political activism, counter-terror discourses in Malaysia also adopted the religious and communal vernaculars of Quranic hermeneutics, conspiracy, and millenarianism, dramatically altering the terms and stakes of security.

Defining Authority: The Islamic Bureaucracy and Experts in Counter-Terror

In my interview with then head of the counter-terror division of Malaysia's Special Branch, Ayob Khan Mydin Pitchay (henceforth Ayob Khan), I asked him about broader P/CVE policies after he told me that law enforcement could only do so much for counter-terrorism as the key was in tackling the ideology. He responded by lamenting that the religious authorities were "not aggressive" in monitoring radical teachings, claiming that "We can't do anything. We are the police. *Religious affairs rightly belong to the religious authorities* . . . but they are not aggressive enough."[6] This quote demonstrates not only a conception of terrorism as a religious problem but also a deference in authority by the police to the religious bureaucracy, despite itself being the most instrumental player in Malaysia's counter-terrorism.

In this section, I will focus on this question of "Islamic" authority in counter-terror by outlining how the Islamic bureaucracy and theological expertise were incorporated into Malaysia's counter-terror operation as three sources of authority: fatwas as the exegetical authority, the Jabatan Kemajuan Islam Malaysia (Department of Islamic Development of Malaysia, JAKIM) as institutional authority, and religious experts as the faces of authority. I dwell on this question of authority because, as in any form of security governance, counter-terror's operationalization relies on hierarchies and networks of authority that provide rationalizations to a number of questions. What is the nature of the transgression? How can risks be calculated? How can society be regulated and self-regulate against threats? Who gets a say in the exercise of state coercion in the name of counter-terror? These are questions that fed into the construction of security logics.

Using this approach, my illustration of Malaysia's "Islamized" counter-terrorism also departs from accounts that assume the interlocking of religion and security as the natural product of a (un)holy alliance between religious and political actors, or indicative of a "total approach" of security, where the coercive capacity of the security apparatus is only made possible by the ideological support offered by religious institutions.[7] I argue against such totalizing and arguably cynical conceptualizations of security that assume some unity in purpose among state actors. Instead, borrowing from Huysmans and Sullivan, I propose that the key to understanding a security logic lies in the "little security nothings."[8] That is to say, our analytical optic must be set on the assembly of "diverse governance techniques, legal interventions, knowledge practices and mundane forms of functional expertise" that operationalizes counter-terrorism as if it is primarily an issue in need of theological arbitration.[9]

Fatwas as Textual Authority

Institutionally speaking, the presiding authority of Malaysia's counter-terrorism is the E8 unit of the Special Branch led by Ayob Khan. Formed in 2014, the E8 is devoted exclusively to counter-terror.[10] On the operational level, preventive detention laws such as the Internal Security Act and its replacements, the Security Offences (Special Measures) Act 2012 and the Prevention of Terrorism Act 2015, provide the legal basis for the police to investigate, arrest, and detain (sometimes without trial) suspects of terrorism.[11] Nevertheless, in broader P/CVE efforts, the police continue to rely on the religious authorities for legitimation. For example, in a seminar given by Ayob Khan about IS in the mosque, he mentioned that it is "*wajib* [compulsory] for Malaysian Muslims to follow the ruling of the Majlis Fatwa [fatwa council]."[12] By the ruling, Ayob Khan was referring to the fatwa released by the Jawatankuasa Fatwa Majlis Kebangsaan Bagi Hal Ehwal Ugama Islam Malaysia (National Fatwa Commission, JKF) in 2015.[13] Composed of muftis from all the Malaysian states, representatives from JAKIM, and a handful of legal experts and academics, the JKF is considered the highest Islamic authority in Malaysia.[14] The fatwa states that it is haram (forbidden) for Muslims to get involved with IS because their cause is "antithetical to the teachings of Islam, the practice of democracy, and humanitarian values" and that dying for IS is not considered *syahid* (martyrdom) as their struggle does not fulfill the criteria of jihad.[15] In citing the JKF as if it was the highest authority in counter-terrorism matters, the Malaysian police were handling the challenge of IS as if its appeal to Muslims was mainly on theological grounds.

As the administration of Islamic affairs in Malaysia is constitutionally under the (subnational) state's prerogative, most, if not all, states in Malaysia have released fatwas about IS of their own following the JKF's fatwa. However, most are not gazetted, making them advisories instead of legally binding documents.[16] One notable exception is the fatwa from Selangor's state fatwa council. The gazetted fatwa not only prohibits Muslims from holding "the beliefs, teachings, and ideology" of IS, but it also explicitly threatens legal action under the state's sharia enactment against any Muslims in Selangor found to be associated with IS.[17] Whereas the fatwa does not mention any specific statute, one can surmise that it refers to Section 7 of the Syariah Criminal Offenses (Selangor) Enactment 1995 that penalizes "any doctrine or ceremony or act" that is "contrary to Islamic Law or any *fatwa*." While it is unlikely that the sharia enactment will ever be employed in counter-terrorism due to questions of constitutionality,[18] it is revealing that the fatwa raises the possibility of terrorism being treated as an offence of *akidah* (faith).[19] It suggests that, at least in governing narratives, state actors have hedged their authority in theological reasoning, even as the operationalization of counter-terrorism largely transpires in the language of rule of law as the Penal Code remains the key legal instrument in counter-terror (as we shall see in chapter 6). In other words, the governing of Muslim "hearts and minds" in Malaysia's counter-terrorism is based on the understanding that these "hearts" and "minds" must be reined in within the strictures of a state-defined hermeneutical authority.

JAKIM as Institutional Authority

Another religious authority involved in counter-terror in Malaysia is the federal department of JAKIM—an institution whose origins and role I have discussed in chapter 3. As mentioned above, the JKF is chaired by a JAKIM official, with its members also serving as the secretary and the legal advisor. Echoing Najib's call that the religious institutions must "actively counter terrorism and extremism,"[20] JAKIM proclaimed an "all-out war" on IS, claiming as its mandate the monitoring of "all religious schools, religious education in mosques and religious talks."[21] Its outreach program to explain the "true meaning of jihad in Islam" had reportedly met "more than a million people."[22] It also set up the multiagency Jihad Concept Explanation Action Committee to address "misconceptions about *jihad* (holy war)."[23] JAKIM was also handed a big data project to analyze "Islamic extremism among citizens," further illustrating the state's view that jihadist extremism was primarily a problem of Muslim religiosity.[24]

JAKIM's institutional relevance to counter-terrorism is also bolstered by its housing of the Jawatankuasa Penapisan Bahan Penerbitan Berunsur Islam (Committee for Screening Publications Related to Islam) that monitors all Islam-related publications. As exposure to "dangerous" texts was increasingly seen as part of the radicalization process, the committee became the authority to assess if an Islamic publication was "subversive" enough to warrant banning, although the ultimate decision to ban still resides with the Ministry of Home Affairs (MOHA).[25] For example, in 2017, the committee recommended banning Abdullah Azzam's *Tarbiyah Jihadiyah*, a book tendered in multiple terrorism trials as evidence of the accused's support of terrorism, but that book remains unbanned till this day.[26]

Counter-terrorism even became a justification for JAKIM's importance. A deputy minister cited combating "extremist ideologies like that of IS" as the reason the department requested a budget of more than MYR 1 billion.[27]

Experts as the Faces of Authority

In Malaysia, individual experts are instrumental in two areas of counter-terror: serving as expert witnesses in the prosecution of terrorism crimes and conducting deradicalization programs. Some have acted in those twin capacities. I will go through these roles in more detail below and shall begin with sketching out the social landscape of Malaysia's terrorism expertise. At this point, it is perhaps most helpful to turn to Stampnitzsky's characterization of the idiosyncratic nature of terrorism expertise first: "In sociological terms, the boundaries of the field are weak and permeable. There is little regulation of who may become an expert, and the key audience for terrorism expertise is not an ideal-typical scientific community of other terrorism experts but, rather, the public and the state."[28]

Nevertheless, in most settings, there is still a researcher/practitioner divide—contested and permeable as these roles may be—that maintains a separate/semi-separate realm of expertise to counterbalance the knowledge formations associated with state power and exigencies. Yet, even when compared with regional counterparts, the boundaries of terrorism expertise in Malaysia are fuzzier as there is no researcher/practitioner divide to speak of, not to mention the lack of independent or semi-independent research outfits that host terrorism expertise. One institution that is dedicated to terrorism research in Malaysia is the Southeast Asia Regional Centre for Counter-Terrorism. Still, it is an outfit under the Ministry of Foreign Affairs and largely staffed by civil servants.

Regional comparisons show that Malaysia's situation is not a given. In Indonesia's case, there is the acclaimed Institute for Policy Analysis of Conflict founded by renowned security analyst Sidney Jones, who was formerly involved with the International Crisis Group. Both of these organizations were able to provide in-depth analysis of Islamist militancy in Indonesia, as their institutional independence from the state did not prevent them from having firsthand access to primary sources such as current and former militants, security practitioners, and materials related to the investigation and prosecution of terrorism cases.[29] On the other hand, Singapore's International Centre for Political Violence and Terrorism Research (ICPVTR) hosted within the S. Rajaratnam School of International Studies in the state-funded Nanyang Technological University constitutes what some call the "Singapore School" of terrorism studies.[30] The ICPVTR functions as more than a research institution; it also runs capacity-building programs and even a terrorism database.[31] Whereas there exist critiques that the Singapore School is complicit in a "collusion between scholars and statesmen," the ICPVTR nevertheless provides an institutional home for terrorism expertise outside the state, which is the reason why there is a Singapore School to be scrutinized in the first place.[32]

Compared to the cases described above, terrorism expertise in Malaysia is bounded to the state in almost a closed loop, in that state recognition is tantamount to the accreditation of expertise. Not only that, being inducted into state practices of counter-terror is probably the only way one can get quality access to primary information needed for terrorism research, further blurring the researcher/practitioner divide. This lack of a separate realm for terrorism expertise may partially explain why, despite the hundreds of arrests made, there is still a lack of empirically grounded theorization of the IS phenomenon in Malaysia.[33] The state-dependent nature of terrorism expertise in Malaysia also reinforces its epistemological enclosure and insularity. Without a critical mass of experts that enjoy some form of institutional independence from the state (and from each other), and without successful extraction from a consultancy culture that incentivizes "unchecked opinions" more than substantive research, the field fails to take on a disciplinary nature and the structures of self-governance that come with it.[34] The lack of data access also impedes the formation of a vibrant scholarly community that enables independent critiques of both the field and state practices in counter-terrorism. Under these circumstances, who the state selected as experts is especially crucial in establishing and legitimizing the epistemological assumptions behind counter-terror practices.

Given the lack of a counterbalance, the composition of terrorism expertise in Malaysia is very much reflective of the state's Islamization of counter-terror (in that the matter was treated institutionally as a religious problem). As highlighted in chapter 3, this development has its history in a discursive economy that took "wrong" Islam as the reason for Islamist militancy, a perspective that was given much elite and institutional support. However, the making of terrorism "expertise" as a public good in Malaysia only really began when the state started resorting to open trials to prosecute terrorism offenders in 2013 and launched more public P/CVE campaigns to alert the public about the threats posed by IS. These developments ushered in a search for experts to fulfill the legal role of expert witness and the intellectual role of public communicator to explicate the problem of terrorism to both the courts and the public.

But who gets to qualify as a terrorism expert in what is, at best, a nascent field? Revealingly, in a presentation prepared by the Attorney General's Chamber, one of the challenges noted in the prosecution of terrorism trials was the "lacking in number of experts in terrorism and Islamic teachings. Currently, we have either expert in terrorism or expert in Islamic teaching and not expert in both fields."[35] Going by this information, an ideal terrorism expert is someone who commands both terrorism and Islamic expertise. In practice, however, terrorism expertise in Malaysia slanted more toward the latter. Experts were most valued for their Islamic expertise instead of the usual areas in terrorism studies, such as ideology, organizational dynamics, or the individual and group psychology behind radicalization.[36]

EXPERTS IN PROFILE

A complete profile of every expert involved in counter-terrorism is hard to come by, given the obscurity of the field—not to mention that the government has not released the complete list of the forty-six experts it appointed to the deradicalization panel.[37] My research through open-source data and interviews suggests that most experts actively engaged in counter-terror practices were indeed trained in Islamic studies or were ulamas themselves. This finding fits into a historical pattern that saw religious scholars recruited into Malaysia's deradicalization programs.[38] To demonstrate this deference toward theological expertise, or rather the governmental assumption that terrorism expertise must be built on top of a solid Islamic education,[39] I will discuss the biographies of two of the arguably most well-known state-affiliated counter-terror experts in Malaysia.

The first is an ulama by the name of Ustaz Zamihan Mat Zin Al-Ghari (henceforth Zamihan).[40] Zamihan was involved in the deradicalization programs since 2005 and was seconded from JAKIM to the MOHA Security and Public Order Bureau in 2012. Zamihan graduated from the Mu'tah University in Jordan in Islamic studies and earned his doctorate from the Universiti Kebangsaan Malaysia's Islamic Studies department with a thesis exploring the Wahhabi influence in the Malaysian civil service.[41] His position as an ulama and a functionary within the federal religious bureaucracy meant that Zamihan's vocation was not simply that of a counter-terror practitioner but also a Muslim preacher with a public presence.[42] Zamihan was appointed as the head of the deradicalization panel from 2017 to 2019, which explained the relative emphasis given to religious expertise as he personally opined that having such expertise was crucial in countering IS's ideology.[43]

Another person who enjoys a public reputation for being a terrorism expert in Malaysia is Ahmad el-Muhammady (henceforth Ahmad).[44] Apart from being a practitioner in the deradicalization programs, Ahmad is also a university lecturer at the International Islamic University of Malaysia (IIUM). He obtained his doctorate in Muslim world issues in 2019 based on a thesis submitted to the International Institute of Islamic Thought and Civilisation of IIUM on Jemaah Islamiyah, a militant Islamist movement in Southeast Asia that was responsible for the Bali bombings.[45] Trained in political science at university, Ahmad came from a solid background of religious learning. Before university, he was a student in Malaysia's *pondok* system of Islamic boarding schools.[46] His religious credentials were clearly valued as the courts had addressed him as Ustaz and mentioned that he "specializes in Islamic studies and political science."[47]

Ahmad is also the son of the late Ustaz Muhammad Uthman el-Muhammady (1943–2013) (henceforth Uthman), a highly regarded Islamic scholar who held the position of Distinguished Senior Fellow in the International Institute of Islamic Thought and Civilisation before his passing. A master's graduate in Islamic studies from the University of Malaya, Uthman was conferred two honorary doctorates for his prolific scholarship and efforts in *dakwah* (proselytization).[48] Uthman was one of the earliest participants in Malaysia's deradicalization programs for detained Islamist militants and was deemed "most outstanding" by Ayob Khan, who was in many ways Malaysia's very own counter-terror czar.[49] Following patterns of familial involvement seen in deradicalization programs elsewhere,[50] Ahmad began taking over his father's duties in 2011 when Uthman's health declined.[51]

To further illustrate how religious expertise dominated terrorism expertise in Malaysia, consider this news report in the Malay newspaper, *Harian Metro*, that named eight local experts in deradicalization.[52] Of the eight, four are ulamas: Zamihan, Ustaz Abdullaah Jalil, Ustaz Yunan Abdul Samad, and Ustaz Abdul Rahman Tajuddin. Abdullaah Jalil is a lecturer in Islamic finance and a member of the fatwa research panel of the Majlis Agama Islam Negeri Sembilan (Islamic Council of Negeri Sembilan), while the latter two are independent preachers. The other three—Ahmad, Ahmad Fauzi Abdul Hamid, and Mohd Mizan Aslam (henceforth Mizan)—are all trained in political science but can be considered highly knowledgeable in Islamic studies. Like Ahmad, Mizan is a graduate of Islamic education before writing a doctoral dissertation about the Kumpulan Mujahidin Malaysia (Malaysia Mujahidin Group), an affiliate of Jemaah Islamiyah.[53] He later became the first rector of the Islamic University College Perlis. Mizan was also personally involved in the deradicalization programs, although, in our interview, he did not mention how he got involved.[54] His doctoral thesis showed remarkable access to classified information, indicating close ties with the police.[55] Ahmad Fauzi is a political science professor who has written extensively about Islam and Malaysian politics, and has received considerable religious training himself.[56] Unlike the other two, Fauzi was not involved in the deradicalization programs, although the police had approached him to serve as an expert to analyze materials seized in counter-terror operations.[57] The only outlier is the last person, Mohd Hizam Hanafiah, who, as far as my knowledge goes, is not formally trained in Islamic studies. He is a lecturer in entrepreneurship and an associate of Zamihan's.[58]

This mixture of Islamic and terrorism expertise in Malaysia has encouraged their conflation. Those who could give religious classes were deemed those who could "heal" the "misguided."[59] It is the reason why deradicalization expertise can be used as a proxy to map the sociological landscape of terrorism expertise in Malaysia, even if it is a mistake to equate one form of expertise with the other. Indeed, deradicalization received a lot of attention in the mid- to late 2010s because the minister of home affairs was actively promoting Malaysia's deradicalization success on the international stage, to the point of proclaiming a "97.5 percent" success rate.[60] However, deradicalization expertise remained a field marked by profound ambiguity. There was no adjudication of what qualifies as expertise (education and/or experience?), nor was there a clear divide between scholar and practitioner, cleric and counselor. In many cases, access and expertise were treated as interchangeable, with some of those who participated in the deradicalization programs ending up writing their doctoral dissertations about it.[61]

Unlike in Singapore, where religious scholars involved in rehabilitation programs must undergo training in counseling, the opacity of the selection process and the lack of a formal structure to train or accredit made claims of expertise in Malaysia seem arbitrary by comparison.[62] Indeed, the credentials of Zamihan were questioned after allegations of him abusing and mistreating the detainees surfaced.[63] His checkered history, which included allegedly uttering offensive and racist remarks toward non-Muslims, became a liability when a new government came into power in May 2018.[64] In 2019, Zamihan was terminated from the deradicalization programs and sent back to JAKIM, ending his secondment to MOHA.

EXPERTS IN ACTION

This institutional bias in selecting individuals with religious expertise to serve as authorities in terrorism is not inconsequential. To be sure, these consequences were less about the machination by individuals but rather a product of the institutionalized security logic. I will use one example here to illustrate the policy implications of this "Islamized" security logic. In an interview, a public prosecutor admitted that they needed the experts to determine if the ideology shown within the seized items (mainly publications) "radicalizes people," and to "*tafsir*" if there were indications of support toward any terrorist organization.[65] This demand for expertise to perform *tafsir* (Quranic exegesis) in a legal process indicates a focus on using textual materials to gauge and prove one's radicalism, and the kind of expertise that would qualify as terrorism expertise, namely, strong religious training, which led to the theological frames in which these experts offered their analysis.

Take, for example, this case involving an individual charged for possessing terrorism-related materials.[66] Three experts (two of them academics in Islamic studies) submitted reports to review Abdullah Azzam's book *Tarbiyah Jihadiyah* that was seized from the accused.[67] While the analyses' primary objective was to ascertain claims of terrorist connections, the reports went on to challenge Abdullah Azzam's interpretation of concepts such as jihad, *takfir* (ex-communication), and *tauhid* (oneness of God). They claimed that Azzam's interpretation is "opposed to the methodology of *Ahlus Sunnah Wal Jamaah* upheld by Malaysian Muslims";[68] and that the "literal" and "extreme" Islam he espoused bears "a false image of Islam" and can "influence readers, especially those without a good command of the knowledge of Islam, towards extremist thinking and would encourage them to partake in armed jihad."[69] One of the experts even made a direct indictment of the accused based solely on the evidence that he possessed the book: "My testimony clearly shows that the book *Tarbiyah Jihadiyah* is motivated to encourage the readers to give full support to IS.[70] It also proves that the owner of this book has some association with the group. Thus, I find this book's owner to be a hardcore supporter of IS and is a threat to national security."[71]

My goal here is not to say that these experts alone determined the fate of the accused, as cases were usually prosecuted based on a combination of material and circumstantial evidence. The analytical move here is about locating them institutionally and functionally within a counter-terror regime that routinely turns to religious expertise and experts to arbitrate matters related to Islamist violent extremism. Following Sullivan's point that "objects of political rule . . . are effects of the techniques and knowledge practices that calculate, classify and target them," I argue that what entails these processes of authority-making in Malaysia's counter-terrorism is a (re)definition of the issue on the epistemological level, leading to what I call the *Islamization* of counter-terror.[72]

Defending Authority: Counter-Terror and the Politics of Theological Defense

The Islamization of counter-terror in Malaysia selects for not only the kinds of institutions and expertise drawn into daily counter-terrorism practices but also the framing of terrorism itself. This framing is one that employs Islamic mythologies, idioms, and exegesis to depict IS as a religious and cosmological foe. As a result, terrorism is condensed and clarified in state narratives as a product of internal intra-Muslim doctrinal differences (or deviations) and, by that logic, implicitly as a crisis peculiar to Muslim societies. This section discusses this framing as well as the politics it generated. By *politics* I refer to how counter-terrorism devolved into an arena in which intra-Muslim differences and rivalry over theological issues played out. In other words, the defense of (state) Islam and its authoritative forms became the dividing line between the state and its jihadist "enemies," as well as between Muslim elites jostling to (re)define Islamic orthodoxy.

The politics that unfold in counter-terrorism is one of theological defense, something I will illustrate in two steps. First, I will discuss what is considered the most authoritative P/CVE text in Malaysia, a booklet entitled *Jihad dan Konsepnya* (Jihad and its concepts) published by JAKIM in collaboration with the Mufti's Department of the Federal Territories, the Royal Malaysian Police, and the National Security Council.[73] Through discourse analysis, I highlight how the document interprets terrorism as a conflict between religious interpretations. The document also narrates the issue of terrorism within a crisis discourse of the Muslim world that reproduces the ontological security-seeking motifs we discussed in previous chapters, albeit with a millenarian twist. Second, I provide an insight into the intra-Muslim rivalry that animated the politics of counter-terror in Malaysia. In doing so, I highlight that, as counter-terrorism moved discursively into the realms of defending "Islamic" authority, the enterprise was grafted onto ongoing religio-political contestations between two camps of religious elites, further complicating notions of authority and expertise in an already contentious field.

Counter-Terror as the Defense of Jihad

Published in 2015, the primary purpose of the booklet *Jihad and Its Concepts*,[74] as its title suggests, is to debunk erroneous interpretations of jihad. It does so by reproducing the JKF's fatwa in its pages, arguing that "confusion in understanding the real concept of jihad and martyrdom according to the principles of sharia" is why Malaysian Muslims came to support IS (11). To tackle the issue, the authors cited the opinion of Muslim thinkers such as Yusuf al-Qaradawi (1–2) and Hasan al-Banna (5) and listed multiple ways through which jihad can be undertaken.[75] They include offensive and defensive jihad, jihad against *nafsu* (desires), and jihad through education and philanthropy (3–4). Nevertheless, if correcting misinterpretations of Islam is what it sets out to do, the booklet's authors made no reference to the ideology of IS at all.[76] Instead, it proclaims that "the decision to wage jihad belongs exclusively to the political rulers," hermeneutically sealing any possibility of conceptualizing jihad beyond the language of the nation-state that undergirds the international legal order (23).[77] In short, the defense of exegetical truth is made tantamount to the defense of the prevailing statist order.

Mimicking developments in Saudi Arabia and even within intrajihadist debates, the figure of the *khawarij* (or *kharijites*) loomed large in the booklet's treatment of IS, as they were called the "*khawarij* of the modern day" (11).[78] The *khawarij*, which translates to "exiters," or those who rebelled, first emerged in the early history of Islam during the events of the First Fitna. Unsatisfied with the cease-fire and mediation between the fourth Rashidun Caliph, Ali, and Muawiyah, the *khawarij* rebelled against both. The rebellion was eventually put down, but it resulted in the assassination of Ali. These events cemented the negative symbolism of the *khawarij* in both Sunni and Shiite discourses, as the movement represents a total repudiation of authority and a harbinger of Muslim disunity and violent contention. Reflecting on the term's longevity in Muslim religio-political discourses in Egypt, Kenney writes: "Kharijism raises some of the most sensitive questions about modern Muslim identity because it explicitly evokes the dichotomy of good Muslim versus bad Muslim. It also directly connects this religious identity with a political one. A Kharijite is not only a misguided believer but a dangerous citizen as well. . . . A bad Muslim is a bad Muslim for all time."[79]

This leitmotif of the "bad Muslim" is also rooted in Malaysian security discourses. As mentioned in chapter 3, the Malaysian government's deployment of the *khawarij* label traces back to its condemnation of the Pan-Malaysian Islamic Party (PAS)'s alleged militancy in the 1980s. Interestingly, as if to prove that *IS* is the *khawarij* reincarnate, the booklet dedicates an entire section to discussing the negative characteristics of the *khawarij*, such as "prejudicial," "easy to label others as heretics," "immature and shallow in thinking," "shallow knowledge in *fiqh* [Islamic jurisprudence]," and "extreme in religious worship" (13–16).

The booklet's comparison between IS and the *khawarij* is not just a rhetorical strategy to demonize the former. Rather, in invoking the mythical and apocalyptic figure of the *khawarij*, the booklet reframes the temporality of counter-terrorism by fusing worldly stakes with an eschatological urgency. For example, the booklet situates the challenge of IS, sectarian warfare in the Muslim world, and the loss of prestige of Muslims within a temporality it calls "realiti umat Islam akhir zaman" (the reality for Muslims in the End Times; 21).[80] One of those listed challenges is that of Muslim disunity—a recurring theme in Malaysia's ethnocentric conception of national security, where the fragmentation of the Malay-Muslims carries the risks of other minority "races" taking advantage of them.[81] This emphasis on unity can be seen from the fact that, despite its harsh condemnation of the *khawariji* as self-righteous and defiant cynics, the booklet's authors did not attempt ex-communication. Instead, they quote a line purportedly from Caliph Ali: "They are our brothers, but they were extreme towards us" (16).

Other than meddling with temporality, "Islamized" P/CVE narratives like these also reframe the spatial dimensions of the problem of terrorism. Much like the crisis discourse employed in the moderate Islam campaigns abroad, the booklet subsumes the concerns of terrorism within a greater concern about the collective image and survival of the *entire* Muslim world. As it is written for a domestic audience, the booklet presents this fear and anxiety more forthrightly than the more eloquent foreign policy narratives we discussed in the previous chapter. For example, its concern about IS lies not in its propensity for violence but rather in how the "Jews and other enemies of Islam" will take advantage of the situation to propagate Islamophobia (20). Such views were not far off from widespread conspiracy theories in Malaysia and elsewhere that IS was "manufactured" to sow disunity, discordance, and the downfall of the Muslim world.[82] For example, when responding to a question by the audience at a local event about former US Secretary of State Hillary Clinton purportedly "claiming that Al-Qaeda is the creation of America," the then counter-terror chief of the police said, "We all know that, without needing to refer to scripture, who are the enemies of Islam: The Jews and them."[83] These concerns about Islamophobia are presented in the booklet alongside vivid descriptions of a Muslim community weakened in all aspects (economy, social, and technology) and tarnished in reputation, thus ultimately having to "succumb to its enemies" (21–22). If losing to the *khawarij* entails cosmological stakes, not being able to handle the Islamophobia that emerges out from outbreaks of Islamist terrorism has its worldly stakes too.

For solutions, the authors referenced the concept of *wasatiyyah* raised in Najib's moderation campaign and Qaradawi's *fiqh al-awlawiyyat*,[84] and claimed that Muslims must channel their energy away from violence and toward rectifying their weaknesses (22–23). Such messaging echoes Mahathir's constant appeal that, instead of "getting mad," Muslims must "get even" on scientific and technological grounds, thus merging the counter-terror agenda with a broader recognition-seeking motif of securing a respectable status for Muslims. Revealingly, the cover of the booklet is filled with images celebrating scientific modernity, featuring shipyards, laboratories, and hazmat suits. When read as a genuine religio-political agenda, the Islamized P/CVE narratives we see in the booklet reflect a much larger concern than merely preserving Islam's "true" interpretations. They also reveal a preoccupation with intra-Muslim unity and the civilizational defense of Islam. Unwittingly, the booklet's identitarian understanding of terrorism also shifts the locus of Muslim radicalization from the individual to an abstract collective (the *ummah*, the nation), leaving out any mention of the lifeworlds or agency of individual Muslims, making it less effective in dealing with the atomized nature of IS-inspired radicalization in Malaysia, something we will return to in the final chapter.[85]

Counter-Terror as Intra-Muslim Politics

The portrayal of counter-terror as defending Islam did not just result in (imaginary) lines being drawn between the Malaysian state and IS. It also exposed counter-terror to the vagaries of intra-Muslim divides and rivalries within Malaysia. Regarding the divide, I am not referring to political divides denoted by party politics but rather a broader theological divide that has its roots in the *kaum tua/kaum muda* (old faction/young faction) contestations since the early twentieth century.[86] However, that rivalry has evolved into an intra-ulama contest in the contemporary setting, due to both the state's co-optation of and capture by the ulamas, blurring the pro- and antiestablishment battle lines of the past.[87]

Without going too deep into the topic, the fault line can be summarized as between two camps. On one end, there is the traditionalist camp consisting of religious scholars who call themselves Ahlus Sunnah Wal Jamaah (ASWJ)[88] that lean toward the Ashaarite school in issues of theology and the Shafi'e schools in matters of jurisprudence, while generally accepting the three other *mazhabs*, or schools of jurisprudence (Maliki, Hanafi, and Hambali), as canon. On the other end, there is a Salafi-oriented camp composed of Perlis mufti Mohd Asri Zainul Abidin (henceforth Asri), UMNO party member Ustaz Fathul Bari, and several well-known independent preachers who advocate a position that Muslims should not be restricted to any particular *mazhab*.[89] According to political scientist Maznah Mohamad, the contest between the two groups lies not in differences "in the philosophical or epistemic basis of Islam itself," but rather "in the practice of Islam, in its guidelines, and in its prescriptions."[90]

As counter-terror became the "locus of competition" between the ASWJ and the Salafis, it is precisely matters of rituals and *tafsir* (Quranic exegesis) that coated P/CVE discourses in Malaysia.[91] Leveraging their strategic connections within the security establishment and the global suspicion against Saudi Arabia as the exporter of Wahhabi, if not radical, Islam, the pro-ASWJ figures propagated the idea that Salafi/Wahhabi teachings were the "gateway to violent extremism," a viewpoint tacitly supported by the then counter-terror chief.[92] In briefings and seminars conducted by the traditionalists, stakeholders were asked to be cautious of Salafi-Wahhabi teachings (with little effort made to distinguish between the two). For example, a presentation given during an event organized by the Department of Federal Territories Islamic Affairs at the National Mosque portrayed the boundaries between violent and nonviolent forms of Salafism as porous, with the nonviolent form metaphorically described as *madu dicampur racun* (honey mixed with poison).[93] The three elements that form the Salafi understanding of *tauhid* (oneness of God)—*tauhid rububiyyah* (Lordship), *tauhid 'uluhiyyah* (Oneness), *tauhid asma' wa sifat* (ownership of His names and attributes)—and *tauhid al-hakimiyyah/mulkiyah* (God's sovereignty), which was attributed to Sayyid Qutb's teachings, were identified as the basis of IS's *takfir* (ex-communication of Muslims) methodology and, by extension, the rationale for its violent extremist methods.[94]

Theological leanings clearly affected the contours of P/CVE narratives and one's interpretation of the issue. For example, in seminars given by Fathul Bari, a pro-Salafi figure who was a member of the Prevention of Terrorism Act Board,[95] the themes of jihad misconception and IS as *khawarij* were raised, but discussions of *tauhid* were omitted altogether.[96] After conducting a short-lived research on the topic,[97] another academic rumored to be close to the Salafi circles, Maszlee Malik,[98] also disputed the claim that Salafism was responsible for the phenomenon and argued that debunking the "Caliphate state" discourse should be given greater priority.[99]

Among the most disparaging critics of Salafi-Wahhabism was Zamihan, who wrote in a book that the doctrine was directly responsible for instigating global jihad.[100] He drew parallels between the violent state-building process of the Saudi kingdom that was undertaken by the Al-Saud clan and Muhammad Abdul Wahab, the founder of Wahhabism, and that of IS and other jihadist groups, pointing out that the former, too, had set out on a violent conquest to rid the Arabian peninsula of practices of *shirk* (polytheism) and *bid'ah* (blasphemous innovation).[101] To be sure, accusing "Arab" interpretations of Islam as subversive is not without its historical precedence in the region,[102] nor is the claim that Salafism is culpable for terrorism unique to Zamihan (Zamihan's book quote at length from several "secular" scholars, including Karen Armstrong and Fawaz Gerges).[103] A key contention between the traditionalists and the Salafis is that practices by the former such as *tahlil, zikir, ziarah kubur, Maulidur Rasul* are all considered *bid'ah* by the latter. This perceived puritanism was cited by some as the reason for radicalization toward IS's *takfiri* ideology, because its adherents have "no qualms slaughtering other Muslims" to defend the purity of religion.[104] Nevertheless, Zamihan's condensation of the cause of Muslim radicalism to rather technical and academic discussions of faith and rituals[105] also contradicted his own observations (and the observations of many of those involved in the deradicalization programs) that the detainees were relatively shallow in their religious knowledge.[106]

The confrontation between the ASWJ and the Salafis—neither side being controversy-free—was not without physical ramifications.[107] In 2018, a raid was conducted by E8 on a Yemeni-linked Salafi madrasah in Perlis based on accusations that it was spreading the "Salafi jihadi ideology."[108] In a statement by the police, examples cited of the madrasah's extreme teachings included the rejection of democracy and secular education, as well as sartorial matters, such as the banning of "men and women from wearing trousers."[109] Notably, that prohibition against trousers was listed as one of the key deviancies of the Salafi-Wahhabi doctrine by Zamihan.[110] The arrest also prompted questions about the complicity of the Perlis religious authorities (exacerbated by the mufti's reputation as a pro-Salafi figure),[111] who reportedly allowed the operation of the madrasah and had made a MYR 100,000 donation to it.[112] Perlis Mufti Asri responded by challenging the impartiality of E8 with tacit suggestions that Ayob Khan was working in cahoots with Zamihan, leveraging the fact that no suspect from the madrasah was ever charged for terrorism.[113]

These rivalries also refracted the meaning of "moderate Islam" in the minds of counter-terror practitioners. This is captured in the printout of a PowerPoint slide shown to me by an academic close to the ASWJ camp, who was himself involved in the deradicalization programs.[114] The slides were used in one training session he conducted in the military academy in Malaysia on the issue of Muslim radicalism, and he used them to explain the problem to me during an interview. In the slide (see Figure 2), the ASWJ's brand of Islam is depicted as "moderate" Islam under siege by secularism, pluralism, and human rights from the left; and by IS, deviant teachings, and Shiism from the right. The effects of counter-terror's Islamization can be seen from the fact that, while said academic is not, strictly speaking, an ulama or religious studies scholar, his typology of radicalism mimicked that of the crisis discourse mentioned above, with a similar emphasis placed on defending what is deemed "official" or "moderate" Islam. In other words, said moderate Islam was made the Archimedean center of a security logic that visualizes and compartmentalizes the problem of violent Islamist radicalization as one among many assaults against the theological foundations of the Muslim faith. Unlike the Western view, the threat from jihadist violent is not viewed as *exceptionally* dangerous, although, in this view, his arguably conservative understanding of Islam is under *exceptional* challenges, hemmed in the middle by liberal and radical forces. Interestingly, during our conversation, the academic also disputed elements of IS's millenarian ideology,

FIGURE 2 Reproduced diagram showing a lecturer-cum-deradicalization practitioner's visualization of radicalism in Islam. Cursive fonts refer to handwritten remarks made by the informant. For clarity, the diagram puts ASWJ in the middle of a left/right divide. The threats he identified on the right are Shiism, Salafism, *Ajaran Sesat* (deviant teachings) and Al-Arqam. Source: The diagram was a printout from a presentation slide that was annotated and given to the author during the interview. Reproduced from fieldnotes, Interview with Academic A, May 9, 2019.

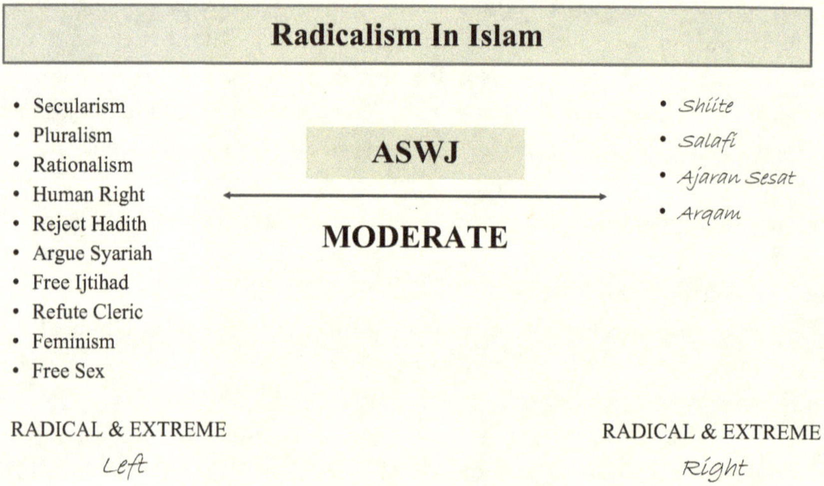

such as their reading of the signs of the End Times and the location where the messianic figure of the Mahdi would emerge, and vaguely offered his own reading of the eschatology.[115] The stakes of security have extended to the cosmological realm, it seems.

Conclusion

This chapter demonstrates that the "Islamization" of counter-terror in Malaysia is not a predetermined outcome but originated within a security assemblage that handpicked, authorized, and deferred to religious actors, institutions, and expertise in the practice of counter-terrorism. The institutionalization of such a security logic shifts discourses about Muslim radicalization in Malaysia toward the textual and theological dimension, centering hermeneutical questions (and authority) in P/CVE discourses at the expense of further interrogation of (radical) Muslim lifeworlds and agencies. By framing the stakes of the fight in religio-existential terms, intra-Muslim contestations over theology and political influence colored the workings of Malaysia's counter-terror regime and shaped perceptions of its legitimacy, especially among Muslims.

Besides highlighting the discursive and practical implications that cascaded from these processes of authority-making in security, this chapter also offers a glimpse into the worldview of a Muslim-led security apparatus that had to execute the Global War on Terror *as* Muslims. As we have seen, the fact that these security practitioners were fighting a "war" that also stigmatized their identity and religion was not lost on them. These sentiments found their way into the ways in which terrorism is conceptualized in Malaysia. Their status as professionals did not preclude Malaysian counter-terror practitioners from seeing themselves as the protectors of Islam's good image and of "moderate Islam" itself, a notable extension of the ethos of Mahathir's stigma-correction enterprise since the 1980s. The next chapter will dive deeper into how this "Islamized" security logic is operationalized as counter-terrorism via governing narratives, and what deeper functions those narratives serve.

SIX

The Anatomy and the List

The Making and Unmaking of Terrorists in Malaysia's Counter-Terrorism

The previous chapter showed how the Malaysian state relied on religious authorities and expertise to frame counter-terrorism as a struggle to defend Islam against theological deviance. However, these insights only highlight the institutional and discursive contours of the field without demonstrating how the security logic and held beliefs of practitioners are translated into governance. It is to governance we now turn. By *governance* I refer to the discursive practices that deal with the "everyday ordering of diverse individual subjectivities, populations, and things."[1] To conceptualize counter-terror as governance, this chapter dives into microgovernmental sites where the "terrorist" is rendered "knowable, stable, and governable" to inform the daily practices of detection, identification, management, neutralization, and rehabilitation.[2] I locate these efforts within three functional areas of counter-terrorism: prevention, preemption, and rehabilitation. In tracing how this "Islamized" security logic is operationalized, this chapter engages with the deeper question of how terrorism is conceived as a problem of governance in Malaysia. Not only that, approaching counter-terrorism via what I call "subject-making" discourses, I demonstrate that the field is laden with knowledge practices that are geared at attaining not only physical but also ontological security for the Muslim state.

This chapter proceeds in four sections. The first section illustrates the nature of the "Muslim terrorist" as an ontological stranger to the Malaysian state. It then argues that counter-terrorism is operationalized via subject-making discourses that render the terrorist governable in biopolitical, judicial, and redemptive terms. The second section addresses the *preventive* component of Malaysia's counter-terror regime by examining state publications that attempted to deal with the perceived risk of soldiers and youths getting radicalized, which led to biopolitical narratives that deconstruct the "radical" through cognitive-behavioral indicators. The third section highlights the *preemptive* aspect that unfolds within the courtroom where the terrorist is affirmed as a (il)legal entity, often based on postulations about the accused's "dangerous" convictions through associations and possessions. Last, we turn to the *rehabilitative* component as I examine Malaysia's deradicalization programs as technologies of reform and redemption—one that projects state power as both punitive and pastoral, and processes the terrorist as schematically knowable and religiously redeemable.

Counter-Terror as Subject Making: Demystifying Strangeness in Security

In the theory chapter, I argued that counter-terrorism, more so in the context of countering Muslim radicalism within a Muslim state, revolves around an enterprise of *ordering*.[3] This understanding goes against Stampnitzsky's observation that counter-terrorism is shrouded in a politics of "anti-knowledge" that "rejected the very possibility of knowing terrorists."[4] Indeed, I contend that the enterprise is premised precisely upon the possibility of *knowing* the terrorist to the point of being able to epistemically arrest it in some degree of bodily, legal, and reformative certainty. In other words, counter-terrorism performs an ontological security-seeking role in practice as it tames the liminality of the terrorist discursively by treating the entity as if it is amenable to detection, deciphering, and deprogramming. This form of subjectivation, problematic as it is, helps inform counter-terrorism in Malaysia (and elsewhere) that is *operationally* reliant on the logic of speculative risks.[5]

Speculation becomes politically tricky when dealing with the question of Muslim radicalization within a Muslim-majority body politic. Given that terrorism suspects in Malaysia mainly came from the majority Malay-Muslim community, the cultural mechanisms of "othering" used to securitize Islam in Muslim-minority societies cannot be replicated in Malaysia. Nor is penalizing Muslim piety fair or feasible, as social professions of faith are common in Malaysia's growingly conservative

Malay-Muslim community.[6] Thus, this entity of the Malay-Muslim terrorist occupies a position of ontological strangeness, a situation Combes calls threatening "*bodies that are at once like us yet not like us*" (emphasis mine).[7] In this case, the "terrorist/stranger" dissolves the self/other boundaries that the Malay-Muslim majoritarian state typically uses to demarcate the boundaries of dangers. Take, for example, the habitual reading of "Chineseness" as a marker of Communist terror—a trope that began in the Emergency period in the 1940s and still lingers on today.[8] The unknowability of the Malay-Muslim terrorist, therefore, disrupted the Malaysian state's claim to be the provider of ontological security, fostering the need for official discourses of subject making to reimagine the Muslim terrorist as a knowable and governable subject.

I have discussed this concept of ontological "strangeness" in chapter 1 and will not repeat it in detail here. In short, my usage draws on Huysmans's understanding of security as a "hermeneutical problem" to address the ontological ambiguity of the citizen-cum-IS supporter who transgresses the insider/outsider, civilian/combatant, and friend/enemy boundaries assumed under the fixtures of the nation-state system.[9] The categorical ambiguity of the Muslim citizen-cum-IS-supporter is undergirded by two factors in Malaysia. The first stems from their pledge of allegiance toward a different Islamic polity as core members of a (self-regarded) Muslim nation-state. Such a pledge challenges the insider/outsider and sovereign/subject boundaries marked by conventional ideas of citizenship. Moreover, the pledge was "strange" as it was pronounced in religious terms with very little regard for the usual totems of national citizenship, such as bureaucratic strictures (instead, many IS supporters would do the opposite by burning their passports), and national(ist) understandings of loyalty, rights, and solidarity.[10] Yet, because terrorism studies have thus far only looked at situations where excommunication of terrorists is executed based on persistent insider/outsider boundaries (the Brown Muslim subject having their citizenship revoked by an Anglo-European government), the literature has largely not dealt with situations where notions of "Muslimness" complicate such boundaries.[11]

The second factor for strangeness is the multiplicity of channels through which an individual's association with terrorism is assumed. The person could be a funder, a migrant, a sympathizer, a foreign fighter, a domestic operative, or just an acquaintance. Such variegated pathways of participation complicate simple friend/enemy distinctions and civilian/combatant categorizations because questions of intention, conviction, and complicity are difficult to ascertain, more so given the relative absence of terrorist attacks in Malaysia. To add, expressions of pan-Muslim solidarity and humanitarian concerns toward the Syrian Civil War were a prevalent part of Malaysia's public discourse, which made it impossible for the authorities to criminalize such activities as showing propensity toward terrorism. Considering the ontological liminality surrounding the entity of the "terrorist," counter-terror practices have to assume an *ordering* role. They must demystify the "citizen-terrorist' by making legible the phenomenon of radicalization in cognitive and behavioral terms, thus harmonizing the subject within the vocabularies of biopolitical, legal, and rehabilitative interventions.[12] In other words, for counter-terror to function as governance, the definitive labelling of *who* is a terrorist is less important than identifying the *bodily contingencies* that gave rise to the entity.

In the following three sections, I will approach three forms of state subjectivation that deconstruct, define, and depict the terrorist as a biopolitical, judicial, and redemptive subject, respectively. These three discursive modes of subject making domesticate the strangeness of the terrorist within social, legal, and pastoral modes of governance, which, in turn, corresponds to the preventive, preemptive, and rehabilitative goals of counter-terrorism. We will first look at *biopolitical* schemas that decompose and reconstruct the potentiality of the radical into a set of observable and measurable traits, which enables preventive "terrorist spotting" to be undertaken in purported vulnerable populations, such as the army and the youth. Then, we track a legal regime that establishes the terrorist as a *judicial* subject in the terms of law and order, thereby arresting the speculative danger of the "radical" through the state's exercise of its punitive power. Last, we venture into an area usually called "deradicalization." I illustrate how the terrorist is reimagined as a *redemptive* subject upon whom the technologies of confession and reform are applied, so that the stranger can be reverse-engineered back into a good citizen. Methodologically, my analyses rely almost entirely on close readings of primary materials such as court judgments, policy documents, and deradicalization manuals. They are also supplemented by background information gleaned from close to fifty interviews consisting of Special Branch officers, lawyers, public prosecutors, deradicalization experts, Home Ministry officers, judges, academics, bureaucrats, and family members of detainees.

Spotting the "Terrorist": You Will Know One When You See One

As the number of IS-related arrests spiked in Malaysia in the mid-2010s, there were two demographic groupings the government was particularly concerned with: the youth and the military. Concern about the former stemmed from the relatively young age of identified IS supporters, many of whom were in their twenties.[13] There were even reported instances of teen involvement, which included a fourteen-year-old reportedly wanting to join IS by eloping with a twenty-two-year-old student; a case of a sixteen-year-old taking a hostage in the name of IS; and a nineteen-year-old who became the leader of a cell planning a pipe bomb attack.[14] The military was also met with the news that fourteen of its members were charged with terrorism-related crimes in 2014 and 2015—a period that coincided with IS declaring its caliphate and at the peak of its territorial and operational gains.[15] Fears about IS's infiltration of the military were unsurprising, given the public memory of the al-Maunah incident, which also involved military personnel (see chapter 3).[16]

Two government publications that were released amid the panic of IS's penetration into these two demographics deserve a critical analysis here. Both were guidelines intended to foster vigilance and (self)-policing of ostensibly vulnerable communities. In some ways, these publications are products of the larger Preventing/Countering Violent Extremism (P/CVE) milieu, with the United Kingdom's Prevent policy being its most notable (and controversial) example. However, unlike Prevent, they do not enforce any statutory duties. Also, unlike how Prevent securitized sociocultural traits of the Muslim community as the suspicious "other" of British-ness,[17] the search for the Muslim "radical" in Malaysia had no outlying sociocultural, racial, or religious markers that could be used to identify a suspect population within its Malay-Muslim-majority society. I argue that this unknowability of the stranger necessitates a kind of high-resolution discursive sculpturing, which separates Malaysia's P/CVE narratives from the broad brushes in the West that simply treat indicators of "Muslimness" as suspicious. The detailed sculpturing can be seen in how the two publications craft the biopolitical subject of the terrorist in almost anatomical precision, listing attributes that range from cognitive traits to behavioral cues. As we shall see, within these narratives, traces of an "Islamized" security logic are peppered throughout.

Radical Spotting in the Army

The first publication to be examined here is a thirty-one-page booklet entitled *Kami Warga ATM Tolak Daesh (ISIS)* [The Malaysian Army rejects Daesh (IS)], which comes with a fourteen-page FAQ section about IS.[18] Published in 2017, the booklet was produced by a special task force within the intelligence unit of the Malaysian Army Forces, formed in 2014 to communicate with members of the army about the dangers of IS.[19] Its publication followed a litany of prohibitions and directives issued by the army that warned military personnel against involvement with IS (p. D). The booklet begins with a primer of IS's ideology and history (including the "truths" behind their narratives) and dedicates an entire section to listing down the "indicators" and "early signs" of someone prone to support IS (11–17). Divided into four subsections (personality, religiosity, social media, and possessions), the thirty-three descriptors provided are pretty detailed. Some of them are listed here:

1. Antisocial and likes to participate in religious activities outside of the squad (13)
2. Behavior changes when jihad is discussed and likes to talk about the brutalities of war within the Middle East (13)
3. Likes to praise Salafi figures and talks about IS's struggles as if their struggle represents Islam
4. Hatred toward Shiites (13)
5. Starts to borrow money for suspicious reasons (13)
6. Applies for holidays suddenly to go to the Middle East or Sabah (14)[20]
7. Possesses books that talk about jihad, the Islamic caliphate, and the resurgence of the Imam Mahdi (14)
8. Demonstrates displeasure with the occupation, policy, welfare, and leader of the force
9. Starts to accuse certain religious practices as *bid'ah* (15)
10. Shows affinity toward religious groups that are outside of the ahli Sunnah Waljamah (15)
11. Thinks that the Malaysian government is *kufr* (disbeliever) and admires the caliphate system (15)
12. Joins WhatsApp groups with religiously infused names (16)
13. Uses the black flag logo for WhatsApp and Telegram or uses jihad-related mottos in social media (16)
14. Having multiple phone numbers and social media accounts without concrete justification (14, 16)

Needless to say, any governmental project that tries to prescribe indicators of radicalization has always been contentious, as it may end up criminalizing differences while reinforcing preexisting norms, prejudices, and hierarchies. For example, Martin criticizes the Prevent policy's "linear, teleological" understanding of radicalization, which led to, on the one hand, visions of population "(re)generation" centered on an "assumed unthreatening, normalised British identity," and, on the other hand, active intervention on those (especially Muslims) who transgressed such normality.[21] Yet even Prevent's guidance document has only six to seven radicalization indicators, which compares meagerly to the long list provided by this booklet.[22] I argue that this gap speaks to the problem of the stranger that the Malaysian state faces, whereby greater ontological undecidability of the "terrorist" resulted in a high(er) definitional pinpointing of the emerging "radical," so that a sense of ontological security can be restored.

Traces of the Islamized security logic charted in this book also made its way into the booklet. The booklet's depiction of the radical as someone disinterested in "*worldly affairs* because they find it meaningless" (emphasis mine) drew upon long-standing tropes and imaginaries of the religious fanatic who saw no point in temporal pursuits (15). The emphasis on religiosity as a marker of radicalization can be seen in how the booklet lays out a string of religious practices, interests, and utterances as observable behavioral traits of radicalism. The booklet also expresses caution about Salafi influences, highlighting *bid'ah* pronouncements and interest in non-ASWJ Islamic organizations as indicators of radicalization (15).[23] Given that a leaked report claims that Salafi-Wahabi thinking has infiltrated the army and may pose a risk of radicalization, such alarmism is not surprising.[24]

In fulfilling its "Spot the Radical" function, the booklet delineates the problem of radicalism as much as it depoliticizes it, turning the issue into a matter of religious and behavioral deviancies. Its focus on the radical's supposedly "misguided" piety justifies the booklet's pastoral tone. The booklet reminds its readers how Islam is "simple," "antiviolence," and "moderate," and that there are "no shortcuts to heaven" (27). This emphasis on curating the meaning of religion is further seen in the preventive measures suggested by the authors, such as vetting the preachers invited to the army and making spot checks at religious teaching centers outside of the army (23–24). Interestingly, the booklet also proposes programs that instill love toward the "country, institutions, family, and society," implying that its authors saw a dialectical opposition between the state's version of such values and the terrorist's (24). Nevertheless, hinting at this dialectical opposition is the furthest the booklet will go in recognizing the attraction of IS as a politically revolutionary movement and not just as a false peddler of martyrdom.[25]

Radical Profiling Among the Youths

The second publication of interest is the *Garis Panduan Pencegahan Fahaman Radikalisme Dan Ekstremisme Dalam Kalangan Belia Dan Masyarakat* [Guideline to prevent radicalism and extremism among Youths in Malaysia] (henceforth GPR), published by the Institute for Youth Research Malaysia (IYRES) under the Ministry of Youth and Sports.[26] Unlike the army's booklet, which is mainly for internal circulation, the GPR has a broader intended audience: it targets not only the youth but also various stakeholders, including parents, NGOs, and the government. The GPR's primary objective is to provide resources to help safeguard youths from radicalization through increased awareness and monitoring from all parties (18–21). This guideline was formulated after three studies were (co)-conducted and sponsored by IYRES, with its results published as a report. The first two were surveys conducted with youths and university graduates to assess their understanding of and receptivity to IS's ideology. The third was a psychometric profiling of forty-two youth detainees associated with terrorism crimes through surveys and in-depth interviews (only eleven were subjected to the latter).[27]

Upon closer inspection, it would appear that these studies assumed a great deal about the problem even before the fact-finding began. Religious deviance and misinterpretation were pushed to the forefront as key factors of radicalization. For example, in a survey of 1,200 Muslim youths entitled "Islamic Education and the Involvement of Youths in Radical Islamic Movements," the questionnaire proceeds in this sequence: (1) if their parents gave them religious education, (2) if they understood the true concept of jihad, and (3) if they agreed with IS's legitimacy and their concept of jihad.[28] In a later section, the questionnaire asks the respondent whether they support IS, and whether they would join the group if given the opportunity.[29] The research design is not only methodologically contentious in that it presumes a direct association between the respondent's religious education and their "radical beliefs"; it also strays into ethically dubious territory as the questions may condemn the respondent to considerable risk of self-incrimination.

The IYRES report also contains a section dedicated to the psychometric profiling of the youth detainees that measures "misinterpretation of religion" but with little elaboration of the "correct" interpretation.[30] Tellingly, this section in the report is followed with a triangular diagram that depicts the three concepts of *tauhid* associated with Salafi teaching and *tauhid al-hakimiyyah/mulkiyah* (God's sovereignty) forming the base for IS's ideology.[31] This appears to be a call-back to the rationale that P/CVE success hinges on mounting a defense against Salafist Islam, something we discussed in the previous chapter. The report also claims that, without any qualifiers, these understandings of *tauhid* would lead to implications such as "rejecting democracy"; "killing Yazidis, Shiites, Christians, and people of other faiths"; and "rejecting the constitution and man-made *toghut* [tyrannical] laws."[32]

Using results from the psychometric profiling study, the GPR (much like the army booklet) also presents a relatively detailed image of the emerging "radical." It describes sixteen indicators found in youths who "are most vulnerable with radical ideas" (15). Such an individual has low self-esteem; has a poor relationship with parents and friends; is narcissistic, judgmental, sensitive, and impulsive; misunderstands religion; and has an aptitude for change and redemption (15). While these attributes are arguably risk factors, the focus on vulnerabilities in character reveals how the GPR's authors conceptualize radicalization as a passive activity in which vulnerable youths are always at risk of being enticed and misled by malevolent forces. Unsurprisingly, monitoring features heavily in the GPR's recommendation section. The section on psychometric profiling encourages self-awareness from individuals, increased vigilance from parents and civil society, and more monitoring from the government on speakers, publications, religious institutions, and the online space (18–21). The report's character-centric view of radicalism might explain why its psychometric study of the forty-two youth detainees omits analyses of their socioeconomic backgrounds.

This approach to understanding radicalism reflects an ethos Dillon calls the biopoliticization of emergent life.[33] In this understanding, the human body is understood not as a vessel of lived experience, but as a "continuously emergent body-in-formation" capable of "becoming danger," thus reinforcing the state's anxiety toward the stranger's ontological undecidability.[34] Such anxiety is precipitated by a sense that "evil is omnipresent and radically undecidable," necessitating the "radical spotting" exercises discussed above to act as moral sentries that "stand guard biopolitically over the threat that life poses to life itself."[35] This latent fear of the youth as emergent terrorists can be seen in the government's panic over IS's purported targeting of universities, resulting in dire warnings from authorities and academics alike.[36] Given that this demographic is supposedly the most highly educated crop of the population, this idea of university students falling prey to IS's propaganda only amplified the state's anxieties over the radical undecidability of the emerging terrorist. These concerns also reveal internalized ideas about Muslim vulnerability and youth gullibility toward religious extremism. These latent assumptions, in turn, foreclosed the exploration of a more significant point: very few of those detained for terrorism offences in Malaysia were educated at the tertiary level, a point I will return to in the concluding chapter.[37]

Convicting the Terrorist: Establishing Dangerous Convictions?

If the making of the terrorist as a biopolitical subject reimagines the stranger as a detectable and comprehensible risk, the making of the terrorist as a judicial subject moderates the entity's ontological strangeness through anchoring it within the certainties of law. In other words, if a biopolitical strategy is about securing a population against its own liminality, the judicialization of terrorism is about fixing such liminality within a language of law and order. Nevertheless, in contrast to the preventive biopolitical discourses that sought to sculpture the emerging terrorist by breaking down its bodily attributes, the judicial discourses of counter-terror sought instead to agglomerate a variety of pathways, motives, methods, convictions, and affiliations under the legal category of "terrorism." In the following, I will show how the judicial subject of the terrorist is ontologically and epistemologically constructed through a combination of broad-ranging laws, strict liability clauses, and associational mapping. The "strangeness" of the terrorist is stripped off by a legal framework operationalized in a flurry of gazettes and lists, buttressed by expert indictment of one's religious "deviancy."

The judicialization of terrorism is a salient feature during Malaysia's addressing of the IS threat (2013 onward) because it coincided with a time when public trials became the main avenue to formally establish the legal subject of the terrorist. Such a change was precipitated by the repeal of the Internal Security Act (ISA) and its replacement by the Security Offences (Special Measures) Act (SOSMA) in 2012.[38] While the Malaysian Penal Code has incorporated terrorism offences since 2007, it was only until SOSMA was gazetted as the procedural code for security offences that terrorism suspects were tried in courts. Two changes complemented this shift from designating a terrorist purely through ministerial diktat during the ISA period to the practice of open trials. First, counter-terrorism has enjoyed increased publicity. Most police raids were now followed by the unprecedented release of public statements and media reports that provided basic information about the arrestees, such as age, location, occupation, and gender. The fact that 256 cases were prosecuted in open court by 2021 also fostered substantial public awareness of terrorism cases.[39] Such visibility of counter-terror performances, albeit with limited transparency, was a marked departure from the obscurity surrounding the roughly one hundred individuals arrested for their alleged association with Jemaah Islamiyah (JI) in the early 2000s.[40] Having a visible facet in counter-terrorism meant that discursive demystification of the stranger was now an essential aspect of the enterprise. With counter-terror operations now exposed to the prying eyes of a Muslim-majority public who often viewed these preemptive arrests with suspicion, the determination of the judicial subject of the terrorist in court also played a part in conveying legibility about the terrorist problem. In a way, the courts became a place to address the question: *When does a civilian cross over to "enemy" territory*?

Second, the nature of jihadist extremism within Malaysia also shifted drastically. Unlike the JI network that was organized around kinship and quasi-kinship networks, IS's more atomized and disorganized membership, when coupled with the high-profile reporting and the diverse profiles that surfaced, created a perception that anyone could be a terrorist.[41] In this context of increased publicity and unpredictability, I argue that the judicial subject-making discourse of the terrorist performs a vital ontological security-seeking function as it consolidates an array of bodily dangers into one single (un)lawful entity.

Coding Terrorism: Definitions and Grey Zones

The legal definition is key to fixing the terrorist as a judicial subject. Elsewhere, I have traced how definitions of terrorism have changed in Malaysia from the ISA's semantical focus on banditry to the contemporary definition modeled after the UK's definition.[42] The offense of terrorism is only incorporated into the Malaysian Penal Code as late as 2007. In the Penal Code, terrorism is defined through a long list of acts, from inducing "serious bodily injury" to disrupting "communications infrastructure, banking or financial services, utilities, transportation or other essential infrastructure." However, these acts can only constitute a terrorism offence if they were conducted to advance "a political, religious or ideological cause" within and beyond Malaysia.[43] Nonetheless, this backstop instituted to prevent legal overstretching did not result in stringent controls over the law's exercise.[44] Compared to the biopolitical discourses described above that created high-resolution depictions of the terrorist, the judicial route actually offered less scrutiny and clarity for two reasons.

First, there remains a legal grey zone where the legal fixing of the terrorist can happen extrajudicially. In 2015, the practice of preventive detention was revived in Malaysia following the enactment of the Prevention of Terrorism Act (POTA), and the Prevention of Crime Act (POCA) 1959 amendment that permitted the latter's use on terrorism crimes. Instead of the courts, both statutes rely on a board to decide if an individual can be detained for up to two years (which can be renewed indefinitely) for engaging in the "commission or support of terrorist acts."[45] According to my informants, these laws were used when the evidence against the suspect was "less convincing," and most of those detained under POTA or POCA were considered to be less "hardcore" ideologically.[46] Whereas the number of people subjected to POTA and POCA was relatively small,[47] the fact that these laws were used, including in one instance on a court-acquitted individual,[48] reveals how counter-terror in Malaysia still has room for extrajudicial measures, despite having moved past the cover of the ISA in recent years.[49]

Second, public trials conducted under SOSMA have been criticized for their lack of rigor and due process. Revealingly, they led to many guilty pleas,[50] which also meant less scrutiny and pushbacks on how the judicial subject of the terrorist was established by investigative and judicial processes in the first place.[51] Cases tried under SOSMA remain challenging for the defense as a result of several special provisions that favor the prosecution,[52] including a detention period of 28 days for investigation with a delay of access to legal representation up to 48 hours; denial of bail for the accused; and the lowering of usual standards of evidence admissibility.[53] The denial of bail means that the accused will be detained as long as the legal process is ongoing, including when the accused is acquitted but the prosecution decides to appeal the case. One can easily spend four to five years in detention before the legal process exhausts itself. Take, for example, the case of Nor Azmi Jailani, a soldier charged with terrorism for involvement in a conspiracy to "kidnap top government officials."[54] He was arrested in 2015; acquitted in the High Court in 2017, which was overturned in 2019; and was sentenced to twelve years in jail in the Federal Court in 2020. That was five years in detention just for the trial. The protracted process discourages detainees who received lower sentences from appealing their cases. That was reportedly the case for Mohd Zulkifli Shafie, who was sentenced to two years in jail for donating MYR 200 to a friend of whose involvement with IS he has since claimed ignorance.[55]

Trials conducted under SOSMA also admit hearsay evidence, which can include "uncorroborated testimony of a child," statements made to agents provocateurs, and statements given by the accused "at any time" with no exceptions for "evidence obtained under duress."[56] These statements significantly hampered the accused's ability to muster an effective defense. In some cases, the accused had to defend themselves against their own statements made during interrogation, which is inadmissible as evidence under normal circumstances. Whereas I have not found any concrete evidence of physical abuse, my informants have claimed that the detainees—most of whom were not seasoned militants or criminals—were subjected to significant psychological pressure during the interrogation period that lasted up to twenty-eight days under SOSMA.[57] Such treatments raise the question of whether the detainees were giving statements against their own will or interest. When combined with the detainees' limited access to legal resources due to their lower socioeconomic backgrounds, these disadvantages often lead them to believe that pleading guilty in hopes of receiving a lighter sentence is the best option available.[58] Tellingly, even the perpetrators of Malaysia's only successful IS-related bombing pleaded guilty, despite the ominous prospect of facing a maximum thirty-year jail sentence under those charges.[59]

Convicting Terrorism: Lists and Workarounds

Counter-terror trials in Malaysia rarely mulled over definitional issues. This is because, in most cases, the establishment of a terrorism offence did not seek to qualify the trifecta established in the penal code: *act* or threat of action (to cause bodily or property damage), *intention* (to spread public fear or intimidate the government), and *conviction* (to advance a political, religious and ideological cause).[60] Despite the importance of the element of conviction as it illuminates the ideological basis of the terrorist act, the issue was rarely raised in trials. To be sure, there were exceptions in which acts purportedly conducted "to free Malaysia from a *kafir* government" or to "launch an attack on a sovereign Democratic state" were considered tantamount to terrorism.[61] However, in most cases, a workaround was implemented based on what Sullivan calls the "Law of the List."[62] Studying the implementation of the UN Security Council ISIL [The Islamic State of Iraq and the Levant] Al-Qaida Sanctions List (UNSC List), Sullivan argues that the UNSC List bypasses the thorny issue of defining terrorism by pushing "the epistemological question of terrorism to one side, [and] by providing a legal technology for knowing and countering global terrorism (listing) without ever having the need to define it."[63]

Put simply, having a list of designated terrorist organizations at hand obviates the need to define terrorism by the letter of the law. Notably, Sullivan calls the UNSC List a "legal black hole" defined by the law's absence.[64] With the "enemy" of the state listed, what is left for counter-terror is the "technical problem of effective list administration and preemptive security practice that [requires] expert calibration."[65] Indeed, in Malaysia, designated terrorist lists were often treated as *the definition of terrorism itself*. The Penal Code's definition of a terrorist and terrorist group includes any "specified entity" designated so under Section 66B and C of the Anti-Money Laundering, Anti-Terrorism Financing and Proceeds of Unlawful Activities Act (AMLA) 2001.[66] While Section 66C of AMLA elaborates on the law's purpose, which is to expedite Malaysia's implementation of the UNSC List,[67] the minister of home affairs still holds absolute prerogative over who and what groups got listed ultimately.

Operationalizing counter-terror through the technology of the list also flattens the "terrorist." By judicializing the UNSC List, determining terrorism no longer hinges on establishing the trifecta of act, intention, and conviction, but rather on which terrorist or terrorist group on the UNSC List the accused was affiliated with. Such affiliation can be in the form of membership, expressions of support, donations, acts of harboring, or even the possession of items and publications that display "symbols associated with a terrorist group, terrorist act or ideology of a terrorist group."[68] These strict liability clauses, not unlike those found in drug offences, combine both criminalization and preemption. They also led to the marginalization of the element of intention and conviction in proving an act of terrorism, as the ideology of the accused was often established by proxy via their possessions or affiliations. Many individuals were charged based on the contents on their mobile phones, and in one case, even for possessing T-shirts containing IS elements.[69] Notwithstanding the occasional strangeness on the procedural end, these judicial discourses helped moderate the ontological strangeness of the terrorist by diminishing its undecidability via utterances of legal certainty.

This reliance on the UNSC List also intersects with the Islamization of counter-terror I discuss in the preceding chapter as religious experts were frequently brought in to ascertain if the items or publications seized were linked to terrorist ideology or terrorist groups.[70] For example, in a high-profile case involving a university student,[71] the prosecution constructed a case by showing through expert reports that each of the twelve books seized from the accused was ideologically affiliated to Al-Qaeda, JI, or IS.[72] In another case, expert reports on the contents of *usrah* (Islamic study groups) sessions attended by the accused were tendered in court, with the expert making extensive notes on how the teachings in those sessions had deviated from the Quran.[73] The fact that clerics and Islamic studies scholars were brought in to assess these items also meant that radicalism was ultimately framed in terms of theological deviancy, Islamizing counter-terrorism in the process.

Interestingly, despite their continued dependence on terrorism experts, some judges have acknowledged the idiosyncrasies of these procedures. For example, one judge asked in his written statement why none of the books tendered as evidence was banned by the Home Ministry if they "were related to and contained elements of terrorism."[74] Another judge also remarked on the superfluous nature of "terrorism expert" testimonies, claiming "I have also perused the 43 images in question which blatantly depicts weapons and Islamic State symbols. Quite obviously, *even without the benefit of expert opinion evidence*, the prosecution would be able to persuade the court to rule that the said images are those associated with the terrorist group known as the Islamic State" (emphasis mine).[75] Nevertheless, ideas about terrorism being a matter of religious misguidance and deviance remained ingrained in judiciary practices and discourses. For example, some judges would advise the convicted to learn about the "true meaning of jihad," further reproducing the idea that counter-radicalization could be achieved through correcting Islamic interpretations.[76] This habitual deference to theological expertise is also seen in this anecdote relayed by one judge in an interview. Mentioning one case in which an accused—who was purportedly an Islamic studies professor[77]—challenged him on the propriety of his practice of Islam, the judge told me "he felt very small" and had to consult with his *ustaz* (Islamic teacher) before responding to the accused the next day.[78]

Before closing this section, I should stress that my analysis here is not a commentary on the innocence or guilt of the parties involved, nor am I claiming that these procedurals necessarily created a farce out of the trials.[79] What I am concerned with here is how the state establishes the judicial subject of the terrorist: a process wherein, despite having a rather detailed legal definition, the judicial subject of the terrorist is often reduced to their possessions, affiliations, connections, and (primarily virtual) expressions.[80] In other words, the discursive making of the terrorist occurs mainly in the mapping of associates, affiliates, and sympathizers and not in the interpretation of context, conviction, and agency.[81] An outcome of this is the underplaying of *ideology*, which ironically means there is no serious political grappling with the social mainstreaming of many exclusivist narratives that may fuel radicalization (even if not entirely in a "conveyor belt" fashion), let alone a resolute defense of Malaysia's constitutional status as a multicultural democracy.[82]

Reforming the Terrorist: Deradicalization as the Technology of Redemption

Apart from enacting a governing discourse of behavioral spotting and legal preemption, the Malaysian state has taken one step further to conquer the ontological strangeness of the terrorist through a discourse of rehabilitation that narrates the entity as a malleable and redemptive subject. The workings of this discourse can be seen in Malaysia's deradicalization program, which is informed by institutional logics that understood radicalization as a product of religious misguidance and character weakness. Before we start, I am well aware that *deradicalization* is a contentious term, with its methods, success claims, and ethical foundations subjected to considerable scrutiny. *Disengagement*, for example, is mooted as a more precise term to describe what these programs achieved.[83] I decided to follow the Malaysian state's terminology of *deradicalization* because it reflects the governmentality behind the program, which is to reverse radicalization. Examining deradicalization also offers a window to understand bifocal nature of the national security state. If in the biopolitical and legal schemes above one encounters the insecure Schmittian state seeking to exceptionalize the terrorist threat for prevention and preemption, in deradicalization one witnesses the high modernist confidence of a gardening state assured of its pastoral power.[84]

The POTA Program

This section examines the deradicalization program designed for the POTA detainees. As mentioned above, POTA allows for the detention of up to two years of anyone believed to have "engaged in the commission or support of terrorist acts involving listed terrorist organizations in a foreign country or any part of a foreign country,"[85] signifying its focus on countering the foreign fighters phenomenon.[86] Despite constituting only a subset of Malaysia's terrorism detainees,[87] POTA is chosen as my focus here mainly for three reasons. First, there is reason to believe that the POTA module is not too different from the deradicalization program for other terrorism detainees, as the agencies involved are essentially the same: the police, the Ministry of Home Affairs (MOHA), and the Prisons Department (JPN). Be it SOSMA or POTA detainees, all terrorism-related cases were handled by E8 in the police and the radical and high-risk detainees division of the JPN.

Second, unlike the usual secrecy surrounding most counter-terror programs, the POTA deradicalization program enjoyed considerable publicity, allowing unprecedented access into its inner workings. The relative openness conferred to POTA coincided with the Najib government's effort to link Malaysia's counter-terror success with its Global Movement of Moderates campaign (see chapter 4). Notwithstanding the lack of concrete evidence,[88] the Malaysian government proclaimed a "97.5 percent" deradicalization success rate.[89] These claims were shared abroad, with the BBC echoing the claim in a report.[90] The governments of India and New Zealand also expressed interest in learning from Malaysia.[91] The UN Security Council Counter-Terrorism Committee Executive Directorate also named Malaysia, alongside Singapore, as having developed "effective government programmes to rehabilitate and reintegrate terrorist inmates into society through preventive/administrative detention."[92]

Malaysia's well-respected deradicalization "success" necessitates a deeper look into its mechanics and operations. Fortunately, with Najib's campaign came an eagerness for policy sharing. In 2016, MOHA published the manual of the deradicalization program in four languages (Malay, English, Arabic, and French), while a paper on Malaysia's policy on counter-terrorism was published under the authorship of the minister of home affairs.[93] I obtained a copy of the English edition of the manual and secured interviews with practitioners directly involved with the program, including MOHA officers, the police, and rehabilitation experts, which enabled me to cross-reference the manual's content with the practitioners' feedback.[94] Borrowing Foucault's understanding of governmentality as embedded in discourses, I argue that my limited access[95] is still sufficient to provide a glimpse into the ensemble of "procedures, analyses and reflections" that operationalizes this idea of deradicalization.[96]

Third, POTA, unlike SOSMA, has an explicit focus on rehabilitation. According to its manual, there is even a module called "Detention as Rehabilitation" in the POTA program.[97] To clarify, POTA and SOSMA detainees in Malaysia experience two different routes of law enforcement. SOSMA detainees are charged in court and must serve their full sentence if convicted, meaning that their incarceration is independent of their rehabilitation. By contrast, POTA detainees are evaluated at the end of the (nominally voluntary) deradicalization program,[98] which serves as the basis for a report recommending the suspension or continuation of their detention—a matter to be decided by the POTA Board.[99] As far as my research goes, the board is not involved in the daily operations of the program, nor do they meet with the detainees under normal circumstances, which makes the evaluation report incredibly influential in determining the fate of the detainee. Furthermore, there is no room for judicial review of the POTA Board's decision.[100] It is also unclear how the membership of the board is decided. According to the law, the POTA Board must be chaired by a "legally qualified person with at least fifteen years experience in the legal field," a deputy chairman, and three to six members.[101] Despite calls for transparency,[102] thus far, nominations to the board remain an obscure matter, and the two POTA Board members I have encountered, one of them Fathul Bari (who appears in chapter 5) and another who has requested anonymity, were both members of the ruling party when they were appointed.

According to the manual, the POTA deradicalization is a two-year program divided into three phases: orientation (not exceeding six months), reinforcing *sahsiah* (character) (months 7–12), and reinforcing *sahsiah* and self-development courses (months 12–24). Whereas the manual only serves as a guideline for practitioners, and some departures do happen in practice, it does reflect the general structure of the program.[103] For example, as the manual suggests, the actual program operates on a tripartite framework. The weekly programs are divided between the JPN, the police, and MOHA, with the three agencies providing 40 percent, 40 percent, and 20 percent of the detainee's final scoring, respectively.[104] Table 2 provides a summary of the program as outlined in the manual.

TABLE 2 A Snapshot of the POTA Deradicalization Program

Modules	Examples of submodules	Agency responsible
PHASE ONE		
Shaping Oneself	• The need for discipline • Act based on necessity, not wants • Resign and give in to accept detention	JPN
Self-Reflection	• Exploring and correcting own mistakes • Gratefulness	JPN
Self-Management	• Emotional management • Stress management	JPN
PHASE TWO		
Social Skills	• Empathy skills • The skill to choose the right friends	JPN
Moral (for non-Muslim detainees only)	• Practicing moral values • Rational thinking	JPN
Spirituality (Muslim detainees only)	• The role of the Muslim in religion, self, family, society, and country • *Wasatiyyah*	JPN
Criminal Behavior	• Awareness of the law • Think before you act • Detention as rehabilitation	JPN
Security I	• Peace is the foundation for the prosperity of the country • The legal system of Malaysia • Security is a collective responsibility	Police
Thought I	• The *akidah* of Ahli Sunnah Wal Jamaah • The dangers of religious extremism • *Fiqh al-awlawiyyat* • The concept of jihad according to Islam	MOHA

Modules	Examples of submodules	Agency responsible
Psychology I	• Managing unfinished business • Anger management • Managing spiritual confusion	MOHA
	PHASE THREE	
Family	• Happy family, prosperous nation • My home is my paradise	JPN
Social	• The beauty of a plural society • United we stand, divided we fall	JPN
Career	• Where do I go from here • Work ethics	JPN
Nationhood	• The importance of understanding the constitution and laws of Malaysia • Love for the country	JPN
Security II	• Terrorism and its impact on self, family, society, religion, race, and country. • Assessment of the level of rehabilitation using the Digital Voice Stress Analysis method.	Police
Security III	• Democracy in Islam • Moderation in a plural society • Actions considered as against the Yang Dipertuan Agong	Police
Thought II	• Methods of interpreting the Quran and the Hadith • Differences in the opinions of scholars • The concept of a Martyr	MOHA
Psychology II	• The ideal character • Identity • Managing conflict	MOHA

Source: MOHA, *Deradicalisation Module.* Table does not contain the full program.

The program's wide-ranging modules reflect its ambition to achieve comprehensive reform, from instilling discipline to strengthening religious knowledge, cultivating patriotism, and reforming character. Yet, despite the plan's holistic nature, addressing "religious misconceptions" remains the main objective of rehabilitation, as the minister of home affairs emphasized in a paper.[105] The religious component is handled by all three agencies, each with religious officers of their own, although the police and MOHA officers (who also drew from a range of external experts, some of whom were discussed in the previous chapter) are the ones who tackle the most challenging issues (see Thought and Security Modules in Table 2).[106] This emphasis on rehabilitating religious interpretations stemmed from the authorities' understanding of the terrorism detainees as belonging to the special category of "ideological offenders"— a designation used to justify their preemptive and segregated detention.[107]

Themes present in Malaysia's P/CVE discourses, such as *wasatiyyah* (moderation), *fiqh al-awlawiyyat* (prioritization in Islamic jurisprudence), and the "proper" concept of jihad, can all be found in the module, revealing a porosity that exists between political discourses and operational practices of counter-terror. Interestingly, the manual also demonstrates a preoccupation with what terrorism will do to Malaysia's status. One of the modules aims to educate the detainees on how terrorism can result in Malaysia being "viewed as a country that produces terrorists," thereby risking its globally celebrated status as a "peaceful, prosperous, and developed" nation.[108]

Deradicalization as Redemption?

One way to understand Malaysia's deradicalization programs is to observe how it envisions the terrorist as a redemptive subject. *But how, and to whom, will the "deradicalizing" subjects be redeeming themselves*? A conceptually productive place to begin with is Foucault's writings about the ritual of confession: "The confession is a ritual of discourse in which the speaking subject is also the subject of the statement; it is also a ritual that unfolds within a *power relationship*, for one does not confess without the presence (or virtual presence) of a partner who is not simply the interlocutor but the authority who requires the confession, prescribes and appreciates it, and intervenes in order to judge, punish, forgive, console, and reconcile . . . and finally, a ritual in which the expression alone, independently of its external consequences, produces intrinsic modifications in the person who articulates it" (emphasis mine).[109] Writing about the Prevent Strategy in the UK, Elshimi also argues that a confessional element exists in the mentoring relationship between the expert and the citizen. The "confession" of the mentee was "recorded, codified for analysis, and reproduced into the body knowledge of radicalisation, ultimately augmenting the 'Truth' of radicalisation," with their salvation offered in return.[110]

In POTA, deradicalization operates as a confessional technology in two evident ways. First, the modules in the program require the detainees to practically *confess*.

Except for phase 4, which encompasses community service, most of the modules in the deradicalization program require the detainees to participate as discussants and share their experiences and opinions. In the earlier phases of the detention, detainees are asked to partake in sessions entitled "resign and give in to detention" and "exploring and correcting own mistakes."[111] The modules are designed in a way that encourages detainees to narrate their experiences. In another session about "love for the country," the detainees are asked to list "the impact and consequences if there is no love for the Country" and "the activities which can increase the love for the Country."[112]

These activities are akin to confessions, not only because they occur within in a power relationship between the confessor and the listener, but also because they involve the extraction of certain "truths" from the confessor (e.g., the admission of guilt, the love for the nation) that cement the confessional dynamic. As Elshimi summarizes, "In the confession, the agency of domination does not reside in the person who speaks, but in the one who questions and listens: Confessing does not set you free, but makes you a subject of power."[113] As the detainees' treatment and prospect of freedom are assessed based on their performances in these confessional practices,[114] the act of confessing is directly linked to their "emancipation," both therapeutically and literally. Their verbalizations of "self, family, society, religion, race, and Country" in these sessions are as much an act of the detainee redeeming oneself as it is the state's window to the redemptive subject, for they serve as direct measures of one's progress in "deradicalization."[115] In other words, these rituals of confession created "truths" out of the detainee's performances of redemption, fulfilling the state's pastoral vision of subject redeemability in the process.[116]

Given Malaysia's emphasis on postrelease contact and care of former detainees, the subject's redemption often manifested as lifelong entanglement with the state.[117] One deradicalization practitioner even mentioned that he would "stay in touch" with his detainees "forever" and some had become his "best friends."[118] This mixture of coercive and pastoral care can be seen in one vignette told by Ayob Khan, the former head of E8, in a media interview after he was promoted to the position of chief police officer for the state of Johor. Recounting his visit to one of the former JI detainees, Abdul Matin Anol Rahmat (aka Pak Abu), when he was in Ulu Tiram, Johor, for official business in 2020,[119] Ayob Khan said:

> When I went with my team to Pak Abu's house, his door and gate were closed. We called for him, but he did not come out. Instead, his wife came out crying, asking if we were to arrest her husband. I said, "No, we came here to visit Pak Abu." She then fetched her husband, who was surprised to see me and came and hugged me while greeting me (he calls me Pak Ayob). I asked him why he had not visited me at the police headquarters now that I had transferred to Johor, and he said he was too embarrassed to go see a chief police officer.[120]

If performing redemption is key to the rituals of radicalization, *what does this redeemed subject look like?* According to the manual, the individual will be a loyal citizen above all, whose primary allegiance lies with the nation (it is telling that in the manual, the word "Country" is capitalized) and its symbols, such as the Constitution and the constitutional monarch as the head of state. The detainee is reminded to appreciate "that Malaysia is a Country that is peaceful and prosperous" and that their action should only be directed at preserving the nation's peace as the foundation of its prosperity and growth.[121] In the program's manual, the dangers of radical thinking are always in reference to the nation.[122] For example, participating in wars abroad is depicted as "illegal" and "will give rise to a negative perception of the authority of the Country."[123] Interestingly, when I asked counter-terror practitioners if they remembered any detainee who was particularly "hardcore," the example I was always given was that of an individual who refused to even sing the national anthem.[124] It appears that the kind of subjectivity the POTA program seeks to inculcate trades the radical's supposed reverence for the universal, as expressed through militant pan-Islamism, with a focus on the patriotic.

When viewed as a whole, the module also contains echoes from the past in an embedded developmental logic. It make subtle references to a *Homo economicus* ethos in its appeal to the detainees to strengthen their discipline, to be "grateful for their career," and to embed themselves in the household as their "paradise."[125] These are all themes that hearken back to the neoliberal sensibility of the Melayu Baru (New Malay) discourse that has emerged since the 1980s, during a period of rapid (Malay) middle-class creation and expansion.[126] The messaging is also reminiscent of Mahathir's many exhortations we saw in chapter 3. Even in P/CVE narratives, one can hear his plea to the Malay-Muslims to trade their fanaticism for pragmatism; their preoccupation with after-worldly salvation for worldly industry and entrepreneurialism; and their frustrations with the powerlessness of the Muslim world for the will to recover Islam's dignity through making scientific and technological breakthroughs, all while elevating Malaysia's status.

Counter-Terrorism as Order Making: Theoretical Innovations and Empirical Insights

This chapter explored how counter-terror functions via subject-making discourses that fulfill preventive, preemptive, punitive, and rehabilitative goals. One can even argue that these discourses actually make up the assemblage we call "counter-terror." Three types of discourses were discussed: biopolitical discourses that deconstruct the anatomy of the terrorist into its discernible cognitive and behavioral parts; judicial discourses that agglomerate different pathways, motivations, and forms of association into a legalistic terroristic whole; and redemptive discourses that oversee the "unmaking" of the terrorist through performative acts of confession and reform. As these discourses of psychometrics, law, and pastoral redeemability take on an Islamized vernacular, they help us understand the Islamization of security not as a process of epistemological colonization, but one of bureaucratic hybridization.[127] Thus, the Malaysian case is highly instructive because, unlike in Western settings where Islam is casted away as the "other" of national values and identity, in Malaysia we witness Islam interwoven into security logics that informed the state's efforts to find, determine, and rehabilitate the terrorist.

The chapter also offers theoretical and methodological innovations in its departure from the counter-terror literature that usually focuses on how the Schmittian exception is constructed in security discourses. By approaching counter-terror *interpretively* through deep analysis of primary materials, I demonstrate that counter-terror's operationalization does not always depend on a rendition of the threat as extraordinary and nebulous. Instead, it entails a demystification of the terrorist within an operational field textured and informed by behavioralist thinking and pastoral practices. In this turn toward the *ordering* function of security, my approach flips the critical security lens that usually interrogates what security practices do *to* its subjects by asking, What does security do *for* the (Muslim) state? In my case, I argue that it performs the ontological security-seeking function of demystifying the "strangeness" of the Muslim terrorist by domesticating it discursively within the framing of a religious deviant or a misguided youth. Nevertheless, these logics that aimed for anatomical and psychological precision can manifest as logical leaps and wishful thinking. In the book's final chapter, I will review the practical implications of Malaysia's Islamized security, as well as the theoretical returns of approaching questions of religion, security, and politics through the lens of ontological security.

CONCLUSION

Islam In, and Beyond, the Politics of Counter-Terror

> Macron is not showing that he is *civilised*. He is very *primitive* in blaming the religion of Islam and Muslims for the killing of the insulting school teacher. (emphasis mine)
>
> —Mahathir Mohamad[1]

In 2020, the outspoken former Malaysian Prime Mahathir Mohamad got into a controversy again for saying on Twitter (now X) that "Muslims have a right to be angry and to kill millions of French people for the massacres of the past."[2] For context, Mahathir was criticizing French President Emmanuel Macron's alleged anti-Islam policies after the death of teacher Samuel Paty at the hands of a self-radicalized individual, who committed the killing based on rumors that the teacher had humiliated the Prophet Muhammad by showing *Charlie Hebdo* cartoons in class.[3] As the global media descended on Mahathir's outrageous words, what came through was another picture of Muslim fanaticism, reinforcing this stereotype that the community is uniquely prone to violent outbursts.[4] But if one reads the essay on Mahathir's blog in full, a different picture emerges: his outburst was less tied to emotive concerns of defending the sacred, nor was it simply a case of "anti-West" zeal.

Two observations support this argument. First, Mahathir followed that sensationalist "killing for revenge" line by saying, "But by and large the Muslims have not applied the 'eye for an eye' law."[5] Second, Mahathir's defense of his coreligionists in France was clearly enveloped by an ontological security-seeking motive. The epigraph above illustrates this nicely, with its somewhat bizarre labeling of Macron as "uncivilized" and "primitive" (Mahathir's own words). Those terms show that Mahathir's claim—that Muslims have a right to be angry and violent—was also meant to emphasize that most Muslims were *not* angry or violent, despite colonial injustices. In other words, Mahathir was inverting the moral judgment by insisting that Muslims are the "civilized" ones when compared to the supposedly secular, "enlightened" French president. Whatever one may think of Mahathir's extrapolations, his essay was clearly couched in an implicit lament of Islam's stigmatization, wherein the onus to prove one's "civilized" status, in his view, almost always fell on the Muslims. One saw that in how, despite all its violence and scandals, the main perpetrators of the Global War on Terror (GWOT) mainly had to contend with how it was a strategic miscalculation and not a decades-long campaign of grotesque brutality.[6]

What the anecdote above and this book have shown through Malaysia's politics of counter-terror is that assumptions of religion's salience in politics and security is nowhere as straightforward and determinative as imagined. Instead of having this laser-focused, identitarian obsession over how this pan-Muslim community of the *ummah* animates Muslim politics,[7] analysts should be more sensitive to how perceptions of stigmatization still linger in Muslim political discourses and state behavior. For example, Islam is securitized in Malaysia not because it is uniquely volatile element for governments. Rather, it emerged as a paradox: *the more Muslim regimes tried to correct Islam's perceived stigmatization, the more they prioritized Islam as an object of governance, and the more religious actors and concerns gained influence to further their Islamization project.* Even as the GWOT winds down (at least as a priority for the United States as it pivots toward the China "threat"), the governmentality and elite sentiments behind Malaysia's politics of counter-terror will have a long afterlife. For example, combatting Islamophobia remains a high priority in the current Madani administration headed by Anwar Ibrahim; whatever his differences with Mahathir are, both found this status trap of having to seek recognition in "Islamic" (and at times, Islamist) terms inescapable.[8]

The Politics of Counter-Terror? A Recap

What is the *politics* of counter-terror that this book interrogated? To recap, I started with the question of how Islam is assimilated into Malaysia's counter-terror practices but ended up providing a historically situated and practice-centric account of the intertwining processes of the securitization of Islam and the Islamization of security. By the *securitization of Islam*, I refer to how the Malaysian state came to see the cultivation of "good" Islam and the remediating, removing, or reforming of "bad" Islam as a security imperative. On the *Islamization of security*, I illustrate how counter-terror discourses and practices within Malaysia have actively deferred to and incorporated Islamic institutions, actors, and expertise in its operationalization.

These two processes converged to form a counter-terrorism regime grounded in a distinct security logic: that terrorism is primarily a product of *religious* misinterpretation and deviance, and thus requires predominantly "religious" solutions. I situate this development historically within the *problématique* of Islam's stigmatization, arguing that, with its Eurocentric cultural hierarchies and an imperial history of racializing Muslims, the modern international order has instituted a sense of ontological insecurity among many postcolonial Muslim elites. In the case of Malaysia, this fueled an ontological security-seeking agenda, which spearheaded two developments since the 1980s. First, Malaysia witnessed a slew of state-led Islamization projects that was explicitly about demonstrating Islam's compatibility with industrial modernity. The second is the gradual making of a national security regime that securitized forms of Islamic unorthodoxy as threats to the state's ambition to "moderate" and "modernize" a brand of regime- and development-friendly Islam.

This book eschews simple causal dynamics but instead sketches out a complex picture of state building, recognition seeking, and security operationalization that informs Malaysia's counter-terror politics as unfolding on three levels: the macrohistorical, the mesoinstitutional, and the microgovernmental. On the *macrohistorical* level, the GWOT as a moral exceptionalist discourse intensified Islam's stigmatization in the postcolonial international order. The singling out of radical Islam as the universal enemy of international society led to strategies by Muslim states that were perceived as "bandwagoning," which I argue were actually ontological security-seeking projects running alongside instrumentalist calculations. For example, Malaysia launched a global "moderate Islam" campaign partly to bandwagon with the Preventing/Countering Violent Extremism (P/CVE) enterprise, but partly also to counter Islam's stigmatization.

On the *mesoinstitutional* level, I charted how an underlying motive of recognition seeking has driven state-led modernist Islamization projects that anchored the governance of Malay-Muslims within bureaucratic structures that regulate Islam, on the other hand, and normalized the idea that Muslim radicalism is a product of "deviant" or "deviated" Islam, on the other. Last, on the *microgovernmental* level, I tracked the culmination of these elite mindsets and state-building trajectories in Malaysia's counter-terror regime through a "thick" study of its biopolitical, judicial, and rehabilitative discourses in the 2010s when Malaysia was facing a wave of

Islamic State (IS)-linked militancy. Through a critical reading of primary sources and interview data, I illustrated the workings of an "Islamized" counter-terror regime in its preventive, preemptive, and rehabilitative components. In this thorough mapping and investigation of counter-terror practices, I denaturalize two ideas about counter-terrorism that are still prevalent in a large swath of security and political science writings: that we can know a priori what counter-terror practices are and how they operate, and that these practices are only about attaining physical security for the state (when in fact, they also fulfill ontological security needs, as chapter 6 demonstrates).

This book's eclectic picture of Malaysia's counter-terror politics does not home in on any particular level of analysis but rather engages with a porosity that runs across the three levels. In doing so, I demonstrate how social concerns of status and religion by Muslim elites have crisscrossed with, and trickled into, security practices. These practices often manifest as narratives that outline the problem of Muslim radicalism in biopolitical, legal, and rehabilitative discourses. They undergird this security assemblage we often knew by its shorthand: counter-terrorism. In other words, starting with *how* counter-terrorism is conducted in Malaysia, I gained insight into *why* it is conducted so—an answer gleaned through the historical-sociological unpacking of state-religion relationship and discourse analysis of daily governing narratives.

The complex framework this book employs broadens instrumentalist and realist accounts of counter-terror that often treat the subject matter as a matter of threat elimination or political opportunism. Unlike those approaches, I am less interested in the questions of how counter-terror is politicized, or who politicized it. By anchoring my multilevel and multisite inquiry of security within social questions of identity, status, and governance, my analysis paints a picture of a social world in which terrorism necessitated a global "war," Islam required "moderation," and the Muslim "terrorist" demanded discursive demystification. Such is the social world Muslim elites and security practitioners must contend with as they navigated questions of identity, status, and governance while performing counter-terrorism. Indeed, this book shows that even an area of study that is as "parochial" as, or as taken as "common sensical" as,[9] counter-terrorism can still produce fruitful theorizations about questions of status, religion, and international security.

Rethinking Counter-Terror: Escaping the Straitjacket of Moderate Islam?

Before we reflect on broader theoretical implications, it is worth exploring what are the real-world stakes to my findings about Islam and counter-terror. Aspects of this question have been unpacked by Cavanaugh, who argues that the "myth" of religious violence establishes a dichotomy between "peace-loving secular reasonableness" on one side, and "irrational religious fanaticism" on the other.[10] As the dichotomy does not bear any historical scrutiny, the exceptionalization of religious violence obfuscates more than it clarifies for any analysis of political violence, which often leads to disastrous policymaking.

For many of its Muslim purveyors, the discourse of moderate Islam is precisely about challenging this dichotomy. However, the discourse also creates distortions due to how the idea of moderate Islam is intrinsically wedded to the P/CVE complex.[11] What I mean by *distortions* here is not so much about how moderate Islam campaigns were badly instrumentalized for P/CVE policy goals, which scholars have addressed.[12] Instead, it concerns broader issues of how the politics of counter-terror generates worldviews and myopias that perpetuate the securitization and stigmatization of Islam—even when pursued with "good intentions" and by Muslim actors themselves—thereby deepening the alienation of Muslim populations and offering no clearer understanding of the evolving issue of violent extremism. Here I will discuss two of these distortions: one about the culturalization of counter-terrorism, and another about official interpretations of IS-linked Muslim militancy in Malaysia.

Moderate Islam and the Culturalization of Counter-Terrorism

The discourse of moderate Islam distorts our understanding of the problem of Muslim militancy. It helped sustain the GWOT as, in the words of journalist Mark Danner, a "forever war" that was not based on the frank appraisal of the real enemy but focused "on the mirror of our own obsessions."[13] The discourse does so by *globalizing* as well as *culturalizing* counter-terrorism. It globalizes because it fuels a global search for, or cultivation of, moderate Islam to combat "global terrorism." At the same time, the moderate Islam campaigns also culturalized the issue, as the underlying logic is that "Muslim" resources are key to fighting terrorism—an understanding of terrorism often constricted to the Islamist type.

In this security geography, the world is implicitly divided into two zones: the West that has to deal with its "Muslim problem," and the Muslim world where the problem is thought to have originated, thence from which solutions can also be found. This geo-locating of the solution in the Muslim world has led to various versions of "counter-terror-friendly" Islam, as seen in Malaysia's *wasatiyyah* campaign that is discussed in this book, or in state-sponsored efforts to promote Indonesia's Islam Nusantara and Morocco's Islam.[14] These branding efforts have policy consequences. For instance, Morocco has trained and exported imams to various West African states and, until 2020, to France.[15] The policy stemmed from Morocco's success in promoting its brand of Islam through a cultural lens, with Moroccan political actors actively pitching its "Sunni-Maliki-Ash'ari-Sufi Islam" heritage against the ostensibly more dogmatic and "radical" Salafi and Wahhabi streak from the Gulf.[16]

My critique of the culturalization of counter-terror does not mean Islam is above integration and hybridization with local cultures. Historians and anthropologists have shown that it clearly does. Rather, my point here is to stress that the culturalization of moderate Islam, when operationalized within the GWOT paradigm, distorts our view of Islamist militancy. These campaigns advance the idea that transnational Islamist terrorism is a global problem in need of a religio-cultural solution (instead of political or socioeconomic ones). However, studies have shown that, despite having cross-border manifestations and a globalist rhetoric in its propaganda, Islamist militancy often exhibits (or is reinforced by) localized roots and entanglements.[17] To think that one cultural model of Islam can solve these problems also exonerates governments, both Muslim and non-Muslim ones, from the responsibility of dealing with the social conditions that led to Muslim radicalization. Worse, such thinking will force these governments to act as if the issue has only to do with Islam, leading to contentious practices of faith policing.[18]

This culturalist view also reinforces the idea that Malaysia's relative security from terrorist attacks is because the country practices moderate Islam, a view that still enjoys some social currency abroad. The perspective is problematic for two reasons. First, it takes an ahistorical view of Muslim militancy by assuming that it is a latent threat within Muslim communities and that the baseline of danger is similar in all contexts as long as there are Muslims. Chances are, such thinking exaggerates Malaysia's "success" and overlooks the fact that the outcome is less about the kind of Islam the country practices and more about the absence of what scholars call "conflict capital"—the legacy of enduring Muslim-led insurgencies—that distinguishes Malaysia from cases like Indonesia, Mindanao, or southern Thailand.[19]

Second, using the security lens to interpret a nation's practice of Islam engenders many pitfalls. On the one hand, it invites alarmist projections. On the other hand, celebrating counter-terror success as the "be-all and end-all" of policy also risks blinding policymakers to religiopolitical trends that, though nonviolent, are dangerous in themselves for their effects on minority rights, civil liberties, and institutional integrity.[20] In other words, the tunnel vision anchored in counter-terrorism does not tell us much about the moving relationship between religion, politics, ideology, and the modalities of violence. Granted, these dynamics are well-debated in scholarship.[21] But it is difficult to press for more substantial and nuanced changes in P/CVE policies in Muslim states if we do not interrogate where the prevailing security logics came from. And as I have shown in this book, importing insights from how Islam is securitized in the West does not help either because they are outwardly similar outcomes that are underpinned by different institutional concerns and logics. Denouncing a "colonial" security logic in toto might provide the rhetorical flourish to demonstrate criticality, but it offers little empirical insight to improve governance in Muslim-majority settings in such a way that the *authoritarianisms* pursued by both strong states and the Muslim militants are kept in check.

The Blind Spots of Islamized Counter-Terror?

The second distortion is directly related to Malaysia's "Islamized" counter-terrorism this book documented in great detail. Framing religious misinterpretation as the main pathway to radicalization obscures the social geography that produced the kind of radical and violent Muslim political activism that defined Malaysia's IS phenomenon in the 2010s. By assuming that doctrine has a particular hold over Muslims, this mindset ushered in a governmentality that takes governing Muslims and policing Islam as more or less the same thing (which they are not). This book has shown that this mindset, while sustained by institutional configurations and practices, also originated from a sense of ontological insecurity deep within the modernist elites of the long-ruling United Malays National Organisation (UMNO). As emblematized by our portraiture of Mahathir in chapter 3, these elites were wary about the stakes of Islam's misinterpretation toward their developmentalist goals. Their fears of this streak of fanaticism imagined to be latent within Malay-Muslim bodies, in turn, made its way into the way they govern.

Put differently, this framing of terrorism as a religious problem is a product of raison d'état (reasoning from the state's perspective). Raison d'état is also what Li detects as an original sin in terrorism studies.[22] But what happened in Malaysia is the inverse of what terrorism studies is often criticized for doing. Whereas terrorism studies is accused of leaning too much into predictive profiling to satisfy the security imperatives of the national security state, counter-terror practitioners in Malaysia, in contrast, saw little value in reading into the social profiles of these individuals. As I observed in my fieldwork, the argument that Muslim radicalization is ultimately a product of theological misinterpretation and shallow religious learning prompted security practitioners to conclude that so-called IS supporters/sympathizers were "impossible to profile."[23] For them, profiling offers no actionable correlation, let alone solid causal relationships, that can tell them who the next radical will be. Even so, as chapter 6 illustrated, this did not stop state agencies, such as the army and the Ministry of Youth, from creating detailed biopolitical projections as to how a potential terrorist might look, act, and behave.

Explaining violent radicalization as a product of religious misinterpretation also implies that anyone who joined a religiously denominated violent movement must be driven by religious motivations. Such an explanation left no radical unexplained and demystifies the strangeness of the Muslim terrorist. It also explains the security apparatus's almost paternalistic view of the problem, as they interpret such forms of activism as emotive, juvenile, and misguided. Yet this inclusive reasoning (in that it accounts for *every* case) also precludes a more comprehensive view of the phenomenon. One of those dimensions excluded is that of *class*. In my interviews, one common observation from those who had contact with the IS detainees is that most were from a lower socioeconomic status. They were less likely to enroll in tertiary education and were more likely to hold menial jobs. Their socioeconomic background also explains why most did not have families that could support a protracted legal campaign, causing many to plead guilty to their charges despite the heavy penalties.[24] In fact, in one interview with a journalist, one detainee who was sentenced to five years in prison claimed that his family could not even afford to visit him once due to financial difficulties.[25]

To probe deeper into this issue of class, we must examine the profiles of the IS-linked detainees. At this point, it is worth revisiting the argument that "profiling" these individuals is analytically unproductive, or worse, ethically problematic. Whereas looking at a dataset of individuals of a movement does not tell us who the next participant will be, it tells us something about the movement, like how political party membership (including its decline) tells us about the state of politics within a particular national or subnational setting.[26] As Li and Hegghammer have shown in their studies of jihadists in the Bosnian War and Saudi Arabia's experience with violent jihadism, respectively, the analysis of the biographical data of the participants of the jihad can be uniquely productive insofar as the goal is to understand the *politics* and not the person.[27] Li, in particular, has warned against a way of studying jihadism that desanitizes its politics: "Without rendering legible the *political nature* of jihadi projects, its focus on doctrine becomes deterministic; its analysis of propaganda tends toward voyeurism; its study of tactics redounds to incoherent moralism; and its focus on individual motivations is atomistic" (emphasis added).[28]

Surveying the Landscape of Malaysia's "Islamic State" Problem

Whereas I can only offer some preliminary findings here as a deeper study with better data access is needed for conclusive results, a cursory survey of the occupational status of the 130 individuals who were charged with "terrorism" crimes (see Figure 3) supports my observation that there is a class dimension to the issue.[29]

Putting together these profiles, one can say that IS-linked activism in Malaysia had mobilized, though not exclusively, a subaltern class of young people from lower socioeconomic backgrounds.[30] Even as the distribution of the occupational classes of this dataset largely matches the labor force structure in Malaysia,[31] what stands apart is that the unemployed are overrepresented in the sample (10 percent),

FIGURE 3 Occupational Classes of 130 Malaysians Charged for IS-linked Terrorism Crimes from 2013 to 2021

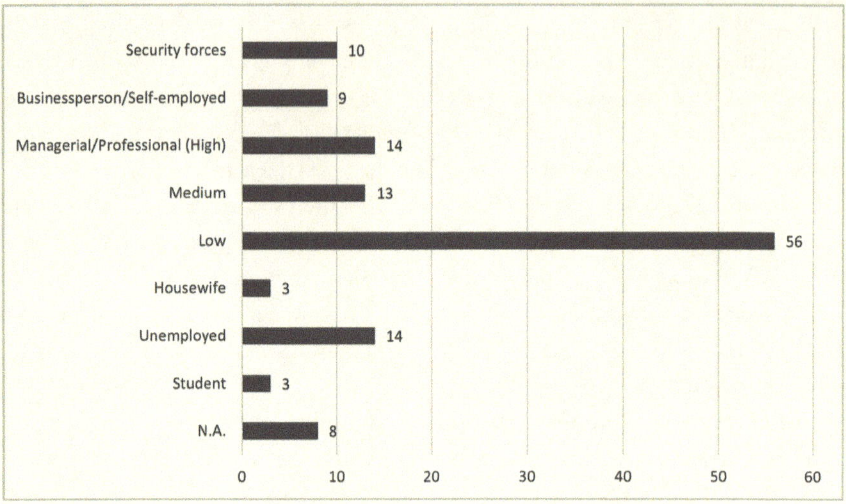

as Malaysia's unemployment rate prior to the COVID-19 pandemic was around 3–3.5 percent.[32] Given that most of those documented here belong to the lower occupational classes, they were most likely not educated to the tertiary level. Using the fact that the median age of dataset is at a relatively young age of thirty-one, we can infer that the proportion of those having tertiary education is much lower than the national tertiary education enrollment rate of 45 percent (as of 2015).[33]

Demographically, the individuals from this dataset are quite distinct from the urbane, middle-class *dakwah* (proselytization) activists whom Olivier Roy calls neofundamentalists.[34] Those activists caught the most interest in writings about Islam in Malaysia because they are the major pushers of Malaysia's political and social praxis of Islam toward a conservative and purity-driven direction.[35] But the continued focus on the neofundamentalists, as a result of negating the class dimension, will result in one making premature and unsubstantiated connections between expressions of urban middle-class fundamentalist attitudes and violent extremism, creating a policy dead-end for those who regard *both* as needing intervention. Those wishing to address violent extremism would find themselves directing inordinate focus on exclusivist urban middle-class circles who, while politically influential, are not extreme in their methods—nor were they generally targets of successful IS recruitment.[36] Meanwhile, those seeking to challenge problematic expressions of Muslim majoritarianism often end up frustrated,[37] as exclusivist and even far-right actors deflect criticism by (wrongly) claiming Islamophobia and (rightly) arguing that they are not terrorists, even if that misses the point entirely.[38]

To be sure, Malaysia's findings were not unique when compared to the profiles of far-right or Islamist militants in places such as the US and Europe, which tend to lean toward the more socially marginal groupings.[39] However, it does set Malaysia apart from other Muslim states, whose jihadist membership tends to have a higher representation from the university educated. For example, in a study of the profiles of 759 Saudi foreign fighters from leaked IS documents, close to half of the individuals (45 percent) were considered undergraduates.[40] Malaysia's "subaltern" IS landscape also deviates from two popular theories of radicalization derived from the Muslim world: the "engineers of jihad" and "deadly clerics" theses that are rooted in explanations of relative deprivation and blocked ambitions, respectively.[41] The former cannot account for the fact that most of those in the Malaysian sample do not have a university education, which means that focusing on the overrepresentation of engineers in jihadist movements elsewhere has little analytical or even policy value in tackling the IS phenomena in Malaysia. Malaysia does not exhibit the "deadly clerics" problem (clerics radicalizing due to frustrated career ambitions) either. Malaysia's IS landscape was notably devoid of charismatic religious figures, unlike in Indonesia, where revered scholarly figures like Abu Bakar Basyir and Aman Abdurrahman presided over as emirs of militant movements, even if only in a spiritual capacity.[42] The insufficiency of these explanations only strengthens the need to investigate the "subaltern" dimension of Malaysia's IS problem.

LOOKING DEEPER INTO CLASS

Reintroducing the class dimension for the Malaysian case is important for two reasons. First, it expands our comparative and theoretical horizons. As mentioned above, the average Malaysian IS member is much closer demographically to the profile of Islamist extremists in Western societies in terms of their socioeconomic marginality.[43] This suggests the Malaysian case fits better in Olivier Roy's explanation of Europe's IS problem: *the Islamization of radicalism*.[44] Roy argues that "rebellious youths have found in Islam the paradigm of their total revolt," and these youths were characterized by their origins in working-class neighborhoods, a born-again religious fervor, and experience with petty crime.[45] One can see the same socioeconomic marginality in the profiles of the trio involved in Malaysia's only successful case of IS-linked terrorist attack in that wave during the 2010s.[46]

The first profile is the alleged "mastermind" of the attack: Muhammad Wanndy Muhammad Jedi (1990–2017, henceforth Wanndy). Wanndy was called Malaysia's "top IS operative" in Syria until he was killed by an airstrike in April 2017. By all accounts, Wanndy appeared to have had a rough childhood, having grown up in a poor, single-parent household after his father died when he was ten years old.[47] He was reclusive and short-tempered, and was eventually expelled from school.

According to Gunaratna, Wanndy only grew pious after his mother's death in 2013 and went to Syria with his wife a year after, but not before relatives accused him of stealing his mother's belongings.[48] After posting about his travels and life in the "caliphate" online, Wanndy gained a substantial following, which propelled him to prominence as a recruiter and cell leader for IS's Malaysian supporters on social media. Wanndy's young age, rural background, and ability to recruit and mesmerize those older and more educated than him is reminiscent of Mohamed Amin Mohamed Razali, who led the bizarre siege by Al-Maunah in the early 2000s at the age of twenty-nine (see chapter 3).[49]

The two operators of the attack—Imam Wahyudin bin Karjono (twenty-one as of 2017, henceforth Wahyudin) and Jonius Ondie @ Jahali (twenty-four as of 2017, henceforth Jonius)—also appeared to have come from disadvantaged backgrounds.[50] According to court documents, Wahyudin from Puchong, Selangor, was raised in a single-parent household, had not completed his education,[51] and was unemployed. Jonius, a factory operator from Sabah, was a new convert to Islam and was only educated to Standard Two at the primary level.[52] Both of them were allegedly "former drug offenders."[53] The trio fits perfectly into Roy's typology of "Islamized" rebellious youths with troubled upbringings.

Second, the omission of class also reduces a complex social phenomenon to the catch-all, static vocabularies of "terrorism" or "violent extremism." I have argued elsewhere that Malaysia's IS cohort represents a discontinuity from the militancy of the Jemaah Islamiyah period in the early 2000s, a change these umbrella terms seem ill equipped to explain.[54] Also, to focus on the terrorism bits without a sociological understanding also means refusing to reckon with Malaysia's largely subaltern IS membership and activism. What we get instead is an analytical optic overshadowed by a preoccupation with the illegality of the movement. By focusing mainly on the criminality of what is fundamentally a *political* cause undertaken by the less privileged, we risk confining the notion of political activism to the methods employed by the middle class and above.[55]

Let me offer two caveats, lest this focus on the class question be misunderstood. First, I am not arguing that these IS-linked individuals were immune to the broader social milieu and that class position alone explained their sociopolitical attitudes.[56] The IS phenomenon is not a product of class consciousness, and socioeconomic indicators alone cannot predict "radical" outcomes. Second, I am in no way saying these actors were not religious, or that their claim to religiously driven goals were insincere or illegitimate. These are psychological and normative assessments a scholar of politics is not qualified to make. But in assuming that doctrine determines politics, one stops engaging with the multitudes of Muslim politics, not least the relationship with "broader discursive and social formations in which religion has a prominent—and problematic—role."[57] In other words, overlooking the class dimension will result in a constricted understanding of Muslim politics.

Peering into their class backgrounds does not mean we must accept, agree, or even sympathize with these individuals. Understandably, one might find their goals or methods abhorrent. But in not looking closer at the social landscape of Malaysia's IS phenomenon, we risk naturalizing this idea that violent jihadism is an unavoidable fringe offshoot of conservative religiosity. Even if one finds negative social implications in either militancy or ultraconservative religiosity, putting them on a sliding scale view of religiosity provides an analytical resolution to neither, as the space between religiosity and political behavior is always mediated by a variety of factors.[58] Moreover, there is also the question of equity on the policy front. Suppose counter-terror measures, with their heavy penalties, preemptive ethos, and alleged entrapping methods, were disproportionately targeted at the lower rungs of society; state policies may end up alienating those they were supposed to reach and moderate.[59] In addition, with the overarching "misinterpretation of Islam" explanation in place, current P/CVE discourses often characterize radicalization as an outcome of character weaknesses and individual naivete: traits often used to stigmatize the underclasses.

Rethinking Religion and Muslim Politics: Two Insights

This book can also be read as an enterprise of *recentering* for three reasons. First, it recenters the GWOT in the experience of a postcolonial Muslim state, Malaysia. Second, it recenters security from a realist understanding to one grounded in ontological security, arguing that Malaysia's bandwagoning in the GWOT is not just about elites pursuing the interest of regime preservation but also reflects a long-standing quest to correct Islam's stigmatization. Third, it recenters counter-terrorism at the level of local practices and discourses to interrogate the institutional and epistemological relationship between Islam and counter-terrorism in Malaysia. These "recenterings" are not just for the sake of diving into the details of the Malaysian case. Theoretically, they help us understand how religion's integration with security (or governance) is not simply the product of opportunistic politicization and instrumentalist securitization, as political science literatures tend to suggest. Rather, these are long-term processes intertwined with elite recognition-seeking efforts and state-building trajectories. In the following two subsections, I will reflect on these insights about state-religion relationships, postcolonial international relations, and security governance, and how they may advance our understanding of Islam's relationship with Muslim state behavior and state security.

Religion, Ontological Security, and Muslim State Behavior

Thus far, critical investigations of authoritarian security practices in postcolonial Muslim states often attribute these practices to either the lingering presence of colonial institutions, dependencies and ways of being, or to the bumpy transition from a secular colonial past to a postcolonial communitarian present.[60] However, harping on the continuity of colonial influence or the traumatic rupture between the "secular colonial" and the "religious postcolonial" may risk robbing postcolonial state actors of their agency. This book enters this topic in such a way that brings the question of identity, religion, and postcoloniality back into our understanding of contemporary security practices without treating any of those variables as determinative. It shows how the perspective of ontological security can be uniquely productive in theorizing how religion matters in a postcolonial world order, both as an (stigmatized) identifier of Muslim identity as well as a constructed master category through which security governance had evolved around.

The postcolonial Malay-Muslim elites I highlighted in this book are those who needed to manage the transition from colonial to postcolonial and, in so doing, navigated situations, interests, and environments where the lines between "secular" and "religious" were never entirely clear.[61] For example, studies that try to capture the normative differences between secular and religious counter-terror actors—sometimes taken as labels to signify the Global North and South respectively—often place too much emphasis on ascriptive identity differences. My case study shows that interactions between secular and religious actors in international relations are not always defined by dynamics of accommodation or conflict due to fundamental value disagreements on the two sides. Rather, they are structured by *social* understandings of identity differences ("Muslim," "Western," "civilized"), which, by virtue of their historical production within a hierarchical environment, translate into different incentives and pressures.[62] Viewing a globalized enterprise such as the GWOT from the non-Western (Muslim) margins provides the avenue to explore such complicated dynamics. Even as the state was enjoying expansions in power and social legitimacy in international society due to its counter-terror prowess, Malaysia's self-embraced Islamic identity and its keen participation in what is understood implicitly as a civilizing mission targeted at Muslims also generated a profound sense of status anxiety among the Muslim elites.

More interestingly, what emerges in this book is that Malaysia's "Muslimness" does not determine state behavior as such in any straightforward way. Despite its elites clearly feeling and internalizing the stigma of being Muslim, they did not opt for the more radical paths of either reforming oneself in the "secular" image of the West (as in the case of Kemalist Turkey), or adopting a renegade status to repudiate the stigma (as in the case of postrevolution Iran).[63] Instead, Malaysia picked a middle path of *reforming to impress*. This was done through a slew of state-led Islamization projects in the 1980s and 1990s. Even as those projects were aimed at instilling cultural change to foster a more industrial, entrepreneurial Malay-Muslim populace to correct Islam's stigmatization, it also had the effect of augmenting Malaysia's identification with its Muslim identity, which explains why religion is becoming a more salient factor in Malaysia's domestic and international politics. Perceived success in becoming both "Islamic" and "modern" also bolstered confidence for a more assertive foreign policy posture, wherein Malaysian leaders, especially Mahathir, started to champion for the needs and grievances of the global South and the Muslim world. After Mahathir's (first) retirement in 2003, successive administrations also strove to claim the mantle of being a (moderate) Islamic state to counter the GWOT's intensified stigmatization of Islam. Granted, these discursive and institutional maneuverings did not resolve the problem of ontological insecurity of the Malaysian Muslim elites. But they explain Malaysia's Islamization that ironically transpired under the watch of what was initially a secular ethnonationalist party, UMNO, instead of its more ideologically committed Islamist opponent.

Put differently, the Malaysian case, as with many other postcolonial Muslim states, shows that status-seeking endeavors with a Western audience (real or imagined) in mind do not necessarily entail Muslim state actors reducing or moderating their association with Islam. Rather, all evidence indicates that operating from a stigmatized social position sharpens one's association with the stigmatized marker because recognition seeking is preceded by the internalization of sedimented and unsurmountable identity differences (e.g., East/West, secular/religious, Muslim/non-Muslim) in the international order.[64] Understanding that a stigma correction motive undergirded Malaysia's state-religion relationship and its rhetorical deployment of the moderate Islam discourse also provides an important corrective to the religious soft power literature that often depicts the employment of religion in foreign policy within a realist and almost cynical framing.[65] Whereas there is no doubt that Muslim political actors have realpolitik interests in their minds, they are nonetheless still social actors inhabiting an international order organized around formal and informal hierarchies often predicated on material, racial, and sociocultural differences.[66] Disregarding the stigmatizing effects of the GWOT on Muslims when analyzing the actions of Muslim states distorts our understanding of the interest calculus among Muslim state elites, including those not considered Islamists.

The longevity of East-West inequalities and the cultural dominance of the latter suggests that ontological security seeking will remain a driver of Muslim state behavior.[67] In the case of Malaysia, seeking ontological security did not just drive the trajectory and forms of Islamization undertaken by the state; it also fostered Islam's securitization that resulted in the narrowing of (state-defined) Islamic orthodoxies and in state and social intolerance of perceivably "deviant" movements. The cascading effects of these developments, which included the increasing persecution of "liberal" Muslim movements, are well documented elsewhere.[68] My argument here is simply that Islamism or conservative Muslim religiosity alone is insufficient to account for all these developments. The question is not so much if Islam is present (or how much)—which often unjustly flattens Muslim political actors into a dichotomy of the "Islamist" and "liberal/secular" types—but Islam *where, when,* and *how*? This emphasis on the spatiotemporal dimension of religion informs this book's multiscalar inquiry of Islam and counter-terrorism in Malaysia. It also reminds us that the social geography of the Muslim world matters. Malaysia's spatial distance from the Middle East and North African (MENA) region is echoed in its discourses about moderate Islam—discourses that also sought to decenter Islam symbolically from its MENA associations.

The Securitization of Islam in Muslim-Majority Settings

This book also contributes to the study of the securitization of Islam by highlighting its dynamic within Muslim states. In Western/Muslim-minority settings, the securitization of Islam often occurred as a result of the Muslim other being racialized or constructed as "a negation of an *idealised* Western secular self," or, worse, as separatist and segregationist elements in places like India and China where authoritarian regimes increasingly adopt oppressive assimilationist policies in the name of nation building.[69] In Muslim-majority settings, however, Islam's securitization is usually attributed to either assertive secularism, as in the case of Kemalist Türkiye and the former Soviet nations, or to military dictatorship's oppression of their Islamist opponents, such as in the case of Egypt, Ben Ali's Tunisia, and Suharto's Indonesia.[70]

However, none of those pathways explain the situation in Malaysia. In Malaysia, what we saw is not just authoritarian impulses that led to the securitization of Islam. More accurately, the securitization transpired under elite meditations about the relationship between the state and religion, which was nested within a broader (nationalist) politics of recognition seeking. By uncovering this process, I demonstrate how ostensibly similar outcomes can come from vastly different trajectories. Both Muslim and non-Muslim majority states have tried to manage Islam as if it can be divided into its bipolar good/moderate and bad/radical halves.[71] However, whereas in the West such views about Islam came from historical prejudices and contemporary right-wing populist pressures, in Malaysia, ideas about "right" and "wrong" Islam, while not above the conveniences of domestic political interests, were inseparable from statist project that needed to ensure that right Islam thrived at the expense of "wrong" ones for developmentalist goals. This zeal is witnessed in the forms of Islamization sanctioned by Mahathir's administration that ruled for twenty-two years: bureaucratization, professionalization, corporatization, and the Islamization of the sciences. As discussed in chapter 3, these forms were driven to project an image of Islam compatible with industrial modernity, scientific rationality, and capitalist productivity.

The securitization of Islam in Malaysia also operates in a more complex manner than what the Copenhagen school of securitization theories suggest. In those interpretations, the securitization of religion often involves framing a "sacred referent object" as "existentially threatened," thereby necessitating extraordinary measures of protection.[72] Laustsen and Wæver summarize this process as "religion plus securitization equals ideology."[73] Yet, even as protecting "true" Islam was used to justify security measures, I argue that what we witness in Malaysia is not a simple case of securitizing actors performing speech acts. Rather, these Islamized security narratives are the product of security logics born out of colonial legacies, postcolonial institutional configurations, as well as Muslim elite responses toward Islam's status in the international order. Instead of being just a speech act, the Mahathir administration's securitization of Islam was linked to a broader modernization project—a project he imbued with existential stakes, thereby legitimating greater state curation of Islam. This sense of existentialism is best illustrated by Mahathir's own words: "A better future for the Muslim Ummah requires much more effort and strength. The Quran promised the eternal survival of Islam; this promise does not extend to Muslims."[74]

In other words, the importance of preserving the correct interpretation of Islam was interpreted by Muslim elites within a worldview that understood survival through the memories of unpleasant colonial encounters and the perception and reality of uneven present hierarchies. This understanding of securitization is more expansive than views claiming that religion's securitization is mainly about defending sacred places, rituals, objects, or even doctrine.[75] It might also serve goals of cultivating empathy. If we can acknowledge that there is a recognition-seeking dimension to Islam's securitization in Muslim political discourses (as seen in the opening anecdote of this chapter), then we might be able to comprehend hot-button issues that spark Muslim anger in a way that escape the tautological claim that Muslims are angry *because* they are Muslims.

Epilogue: Status, Security, and Modernity

International relations scholarship has recently taken a strong interest in status, yet that interest generally revolves around rising powers, those who have the means and potential to "get even."[76] This book has shown that even for those who cannot quite get even (which is the case for most Muslim states), status seeking and stigma correction are still important aspects of their politics and policymaking. These perspectives are important for three reasons. First, they remind us that considerations of honor, such as the desire to be recognized as part of the "civilized" amid the moral exceptionalism of the GWOT, need not always result in "muscular" responses like hostile rhetoric or uncooperative, aggressive postures. After all, a sense of status insecurity has driven Malaysia into active participation in the GWOT, although it was animated by a degree of ambivalence toward the enterprise. When the GWOT ended up deepening the mutual distrust between the West and the Muslim states, these unresolved recognition needs fostered polarization among international society even as Muslim and non-Muslim regimes hunted jointly for the universal enemy that is the terrorist.

Second, having a nuanced understanding of Muslim state concerns about status and recognition is important for the prospect of global governance projects, like tackling climate change. If elites' understanding of their position (as Muslims) in the global hierarchy influences how they buy into and operationalize global governance agendas, acknowledging that fact can help cultivate favorable conditions for cooperation. More importantly, it also spells out the stakes that, if there is a shift in the political climate in the Global North that undermines the legitimacy of the climate agenda (the most vulnerable spot being the US),[77] that may reduce the incentive for Muslim states (and the rest) to participate. Muslim state elites might stop seeing reducing carbon emissions as key to being recognized as a responsible (read: "civilized") global actor. Third, it helps us realize that desires for status and recognition, instead of how Islamized these states are, can better explain Muslim state foreign policy. For example, the latter does not quite capture their views about Great Power politics. The Xinjiang issue, which borders on cultural genocide on some accounts, does not corral as many anti-China positions from the Muslim states as some observers (and probably Washington) would hope.[78] Conversely, anti-liberal and anti-West positions keep gaining social currency in Muslim states (and, indeed, among Muslim elites).[79] If one goes back to the problem of stigmatization, where the perceived axis of exclusion is historically drawn around (and by) the Anglo-European world, perhaps this animus is not so incomprehensible.[80]

I will conclude this book with another cursory example of how insights about ontological security can inform analysis of contemporary Muslim politics beyond the US-China competition angle. In the aftermath of the Arab Spring, Arab Muslim regimes have embarked on status-seeking projects by erecting totems of (hyper)modernity. This is seen in the region's launching of a flurry of "smart cities," from Saudi Arabia's Neom to Abu Dhabi's Masdar City and Egypt's yet unnamed new administrative capital.[81] These projects echo the current zeitgeist with their claims of being carbon-free and enthusiastic incorporation of futuristic technologies, such as driverless cars, robot maids, and, in the case of Neom, even an artificial moon at one point.[82] I agree with Jones's assessment in her study of the United Arab Emirates that, far from being just vanity projects, such "monumentalism," in its "imposing architecture, striking visual design, and 'built cities'," was not "merely lip service" but reflective of elite interests to nurture a "creative Arab Renaissance."[83] From an ontological security standpoint, these projects make sense too. As Arab Muslim states situated geographically within a region that has suffered from the stigma of jihadist uprising and violence in the past decades, it is perhaps unsurprising that these regimes, which have projected themselves as reliable counter-terror states (mainly to the West but also to their people), have also opted for these hypermodern constructions.[84] Without dismissing domestic "push" factors such as attracting foreign investments and diversifying their oil-based economy, there also appears to be almost an element of overcompensation here. It is arguable that these Arab Muslim elites are keen to put the stigma associated with the geopolitical chaos of the Arab Spring and the televised brutalities of IS (to which their states contributed significantly in terms of foreign fighters) behind them by reorienting the image of their states toward the future and the futuristic. Such sci-fi humanist pretensions can be seen in how Saudi Arabia's Neom project claims to be the "accelerator of human progress and a vision of what a New Future might look like."[85]

More interestingly, these projects appear to be stripped of any local religio-cultural influences in their cosmopolitan, albeit sterile, aesthetics. This form of architectural deculturalization is significantly different from Malaysia's construction of its own "smart cities" such as Cyberjaya and Putrajaya in the late 1990s. "Malaysian-Islamic" features were ubiquitous in those constructions; unsurprising, as they were part of "an ongoing endeavour to re-establish Malay and Islamic pride and self-respect," echoing the "Islamization as stigma correction" ethos I discussed in this book.[86] These cases underpin this book's argument that considerations of identity and recognition still animate Muslim politics doggedly, with the modernization paradigm looming over Muslim elites' conceptualization of good governance and national security. The dialectical opposition between the image of a medieval suicide-vest-wearing fanatic and a gadget-toting, driverless-car-hailing future citizen remains affixed in global imaginaries, including in societies most stigmatized by this dichotomy.

APPENDIX

Notes on the Terrorism Detainee Dataset

This dataset is composed of 130 individuals (117 males, 13 females) charged in Malaysian courts for terrorism offences between 2013 and 2021. The source of the data came from various news reports and court documents. Non-Malaysians were left out because, whereas the government did charge some under terrorism offences, most of the foreigners detained for suspected terrorism crimes were deported. Thus, I limit my dataset to only Malaysians to ensure consistency and comparability of data. Of all the cases, I only know of one in which the accused was acquitted, but that happened under a technicality. The case involved a police officer accused of withholding information about alleged terrorist acts from the police, and according to official documents and my research, she appeared to be well acquainted with some of the suspected Islamic State (IS) militants.[1] I have decided to include that case in the dataset, not as an indictment of her guilt, but to recognize the individual as part of an IS-related ecosystem within Malaysia.

The primary purpose of this dataset is to make a preliminary survey of the socioeconomic backgrounds of these individuals. I extrapolate the backgrounds of these individuals from their occupations, hypothesizing that the information will be quite revealing of one's educational and income status. Other than the few categories separated out (security forces,[2] housewife, student, unemployed, and not

TABLE 3 Occupational Groupings Based on Their Class Positions

Skill level	Occupational grouping	Median salary (MYR as of 2016)	Prevalence in labor force (%, as of 2016)	Occupational class
Skilled	Managers	5,500	4.6	HIGH
Skilled	Professionals	4,450	12.4	
Skilled	Technicians and associate professionals	2,760	10.3	MEDIUM
Semiskilled	Clerical support workers	2,000	8.2	
Semiskilled	Service and sales workers	1,225	22.4	LOW
Semiskilled	Skilled agricultural, forestry, and fishery workers	1,350	6.2	
Semiskilled	Craft and related trades work	1,500	11.1	
Semiskilled	Plant and machine operators and assemblers	1,485	11.8	
Low-skilled	Elementary occupations	1,100	13.0	

Source: All data based on DOSM, *Salaries*; DOSM, *Labour Force Survey Report 2016* (DOSM, 2017); 2008 Malaysian Standard Classification of Occupations (MASCO-08), https://www.ilmia.gov.my/index.php/en/dashboard-datamart/kilm/indicators/employment-by-occupation.

available), I group the individuals into three occupational classes (high, medium, and low) based on the skilled, semiskilled, and low-skilled categories prescribed by the 2008 Malaysia Standard Classification of Occupations (see Table 3).

However, the three occupational classes do not map neatly onto the three skill categories. I have made some adjustments to the categories to better reflect the unequal and generally low-paying situation of the Malaysian labor market, which only has a median monthly salary of MYR 1,700 (roughly USD 400) according to the Salaries and Wages Survey Report of 2016.[3] To do so, I assign the categories of high, medium, and low occupational classes based on median salary data.

As one can see, the prescribed skill levels do not approximate the social class of the individuals, given the massive wage differences within the skill-based groupings. Moreover, judging by skill level alone omits the fact that many of the so-called semiskilled occupations in Malaysia only earn an income marginally better than the elementary occupations in 2016. By contrast, groups often considered "middle-class," such as managers and professionals, are actually not in the middle in terms of their position in the wage ladder. Also, the fact that an average tertiary-educated person earned about MYR 3,274 in 2016 indicates that most of those in the "medium" and "low" occupational categories are likely educated to the secondary level or lower.[4]

Whereas having most of the IS-related detainees concentrated in the "low" category (see Figure 5) is generally reflective of Malaysia's labor force, it does highlight the subaltern- or proletariat-centric nature of the (disorganized) movement, contrasting it with the membership structure of other forms of political movements that tend to find its most active members from the urban middle class. For example, most, if not all, of Malaysia's parliamentarians have a university degree or above. If the barriers to entering "mainstream" political activity skewed upward, it would appear that IS-linked activism has a downward appeal, which is an interesting observation on its own.

Notes

Introduction

1. "Remarks by President Trump and Prime Minister Najib Abdul Razak of Malaysia Before Bilateral Meeting," September 12, 2017, https://trumpwhitehouse.archives.gov/briefings-statements/remarks-president-trump-prime-minister-najib-abdul-razak-malaysia-bilateral-meeting/ .

2. On the idea of transnational jihadism being international society's common enemy, see Barak Mendelsohn, "Sovereignty Under Attack: The International Society Meets the Al Qaeda Network," *Review of International Studies* 31, no. 1 (2005): 45–68.

3. I refer to Muslim states here as states with a Muslim-majority population.

4. Simeon Kerr, "Saudi Crown Prince Pledges to Rid World of Islamist Terror," *Financial Times*, November 26, 2017, https://www.ft.com/content/0f61de82-d2c7-11e7-a303-9060cb1e5f44.

5. William Booth and Taylor Luck, "To Counter Rise of Islamic State, Jordan Imposes Rules on Muslim Clerics," *The Washington Post*, November 9, 2014, https://www.washingtonpost.com/world/middle_east/to-counter-rise-of-the-islamic-state-jordan-imposes-rules-on-muslim-clerics/2014/11/09/4d5fce22-5937-11e4-bd61-346aee66ba29_story.html.

6. Chaima Lahsini, "Ahmed Abbadi: Morocco Is a Model of Moderate Islam," *Morocco World News*, February 9, 2017, https://www.moroccoworldnews.com/2017/02/207779/ahmed-abbadi-morocco-is-a-model-of-moderate-islam/.

7. Annelle Sheline, "Middle East Regimes Are Using 'Moderate' Islam to Stay in Power," *The Washington Post*, March 1, 2017, https://www.washingtonpost.com/news/monkey-cage/wp/2017/03/01/middle-east-regimes-are-using-moderate-islam-to-stay-in-power/?utm_term=.56c8169408c5.

8. Shamim Adam and Annisa Shukry "Najib Set to Meet Trump as 1MDB Probe Deepens," *Bloomberg*, September 11, 2017, https://www.bloomberg.com/news/articles/2017-09-11/trump-to-meet-favorite-premier-as-malaysian-fund-probe-deepens; "Mr. Najib and Mr. Trump," *The Wall Street Journal*, May 7, 2018, https://www.wsj.com/articles/mr-najib-and-mr-trump-1525732011.

9. See William Cavanaugh, *The Myth of Religious Violence: Secular Ideology and the Roots of Modern Conflict* (Oxford University Press, 2009); Irm Haleem, *The Essence of Islamist Extremism: Recognition through Violence, Freedom through Death* (Routledge, 2012); Jeroen Gunning and Richard Jackson, "What's So 'Religious' about 'Religious Terrorism'?" *Critical Studies on Terrorism* 4, no. 3 (2011): 369–88.

10. See Stuart Croft, "Constructing Ontological Insecurity: The Insecuritization of Britain's Muslims," *Contemporary Security Policy* 33, no. 2 (2012): 219–35; Stuart Croft, *Securitizing Islam: Identity and the Search for Security* (Cambridge University Press, 2012); Stacey Gutkowski, "The British Secular Habitus and the War on Terror," *Journal of Contemporary Religion* 27, no. 1 (2012): 87–103; Luca Mavelli, "Between Normalisation and Exception: The Securitisation of Islam and the Construction of the Secular Subject," *Millennium: Journal of International Studies* 41, no. 2 (2013): 159–81.

11. Sarah Logan, *Hold Your Friends Close: Countering Radicalization in Britain and America* (Oxford University Press, 2023).

12. Out of the five countries that contributed the most foreign fighters to IS, four were Muslim states (Tunisia, Saudi Arabia, Jordan, and Türkiye). Ian Bremmer, "The Top 5 Countries Where ISIS Gets Its Foreign Recruits," *Time*, April 17, 2017, https://time.com/4739488/isis-iraq-syria-tunisia-saudi-arabia-russia/. However, it is important to note that if assessed from the criterion of number of foreign fighters relative to Muslim population, European countries such as Finland, Ireland, Belgium, Sweden, and Austria outperformed the Muslim states. See Efraim Benmelech and Esteban F. Klor, "What Explains the Flow of Foreign Fighters to ISIS?" *Terrorism and Political Violence*, 32, no. 7 (2020): 1465.

13. Kieran McConaghy, *Terrorism and the State: Intra-State Dynamics and the Response to Non-State Terrorism* (Palgrave Macmillan, 2017); Frank Foley, *Countering Terrorism in Britain and France: Institutions, Norms and the Shadow of the Past* (Cambridge University Press, 2013).

14. Victor V. Ramraj, Michael Hor, Kent Roach, and George Williams, eds., *Global Anti-Terrorism Law and Policy* (Cambridge University Press, 2012); Kent Roach, ed.,

Comparative Counter-Terror Law (Cambridge University Press, 2015); Jayson S. Lamchek, *Human Rights-Compliant Counterterrorism: Myth-Making and Reality in the Philippines and Indonesia* (Cambridge University Press, 2019); Fatemah Alzubairi, *Colonialism, Neo-Colonialism, and Anti-Terrorism Law in the Arab World* (Cambridge University Press, 2019).

15. McConaghy, *Terrorism and the State*, 111, 147.

16. Foley, *Countering Terrorism*, 245–51.

17. Kent Roach, *The 9/11 Effect: Comparative Counter-Terrorism* (Cambridge University Press, 2011); Gavin Sullivan, *The Law of the List: UN Counterterrorism Sanctions and the Politics of Global Security Law* (Cambridge University Press, 2020); Jothie Rajah, "Sinister Translations: Law's Authority in a Post-9/11 World," *Indiana Journal of Global Legal Studies* 21, no. 1 (2014): 107–43; Darryl Li, *The Universal Enemy: Jihad, Empire, and the Challenge of Solidarity* (Stanford University Press, 2020); Jothie Rajah, "Law, Politics, and Populism in the U.S.A. P.A.T.R.I.O.T. Act," *Indiana Journal of Global Legal Studies* 26, no. 1 (2019): 61–85.

18. Farish A. Noor, "How Washington's 'War on Terror' Became Everyone's: Islamophobia and the Impact of September 11 on the Political Terrain of South and Southeast Asia," *Human Architecture: Journal of the Sociology of Self-Knowledge* 8, no. 1 (2006): 29–50. See also Roberta Haar, "Explaining George W. Bush's Adoption of the Neoconservative Agenda after 9/11," *Politics & Policy* 38, no. 5 (2010): 965–90.

19. Stacey Gutkowski, "We Are the Very Model of a Moderate Muslim State: The Amman Messages and Jordan's Foreign Policy," *International Relations* 30, no. 2 (2016): 206–26; Annelle R. Sheline, "Shifting Reputations for 'Moderation': Evidence from Qatar, Jordan, and Morocco," *Middle East Law and Governance*, 12 (2020): 109–29.

20. Peter S. Henne, *Islamic Politics, Muslim States, and Counterterrorism Tensions* (Cambridge University Press, 2017).

21. A case can be made against Türkiye's supposedly positive counter-terror cooperation with the US. For example, Türkiye's initial lukewarm response to the IS threat, most evident in its lax border controls that allowed a significant influx of foreign fighters, prompts one to question its degree of cooperativeness with the US, which clearly saw IS as a prominent threat. Türkiye's anti-Kurdish policies also hampered US counter-terror interests, given that the Kurdish militias were key allies in the US's military campaign against IS in Syria and Iraq. See Tim Arango, and Eric Schmitt, "A Path to ISIS, Through a Porous Turkish Border," *The New York Times,* March 9, 2015, https://www.nytimes.com/2015/03/10/world/europe/despite-crackdown-path-to-join-isis-often-winds-through-porous-turkish-border.html.

22. Ann Marie Wainscott, *Bureaucratizing Islam: Morocco and the War on Terror* (Cambridge University Press, 2017), 2.

23. Sarah J. Feuer, *Regulating Islam: Religion and the State in Contemporary Morocco and Tunisia* (Cambridge University Press, 2018), 17; cf. Sarah Feuer, "State Islam in the

Battle Against Extremism: Emerging Trends in Morocco and Tunisia," *Policy Focus* 145 (Washington Institute for Near East Policy, 2016).

24. Wainscott, *Bureaucratizing Islam*, 29; Feuer, "State Islam," 183.

25. Valentina Bartolucci, "Analysing Elite Discourse on Terrorism and its Implications: The Case of Morocco," *Critical Studies on Terrorism*, 3, no. 1 (2010): 127.

26. Cavanaugh, *Myth of Religious Violence*; Olivier Roy, *Jihad and Death: The Global Appeal of Islamic State* (Oxford University Press, 2017).

27. Lisa Stampnitzky, *Disciplining Terror: How Experts Invented "Terrorism"* (Cambridge University Press, 2013); Darryl Li, "A Jihadism Anti-Primer," *Middle East Report* 276 (2015), https://merip.org/2015/12/a-jihadism-anti-primer/.

28. Jennifer Mustapha, *Writing Southeast Asian Security: Regional Security and the War on Terror After 9/11* (Routledge, 2019), 3. On critical terrorism studies, see Jeroen Gunning, "A Case for Critical Terrorism Studies?" *Government and Opposition* 42, no. 3 (2007): 363–93; Richard Jackson, "The Core Commitments of Critical Terrorism Studies," *European Political Science* 6 (2007): 244–51; Richard Jackson, M. B. Smyth, and Jeroen Gunning, "Critical Terrorism Studies: Framing a New Research Agenda," in *Critical Terrorism Studies*, ed. Richard Jackson, M. B. Smyth, and Jeroen Gunning (Routledge, 2009).

29. Elizabeth Shakman Hurd, *Beyond Religious Freedom: The New Global Politics of Religion* (Princeton University Press, 2015), 110; Saba Mahmood, "Secularism, Hermeneutics, and Empire: The Politics of Islamic Reformation," *Public Culture* 18, no. 2(2006): 323–47.

30. Alzubairi, *Colonialism*, 25; Iza Hussin, "'The New Global Politics of Religion': Religious Harmony, Public Order, and Securitisation in the Post-Colony," *Journal of Religious and Political Practice* 4, no. 1 (2018): 103.

31. "In Malaysia, we have a long history of emphasising that moderation—the practice of *wasatiyya*—is a Quranic injunction." Speech given by Najib Razak at the International Conference on Deradicalisation and Countering Violence Extremism, January 25, 2016.

32. Hurd, *Beyond Religious Freedom*, 35.

33. Alexander Wendt, "Anarchy Is What States Make of It: The Social Construction of Power Politics," *International Organization* 46, no. 2 (1992): 425.

34. Colin Wight, *Agents, Structures and International Relations: Politics as Ontology* (Cambridge University Press, 2006), 5.

35. Oded Löwenheim, *Predators and Parasites: Persistent Agents of Transnational Harm and Great Power Authority* (University of Michigan Press, 2007), 176.

36. Mendelsohn, "Sovereignty Under Attack," 54.

37. Farid Hafez, "Unwanted Identities: The 'Religion Line' and Global Islamophobia," *Development* 63 (2020): 9–19.

38. Henne, *Islamic Politics*.

39. Peter Mandeville and Shadi Hamid, *Islam as Statecraft: How Governments Used Religion in Foreign Policy* (Brookings Institution, 2018), 2.

40. See, for example, such a portraiture of the "shrewd autocrat" in Robert F. Worth, "Mohammed bin Zayed's Dark Vision of the Middle East's Future," *The New York Times Magazine*, January 9, 2020, https://www.nytimes.com/2020/01/09/magazine/united-arab-emirates-mohammed-bin-zayed.html.

41. On habitus, I take a wide Bourdieusian definition that denotes a field with "common forms and categories of perception and appreciation, social frameworks of perceptions," See Pierre Bourdieu, "Rethinking the State: Genesis and Structure of the Bureaucratic Field," *Sociological Theory* 12, no. 1 (1994):13.

42. See Ayşe Zarakol, "What Makes Terrorism Modern? Terrorism, Legitimacy, and the International System," *Review of International Studies* 37, no. 5 (2011): 2311–66; Roxanne Euben, "Killing (for) Politics: Jihad, Martyrdom, and Political Action," *Political Theory* 30, no. 1 (2002): 4–35; Cavanaugh, *Myth of Religious Violence*; T. K. Wilson, *Killing Strangers: How Political Violence Became Modern* (Oxford University Press, 2020).

43. Pinar Kemerli, "The Islamist Terrorist as the New Universal Enemy: Discourses on Terror at the United Nations," in *The Oxford Handbook of the History of Terrorism Online Edition*, ed. Carola Dietze and Claudia Verhoeven (Oxford University Press, 2014), 606–26.

44. On the effects of GWOT on Islamophobia, see Khaled A. Beydoun, "Exporting Islamophobia in the Global War on Terror," *New York University Law Review Online* 95, no. 8 (2020): 81–100; Mahmood Mamdani, "Good Muslim, Bad Muslim: A Political Perspective on Culture and Terrorism," *American Anthropologist* 104, no. 3 (2002): 766–75; Adrian Cherney and Kristina Murphy, "What Does It Mean to Be a Moderate Muslim in the War on Terror? Muslim Interpretations and Reactions," *Critical Studies on Terrorism* 9, no. 2 (2016): 159–81.

45. Michael Barnett, "Covid-19 and the Sacrificial International Order," *International Organization* 74, no. S1 (2020): E128–47; Carlos Tornel, "Decolonizing Energy Justice from the Ground Up: Political Ecology, Ontology, and Energy Landscapes," *Progress in Human Geography* 47, no. 1 (2023): 43–65.

46. Catarina Kinnvall and Ted Svensson, "Ontological Security and the Limits to a Common World: Subaltern Pasts and the Inner-Worldliness of the Tablighi Jama'at," *Postcolonial Studies* 20, no. 3 (2017): 341.

47. Croft, *Securitizing Islam*; Mavelli, "Between Normalisation and Exception."

48. Tobias Müller, "Engaging 'Moderates' Against 'Extremists' in German Politics on Islam," *The Review of Faith & International Affairs* 15, no. 2 (2017): 55–65; Gutkowski, "British Secular Habitus."

49. Logan, *Hold Your Friends Close*.

50. Thomas Hegghammer, *Jihad in Saudi Arabia: Violence and Pan-Islamism since 1979* (Cambridge University Press, 2010); Nicola Pratt and Dina Rezk, "Securitizing

the Muslim Brotherhood: State Violence and Authoritarianism in Egypt after the Arab Spring," *Security Dialogue* 50, no. 3 (2019): 239–56.

51. I have discussed the legalist and IR literature above, but for examples of studies of counter-terror that look at other "segmental" policy interests, see Rohan Gunaratna and Muhammad Ali, eds., *Terrorist Rehabilitation: A New Frontier in Counter-Terrorism* (Imperial College Press, 2015); Hamed El-Said, *De-Radicalising Islamists: Programmes and Their Impact in Muslim Majority States* (International Centre for the Study of Radicalisation, 2012); Ann-Sophie Hemmingsen and Karin Ingrid Castro, *The Trouble with Counter-Narratives, DIIS Report* 2017, no. 1 (Danish Institute of International Studies, 2017). I Gusti Bagus Dharma Agastia et al., "Countering Violent Extremism Through State-Society Partnerships: A Case Study of De-Radicalisation Programmes in Indonesia," *Journal of Policing, Intelligence and Counter Terrorism* 15, no. 1 (2020): 23–43.

52. The classic reference for the Copenhagen school is Barry Buzan, Ole Wæver, and Jaap de Wilde, *Security: A New Framework for Analysis* (Lynee Rienner, 1998).

53. "Riding a Tiger," *The Economist*, April 4, 2015, https://www.economist.com/asia/2015/04/04/riding-a-tiger.

54. Marc Lourdes. "Islamic State Launches First Successful Attack in Malaysia," *CNN*, July 4, 2016. https://edition.cnn.com/2016/07/04/homepage2/islamic-state-attack-malaysia/index.html. After the completion of this manuscript, an attack occurred at a police station in Ulu Tiram, Johor on May 17, 2024, killing two officers. The assailant was killed but his family was charged for spreading "Islamic State" ideology. See "5 Family Members of Malaysian Man Who Attacked Police Station Face Terrorism Charges," *Associated Press*, June 19, 2024, https://apnews.com/article/malaysia-attack-police-station-cfe968236c9a489d47f2c6b5ffb01d2b

55. There are challenges to Malaysia's "success" story. For example, Liow writes that, relative to its population, Malaysians joined IS at a higher rate than Indonesia. A Pew Research Survey also found that about 11 percent of Malaysians expressing support for IS, a figure significantly higher than Indonesia, Türkiye, and Pakistan. See Joseph Chinyong Liow "Malaysia's ISIS Conundrum," Brookings, April 21, 2015, https://www.brookings.edu/opinions/malaysias-isis-conundrum/; Jacob Poushter, "In Nations with Significant Muslim Populations, Much Disdain for ISIS," Pew Research Center, November 17, 2015, http://www.pewresearch.org/fact-tank/2015/11/17/in-nations-with-significant-muslim-populations-much-disdain-for-isis/.

56. Bruce Vaughn, "Malaysia: Political Transition and Implications for US Policy," Congressional Research Service, July 28, 2004, 1, https://apps.dtic.mil/sti/tr/pdf/ADA461674.pdf.

57. Similar efforts of religious diplomacy were noted in Indonesia, albeit it became more prominent later with the Islam Nusantara branding. See James B. Hoesterey, "Indonesian Islam as Model for the World? Diplomacy, Soft Power, and the Geopolitics of

'Moderate Islam,'" in Peter Mandaville ed., *The Geopolitics of Religious Soft Power: How States Use Religion in Foreign Policy* (Oxford University Press, 2023).

58. Joseph Chinyong Liow, *Muslim Resistance in Southern Thailand and Southern Philippines: Religion, Ideology, and Politics*, Policy Studies 24 (East-West Center, 2006); Edward Aspinall, *Islam and Nation: Separatist Rebellion in Aceh, Indonesia* (Stanford University Press, 2009); John T. Sidel, *Riots, Pogroms, and Jihad: Religious Violence in Indonesia* (Cornell University Press, 2006).

59. Nathan J. Brown, *When Victory Is Not an Option: Islamist Movements in Arab Politics* (Cornell University Press, 2012).

60. For example, in Malaysia's most notorious political crackdown in recent history, Operasi Lalang (Operation Weeding) in 1987, most of those arrested were Chinese educationalists and members from the secularist Democratic Action Party, including its leader Lim Kit Siang. On Operasi Lalang, see Julian C. H. Lee, "The Fruits of Weeds: Taking Justice at the Commemoration of the Twentieth Anniversary of Operasi Lalang in Malaysia," *The Round Table 97*, no. 397 (2008): 605–15.

61. For the best resource for PAS, see Farish A. Noor, *The Malaysian Islamic Party PAS 1951–2013: Islamism in a Mottled Nation* (Amsterdam University Press, 2014).

62. Singapore, for example, still retains the ISA as its primary counter-terror legislation.

63. Aiming at addressing "the conditions conducive to the spread of terrorism," P/CVE usually carries the connotation that they are soft, preventive measures that separate them from the hard, kinetic measures. See UN Resolution 2178 (2004). For this book, I see no reason to conceptually separate counter-terror from P/CVE, as the goals are the same. "Hard" and "soft" measures are often interlaced with one another, and it is not entirely clear that P/CVE programs, such as the Prevent Strategy in the UK, were devoid of state coercion and violence. See Fahid Qurashi, "The Prevent Strategy and the UK 'War on Terror': Embedding Infrastructures of Surveillance in Muslim Communities," *Humanities and Social Sciences Communications* 5, no. 1 (2018): 1–13.

64. For examples of such studies, see Kumar Ramakrishna, "The Southeast Asian Approach to Counter-Terrorism: Learning from Indonesia and Malaysia," *The Journal of Conflict Studies* 25, no. 1 (2005): 27–47; Jörg Monar, "Common Threat and Common Response? The European Union's Counter-Terrorism Strategy and Its Problems," *Government and Opposition* 42, no. 3 (2007): 292–313.

65. Alex Schmid, "Terrorism—The Definitional Problem," *Case Western Reserve Journal of International Law* 36, no. 2–3 (2004): 375–420.

66. Limor Samimian-Darash and Meg Stalcup, "Anthropology of Security and Security in Anthropology: Cases of Counterterrorism in the United States," *Anthropological Theory* 17, no. 1 (2017): 71.

67. David Scott, *Conscripts of Modernity: The Tragedy of Colonial Enlightenment* (Duke University Press, 2004). 4.

68. On why interrogating state power at its "diffuse, capillary, or 'mobile' mechanisms" does not necessitate the negation of the concept of the state, see Kimberly J. Morgan and Ann Shola Orloff, "Introduction: The Many Hands of the State," in *The Many Hands of the State: Theorizing Political Authority and Social Control*, ed. Kimberly J. Morgan and Ann Shola Orloff (Cambridge University Press, 2017).

69. Rudra Sil and Peter J. Katzenstein, "Analytic Eclecticism in the Study of World Politics: Reconfiguring Problems and Mechanisms Across Research Traditions," *Perspectives on Politics* 8, no. 2 (2010): 419.

70. Ondřej Ditrych, *Tracing the Discourses of Terrorism: Identity, Genealogy and State* (Palgrave Macmillan, 2014), 1.

71. Anna Holzscheiter, "Between Communicative Interaction and Structures of Signification: Discourse Theory and Analysis in International Relations," *International Studies Perspectives* 15, no. 2 (2014): 144.

72. On critical discourse analysis, see Ruth Wodak and Michael Meyer, "Critical Discourse Analysis: History, Agenda, Theory, and Methodology," in *Methods for Critical Discourse Analysis*, 3rd ed., ed. Ruth Wodak and Michael Meyer (Sage, 2016).

73. On maintaining an ethnographic sensibility in political science, see Edward Schatz, "Introduction: Ethnographic Immersion and the Study of Politics," in *Political Ethnography: What Immersion Contributes to the Study of Power*, ed. Edward Schatz (University of Chicago Press, 2009), 5–10.

74. On the concept of "thick" description, see Clifford Geertz, *The Interpretation of Cultures* (Basic Books, 1973), chap. 1; cf. Jef Huysmans, "Security! What Do You Mean? From Concept to Thick Signifier," *European Journal of International Relations* 4, no. 2 (1998): 226–55.

75. "Plans of Action to Prevent Violent Extremism," UN Counter-Terrorism Centre, https://www.un.org/counterterrorism/cct/plans-of-action-to-prevent-violent-extremism.

76. The only institution I have failed to secure an interview with is the Prisons Department.

77. It is widely known that police surveillance of former detainees of terrorism offenses is practiced in Malaysia. Without obtaining police clearance, establishing contact with these individuals can put them at significant risk. Additionally, during my fieldwork, most of the IS-related detainees were still in detention, and I did not have access to them.

78. For example, the family members of terrorism-offense detainees have set up a group called Desak Sampai Mansuh (Push Until Repeal) that advocates for the repeal of security laws and the release of all detainees. Their social media page serves as a good outlet to obtain family and detainee perspectives, although their subjective position as family activists must be taken into account in the analysis.

79. For perspectives on Malaysia's political transition and the coup that reversed it, see Meredith L. Weiss and Faisal S. Hazis, eds., *Towards a New Malaysia? The 2018*

Election and Its Aftermath (NUS Press, 2020); Chin-Huat Wong, "Parliament as Prime Minister's Electoral College: The Defection Game in Malaysia's Democratic Backsliding," *The Round Table 109*, no. 5 (2020): 586–607.

80. On the Official Secrets Act 1972 and its use in covering up political scandals in Malaysia, see Syahredzan Johan, "Time to Replace Official Secrets Act," *The Star Online*, July 11, 2016, https://www.thestar.com.my/opinion/online-exclusive/a-humble-submission/2016/07/11/time-to-replace-official-secrets-act/.

Chapter 1

1. On discussions of the state as a "condition of being," see Iza Hussin, *The Politics of Islamic Law: Local Elites, Colonial Authority, and the Making of the Muslim State* (University of Chicago Press, 2016), 16.

2. On a multidimensional view of the state that also operates as a "sociocultural phenomenon," see Kimberly J. Morgan and Ann Shola Orloff, "Introduction: The Many Hands of the State," in *The Many Hands of the State: Theorizing Political Authority and Social Control*, ed. Kimberly J. Morgan and Ann Shola Orloff (Cambridge University Press, 2017).

3. Joel S. Migdal, *State in Society: Studying How States and Societies Transform and Constitute One Other* (Cambridge University Press, 2004), 16–23.

4. Migdal, *State in Society*, 16–17.

5. Ayşe Zarakol, "What Makes Terrorism Modern? Terrorism, Legitimacy, and the International System," *Review of International Studies* 37, no. 5 (2011): 2315.

6. Andrew Phillips, *War, Religion and Empire: The Transformation of International Orders* (Cambridge University Press, 2011), 52; Darryl Li, "Jihad in a World of Sovereigns: Law, Violence, and Islam in the Bosnia Crisis," *Law & Social Inquiry* 41, no. 2 (2018): 371–401.

7. See Walter Enders, Todd Sandler, and Khusrav Gaibulloev, "Domestic versus Transnational Terrorism: Data, Decomposition, and Dynamics," *Journal of Peace Research* 48, no. 3 (2011): 319–37; Krisztina Kis-Katos, Helge Liebert, and Günther G. Schulze, "On the Origin of Domestic and International Terrorism," *European Journal of Political Economy* 27, no. 1 (2011): S17–S36.

8. Ondřej Ditrych, *Tracing the Discourses of Terrorism: Identity, Genealogy and State* (Palgrave Macmillan, 2014), 90; cf. Christian Reus-Smit, *The Moral Purpose of the State: Culture, Social Identity, and Institutional Rationality in International Relations* (Princeton University Press, 1999).

9. See China's expansion of infrastructural and biopower into Xinjiang in the name of counter-terrorism in Sheena Chestnut Greitens, Myunghee Lee, and Emir Yazici, "Counterterrorism and Preventive Repression: China's Changing Strategy in Xinjiang," *International Security* 44, no. 3 (2020): 9–47; Sean R. Robert, "The Biopolitics of China's 'War on Terror' and the Exclusion of the Uyghurs," *Critical Asian Studies* 50, no. 2 (2018): 232–58.

10. Li, "Jihad in a World of Sovereigns," 374.

11. On the question of social ontologies in international politics, see Colin Wight, *Agents, Structures and International Relations: Politics as Ontology* (Cambridge University Press, 2006).

12. On the importance of biographical narratives to state identity, see Brent J. Steele, *Ontological Security in International Relations: Self-Identity and the IR State* (Routledge, 2008), 10–12; Jelena Subotić, "Narrative, Ontological Security, and Foreign Policy Change," *Foreign Policy Analysis* 12, no. 4 (2016): 610–27.

13. On the question of states having "emotions" or "moral possibilities" that invoke feelings of shame, see Steele, *Ontological Security*, chap. 2 and 3; Alexander Wendt, "The State as Person in International Theory," *Review of International Studies* 30, no. 2 (2004): 289–316; Ayşe Zarakol, "Ontological (In)security and State Denial of Historical Crimes: Turkey and Japan," *International Relations* 24, no. 1 (2010): 3–23.

14. "Malaysia Tables Two Bills as Preemptive Move Against Terrorism," *Bernama*, April 3, 2015.

15. Malaysia's claim of counter-terror success was also boosted by the now lionized "hearts and minds" campaign against the Communist militants in the 1950s. See Wen-Qing Ngoei, "The 'Lessons' of Britain's Counterinsurgency in Malaya: An American Obsession," *Perspectives on History*, July 2, 2019, https://www.historians.org/perspectives-article/the-lessons-of-britains-counterinsurgency-in-malaya-an-american-obsession-july-2019/. On a critical (re)reading of the hearts and minds paradigm, see Jacqueline L. Hazelton, "The 'Hearts and Minds' Fallacy: Violence, Coercion, and Success in Counterinsurgency Warfare," *International Security* 42, no. 1 (2017): 80–113.

16. Migdal, *State in Society*, 18.

17. Pierre Bourdieu, "Rethinking the State: Genesis and Structure of the Bureaucratic Field," *Sociological Theory* 12, no. 1 (1994): 13.

18. James C. Scott, *Seeing Like a State: How Certain Schemes to Improve the Human Condition Have Failed* (Yale University Press, 1998), 3; cf. Joseph MacKay, *The Counterinsurgent Imagination: A New Intellectual History* (Cambridge University Press, 2023).

19. Thomas Lemke, *Foucault, Governmentality, and Critique* (Routledge, 2016), 29.

20. Sarah Logan, *Hold Your Friends Close: Countering Radicalization in Britain and America* (Oxford University Press, 2023).

21. Lemke, *Foucault, Governmentality, and Critique*, 26–29.

22. Peter. A. Jackson, "The Performative State: Semi-coloniality and the Tyranny of Images in Modern Thailand," *Sojourn: Journal of Social Issues in Southeast Asia* 19, no. 2 (2004): 219–253; Peter. A. Jackson, "The Thai Regime of Images," *Sojourn: Journal of Social Issues in Southeast Asia* 19, no. 2 (2004): 181–218.

23. Jackson, "The Performative State," 237.

24. The critique of hypocrisy is a mainstay in critical terrorism studies. They range from accusations of double standards (on what qualifies as terrorism) to states forgoing their human rights commitments in the name of counter-terror. In the case of Muslim

states, failing to live up to the "moderate Islam" rhetoric espoused by elites is another ground for such critique.

25. Fatemah Alzubairi, *Colonialism, Neo-Colonialism, and Anti-Terrorism Law in the Arab World* (Cambridge University Press, 2019); William Vlcek, "A Leviathan Rejuvenated: Surveillance, Money Laundering, and the War on Terror," *International Journal of Politics, Culture, and Society* 20, no. 1 (2008): 21–40; Leila N. Sadat, "Extraordinary Rendition, Torture, and Other Nightmares from the War on Terror," *George Washington Law Review* 75, no. 5 (2007): 1200–48.

26. Barak Mendelsohn, "Sovereignty Under Attack: The International Society Meets the Al Qaeda Network," *Review of International Studies* 31, no. 1 (2005): 45–68; Farish A. Noor, "How Washington's 'War on Terror' Became Everyone's: Islamophobia and the Impact of September 11 on the Political Terrain of South and Southeast Asia," *Human Architecture: Journal of the Sociology of Self-Knowledge,* 8, no. 1 (2006): 29–50.

27. Alzubairi, *Colonialism*, 25–29.

28. Stefano Bonino, "*Prevent*-ing Muslimness in Britain: The Normalisation of Exceptional Measures to Combat Terrorism," *Journal of Muslim Minority Affairs* 33, no. 3 (2013): 385–400.

29. Darryl Li, *The Universal Enemy: Jihad, Empire, and the Challenge of Solidarity* (Stanford University Press, 2020), 196.

30. Brent J. Steele, "'Ideals That Were Really Never in Our Possession': Torture, Honor and US Identity," *International Relations* 22, no. 2 (2008): 243–61; Jelena Subotić and Brent. J. Steele, "Moral Injury in International Relations," *Journal of Global Security Studies* 3, no. 4 (2018): 387–401.

31. Barry Buzan, "Will the 'Global War on Terrorism' Be the New Cold War?" *International Affairs* 82, no. 6 (2006): 1116.

32. Hans Köchler, "The Global War on Terror and the Metaphysical Enemy," in *The 'Global War on Terror' and the Question of World Order*, ed. Hans Köchler (International Progress Organization, 2008), 18; cf. Pinar Kimerli, "The Islamist Terrorist as the New Universal Enemy: Discourses on Terror at the United Nations," in *The Oxford Handbook of the History of Terrorism*, ed. Carola Dietze and Claudia Verhoeven (Oxford University Press, 2014).

33. Samuel P. Huntington, *The Clash of Civilizations and the Remaking of World Order* (Simon & Schuster, 1996), 254.

34. As Zarakol puts it, "the modern state makes 'progress' its business," see Ayşe Zarakol, *After Defeat: How the East Learned to Live with the West* (Cambridge University Press, 2011), 77.

35. Eva Herschinger, *Constructing Global Enemies: Hegemony and Identity in International Discourses on Terrorism and Drug Prohibition* (Routledge, 2011), 1.

36. Ditrych, *Tracing the Discourses of Terrorism*, 5.

37. Ditrych, *Tracing the Discourses of Terrorism*, 6.

38. Zarakol, "What Makes Terrorism Modern?," 2315.

39. Zarakol, "What Makes Terrorism Modern?," 2316.

40. See, for example, the labeling of anarchist terrorism as the "crime against the whole human race" by Theodore Roosevelt; and as "enemies of the human race" by the *New York Times* in 1905 in R. Jensen, "The United States, International Policing and the War Against Anarchist Terrorism, 1900–1914," *Terrorism and Political Violence* 13, no. 1 (2001): 19; Richard Bach Jensen, *The Battle Against Anarchist Terrorism: An International History, 1878–1934* (Cambridge University Press, 2014), 305n35.

41. Phillip Deery, "The Terminology of Terrorism: Malaya, 1948–52," *Journal of Southeast Asian Studies* 34, no. 2 (2003): 231–47.

42. See, for example, Jensen, *Battle Against Anarchist Terrorism*; Richard Bach Jensen, "The International Campaign Against Anarchist Terrorism, 1880–1930s," *Terrorism and Political Violence* 21, no. 1 (2009): 89–109; Richard Bach Jensen, "The International Anti-Anarchist Conference of 1898 and the Origins of Interpol," *Journal of Contemporary History* 16, no. 2 (1981): 323–47.

43. Jensen, "Anti-Anarchist Conference," 327. Barring the United States, the "whole of Europe" was arguably conceived as the entirety of the "civilized" world considering the conference was hosted during the zenith of European imperialism in the late nineteenth century.

44. Li, *The Universal Enemy*, 196–201.

45. On the franchising of the language of the GWOT, see Pablo A. Rodríguez-Merino, "Old 'Counter-Revolution', New 'Terrorism': Historicizing the Framing of Violence in Xinjiang by the Chinese State," *Central Asian Survey* 38, no. 1 (2019): 30–32.

46. Lisa Stampnitzky, *Disciplining Terror: How Experts Invented "Terrorism"* (Cambridge University Press, 2013), chap. 7.

47. Elizabeth Shakman Hurd, "Islam and Foreign Policy in Europe and the United States," *Foreign Policy Analysis* 3, no. 4 (2007): 345–67; Elizabeth Shakman Hurd, *The Politics of Secularism in International Relations* (Princeton University Press, 2008).

48. On Malaysia's Islamization, see Seyyed Vali Reza Nasr, *Islamic Leviathan: Islam and the Making of State Power* (Oxford University Press, 2001); Shanti Nair, *Islam in Malaysian Foreign Policy* (Routledge, 1997).

49. See for example, US Department of State, "Country Report on Terrorism 2018," October 2019, https://www.state.gov/wp-content/uploads/2019/11/Country-Reports-on-Terrorism-2018-FINAL.pdf.

50. On the use of "lists" as a technology in global governance, see Gavin Sullivan, *The Law of the List: UN Counterterrorism Sanctions and the Politics of Global Security Law* (Cambridge University Press, 2020).

51. See "Pakistan: Friend or Foe in the Fight Against Terrorism?," Joint Hearing Before the Subcommittee on Terrorism, Nonproliferation, and Trade and the Subcommittee on Asia and the Pacific of the Committee On Foreign Affairs, July 12, 2016, https://www.govinfo.gov/content/pkg/CHRG-114hhrg20742/html/CHRG-114hhrg20742.htm. There were also repeated attempts in Congress to hold Saudi

Arabia accountable for its links to terrorism, from the unsuccessful bill called the Saudi Arabia Accountability Act in 2007 to the Justice Against Sponsors of Terrorism Act 2016 that enables families of the September 11 to file lawsuits against the government of Saudi Arabia.

52. Prashanth Parameswaran, "US-Malaysia Counterterrorism Cooperation in the Spotlight with Home Minister Visit," *The Diplomat*, September 21, 2019, https://thediplomat.com/2019/09/us-malaysia-counterterrorism-cooperation-in-the-spotlight-with-home-minister-visit/.

53. "US Visa Ban a 'Price to Pay' for Being Islamic: Mahathir," *Agence France-Presse*, September 17, 2002.

54. Eileen Ng. "Gov't Mounts Media Offensive to Assure Investors of Safe Haven," *Agence France-Presse*, February 6, 2002; Pauline Jasudason, "Malaysia Knocks U.S. Airport Checks," *Associated Press News*, October 2, 2002, https://apnews.com/article/1de241fb699b0879cdb21ab35e0f899d.

55. It is interesting to note that Indonesia, the most populous Muslim country in the world, does not participate in both the IMCTC and the Global Coalition Against Daesh. This is most likely due to the Indonesian state's enduring struggle with Islamist militancy, which began ever since the nation's inception. The protracted and complicated nature of the conflict, with military actors playing both sides for their own political interests, also explains why Islamist violence is generally treated as a domestic issue in Indonesia. In addition, former President Joko Widodo's evoking of the Pancasila state (Indonesia's largely secular nationalist founding principles) to counter the Islamist challenge also meant that the government was unlikely to play up its Islamic identity more than necessary. On Indonesia's experience with jihadism, see John T. Sidel, *Riots, Pogroms, and Jihad: Religious Violence in Indonesia* (Cornell University Press, 2006); Quinton Temby, "Imagining an Islamic State in Indonesia: From Darul Islam to Jemaah Islamiyah," *Indonesia* 89 (2010): 1–36. On the Jokowi's government use of Pancasila as a bulwark against Islamist challenge, see Nithin Coca, "The Return of Pancasila," *New Naratif*, July 2, 2018, https://newnaratif.com/journalism/the-return-of-pancasila/.

56. "About IMCTC," https://web.archive.org/web/20200924104332/https://www.imctc.org/English/About.

57. "Saudi Arabia," at https://theglobalcoalition.org/en/partner/saudi-arabia/. Information on airstrikes now deleted.

58. Tunisia was the largest contributor of foreign fighters to IS, but the internal weakness of its postrevolution state arguably did not afford it the luxury to participate in external military campaigns. The global celebration of its new constitution passed in 2015 as an achievement of "pluralistic democracy," which included a Nobel Peace Prize, probably helped deflect the stigma considerably. See "The Nobel Peace Prize for 2015," https://www.nobelprize.org/prizes/peace/2015/press-release/.

59. Cole Bunzel. *The Kingdom and the Caliphate: Duel of the Islamic States* (Carnegie Endowment for International Peace, 2016).

60. "82 Partners United in Ensuring Daesh's Enduring Defeat," https://theglobalcoalition.org/en/partners/. The IMCTC and the Global Coalition Against Daesh has overlapping members such as Malaysia, Saudi Arabia, Egypt, Jordan, and Türkiye. Oddly enough, Pakistan is a member of the IMCTC but not the Global Coalition, despite being a key ally of the US.

61. Here I echo Phillips's call on the need to acknowledge global jihadism's systemic challenge: "The jihadist assault on the state system evolved out of a sweeping philosophical critique of secular modernity, and the extent of the jihadists' animus towards the supposed materialism and idolatry of the modern world must not be downplayed, lest one lose sight of the movement's uncompromisingly anti-systemic character." See Phillips, *War, Religion and Empire*, 288.

62. Barack Obama, "Statement by the President," August 7, 2014, https://obamawhitehouse.archives.gov/the-press-office/2014/08/07/statement-president. This association with barbarism was most keenly felt when terms associated with meanings of savagery such as "genocide" and "religious cleansing" were pronounced, including by the UN. See "UN Human Rights Panel Concludes ISIL Is Committing Genocide Against Yazidis," June 16, 2016, https://news.un.org/en/story/2016/06/532312.

63. See Nina Shea, "Barbarism 2014: On Religious Cleansing by Islamists," *World Affairs* 177, no. 4 (2014): 34–46.

64. R. D. Laing, *The Divided Self* (Penguin, 1990), 39.

65. Anthony Giddens, *Modernity and Self-Identity: Self and Society in the Late Modern Age* (Polity, 1991), 53.

66. Giddens, *Modernity and Self-Identity*, 54.

67. Giddens, *Modernity and Self-Identity*, 55

68. Giddens, *Modernity and Self-Identity*, 55.

69. Jef Huysmans, "Security! What Do You Mean? From Concept to Thick Signifier," *European Journal of International Relations* 4, no. 2 (1998): 233–34.

70. Jelena Subotić, "Narrative, Ontological Security, and Foreign Policy Change," *Foreign Policy Analysis* 12, no. 4 (2016): 610–27; Caterina Kinnvall, "Globalization and Religious Nationalism: Self, Identity, and the Search for Ontological Security," *Political Psychology* 25, no. 5 (2004): 721–47; Marco Vieira, "(Re-)imagining the 'Self' of Ontological Security: The Case of Brazil's Ambivalent Postcolonial Subjectivity," *Millennium: Journal of International Studies* 46, no. 2 (2018): 142–64.

71. Steele, *Ontological Security*, 71–73.

72. Steele, *Ontological Security*, 20.

73. The idea of state personhood, in that states can be treated conceptually as psychological persons with cognitive and mental attributes of a person in the study of international politics, is advocated in a seminal text by Alexander Wendt. See Wendt, "The State as Person."

74. Zarakol, "Ontological (In)security and State Denial," 3.

75. Steele, *Ontological Security*, 52.

76. Steele, *Ontological Security*, 149.

77. "Most communities in the world exist in a constant state of identity struggle. While it is extremely difficult to live up to the standards of modernity—which, despite its universal language, has undeniable Western origins and therefore carries certain assumptions about proper social and institutional configurations—without feeling inauthentic, it is also almost impossible to be authentically non-Western." Zarakol, *After Defeat*, 5.

78. Zarakol, *After Defeat*; Ayşe Zarakol, "What Made the Modern World Hang Together: Socialisation or Stigmatisation?," *International Theory* 6, no. 2 (2014): 311–32; cf. Erving Goffman, *Stigma: Notes on the Management of Spoiled Identity* (Simon & Schuster, 1963).

79. Zarakol, *After Defeat*, chap. 2.

80. Zarakol, *After Defeat*, 15.

81. Zarakol, *After Defeat*, 6.

82. Zarakol, *After Defeat*, 4.

83. John M. Hobson and J. C. Sharman, "The Enduring Place of Hierarchy in World Politics: Tracing the Social Logics of Hierarchy and Political Change," *European Journal of International Relations* 11, no. 1 (2005): 92.

84. One exception here is Vieira's exploration of the sense of "lack" perceived by Brazil's political elites due to their internalization of the global racial hierarchy, which they later translated into fantasized narratives of the "self" in Brazilian foreign policy aimed at bridging this gap with an imagined Western "other." See Vieira, "Brazil's Ambivalent Postcolonial Subjectivity." Zarakol, who spearheaded the use of the concept in IR, focuses her case studies on Türkiye, Russia, Japan, and Thailand, none of which were actually colonized. See Zarakol, *After Defeat*; Ayşe Zarakol, "Revisiting Second Image Reversed: Lessons from Turkey and Thailand," *International Studies Quarterly* 57, no. 1 (2013): 150–62.

85. Cemil Aydin, *The Politics of Anti-Westernism in Asia: Visions of World Order in Pan-Islamic and Pan-Asian Thought* (Columbia University Press, 2007); Cemil Aydin, *The Idea of the Muslim World: A Global Intellectual History* (Harvard University Press, 2017).

86. On colonialism and the racialization of Muslims, see Aydin, *Idea of the Muslim World*; Edward Said, *Orientalism* (Penguin, 2003); Andrew Delatolla and Joanna Yao, "Racializing Religion: Constructing Colonial Identities in the Syrian Provinces in the Nineteenth Century," *International Studies Review* 21, no. 4 (2019): 640–61.

87. On global Islamophobia, see Faisal Devji, "From Xinjiang to Germany: How Did Islamophobia Become a Global Phenomenon?," *The Guardian*, March 27, 2020, https://www.theguardian.com/commentisfree/2020/mar/27/xinjiang-germany-islamophobia-global-phenomenon.

88. Mohamad Abu Bakar, "Without Lenin and Locke: The Impacts of Islamic Resurgent on International Politics," *TAFHIM: IKIM Journal of Islam and the Contemporary World* 1, no. 4 (2015): 57.

89. US Department of State, "Struggle of Ideas in the Islamic World," *Country Reports on Terrorism 2007*, April 30, 2008, https://2009-2017.state.gov/j/ct/rls/crt/2007/104114.htm.

90. Ahmet T. Kuru, *Islam, Authoritarianism, and Underdevelopment: A Global and Historical Comparison* (Cambridge University Press, 2019). Please note that I am not disputing Kuru's thesis on state-ulama alliance here, which is convincing, but rather making an observation on the ease with which the Muslim world can be treated as a bloc fitted for unitary explanations, just like many accounts about the "West."

91. Peter Mandaville, *Transnational Muslim Politics: Reimagining the Ummah* (Routledge, 2001); Olivier Roy, *Globalized Islam: The Search for a New Ummah* (Columbia University Press, 2004); Reza Pankhurst, *The Inevitable Caliphate? A History of the Struggle for Global Islamic Union, 1924 to the Present* (Oxford University Press, 2013); Mona Hassan, *Longing for the Lost Caliphate: A Transregional History* (Princeton University Press, 2016).

92. Guy Martin, *African Political Thought* (Palgrave Macmillan, 2012), chap. 4; Valeria Sinclair-Chapman and Melanye Price, "Black Politics, the 2008 Election, and the (Im)Possibility of Race Transcendence," *PS: Political Science & Politics* 41, no. 4 (2008): 739–45; Andra Gillespie, ed., *Whose Black Politics? Cases in Post-Racial Black Leadership* (Routledge, 2010). To be sure, I am not dismissing the histories and struggles of Black internationalist "worldmaking," but rather pointing out how the enterprise has largely settled within a national or continental form. On Pan-Africanism as internationalist politics, see Adom Getachew, *Worldmaking After Empire: The Rise and Fall of Self-Determination* (Princeton University Press, 2019); Robbie Shilliam, *The Black Pacific: Anti-Colonial Struggles and Oceanic Connections* (Bloomsbury Academic, 2015).

93. Aydin, *Idea of the Muslim World*, 5.

94. Said, *Orientalism*, 83.

95. Elizabeth Shakman Hurd, "Appropriating Islam: The Islamic Other in the Consolidation of Western Modernity," *Critique: Critical Middle Eastern Studies* 12, no. 1 (2003): 40.

96. These political expressions of pan-Islam, however, tend to be confined to local political aspirations. See Anthony Reid, "Nineteenth Century Pan-Islam in Indonesia and Malaysia," *The Journal of Asian Studies* 26, no. 2 (1967): 267–83; Chiara Formichi, "Pan-Islam and Religious Nationalism: The Case of Kartosuwiryo and Negara Islam Indonesia," *Indonesia* 90 (2010): 125–46.

97. Zarakol, *After Defeat*, 146–48.

98. Norshahril Saat, *The State, Ulama and Islam in Malaysia and Indonesia* (ISEAS Yusof Ishak Institute, 2018), 117–20; Hania Sobhy, "Secular Façade, Neoliberal

Islamisation: Textbook Nationalism from Mubarak to Sisi," *Nations and Nationalism* 21, no. 4 (2015): 805–24.

99. Joseph Chinyong Liow, *Piety and Politics: Islamism in Contemporary Malaysia* (Oxford University Press, 2009); Gregory Starrett, *Putting Islam to Work: Education, Politics, and Religious Transformation in Egypt* (University of California Press, 1998).

100. The idea that statehood is always "in the making" is not new. See Julia Gallagher, *Zimbabwe's International Relations: Fantasy, Reality and the Making of the State* (Cambridge University Press, 2017).

101. Roy, *Globalized Islam*; Salwa Ismail, *Rethinking Islamist Politics: Culture, the State, and Islamism* (I. B. Tauris, 2006).

102. On state-driven Islamization, see Nasr, *Islamic Leviathan*; Maznah Mohamad, *The Divine Bureaucracy and Disenchantment of Social Life: A Study of Bureaucratic Islam in Malaysia* (Palgrave Macmillan, 2020); Ahyan Kaya, "Islamisation of Turkey under the AKP Rule: Empowering Family, Faith and Charity," *South European Society and Politics* 20, no. 1 (2015): 47–69.

103. Imran Said, "Malaysia's Struggle to Preserve Religious Pluralism," *Quillette*, January 6, 2019, https://quillette.com/2019/01/06/malaysias-struggle-to-preserve-religious-pluralism/.

104. Nair, *Islam in Malaysian Foreign Policy*, 55; cf. David Delfolie, "Malaysian Extraversion Towards the Muslim World: Ideological Positioning for a 'Mirror Effect,'" *Journal of Current Southeast Asian Affairs* 31, no. 4 (2012): 3–29.

105. Rebecca Adler-Nissen, "Stigma Management in International Relations: Transgressive Identities, Norms, and Order in International Society," *International Organization* 68, no. 1 (2014): 143–76.

106. Adler-Nissen, "Stigma Management," 168.

107. On Mahathir as a Third World iconoclast, see Johan Saravanamuttu, "Malaysia's Foreign Policy in the Mahathir Period, 1981–1995: An Iconoclast Come to Rule," *Asian Journal of Political Science* 4, no. 1 (1996): 1–16.

108. Wen-Qing Ngoei, *Arc of Containment: Britain, the United States, and Anticommunism in Southeast Asia* (Cornell University Press, 2019); Francis Kok-Wah Loh, "Malaysia After Mahathir: Late Democratization Amidst Development, the Strong Developmental State, and Developmentalism," in *Democracy or Alternative Political Systems in Asia: After the Strongmen*, ed. Hsin-Huang Michael Hsiao (Routledge, 2013).

109. Adler-Nissen, "Stigma Management,"153.

110. Michael G. Peletz, *Islamic Modern: Religious Courts and Cultural Politics in Malaysia* (Princeton University Press, 2002), 277.

111. On Malaysia's "Islamic modernities," see Peletz, *Islamic Modern*; Patricia Sloanne-White, *Corporate Islam: Sharia and the Modern Workplace* (Cambridge University Press, 2017); Wai Weng Hew, "Islamic Ways of Modern Living: Middle-Class Muslim Aspirations and Gated Communities in Peri-Urban Jakarta," in *Jakarta:*

Claiming Spaces and Rights in the City, ed. Jörgen Hellman, Marie Thynell, and Roanne van Voorst (Routledge, 2018).

112. Zarakol, *After Defeat*, 192.

113. Oxford English Dictionary (Online Edition), "Moderate," https://www.oed.com/view/Entry/120601?rskey=Cjo3ZQ&result=2&isAdvanced=false#eid.

114. See examples of the use of these labels in Amy L. Freedman, "Civil Society, Moderate Islam, and Politics in Indonesia and Malaysia," *Journal of Civil Society* 5, no. 2 (2009): 107–27; Dilshod Achilov and Sedat Sen, "Got Political Islam? Are Politically Moderate Muslims Really Different from Radicals?" *International Political Science Review* 38, no. 5 (2017): 608–24; Robert W. Hefner and Patricia Horvatich, eds., *Islam in an Era of Nation-States: Politics and Religious Renewal in Muslim Southeast Asia* (University of Hawai'i Press, 1997).

115. Mohammad Hashim Kamali, *The Middle Path of Moderation in Islam: The Qur'ānic Principle of Wasaṭiyyah* (Oxford University Press, 2015), 1.

116. Rosemary R. Hicks, "Comparative Religion and the Cold War Transformation of Indo-Persian 'Mysticism' into Liberal Islamic Modernity," in *Secularism and Religion-Making*, ed. Markus Dressler and Arvind Mandair (Oxford University Press, 2011).

117. Mark Woodward, Muhammad Sani Umar, Inayah Rohmaniyah, and Mariani Yahya, "Salafi Violence and Sufi Tolerance? Rethinking Conventional Wisdom," *Perspectives on Terrorism* 7, no. 6 (2013): 58–78.

118. Tobias Müller, "Engaging 'Moderates' Against 'Extremists' in German Politics on Islam," *The Review of Faith & International Affairs* 15, no. 2 (2017): 62. On racialization of Muslims in P/CVE policies, see Martijn de Koning, "'You Need to Present a Counter-Message': The Racialisation of Dutch Muslims and Anti-Islamophobia Initiatives," *Journal of Muslims in Europe* 5, no. 2 (2016): 170–89.

119. Annelle Sheline, "Middle East Regimes Are Using 'Moderate' Islam to Stay in Power," *The Washington Post*, March 1, 2017, https://www.washingtonpost.com/news/monkey-cage/wp/2017/03/01/middle-east-regimes-are-using-moderate-islam-to-stay-in-power/?utm_term=.56c8169408c5.

120. Annelle R. Sheline, "Shifting Reputations for 'Moderation': Evidence from Qatar, Jordan, and Morocco," *Middle East Law and Governance*, 12 (2020): 129.

121. On Islam as soft power, see Peter Mandaville and Shadi Hamid, *Islam as Statecraft: How Governments Use Religion in Foreign Policy* (Brookings Institution, 2018).

122. Zarakol, *After Defeat*, 10.

123. I am not disputing the fact that cultural specificities can be found in sociopolitical expressions of both democracy and Islam. Rather, my point is to highlight how these two signifiers of universalism are treated differently in contemporary political discourses. Democracy is usually invoked without any references to cultural specificities, while Islam is only treated as a public good in Anglo-European discourses if there is a value-added component such as being "moderate" or "Sufi." On the Eurocentrism of

democracy and its cognates, see Dipesh Chakrabarty, *Provincializing Europe: Postcolonial Thought and Historical Difference* (Princeton University Press, 2000).

124. Ann Marie Wainscott, *Bureaucratizing Islam: Morocco and the War on Terror* (Cambridge University Press, 2017); Stacey Gutkowski, "We Are the Very Model of a Moderate Muslim State: The Amman Messages and Jordan's Foreign Policy," *International Relations* 30, no. 2 (2016): 206–26; James B. Hoesterey, "Islamic Soft Power in the Age of Trump: Public Diplomacy and Indonesian Mosque Communities in America," *Islam and Christian–Muslim Relations* 31, no. 2 (2020): 191–214.

125. Wainscott, *Bureaucratizing Islam*; Sheline, "Shifting Reputations"; Stella Athanasoulia, "From 'Soft' to 'Hard' to 'Moderate': Islam in the Dilemmas of Post-2011 Saudi Foreign Policy," *Religions* 11, no. 4 (2020): 211, https://doi.org/10.3390/rel11040211.

126. Iza Hussin, "Translating Public Order: Colonial, Transnational, and International Genealogies," *Political Geography* 75 (2019): 9.

127. Eqbal Ahmad, "Revolutionary War and Counter-Insurgency," *Journal of International Affairs* 25, no. 1 (1971): 8.

128. Claudia Aradau and Rens van Munster, "Governing Terrorism Through Risk: Taking Precautions, (un)Knowing the Future," *European Journal of International Relations* 13, no. 1 (2007): 90.

129. Migdal, *State in Society*; Katrina Riddell, *Islam and the Securitisation of Population Policies: Muslim States and Sustainability* (Ashgate, 2009).

130. Oded Löwenheim, *Predators and Parasites: Persistent Agents of Transnational Harm and Great Power Authority* (University of Michigan Press, 2007), 219.

131. Mark Bevir, *A Theory of Governance* (University of California Press, 2013), 1.

132. "Governance is a cultural practice because it is meaningful activity. It is a historical practice because this activity is contingent" (Bevir, *A Theory of Governance*, 156).

133. For a meditation on the methodology of reading paperwork, see Nick Cheesman, "Reading Paperwork Realistically," *Politics, Groups, and Identities* 9, no. 4 (2021): 835–40.

134. Bevir, *Theory of Governance*, 37.

135. On the politics of memory and trauma, see, for example, Duncan Bell, ed., *Memory, Trauma and World Politics: Reflections on the Relationship Between Past and Present* (Palgrave Macmillan, 2006).

136. Jim Marlow, "Governmentality, Ontological Security and Ideational Stability: Preliminary Observations on the Manner, Ritual and Logic of a Particular Art of Government," *Journal of Political Ideologies* 7, no. 2 (2002): 256.

137. Ayşe Zarakol, "States and Ontological Security: A Historical Rethinking," *Cooperation and Conflict* 52, no. 1 (2017): 61.

138. Zarakol, "States and Ontological Security," 58.

139. Barry Buzan, Ole Wæver, and Jaap de Wilde, *Security: A New Framework for Analysis* (Lynee Rienner, 1998), 24; Luca Mavelli, "Between Normalisation and

Exception: The Securitisation of Islam and the Construction of the Secular Subject," *Millennium: Journal of International Studies* 41, no. 2 (2013): 164.

140. Aradau and van Munster, "Governing Terrorism," 97.

141. Jef Huysmans, "What's in an Act? On Security Speech Acts and Little Security Nothings," *Security Dialogue* 42, no. 4–5 (2011): 375.

142. Huysmans, "What's in An Act?," 377–79.

143. For examples of accounts that presume that states exercise hegemony over meaning in the 9/11 context, see Jennifer Mustapha, *Writing Southeast Asian Security: Regional Security and the War on Terror After 9/11* (Routledge, 2019); Ronald R. Krebs and Jennifer K. Lobasz, "Fixing the Meaning of 9/11: Hegemony, Coercion, and the Road to War in Iraq," *Security Studies* 16, no. 3 (2007): 409–51.

144. Zygmunt Bauman, *Modernity and Ambivalence* (Polity, 1991), 64.

145. Bauman, *Modernity and Ambivalence*, 63. Emphasis mine.

146. Bauman, *Modernity and Ambivalence*, 65.

147. Huysmans, "Security!," 241.

148. Zarakol, "What Makes Terrorism Modern," 2315.

149. Nicholas Chan, "In Moderation of 'Strangers': Terrorism, Ontological (In)Security and Counter-Narratives in Malaysia," *Critical Studies on Security* 8, no. 1 (2020): 33.

150. Bauman, *Modernity and Ambivalence*, 69–70.

151. ML deRaismes Combes, "Encountering the Stranger: Ontological Security and the Boston Marathon Bombing," *Cooperation and Conflict* 52, no. 1 (2017): 127.

152. On the "othering" of Muslims, see Denise Maia Carter, "(De)constructing Difference: A Qualitative Review of the 'Othering' of UK Muslim Communities, Extremism, Soft Harms, and Twitter Analytics," *Behavioral Sciences of Terrorism and Political Aggression* 9, no. 1 (2017): 21–36; Derek M. D. Silva, "The Othering of Muslims: Discourses of Radicalization in the *New York Times*, 1969–2014," *Sociological Forum* 32, no. 1 (2017): 138–161.

153. Most of those arrested for involvement in Muslim militancy in Malaysia are, though not exclusively, Malays, due to the Malays being the majority Muslim population in the country. This ethnoreligious conflation reflects Malaysia's contentious ethnic politics, where a colonial-era constitutional definition of Malays as necessarily Muslims, and that being Malay comes with special privileges, obscures the interethnic diversity within the Malaysian Muslim landscape. Further discussion of Malaysia's ethnoreligious identity politics will follow in later chapters.

154. Amira Jadoon, Nakissa Jahanbani, Elina Noor, Marley Carroll, and William Frangia, *Risks, Recruits, and Plots: Understanding and Mitigating the Influence of the Islamic State in Malaysia* (Combatting Terrorism Center, US Military Academy, 2022), 23.

155. On the historical background of Muslim militancy in Southeast Asia, see Joseph Chinyong Liow, "Muslim Resistance in Southern Thailand and Southern Philippines: Religion, Ideology, and Politics," *Policy Studies* 24 (East-West Center, 2006).

156. Bauman, *Modernity and Ambivalence*, 27. cf. Amir Weiner, "Introduction: Landscaping the Human Garden," in *Landscaping the Human Garden: 20th Century Population Management in a Comparative Framework*, ed. Amir Weiner (Stanford University Press, 2003).

157. For example, the Singaporean statesman Lee Kuan Yew is known for his eugenicist's concern of Singapore's gene pool, as seen in this quote: "If you don't include your women graduates in your breeding pool and leave them on the shelf, you would end up a more stupid society. . . . So what happens? There will be less bright people to support dumb people in the next generation. That's a problem." See "Policies for the Bedroom and Beyond," *Today Online*, March 23, 2015, https://www.todayonline.com/rememberinglky/policies-bedroom-and-beyond. His plans sought to increase "fertility for university-educated women and [had] provided major subsidies for the voluntary sterilization of poor and uneducated parents." J. John Palen, "Fertility and Eugenics: Singapore's Population Policies," *Population Research and Policy Review* 5 (1986): 3.

158. Saudi Arabia is a prime example of such "openness." On the case studies it generated, see Christopher Boucek, "Saudi Arabia's 'Soft' Counterterrorism Strategy: Prevention, Rehabilitation, and Aftercare," *Carnegie Papers* no. 97 (Carnegie Endowment for International Peace, 2008); Christopher Boucek, "Counter-Terrorism from Within: Assessing Saudi Arabia's Religious Rehabilitation and Disengagement Programme," *The RUSI Journal* 153, no. 6 (2008): 60–65. For a King's College London study that covers eight Muslim states, including Malaysia and Saudi Arabia, see Hamed El-Said, *De-Radicalising Islamists: Programmes and Their Impact in Muslim Majority States* (ICSR, King's College London, 2012).

159. By *governmentality*, I refer to the "systematic and regulated practices of government" that also "points to elements of calculation or to a rational knowledge of the entities to be governed." See Lemke, *Foucault, Governmentality, and Critique*, 18; cf. Michel Foucault, *Security, Territory, Population: Lectures at the Collège de France, 1977–78*, trans. Graham Burchell (Palgrave Macmillan, 2007); Mitchell Dean, *Governmentality: Power and Rule in Modern Society* (Sage, 2008).

160. Michel Foucault, *Society Must Be Defended: Lectures at the Collège de France, 1975–76*, trans. David Macey (Picador, 2003), 252.

161. Foucault, *Security, Territory, Population*; Colin Gordon, "Governmental Rationality: An Introduction," in *The Foucault Effect: Studies in Governmentality*, ed. Graham Burchell, Colin Gordon, and Peter Miller (University of Chicago Press, 1991); Michel Foucault, "Truth and Power," in *The Foucault Reader*, ed. Paul Rabinow (Pantheon Books, 1984).

162. See examples of these studies in Edward J. Lemon, "Building Resilient Secular Citizens: Tajikistan's Response to the Islamic State," *Caucasus Survey* 4, no. 3 (2016): 261–81; Edward Lemon and Hélène Thibault, "Counter-Extremism, Power, and Authoritarian Governance in Tajikistan," *Central Asian Survey* 37, no. 1 (2017): 137–59.

163. Sullivan, *The Law of the List*, 17. cf. Aihwa Ong and Stephen J. Collier, eds., *Global Assemblages: Technology, Politics, and Ethics as Anthropological Problems* (Blackwell, 2005); Saskia Sassen, *Territory, Authority, Rights: From Medieval to Global Assemblages* (Princeton University Press, 2006).

164. Limor Samimian-Darash and Meg Stalcup, "Anthropology of Security and Security in Anthropology: Cases of Counterterrorism in the United States," *Anthropological Theory* 17, no. 1 (2017): 61.

165. I use the term *preemptive* instead of *punitive* because, while Malaysia has thus far suffered one IS-related attack, close to five hundred arrests (as of 2021) have been made on individuals suspected to have committed a terrorism crime. Thus, preemption better encapsulates the modus operandi here.

166. Mara Loveman, "The Modern State and Primitive Accumulation of Symbolic Power," *American Journal of Sociology* 110, no. 6 (2005): 1651–83.

167. Wainscott, *Bureaucratizing Islam*; Sarah J. Feuer, *Regulating Islam: Religion and the State in Contemporary Morocco and Tunisia* (Cambridge University Press, 2018); Thomas Hegghammer, *Jihad in Saudi Arabia: Violence and Pan-Islamism since 1979* (Cambridge University Press, 2010).

168. Markus Dressler and Arvind Mandair, "Introduction: Modernity, Religion-Making, and the Postsecular," in *Secularism and Religion-Making*, ed. Markus Dressler and Arvind Mandair (Oxford University Press, 2011), 19.

169. Lemke, *Foucault, Governmentality, and Critique*, 13.

170. On pastoral power, see Mark Bevir, "Foucault, Power, Institutions," *Political Studies* 47 (1999): 345–59.

Chapter 2

1. Julia Stephens, *Governing Islam: Law, Empire, and Secularism in South Asia* (Cambridge University Press, 2018); Thomas David DuBois, "Hegemony, Imperialism, and the Construction of Religion in East and Southeast Asia," *History and Theory* 44, no. 4 (2005): 113–31.

2. Talal Asad, *Genealogies of Religion: Discipline and Reasons of Power in Christianity and Islam* (Johns Hopkins University Press, 2009).

3. Markus Dressler and Arvind-Pal S. Mandair, "Introduction: Modernity, Religion-Making, and the Postsecular," in *Secularism and Religion-Making*, ed. Markus Dressler and Arvind-Pal S. Mandair (Oxford University Press, 2011); Jeremy Menchik, "The Constructivist Approach to Religion and World Politics," *Comparative Politics* 49, no. 4 (2017): 561–81; Tomoko Masuzawa, *The Invention of World Religions: Or, How European Universalism Was Preserved in the Language of Pluralism* (University of Chicago Press, 2005); Elizabeth Shakman Hurd, "The Political Authority of Secularism in International Relations," *European Journal of International Relations* 10, no. 2 (2016): 235–62.

4. See Muhammad Luttfi Abdul Khalid, "IPeguam Dukung Aspirasi Tun Ahmad Fairuz untuk Daulatkan Islam" [IPeguam maintain the aspiration of Tun Ahmad

Fairuz to strengthen Islam], *Ismawebnet*, April 3, 2017, https://ismawebnet.wordpress.com/2017/04/03/ipeguam-dukung-aspirasi-tun-ahmad-fairuz-daulatkan-islam/; Moustapha Abbas, "Bukti Islam Terjulang di Bumi Pahang Sejak Ratusan Tahun Yang Lalu" [Islam was erected in the face of Pahang since hundreds of years ago], *The Patriots*, October 24, 2019, https://www.thepatriots.asia/bukti-islam-terjulang-di-bumi-pahang-sejak-ratusan-tahun-yang-lalu/.

5. Chiara Formichi, *Islam and Asia: A History* (Cambridge University Press, 2020), chap. 1–3; Leonard Andaya, *Leaves of the Same Tree: Trade and Ethnicity in the Straits of Melaka* (University of Hawai'i Press, 2008); Leonard Andaya, "Kingship-Adat Rivalry and the Role of Islam in South Sulawesi," *Journal of Southeast Asian Studies* 15, no. 1 (1984): 22–42.

6. Ahmad Fauzi Abdul Hamid, "The Impact of Sufism on Muslims in Pre-colonial Malaysia: An Overview of Interpretations," *Islamic Studies* 41, no. 3 (2002): 467–93; Farish A. Noor, "From Majapahit to Putrajaya: The Kris as a Symptom of Civilizational Development and Decline," *South East Asia Research* 8, no. 3 (2000): 239–79; Barbara Watson Andaya and Leonard Y. Andaya, *A History of Malaysia* (Palgrave Macmillan, 2017), 56–61.

7. Iza Hussin, *The Politics of Islamic Law: Local Elites, Colonial Authority, and the Making of the Muslim State* (University of Chicago Press, 2016), 53.

8. Abdul Hamid, "The Impact of Sufism," 485.

9. Carolina López C., "The British Presence in the Malay World: A Meeting of Civilizational Traditions," *SARI*, 19: 11; Andaya and Andaya, *History of Malaysia*, 27.

10. Noor, "From Majapahit to Putrajaya," 252–53; Khairudin Aljunied, *Islam in Malaysia: An Entangled History* (Oxford University Press, 2019), 134; cf. A. C. Milner, "Islam and Malay Kingship," *The Journal of the Royal Asiatic Society of Great Britain and Ireland* 1 (1981): 46–70.

11. Noor, "From Majapahit to Putrajaya," 245n14; Anthony Milner, *The Invention of Politics in Colonial Malaya* (Cambridge University Press, 2002), 103.

12. Milner, *Invention of Politics*, 148.

13. Noor, "From Majapahit to Putrajaya," 246n15.

14. James C. Scott, *The Art of Not Being Governed: An Anarchist History of Upland Southeast Asia* (Yale University Press, 2009), 4.

15. On how modern states are ontologically difference from premodern ones, see Ayşe Zarakol, "States and Ontological Security: A Historical Rethinking," *Cooperation and Conflict* 52, no. 1 (2017): 58–61. Giddens's discussion of the modern state as "reflexively monitored systems which ... follow coordinated policies and plans on a geopolitical scale" and that its *modern* nature lies in how it operates based on "regularised control of social relations across indefinite time-space distances" serves as a good contrast from its premodern forms. See Anthony Giddens, *Modernity and Self-Identity: Self and Society in the Late Modern Age* (Polity, 1991), 15–16.

16. T. N. Harper, *The End of Empire and the Making of Malaya* (Cambridge University Press, 1999); Jomo Kwame Sundaram, *A Question of Class: Capital, the State, and Uneven Development in Malaya* (Oxford University Press, 1986).

17. Hussin, *The Politics of Islamic Law*, 16. On the colonial "science" of census taking and communal zoning, see Charles Hirschman, "The Making of Race in Colonial Malaya: Political Economy and Racial Ideology," *Sociological Forum* 1, no. 2 (1986): 330–61; Ellen C. Cangi, "Civilizing the People of Southeast Asia: Sir Stamford Raffles' Town Plan for Singapore 1819–23," *Planning Perspectives* 8, no. 2 (1993): 166–87.

18. Donna J. Amoroso, *Traditionalism and the Ascendancy of the Malay Ruling Class in Colonial Malaya* (NUS Press and SIRD, 2014), 51.

19. Farish A. Noor, *Data-Gathering in Colonial Southeast Asia 1800–1900: Framing the Other* (Amsterdam University Press, 2019), 207.

20. Iza Hussin, "The Pursuit of the Perak Regalia: Islam, Law, and the Politics of Authority in the Colonial State," *Law & Social Inquiry* 32, no. 3 (2007): 759–88.

21. Mary P. Callahan, "State Formation in the Shadow of the Raj: Violence, Warfare, and Politics in Colonial Burma," *Southeast Asian Studies* 39, no. 4 (2002): 513–36.

22. Amoroso, *Traditionalism*, 66.

23. Amoroso, *Traditionalism*, 52–53, 95. This patrimonial attitude to curate and conserve on behalf the "natives" can be found even with the early operatives of the British East India Company, such as Stamford Raffles. In his book *The History of Java* (1817), Raffles regarded the Javanese as "a once-great civilisation that eventually fell to ruin, but was a great civilisation nonetheless, and one which deserved to be *rescued* by the British." See Farish A. Noor, *The Discursive Construction of Southeast Asia in 19th Century Colonial-Capitalist Discourse* (Amsterdam University Press, 2016), 78.

24. Stephens, *Governing Islam*, 16.

25. Hussin, *The Politics of Islamic Law*, 26; Robert Hefner, *Civil Islam: Muslims and Democratization in Indonesia* (Princeton University Press, 2000), 31–34.

26. Hussin, *The Politics of Islamic Law*, 236.

27. Tamir Moustafa, *Constituting Religion: Islam, Liberal Rights, and the Malaysian State* (Cambridge University Press, 2018); Ahmad Fauzi Abdul Hamid, "Shariaization of Malay-Muslim Identity in Contemporary Malaysia," *JMBRAS* 91, no. 2 (2018): 49–78; Maznah Mohamad, "Making Majority, Undoing Family: Law, Religion and the Islamization of the State in Malaysia," *Economy and Society* 39, no. 3 (2010): 360–84.

28. Hussin, *The Politics of Islamic Law*, 30–35.

29. Hussin, *The Politics of Islamic Law*, 89.

30. Moshe Yegar, *Islam and Islamic Institutions in British Malaya: Policies and Implementation* (Magnes, 1979); Yuki Shiozaki, "The Historical Origins of Control over Deviant Groups in Malaysia: Official Fatwá and Regulation of Interpretation," *Studia Islamika* 22, no. 2 (2015): 205–32; Maznah Mohamad, *The Divine Bureaucracy and Disenchantment of Social Life: A Study of Bureaucratic Islam in Malaysia* (Palgrave Macmillan, 2020), 33–46.

31. During British colonialism, the population of Malaya expanded significantly through an almost laissez-faire immigration policy to support the burgeoning mineral and tin industry and later cash-crop economy. Many of these immigrants came from the southern provinces of China and the Indian subcontinent due to political instability and economic pressures in those regions. See Harper, *The End of Empire*, 24; Sundaram, *Question of Class*, chap. 6–7.

32. Milner, *Invention of Politics*, 137–92.

33. Julia Stephens, "The Phantom Wahhabi: Liberalism and the Muslim Fanatic in Mid-Victorian India," *Modern Asian Studies* 47, no. 1 (2013): 22–52.

34. Khairudin Aljunied, *Radicals: Resistance and Protest in Colonial Malaya* (Northern Illinois University Press, 2015), 27.

35. Harper, *The End of Empire*, 21. Nevertheless, there were competing accounts about the role of religion in these conflicts. For example, Cheah and Abdul Hamid downplay religion as a motivating factor in the Kelantan uprising. Gopinath opines that religion explains the mobilizing success of the Pahang rebellion. See Cheah Boon Kheng, *To' Janggut: Legends, Histories, and Perceptions of the 1915 Rebellion in Kelantan* (NUS Press, 2006); Ahmad Fauzi Abdul Hamid, "Malay Anti-Colonialism in British Malaya: A Re-appraisal of Independence Fighters of Peninsular Malaysia," *Journal of Asian and African Studies* 42, no. 5 (2007): 375; Ananda Gopinath, *Pahang 1880–1933: A Political History* (Malaysian Branch of the Royal Asiatic Society, 1991), 133–70.

36. On Burhanuddin's multifaceted political trajectory, see Farish A. Noor, *The Malaysian Islamic Party 1951–2013: Islamism in a Mottled Nation* (Amsterdam University Press, 2014), chap. 1.

37. The definitive account of the dispute belongs to William Roff's study of the *kaum tua* (old faction) versus *kaum* muda (young faction) contest, whereby ulamas linked to the ruling class clashed, mainly in polemics, with a group of young, urban-centric, cosmopolitan Muslim intellectuals who capitalized on the print media to spread their Islamist reformist ideas. See William R. Roff, *The Origins of Malay Nationalism* (University of Malaya Press, 1967), 56–90; William R. Roff, "Kaum Muda–Kaum Tua: Innovation and Reaction Amongst the Malays, 1900–41," in *Readings on Islam in Southeast Asia*, ed. Ahmad Ibrahim, Sharon Siddique, and Yasmin Hussain (ISEAS, 1985), 123–29.

38. Milner, *Invention of Politics*, 145.

39. Roff, *Malay Nationalism*, 79; Milner, *Invention of Politics*, chap. 6 and 7.

40. Anthony Reid, "Nineteenth Century Pan-Islam in Indonesia and Malaysia," *The Journal of Asian Studies* 26, no. 2 (1967): 267–83; Cemil Aydin, *The Politics of Anti-Westernism in Asia: Visions of World Order in Pan-Islamic and Pan-Asian Thought* (Columbia University Press, 2007); Cemil Aydin, *The Idea of a Muslim World: A Global Intellectual History* (Harvard University Press, 2017).

41. Muhamad Ali, *Islam and Colonialism: Becoming Modern in Indonesia and Malaya* (Edinburgh University Press, 2016), 10.

42. Milner, *Invention of Politics*, 183–87.

43. Milner, *Invention of Politics*, 184.

44. Abdul Hamid, "Malay Anti-Colonialism," 392. Aljunied and Roff made similar observations about the limited reach of *kaum muda*'s intellectual project. See Aljunied, *Radicals*; Roff, "Kaum Muda–Kaum Tua."

45. Firdaus Abdullah, *Radical Malay Politics: Its Origins and Early Development* (Pelanduk, 1985), 30.

46. On UMNO's and, by extension, Malay dominance in Malaysian politics, see Chin-Huat Wong, James Chin, and Norani Othman, "Malaysia—Towards a Topology of an Electoral One-Party State," *Democratization* 17, no. 5 (2010): 920–49; William Case, "UMNO Paramountcy: A Report on Single-Party Dominance in Malaysia," *Party Politics* 2, no. 1 (1996): 115–27.

47. In 1963, the Federation of Malaya's eleven states in Peninsular Malaya were combined with Sabah, Sarawak, and Singapore to form the federation of Malaysia. Singapore left the federation in 1965. As this section covers both the Malayan (1957–1963) and Malaysian (1963–onward) period, the term "Malaysia" will be used for consistency.

48. Benedict Anderson, *Imagined Communities: Reflections on the Origin and Spread of Nationalism* (Verso, 2006), 22–26. Benedict Anderson, "The Nation and the Origin of National Consciousness," in *The Ethnicity Reader: Nationalism, Multiculturalism and Migration*, ed. Montserrat Guibernau and John Rex (Polity, 2010), 56.

49. Anderson, *Imagined Communities*, 37.

50. John Kelly, "Time and the Global: Against the Homogeneous, Empty Communities in Contemporary Social Theory," *Development and Change* 29, no. 4 (1998): 866.

51. Kelly, "Time and the Global," 867.

52. Naeem Inayatullah and David L. Blaney, *International Relations and the Problem of Difference* (Routledge, 2004), chap. 2 and 3.

53. Ayşe Zarakol, *After Defeat: How the East Learned to Live with the West* (Cambridge University Press, 2011), 41.

54. Zarakol, *After Defeat*, 91.

55. J. P. Nettl and Roland Robertson, "Industrialization, Development or Modernization," *The British Journal of Sociology* 17, no. 3 (1966): 274–91.

56. Vieira writes that this desire for non-Western authenticity is doomed to disappoint those who pursue it: "These processes of postcolonial self-identification are necessary fantasies that work to psychologically ameliorate the anxiety generated by the subject's permanent desire to fill up with meaning their existential lack, generated by their stigmatised position in the system of Western (post-)coloniality. For Lacan the fulfilment of a whole and authentic 'self' is always a desired, albeit impossible, project." See Marco Vieira, "The Decolonial Subject and the Problem of Non-Western Authenticity," *Postcolonial Studies* 22, no. 2 (2019): 158.

57. Adom Getachew, *Worldmaking After Empire: The Rise and Fall of Self-Determination* (Princeton University Press, 2019), 4–5.

58. Brent J. Steele, *Ontological Security in International Relations: Self-Identity and the IR State* (Routledge, 2008), 19.

59. On the development of Malaysia's consociational model, see William Case, *Elites and Regimes in Malaysia: Revisiting a Consociational Democracy in Malaysia* (Monash Asia Institute, 1996), chap. 2.

60. On Malaysia's first government change in 2018, see Chin-Huat Wong, "The Rise, Resilience and Demise of Malaysia's Dominant Coalition," *The Round Table 107*, no. 6 (2018): 755–69.

61. Harry J. Benda, "Political Elites in Colonial Southeast Asia: An Historical Analysis," *Comparative Studies in Society and History* 7, no. 3 (1964): 234.

62. Dan Slater, *Ordering Power: Contentious Politics and Authoritarian Leviathan in Southeast Asia* (Cambridge University Press, 2010).

63. Scholars have argued that Malaysia's strong state capacity were laid during the Communist Insurgency period, see Dan Slater, "Strong-State Democratization in Malaysia and Singapore," *Journal of Democracy* 23, no. 2 (2012): 21–25; Richard Stubbs, "The Malayan Emergency and the Development of the Malayan State," in *The Counter-insurgent State: Guerrilla Warfare and State-Building in the 20th Century*, ed. Paul B. Rich and Richard Stubbs (St. Martin's, 1997), 50–71.

64. This can be seen during the declaration of Emergency Rule following the May 13 racial riots in 1969. The National Operations Council that was tasked with taking over the administration of the country were dominated by the Malay aristocratic/administrative elites from UMNO. The council included the head of police and the chief of army, both of whom were Malay as well.

65. Hong-Hai Lim, "Ethnic Representation in the Malaysian Bureaucracy: The Development and Effects of Malay Domination," *International Journal of Public Administration* 30, no. 12–14 (2007): 1503–24.

66. For writeups of these profiles, see N. John Funston, *Malay Politics in Malaysia: A Study of the United Malays National Organisation and Party Islam* (Heinemann Educational Books, 1980), 109–16; Francis E. Hutchinson, "Malaysia's Independence Leaders and the Legacies of State Formation Under British Rule," *Journal of the Royal Asiatic Society* 25, no. 1 (2015): 144–45.

67. Funston, *Malay Politics*, 109–11; Hutchinson, "Malaysia's Independence Leaders," 144.

68. Funston, *Malay Politics*, 298–306; Harper, *The End of Empire*, chap. 2.

69. Wu Xiao An, *Chinese Business in the Making of a Malay State, 1882–1941: Kedah and Penang* (Routledge Curzon, 2003).

70. James C. Scott, *Political Ideology in Malaysia: Reality and Beliefs of an Elite* (Yale University Press, 1968), 42.

71. Scott, *Political Ideology in Malaysia*, 42.

72. Scott, *Political Ideology in Malaysia*, 39–44.

73. Zarakol, *After Defeat*, chap. 1 and 2.

74. Dan Slater provides perhaps the best comparative account about elite configuration and state building in Southeast Asia. See Slater, *Ordering Power.*

75. Scott, *Political Ideology in Malaysia*, 163.

76. Benda, "Political Elites."

77. Funston, *Malay Politics*, 40.

78. Getachew, *Worldmaking*, 14–22; Srdjan Vucetic, *The Anglosphere: The Genealogy of a Racialized Identity in International Relations* (Stanford University Press, 2011).

79. Scott, *Political Ideology in Malaysia*, 251.

80. Scott, *Political Ideology in Malaysia*, 153.

81. Dipesh Chakrabarty, *Provincializing Europe: Postcolonial Thought and Historical Difference* (Princeton University Press, 2000), 1–6.

82. On the issue of race in IR theory and practice, see John M. Hobson, "Re-Embedding the Global Colour Line Within Post-1945 International Theory," in *Race and Racism in International Relations: Confronting the Global Colour Line*, ed. Alexander Anievas, Nivi Manchanda, and Robbie Shilliam (Routledge, 2015).

83. Zarakol, *After Defeat*, 56.

84. Zarakol, *After Defeat*, 55.

85. Zarakol writes this of Kemalism's dismissal of the Ottoman Empire, "they downplayed the degree to which Ottoman politics had been pluralistic and representative and instead emphasized the picture of a backward, religious society in need of immediate rescue." See Ayşe Zarakol, "Revisiting Second Image Reversed: Lessons from Turkey and Thailand," *International Studies Quarterly* 57, no. 1 (2013): 159.

86. Shaharuddin Maaruf, *Malay Ideas on Development: From Feudal Lord to Capitalist* (Strategic Information and Research Development Centre, 2014), 142. The most trenchant critique of internalized colonial epistemologies among the postcolonial elites remains none other than Syed Hussein Alatas's magnum opus, *The Myth of the Lazy Native: A Study of the Image of the Malays, Filipinos and Javanese from the 16th to the 20th Century and Its Function in the Ideology of Colonial Capitalism* (Frank Cass, 1977).

87. Hussein, *The Politics of Islamic Law*, 156.

88. Amoroso, *Traditionalism*, 151.

89. Scott, *Political Ideology in Malaysia*, 203.

90. Scott, *Political Ideology in Malaysia*, 203.

91. Anthony C. Milner, "The Impact of the Turkish Revolution on Malaya," *Archipel* 31 (1986): 127.

92. Scott, *Political Ideology in Malaysia*, 181–201; cf. Philip Dwyer and Amanda Nettelbeck, eds., *Violence, Colonialism and Empire in the Modern World* (Palgrave Macmillan, 2018).

93. Scott, *Political Ideology in Malaysia*, 208.

94. Scott, *Political Ideology in Malaysia*, 173.

95. The actual circumstances that led to the riots remain an understudied subject, but scholars have attributed it to the fractious politics between the Malayan Chinese

Association and UMNO, as well as an internal coup within UMNO as a faction of Malay ultras sought to overturn the Tunku's leadership for being too "soft" toward the Chinese. See Anthony Reid, "The Kuala Lumpur Riots and the Malaysian Political System," *Australian Outlook* 23, no. 3 (1969): 258–78; Kua Kia Soong, *May 13: Declassified Documents on the Malaysian Riots of 1969* (Suaram, 2007); R. K. Vasil, *The Malaysian General Elections of 1969* (Oxford University Press, 1972).

96. On these cases, see Zarakol, "Second Image,"; S. V. R. Nasr, *Islamic Leviathan: Islam and the Making of State Power* (Oxford University Press, 2001); Mary P. Callahan, *Making Enemies: War and State Building in Burma* (Cornell University Press, 2003).

97. Moustafa, *Constituting Religion*; Dian A. H. Shah, *Constitutions, Religion and Politics in Asia: Indonesia, Malaysia and Sri Lanka* (Cambridge University Press, 2017).

98. Joseph Fernando, "The Position of Islam in the Constitution of Malaysia," *Journal of Southeast Asian Studies* 37, no. 2 (2006): 249–66.

99. Fernando, "The Position of Islam," 253.

100. Moustafa, *Constituting Religion*, 55. The formation of Malaya in 1957 as a constitutional monarchy occurred under a unique federated arrangement composed of the nine Malay states and two Straits Settlements that were also Crown Colonies, Penang and Melaka. The nine Malay states all have their own monarchs, the sultans, who maintained their position as hereditary rulers and as the nominal head and guardian of Islam and Malay customs in their respective states. The head of state for Malaya (and later Malaysia), the Yang Dipertuan Agong, is selected from one of the nine sultans on a rotational basis. The Yang Dipertuan Agong also serves as the custodian of Islam and Malay customs for the states without Malay rulers, namely, Penang, Melaka, Sabah, Sarawak, and the Federal Territories.

101. Ariffin Omar, *Bangsa Melayu: Malay Concepts of Democracy and Community 1945–1950* (Oxford University Press, 1993), 7–8. Also see note 31 above.

102. Fernando writes that the provision of Islam as the official religion of the federation was insisted on by UMNO for it would have "an important psychological impact on the Malays," see Fernando, "Position of Islam," 258. On the intricacies between colonial rule, Muslim elites, and institutional politics that led to the construction of the Malay-Muslim identity, see Moustafa, *Constituting Religion*, 50–51, and Hussin, "The Pursuit of the Perak Regalia."

103. *Bumiputeras* in Malaysia include not only that of the Malays but also the "native" people of Sabah and Sarawak as defined under Article 161A (6)(7) of the Constitution. There are ongoing debates as to how inclusive the *bumiputera* identity is in practice, considering the perceived relegation of the East Malaysian *bumiputera* to second-class status, as well as the exclusion of the Orang Asli (a collective term referring to the indigenous people such as the Temiar, Semai, and Jakun) in the constitutional definition of *bumiputera,* despite them being one of the earliest settlers of the Malay peninsula. See James Chin, "Second Class Bumiputera? The Taming of the

Dayaks and Kadazandusun of East Malaysia," in *Misplaced Democracy: Malaysian Politics and People*, ed. Sophie Lemiere (SIRD, 2014); Colin Nicholas, "The Orang Asli: First on the Land: Last in the Plan," *Kajian Malaysia* 21, no. 1–2 (2003): 315–29.

104. The prohibition is only one-way. Proselytization of non-Muslims was actually encouraged by state institutions such as the Muslim Welfare Organization of Malaysia and the Islamic Dakwah. See Sophie Lemiere, "Conversion and Controversy: Reshaping the Boundaries of Malaysian Pluralism," in *Proselytizing and the Limits of Religious Pluralism in Contemporary Asia*, ed. James Finucane and Michael F. Feener (Springer, 2014), 54.

105. See Articles 5 to 13 on the fundamental liberty provisions of the Constitution.

106. On the ideology of Islamism, see Andrew Phillips, *War, Religion and Empire: The Transformation of International Orders* (Cambridge University Press, 2011), 270–79; Roxanne Euben, *Enemy in the Mirror: Islamic Fundamentalism and the Limits of Modern Rationalism* (Princeton University Press, 1999).

107. Safie bin Ibrahim, *The Islamic Party of Malaysia: Its Formative Stages and Ideology* (Nuawi bin Ismail, 1981), 107.

108. Y. Mansoor Marican, "Malay Nationalism and the Islamic Party of Malaysia," *Islamic Studies* 16, no. 1 (1977): 298.

109. On PAS's stand on various issues, see Ibrahim, *Islamic Party of Malaysia*; Funston, *Malay Politics*, 134–61. Farish Noor's historical study of PAS, depicts a political party that, while maintaining Islam's centrality in its struggle, is not immune to pragmatic adaptations to global events and local contingencies, see Noor, *Malaysian Islamic Party*.

110. Funston, *Malay Politics*, 172–83; Ahmad Fawzi Mohd Basri, "The United Malays National Organization (UMNO) 1981–1991: A Study of the Mechanics of a Changing Political Culture" (PhD diss., University of Hull, 1992), 80–85; Margaret Roff, "The Politics of Language in Malaya," *Asian Survey* 7, no. 5 (1967): 316–28.

111. Nasr, *Islamic Leviathan*, 11.

112. Noor, *Malaysian Islamic Party*, 56.

113. Funston, *Malay Politics*, 153–54.

114. Hwok-Aun Lee, Edmund Terence Gomez, and Shakila Yacob, "Ethnicity, Economy and Affirmative Action in Malaysia," in *Affirmative Action, Ethnicity and Conflict*, ed. Edmund Terence Gomez and Ralph Prendas (Routledge, 2013), 74.

115. Nasr, *Islamic Leviathan*, 56.

116. *Straits Times*, May 1, 1959, quoted in Fred R. Von Der Mehden, "Religion and Politics in Malaysia," *Asian Survey* 3, no. 12 (1963): 611.

117. Helen Ting Mu Hung, "The Politics of Hudud Law Implementation in Malaysia," ISEAS Working Paper no. 2 (ISEAS–Yusof Ishak Institute, 2016); Jason P. Abbott and Sophie Gregorios-Pippas, "Islamization in Malaysia: Processes and Dynamics," *Contemporary Politics* 16, no. 2 (2010): 135–51.

118. Funston, *Malay Politics*, 147.

119. Amoroso, *Traditionalism*.

120. Geoff Wade, "The Origins and Evolution of Ethnocracy in Malaysia," *The Asia-Pacific Journal* 47, no. 7 (2009): 1–38.

121. Funston, *Malay Politics*, 146.

122. This struggle echoes Zarakol's contention that ontological insecurity is generated neither solely exogenously nor endogenously. For postcolonial elites who were socialized into an international order not of their making, it is usually a combination of both. See Ayşe Zarakol, "Ontological (In)security and State Denial of Historical Crimes: Turkey and Japan," *International Relations* 24, no. 1 (2010): 3–23.

123. Nikki R. Keddie, "The Revolt of Islam, 1700 to 1993: Comparative Considerations and Relations to Imperialism," *Comparative Studies in Society and History* 36, no. 3 (1994): 463–87; Vedi R. Hadiz, "Indonesian Political Islam: Capitalist Development and the Legacies of the Cold War," *Journal of Current Southeast Asian Affairs* 30, no. 1 (2011): 3–38; Behlül Özkan, "The Cold War-Era Origins of Islamism in Turkey and Its Rise to Power," *Hudson Institute*, November 5, 2017, https://www.hudson.org/research/13807-the-cold-war-era-origins-of-islamism-in-turkey-and-its-rise-to-power.

Chapter 3

1. Mahathir Mohamad, "Islam: The Misunderstood Religion," *Islamic Studies* 36, no. 4 (1997): 691. This is the text of a lecture Mahathir delivered at the Oxford Centre of Islamic Studies, Oxford, United Kingdom on April 16, 1996.

2. Kua Kia Soong, *Racism & Racial Discrimination in Malaysia: A Historical & Class Perspective* (Suaram, 2015).

3. Anwar Ibrahim began his political activism as a student leader and later rose to be the leader of one of Malaysia's earliest Islamist social movements, the Angkatan Belia Islam Malaysia (Malaysian Islamic Youth Movement, ABIM). Once seem destined to be a future Pan-Malaysian Islamist Party (PAS) leader, Anwar shocked many of his supporters when he joined PAS's nemesis, the United Malays National Organisation (UMNO), in 1982. His political career in UMNO was initially defined by a meteoric rise that saw Anwar becoming deputy prime minister by 1993, and later by a scandalous downfall in 1997 following an acrimonious break with Mahathir. In a protracted comeback, Anwar became Malaysia's tenth prime minister in 2022.

4. Mahathir Mohamad, *The Challenge* (Pelanduk, 1986), 73.

5. See Joseph Chinyong Liow, *Piety and Politics: Islamism in Contemporary Malaysia* (Oxford University Press, 2009); Kikue Hamayotsu, "Politics of Syariah Reform: The Making of the State Religio-Legal Apparatus," in *Malaysia: Islam, Society, and Politics*, ed. Virginia Hooker and Norani Othman (ISEAS–Yusof Ishak Institute, 2003), 55–79; Shanti Nair, *Islam in Malaysian Foreign Policy* (Routledge, 1997); Seyyed Vali Reza Nasr, *Islamic Leviathan: Islam and the Making of State Power* (Oxford University Press, 2001).

6. Judith Nagata, *The Reflowering of Malaysian Islam* (University of British Columbia Press, 1984); Chandra Muzaffar, *Islamic Resurgence in Malaysia* (Fajar Bakti, 1987); Zainah Anwar, *Islamic Revivalism in Malaysia* (Fajar Bakti, 1987); Hussin Mutalib, *Islam and Ethnicity in Malay Politics* (Oxford University Press, 1990).

7. Joseph Chinyong Liow, "Exigency or Expediency? Contextualizing Political Islam and the PAS Challenge in Malaysian Politics," *Third World Quarterly* 25, no. 2 (2004): 359–72; Joseph Chinyong Liow, "Political Islam in Malaysia: Problematising Discourse and Practice in the UMNO–PAS 'Islamisation Race,'" *Commonwealth & Comparative Politics* 42, no. 2 (2004): 184–205; Farish A. Noor, "Blood, Sweat and Jihad: The Radicalization of the Political Discourse of the Pan-Malaysian Islamic Party (PAS) from 1982 Onwards," *Contemporary Southeast Asia* 25, no. 2 (2003): 200–32; Kikue Hamayotsu, "Demobilizing Islam: Institutionalized Religion and the Politics of Co-optation in Malaysia" (PhD diss., Australian National University, 2005).

8. See a version of my argument at Nicholas Chan, "Rethinking the Causes of Islamisation: Ontological (In)security, Postcoloniality, and Islam in Malaysia," *Journal of Southeast Asian Studies* 54, no. 3 (2023): 419–49.

9. Khoo Boo Teik, *Paradoxes of Mahathirism: An Intellectual Biography of Mahathir Mohamad* (Oxford University Press, 1995), 181–86.

10. Wain's documentation of Mahathir's political journey describes a process that was far from determinant, with his predecessor Hussein Onn doubting him as a successor almost every step of the way. See Barry Wain, *Malaysian Maverick: Mahathir Mohamad in Turbulent Times* (Palgrave Macmillan, 2009), 33–40.

11. Diane K. Mauzy and R. S. Milne, "The Mahathir Administration in Malaysia: Discipline Through Islam," *Pacific Affairs* 56, no. 4 (1983): 627.

12. Figures such as Syed Jaafar Albar, Syed Nasir Ismail, and Rahman Talib were pushing for UMNO to adopt more pro-Malay stances since the 1960s, clashing frequently with the Tunku's more moderate leanings. Nevertheless, it was the young Turks, such as Mahathir and his later deputy, Musa Hitam, who were singled out by the Tunku as the "ultras." See Ahmad Fawzi Mohd Basri, "The United Malays National Organization (UMNO) 1981–1991: A Study of the Mechanics of a Changing Political Culture" (PhD diss., University of Hull, 1992), 150. Mahathir's reentry into UMNO in 1972 was followed by a meteoric rise. He was one of the party's vice presidents by 1975, and following Tunku Abdul Razak's death in 1976, was promoted to deputy president. In government, he was made the minister of education in 1974, deputy prime minister in 1976, and was prime minister by 1981.

13. On the New Economic Policy, see Terence Gomez and Johan Saravanamuttu, eds., *The New Economic Policy in Malaysia: Affirmative Action, Ethnic Inequalities, and Social Justice* (NUS Press, 2013).

14. Dan Slater, *Ordering Power: Contentious Politics and Authoritarian Leviathan in Southeast Asia* (Cambridge University Press, 2010), 150–51.

15. Dan Slater, "Iron Cage in an Iron Fist: Authoritarian Institutions and the Personalization of Power in Malaysia," *Comparative Politics* 36, no. 1 (2003): 80–101.

16. "PAS' Controversial Statements," *The Star Online*, March 5, 2008, https://www.thestar.com.my/news/nation/2008/03/05/pas-controversial-statements. On an analysis of Mahathir's complicated relationship with what is ostensibly known as liberal Islam, see Sven Schottmann, *Mahathir's Islam: Mahathir Mohamad on Religion and Modernity in Malaysia* (University of Hawai'i Press, 2018), 137–41.

17. For this book, the English version will be used as the primary reference. See Mohamad, *The Challenge*. Mahathir's second book was a relatively obscure one, entitled *Panduan Peniaga Kecil* (Guidebook for small business owners), which was published in 1973. The book is where his message that the Malays must be successful economically was channeled into an applied form.

18. Schottmann, *Mahathir's Islam*, 29.

19. Mohamad, *The Challenge*, viii.

20. Mohamad, "Misunderstood Religion," 700; cf. Mohamad, *The Challenge*, chap. 3.

21. Mohamad, *The Challenge*, viii.

22. Mohamad, *The Challenge*, 36.

23. Mohamad, *The Challenge*, 73; Sven A. Schottmann, "God Helps Those Who Help Themselves: Islam According to Mahathir Mohamad," *Islam and Christian–Muslim Relations* 24, no. 1 (2013): 57–69.

24. Mohamad, *The Challenge*, 72.

25. Mohamad, *The Challenge*, 74.

26. Schottmann, *Mahathir's Islam*, 108; Khoo, *Paradoxes of Mahathirism*, 172–73.

27. Ayşe Zarakol, *After Defeat: How the East Learned to Live with the West* (Cambridge University Press, 2011).

28. Zarakol, *After Defeat*, 62.

29. Sven A. Schottmann, "The Pillars of 'Mahathir's Islam': Mahathir Mohamad on Being-Muslim in the Modern World," *Asian Studies Review* 35, no. 3 (2011): 359.

30. Mohamad, *The Challenge*, 114.

31. Junita Mat Rasid, "Dr M: Muslim Nations Can Become Developed and Competitive," *New Straits Times*, November 30, 2019, https://www.nst.com.my/news/nation/2019/11/543419/dr-m-muslim-nations-can-become-developed-and-competitive.

32. Mahathir Mohamad, *The Malay Dilemma: Reprint with a New Preface* (Marshall Cavendish, 2008), 217. Mahathir's penchant for adopting a medical, if not almost "surgical" lens, in his writing is one of his most distinguishing features. See Khoo, *Paradoxes of Mahathirism*, 294–301.

33. Khoo, *Paradoxes of Mahathirism*, 30.

34. Mohamad, *Malay Dilemma*, 217.

35. Michael D. Barr, "Lee Kuan Yew: Race, Culture and Genes," *Journal of Contemporary Asia* 29, no. 2 (1999): 145–66.

36. Mohamad, *Malay Dilemma*, 9.

37. Farish A. Noor, *The Discursive Construction of Southeast Asia in 19th Century Colonial-Capitalist Discourse* (Amsterdam University Press, 2016), 95.

38. Syed Hussein Alatas, *The Myth of the Lazy Native: A Study of the Image of the Malays, Filipinos and Javanese from the 16th to the 20th Century and Its Function in the Ideology of Colonial Capitalism* (Frank Cass, 1977).

39. Alatas, *The Myth of the Lazy Native*, 155. Edited by then–UMNO Youth Chief Senu Abdul Rahman, *Revolusi Mental* is a collection of essays published in 1971, right after the May 13 racial riots and when the government was beginning to implement the New Economic Policy. The book contains a foreword by then–Prime Minister Tun Abdul Razak who claimed that the Malays' backwardness was due to their "lack of knowledge and constrained by their *kolot* [outdated] ways." Calls for reform were framed in an existential language, as the editor writes, "Do the Malays not yet believe their struggle in this country is a struggle for survival, in which only those with the conditions and capabilities are able to make it, just like how Charles Darwin proposed in his theory of Natural Selection?" See Senu Abdul Rahman, ed., *Revolusi Mental* (Utusan, 1971), v, xvii.

40. Alatas, *The Myth of the Lazy Native*, 148.

41. "*If the Malays are to be rehabilitated, all the attitudes and values that have contributed to their present dilemma must be studied, assessed and where necessary, discarded or modified*" (emphasis mine). Mohamad, *Malay Dilemma*, 146.

42. Schottmann, *Mahathir's Islam*, 119–26.

43. Schottmann, *Mahathir's Islam*, 124.

44. In Mahathir's words, "*If we study the histories of the peoples conquered and colonized by the West, one salient fact we will note is their lack of discipline*" (emphasis mine). Mohamad, *The Challenge*, 46.

45. The theme of the West in decline was a recurring feature in Mahathir's thoughts. See Khoo, *Paradoxes of Mahathirism*, 42–46.

46. Mohamad, *The Challenge*, 72.

47. Dale F. Eickelman and James Piscatori, *Muslim Politics* (Princeton University Press, 2004), 37–45; Gregory Starrett, *Putting Islam to Work: Education, Politics, and Religious Transformation in Egypt* (University of California Press, 1998), 8–10.

48. Gilles Kepel, *Jihad: The Trail of Political Islam* (I. B. Tauris, 2002), chap. 4–5; Nagata, *Reflowering of Malaysian Islam*; Liow, *Piety and Politics*; Anwar, *Islamic Revivalism*.

49. Mahathir would later in his life call Islam as practiced by the state institutions in Malaysia "cruel and inconsiderate." Indeed, as Maznah Mohamad observes, in the late 1990s, Mahathir increasingly found himself on the losing side when he clashed with the religious bureaucracy over issues of culture and theology. See Maznah Mohamad,

"A Clamour For Islamic Reform in Malaysia: But in Which Direction Under a Divine Bureaucracy?" *New Mandala*, June 4, 2019, https://www.newmandala.org/a-clamour-for-islamic-reform-in-malaysia-but-in-which-direction-under-a-divine-bureaucracy/; Maznah Mohamad, *The Divine Bureaucracy and Disenchantment of Social Life: A Study of Bureaucratic Islam in Malaysia* (Palgrave Macmillan, 2020), 135–40.

50. Schottmann, *Mahathir's Islam*, 10.

51. Slater, "Iron Cage in an Iron Fist"; Wain, *Malaysian Maverick*.

52. *Konfrontasi* refers to a standoff between Malaysia and Indonesia between 1963 and 1966. It started when President Sukarno of Indonesia opposed the formation of Malaysia in 1963 as a "neocolonial" project. Whereas the two nations avoided an open war, skirmishes broke out. PAS's critique of the government for receiving Western aid then, not to mention Dr Burhanuddin's long-standing ties with many of the Malay nationalists who envisioned a greater Indo-Malaya polity, set the pretext for a government crackdown. See Farish A. Noor, *The Malaysian Islamic Party PAS 1951–2013: Islamism in a Mottled Nation* (Amsterdam University Press, 2014), 58–60.

53. The ISA was a colonial-era law that allowed preventive detention of individuals deemed "in any manner prejudicial to the security of Malaysia." It was repealed in 2012 and replaced with a different set of security laws, which will be discussed in chapter 6. See Section 8(1) of Internal Security Act 1960.

54. In the policy document online, it states that the policy started in 1985. Other sources have placed its initiation in 1983. For the policy document, see *Dasar Penerapan Nilai-Nilai Islam dalam Pentadbiran Negara*, https://www.pmo.gov.my/dokumenattached/Dasar/10DASAR_PENERAPAN_NILAI.pdf. For the other sources, see Schottmann, *Mahathir's Islam*, 6; Nair, *Islam in Malaysian Foreign Policy*, 52n60.

55. Schottmann, "God Helps Those Who Help Themselves."

56. *Dasar Penerapan Nilai-Nilai Islam*, 1–2.

57. Nasr, *Islamic Leviathan*.

58. Nasr, *Islamic Leviathan*, 16–17.

59. Kikue Hamayotsu, "The Political Origins of Islamic Courts in Divided Societies: The Case of Malaysia," *Journal of Law and Religion* 33, no. 2 (2018): 270; cf. Hamayotsu, *Demobilizing Islam*.

60. Officers from JAKIM also serve as chair and secretary to the Fatwa Council.

61. On JAKIM, see Mohamad, *Divine Bureaucracy*, 79–90; Liow, *Piety and Politics*, 48–52; Norshahril Saat, *The State, Ulama and Islam in Malaysia and Indonesia* (Amsterdam University Press, 2018), 55.

62. The allocation for Islamic affairs at the federal level has reached MYR 2 billion in 2025, with JAKIM alone taking approximately half of that funding. See "Govt Allocates RM2b for Islamic Affairs," *Malaysiakini*, October 18, 2024, https://www.malaysiakini.com/news/723188; Mohamad, *Divine Bureaucracy*, 83. The asymmetry between federal and state funding in Islamic affairs mirrors the asymmetry between

Malaysia's national and subnational governments, both being products of Malaysia's centralized federalism. According to Ostwald, the total expenditure of all subnational governments in Malaysia is less than 10 percent of all governmental expenditure. See Kai Ostwald, "Federalism without Decentralization: Power Consolidation in Malaysia," *Journal of Southeast Asian Economies* 34, no. 3 (2017): 500.

63. Mohamad, *Divine Bureaucracy*, 78.

64. Jomo Kwame Sundaram, "'Malaysia Incorporated': Corporatism a la Mahathir," *Institutions and Economics* 6, no. 1 (2014): 73–94.

65. Nasr, *Islamic Leviathan*, 128.

66. Ayşe Zarakol, "Revisiting Second Image Reversed: Lessons from Turkey and Thailand," *International Studies Quarterly* 57, no. 1 (2013): 150–62.

67. Space does not allow me to cover the full spectrum of the dynamics and effects of state-led Islamization in Malaysia. For that, see Liow, *Piety and Politics*; Jason P. Abbott and Sophie Gregorios-Pippas, "Islamization in Malaysia: Processes and Dynamics," *Contemporary Politics* 16, no. 2 (2010): 135–51; Maznah Mohamad, "Making Majority, Undoing Family: Law, Religion and the Islamization of the State in Malaysia," *Economy and Society* 39, no. 3 (2010): 360–84.

68. Michael G. Peletz, *Islamic Modern: Religious Courts and Cultural Politics in Malaysia* (Princeton University Press, 2002), 21. See also Dominik M. Müller, "Bureaucratic Islam Compared: Classificatory Power and State-ified Religious Meaning-Making in Brunei and Singapore," *The Journal of Law and Religion* 33, no. 2 (2018): 212–47; Hew Wai Weng, "Consumer Space as Political Space: Liquid Islamism in Malaysia and Indonesia," in *Political Participation in Asia: Defining and Deploying Political Space*, ed. E. Hansson and M. L. Weiss (Routledge, 2018), 112–29.

69. Saat, *The State, Ulama and Islam*; Abbott and Gregorios-Pippas, "Islamization in Malaysia,."

70. Mohamad, *Divine Bureaucracy*, 3.

71. Max Weber, *Economy and Society: An Outline of Interpretive Sociology* (University of California Press, 1978), 952–54.

72. Johan Fischer, *The Halal Frontier: Muslim Consumers in a Globalized Market* (Palgrave Macmillan, 2011).

73. Mohamad, *Divine Bureaucracy*, 109.

74. Johan Fischer, "Manufacturing Halal in Malaysia," *Contemporary Islam* 10 (2016): 35–52.

75. Müller, "Bureaucratic Islam."

76. See another case of Islam was reinvented alongside "the more universal languages of bureaucracy, cultural globalisation, modern nationalism, marketisation, scientisation, and statisticalisation" in Brunei, in Dominik M. Müller, "Hybrid Pathways to Orthodoxy in Brunei Darussalam: Bureaucratised Exorcism, Scientisation and the

Mainstreaming of Deviant-Declared Practices," *Journal of Current Southeast Asian Affairs* 37, no. 1 (2018): 176.

77. On how the training of sharia court judges and lawyers largely took place in a secular civil law tradition instead of through "classical modes of reasoning," see Tamir Moustafa, *Constituting Religion: Islam, Liberal Rights, and the Malaysian State* (Cambridge University Press, 2018), 43; Mohamad, *Divine Bureaucracy*, 125; Hamayotsu, *Demobilizing Islam*, 63–66.

78. The mufti is considered the highest authority of Islam within the Malaysian states as they serve as the advisors to the Malay rulers on Islamic affairs. However, their power extends beyond giving advice to the rulers, as the mufti's office is also responsible for issuing fatwas that are legally binding for Muslims under state laws.

79. On the *pondoks* (Islamic boarding schools) and madrasahs as "traditional" institutions of Islamic learning in Malaysia, see Ahmad Fauzi Abdul Hamid, "Islamic Education in Malaysia," in *Handbook of Islamic Education*, ed. Holger Daun and Reza Arjmand (Springer, 2018), 745–61.

80. Redzuan Muharam, "Dharshini Cemerlang Ujian Tassawur Islam" [Dharshini excels in Tassawur Islam examination], *Berita Harian*, September 17, 2020, https://www.hmetro.com.my/utama/2020/09/621664/dharshini-cemerlang-ujian-tassawur-islam.

81. Mohamad, *Divine Bureaucracy*, vii.

82. Patricia Sloane-White's works remain the best resource for the topic, especially in capturing of the lifeworld of an ascendent, self-confident "Islamic" capitalist class that emerged as a direct result of Mahathir's Islamization drive, although this class would later become the key drivers of the project too. See Patricia Sloane, *Islam, Modernity and Entrepreneurship among the Malays* (Macmillan, 1999); Patricia Sloane-White. *Corporate Islam: Sharia and the Modern Workplace* (Cambridge University Press, 2017).

83. "Opening Address to the Seminar on Developing Islamic Financial Instruments," speech given by Mahathir Mohamad on April 28, 1986.

84. World Bank, *Malaysia: Islamic Finance and Financial Inclusion* (World Bank, 2020), 19.

85. On the "Islamization of knowledge" project, see Mona Abaza, "Intellectuals, Power and Islam in Malaysia: S.N. al-Attas or the Beacon on the Crest of a Hill," *Archipel* 58 (1999): 189–217.

86. Universiti Sains Islam Malaysia, "Overview," https://www.usim.edu.my/introduction/.

87. The three most recent vice-chancellors of USIM are a chemist, a theoretical physicist, and a food scientist respectively, all trained in Western universities. The current vice-chancellor (as of this writing) is Sharifudin Md Shaarani, a food scientist who received his PhD from the University of Cambridge. It appears that Sharifudin earned

his Islamic credentials through substantial involvement in the halal industry. See "Professor Ts. Dr. Sharifudin Md Shaarani Appointed as USIM Vice-Chancellor," https://www.usim.edu.my/news/professor-ts-dr-sharifudin-md-shaarani-appointed-as-usim-vice-chancellor/.

88. Farish A. Noor, "Re-orienting the 'West'? The Transnational Debate on the Status of the 'West' in the Debates Among Islamist Intellectuals and Students from the 1970s to the Present," *Majalah Al-Jamiah* 47, no. 1 (2009): 1–47; Wiebke Keim, "Islamization of Knowledge—Symptom of the Failed Internationalization of the Social Sciences?" *Method(e)s: African Review of Social Science Methodology* 2, no. 1–2 (2017): 127–54.

89. Hamayotsu, "Political Origins," 269.

90. Greg Felker, "Malaysia's Development Strategies: Governing Distribution-Through-Growth," in *Routledge Handbook of Contemporary Malaysia*, ed. Meredith L. Weiss (Routledge, 2018), 134–38.

91. Nair, *Islam in Malaysian Foreign Policy*, 116.

92. David Delfolie, "Malaysian Extraversion Towards the Muslim World: Ideological Positioning for a 'Mirror Effect,'" *Journal of Current Southeast Asian Affairs* 31, no. 4 (2012): 3–29.

93. Cited in Delfolie, "Malaysian Extraversion," 24n32.

94. "Welcoming Address at the Opening of KL Summit 2019," speech given by Mahathir Mohamad on December 19, 2019. Whereas Mahathir did not name the Arab world specifically, his sentiment toward the region and what it meant for Islam's reputation is well known. Also see Khoo, *Paradoxes of Mahathirism*, 164; Abaza, "Intellectuals," 194.

95. Darren C. Zook, "Making Space for Islam: Religion, Science, and Politics in Contemporary Malaysia," *The Journal of Asian Studies* 69, no. 4 (2010): 1153.

96. Zook, "Making Space for Islam," 1143–66.

97. Yuki Shiozaki, "The Historical Origins of Control over Deviant Groups in Malaysia: Official Fatwá and Regulation of Interpretation," *Studia Islamika* 22, no. 2 (2015): 205–32.

98. Mohamad, *Malay Dilemma*, 151.

99. Mohamad, *Malay Dilemma*, 151.

100. Mohamad, *Malay Dilemma*, 152.

101. Kamarulnizam Abdullah, "National Security and Malay Unity: The Issue of Radical Religious Elements in Malaysia," *Contemporary Southeast Asia* 21, no. 2 (1999): 261–82.

102. Nair, *Islam in Malaysian Foreign Policy*, 152; Engku Ahmad Zaki Engku Alwi, "Kajian Ajaran Sesat Dalam Pengajian Islam: Satu Sorotan" [A note on deviant movements in Islam], *Jurnal Usuluddin* 26 (2007): 1.

103. In 2015, MYR 500 million was spent on an item labeled "policy," whose objective was to "thwart attempts to 'deviate' Muslims by groups deemed 'deviant' and 'threatening national security.'" Mohamad, *Divine Bureaucracy*, 86.

104. "Pencapaian Barisan Nasional Dalam Memartabatkan Islam Dan Keharmonian Agama #JanjiDitepati" [National Front's achievement in strengthening Islam and religious harmony], *Penangkini*, March 25, 2018, https://www.penangkini.com/2018/03/pencapaian-barisan-nasional-dalam_56.html (page no longer available).

105. Mutalib calls *dakwah* "the propagation of the Islamic message and call on Muslims to upgrade their Islamicity." See Mutalib, *Islam and Ethnicity*, 74. "*Dakwah* movements" is often used as a shorthand to label the many active, urban-based Muslim social movements that emerged since the late 1970s. Prominent examples include ABIM, Darul Arqam, Jemaah Tabligh, and others. See Mutalib, *Islam and Ethnicity*, chap. 3; Muzaffar, *Islamic Resurgence*; Nagata, *Reflowering of Malaysian Islam*.

106. For the most informative writings on Arqam, see Ahmad Fauzi Abdul Hamid, "Political Dimensions of Religious Conflict in Malaysia: State Response to an Islamic Movement," *Indonesia and the Malay World* 28, no. 80 (2000): 32–65; Ahmad Fauzi Abdul Hamid, "The Banning of Darul Arqam in Malaysia," *Review of Indonesian and Malaysian Affairs* 39, no. 1 (2005): 87–128; Judith Nagata, "Alternative Models of Islamic Governance in Southeast Asia: Neo-Sufism and the Arqam Experiment in Malaysia," *Global Change, Peace & Security* 16, no. 2 (2004): 99–114.

107. Nagata, "Neo-Sufism," 106.

108. Nagata, "Neo-Sufism," 108.

109. Sharifah Zaleha Syed Hassan, "Constructions of Islamic Identities in a Suburban Community in Malaysia," *Southeast Asia Journal of Social Science* 25, no. 2 (1997): 30.

110. On the relationship between Malaysian politics and state clientelism, see Edmund Terence Gomez and Jomo K. S., *Malaysia's Political Economy: Politics, Patronage and Profits* (Cambridge University Press, 1999).

111. Nagata, "Neo-Sufism," 107–8.

112. Anwar Ibrahim is a classic example of how some *dakwah* movements in Malaysia, despite being ostensibly nonpolitical, kept one foot within Malaysian politics. Once president of ABIM, Anwar was inducted into UMNO in 1982 and rose to become deputy prime minister of Malaysia in 1992. Whereas ABIM maintained its independence from UMNO, it is evident that Anwar's co-optation muted their criticism of the government while enabling their participation in the government's Islamization projects. See Jomo Kwame Sundaram and Ahmed Shabery Cheek, "The Politics of Malaysia's Islamic Resurgence," *Third World Quarterly* 10, no. 2 (1988): 856–60.

113. Abdul Hamid, "Religious Conflict," 51. *Tarbiyah* generally refers to a model of Islamic education popular among Muslim Brotherhood-influenced Islamist movements whereby classes and discussions of religion are organized in small study groups called *usrahs*.

114. For a detailed writing of the saga, see Abdul Hamid, "Religious Conflict"; Abdul Hamid, "Banning of Darul Arqam."

115. Abdul Hamid, "Banning of Darul Arqam," 94. On the ISA, see note 52.

116. For a detailed illustration of the theological disputes between Arqam and the state religious officials, see Abdul Hamid, "Banning of Darul Arqam," 99–104.

117. Hamid, "Banning of Darul Arqam," 114–16.

118. Hamid, "Banning of Darul Arqam," 116.

119. For a view that says it was political, see Abdul Hamid, "Religious Conflict."

120. Mahathir appeared in a dialogue with the chief executive of GISB. See GISB Holdings, "Dialog Y.A. Bhg. Tun Mahathir Mohamad bersama GISBH," July 31, 2023, https://www.facebook.com/gisbhcom/videos/1430088274227111. On Mahathir's defense of GISB, see Austin Camoens, "Police Respond to Dr M's Assertion of Excessive Action Against GISB," *New Straits Times*, October 10, 2024, https://www.nst.com.my/news/nation/2024/10/1117791/police-respond-dr-ms-assertion-excessive-action-against-gisb.

121. Nagata, "Neo-Sufism," 110.

122. Nagata, "Neo-Sufism," 110.

123. Syed Hassan, "Islamic Identities," 30.

124. Nagata, *Reflowering of Malaysian Islam*, 113.

125. Abdul Hamid, "Banning of Darul Arqam," 105.

126. Unit Akidah dan Ajaran Sesat, "Latar Belakang Pengharaman Aktiviti Kumpulan Darul Arqam Malaysia" [The background to the banning of Darul Arqam Malaysia], *Jurnal Penyelidikan Islam* 9 (1995): 47.

127. Abdul Hamid, "Banning of Darul Arqam," 105.

128. Nagata, "Neo-Sufism," 112.

129. Abdul Hamid, "Religious Conflict," 53.

130. On the concept of the gardening state, see Zygmunt Bauman, *Modernity and Ambivalence* (Polity, 1991), 26–30.

131. See Syariah Criminal Offences (Federal Territories) Act 1997; Syariah Criminal Offences Enactment (Johor) 1997; Syariah Criminal Offences Enactment (Selangor) 1995; Syariah Criminal Offences Enactment (Pahang) 2013; Syariah Criminal Offences Enactment (Pulau Pinang) 1996; Syariah Criminal Offences (Takzir) Enactment 2001 (Terengganu); Syariah Criminal Offences Ordinance 2001 (Sarawak).

132. For detailed accounts of the Al-Ma'unah affair, see Elina Noor, "Al-Ma'unah and KMM in Malaysia," in *A Handbook of Terrorism and Insurgency in Southeast Asia*, ed. A. T. H. Tan (Edward Elgar, 2007); Ahmad Fauzi Abdul Hamid, "Islam and Violence in Malaysia," Working Paper no. 123 (S. Rajaratnam School of International Studies, Nanyang Technological University, 2007), 20–24.

133. Raphael Wong, "Death for Al-Ma'unah Man," *The Star Online*, June 27, 2003, https://www.thestar.com.my/news/nation/2003/06/27/death-for-almaunah-man_1. In 2020, thirteen of these men were granted a royal pardon.

134. Amin himself was an ex-army private who was discharged after being court-martialed. His "left" and "right"-hand men during the coup were an ex-police

officer and an active-duty member of the army. It was also reported that the group had attracted some support from the Malaysian armed forces. See "9 Anggota Tentera yang Terlibat Dilucut Jawatan" [9 military officers involved in Al-Ma'unah suspended], *Berita Harian*, July 15, 2000; "The Two Faces of a Cult Leader," *The Straits Times*, July 10, 2000.

135. Malaysia experienced two Emergencies, which were practically "shooting wars" against a Communist insurgency. The most well-known period lasted from 1948 to 1960, while a second Emergency was declared from 1968 to 1989 and concluded with the Peace Agreement of Hat Yai in 1989.

136. Federal Government of Malaysia, *Threat to Muslim Unity and National Security* (Federal Government of Malaysia, 1984), 3–6.

137. On PAS's radicalization during its confrontation with UMNO, see Noor, "Blood, Sweat and Jihad."

138. Federal Government of Malaysia, *White Paper to the Memali Incident* (Federal Government of Malaysia, 1986), 22.

139. "The Opening Ceremony of the International Islamic Symposium," speech given by Mahathir Mohamad on March 5, 1986.

140. Federal Government of Malaysia, *Threat to Muslim Unity*, 2.

141. "We Don't Attach Much Value to New York Times Report, Says Abdullah," *Bernama*, October 11, 2001.

142. Federal Government of Malaysia, *Al-Ma'unah Sesat di Sauk* (Department of Information Malaysia, 2000).

143. It is noteworthy that both the minister and deputy director were highly trained religious scholars. Both were Al-Azhar graduates and doctorate holders in Islamic studies. Abdul Hamid Othman wrote a dissertation at the University of St Andrews entitled "Shāfiʿī and the Interpretation of the Role of the Qur'ān and the Ḥadīth," while Abdul Munir Yaacob wrote a dissertation entitled "Islamic Judiciary with Special Reference to Shari'ah Courts in Peninsula Malaysia" at the International Islamic University of Malaysia.

144. Al-Ma'unah was rumored to have as many as 1,700 members, although that figure might be exaggerated. See Abdul Hamid, "Islam and Violence," 23. There is also no evidence that suggests that most of its members knew that their leadership was planning a coup.

145. "Malaysia Kesan 44 Ajaran Sesat" [Malaysia identified 44 deviant movements], *Berita Minggu*, July 9, 2000.

146. Speech at the opening of the Third Malay-Islamic World Convention, Malacca, by Mahathir Mohamad, October 3, 2002, as cited in Schottmann, *Mahathir's Islam*, 124.

147. "Meeting the Challenges of the 21st Century: Role of Muslim Nations," speech given by Mahathir Mohamad on April 26, 2001, at the Emirates International Forum.

148. Wan Hamidi Hamid, "Lost at the Fringe," *The Straits Times*, July 30, 2000. The then-Defense Minister Najib Razak and the high court judgment also made the observation that (most of the) Al-Ma'unah members were "well educated," see "Anggota Al-Maunah Berpendidikan Tinggi" [Al-Ma'unah members well educated], *Berita Harian*, July 8, 2000. Being "well educated" is nonetheless a subjective judgment. Going by the court documents, one can only safely say that two out of the twenty-nine charged went to university, see *Public Prosecutor v. Mohd Amin Mohd Razali & Ors*, Written Judgment of the Kuala Lumpur High Court, 361.

149. Biodata of the Al-Ma'unah members can be found at "Biodata Anggota Al-Maunah," [Biodata of Al-Ma'unah members] https://komanderperang.blogspot.com/2011/10/biodata-anggota-al-maunah.html. For accuracy, I cross-checked the information with various sources, including newspaper articles and court documents.

150. On the effects of Islam's disenchantment in its bureaucratic forms, which ranged from constrained and contentious interaction with non-Muslims to heightened (state) intolerance of intra-Muslim pluralism, see Mohammad, *Divine Bureaucracy*, 274–75; Ahmad Fauzi Abdul Hamid and Muhamad Takiyuddin Ismail, "Islamist Conservatism and the Demise of Islam Hadhari in Malaysia," *Islam and Christian–Muslim Relations* 25, no. 2 (2014): 170–71.

151. Yuen Meiking, "Ex-PM Cautions Against Turning Islam into 'Police State Religion," *The Star Online*, January 29, 2014, https://www.thestar.com.my/news/nation/2014/01/29/dr-m-educate-muslims-expm-cautions-against-turning-islam-into-police-state-religion.

152. Mohamad, "Misunderstood Religion," 699.

Chapter 4

1. Annelle Sheline, "Middle East Regimes Are Using 'Moderate' Islam to Stay in Power," *The Washington Post*, March 1, 2017, https://www.washingtonpost.com/news/monkey-cage/wp/2017/03/01/middle-east-regimes-are-using-moderate-islam-to-stay-in-power/?utm_term=.56c8169408c5; Farish A. Noor, "How Washington's 'War on Terror' Became Everyone's: Islamophobia and the Impact of September 11 on the Political Terrain of South and Southeast Asia," *Human Architecture: Journal of the Sociology of Self-Knowledge* 5, no. 1 (2006): 29–50; Ann Marie Wainscott, *Bureaucratizing Islam: Morocco and the War on Terror* (Cambridge University Press, 2017).

2. Saba Mahmood, "Secularism, Hermeneutics, and Empire: The Politics of Islamic Reformation," *Public Culture* 18, no. 2 (2006): 331; Mahmood Mamdani, *Good Muslim, Bad Muslim: America, the Cold War, and the Roots of Terror* (Doubleday, 2004).

3. Angel Rabasa, Cheryl Benard, Lowell H. Schwartz, and Peter Sickle, *Building Moderate Muslim Networks* (Rand Corporation, 2007).

4. Malaysia's reputation as the epitome of moderate Islam in the 2000s is alluded to multiple times in Liow's detailed study of political Islam in Malaysia, see Joseph

Chinyong Liow, *Piety and Politics: Islamism in Contemporary Malaysia* (Oxford University Press, 2009), 3, 4, 14.

5. Malaysia's placing on such a pedestal was based on wildly alarmist writings about the threat of radical Islam in Southeast Asia in the early 2000s. For examples of such writings, see Angel Rabasa, "Political Islam in Southeast Asia: Moderates, Radicals and Terrorists," *The Adelphi Papers* 43, no. 358 (2003): 7–82; Rohan Gunaratna, *Inside Al-Qaeda: Global Network of Terror* (Columbia University Press, 2002), chap. 4; Zachary Abuza, *Militant Islam in Southeast Asia: Crucible of Terror* (Lynne Rienner, 2003).

6. The hits dropped to 114 in 2005 and were followed by an overall trend of decline. In 2008, there were only 25 hits, suggesting the waning of (Western) media interest in seeking out moderate Islam. The hits in Factiva picked up again between the years 2014–2017, which coincided with IS's rise and fall, as well as Malaysia's own Global Movement of Moderation campaign, which I will discuss below.

7. Another contender for this position among the Muslim states is Türkiye. Data from World Bank has shown that Malaysia's GDP per capita (in current USD) slightly surpassed Türkiye's in 2001 (USD 3,913 versus USD 3,119), although Türkiye would overtake Malaysia in 2003 until it lost that lead in 2018.

8. On Malaysia's status as a hybrid regime showing characteristics of competitive authoritarianism, see Steven Levitsky and Lucan A. Way, *Competitive Authoritarianism: Hybrid Regimes After the Cold War* (Cambridge University Press, 2010); Dan Slater, "Strong-State Democratization in Malaysia and Singapore," *Journal of Democracy* 23, no. 2 (2012): 19–33.

9. Mustapha Kamal Pasha, *Islam and International Relations: Fractured Worlds* (Routledge, 2017), 4; cf. Edward Said, *Orientalism* (Penguin, 2003).

10. Simon Cameron-Moore, "Analysis—Malaysia PM Welcomed as Voice of Reason by Washington," *Reuters*, May 12, 2002.

11. On a classic writing about "Muslim rage," see Bernard Lewis, "The Roots of Muslim Rage," *The Atlantic*, September 1990, https://www.theatlantic.com/magazine/archive/1990/09/the-roots-of-muslim-rage/304643. On the Bush doctrine, see Norman Podhoretz, "Enter the Bush Doctrine: The Four Pillars of the Bush Doctrine, the President's Strategy for Winning World War IV," *The Wall Street Journal*, September 2, 2004.

12. Hardev Kaur, "Malaysia a Beacon of Stability in the Islamic World," *Business Times*, April 22, 2002.

13. "Interview with L'expansion Magazine of France, Issue of 22 Nov to 6 Dec, 2001," Prime Minister's Office of Malaysia, https://www.pmo.gov.my/ucapan/index.php?qt=%moderate%&m=p&p=all&id=145.

14. On the Mahathir-Anwar breakup, see Jason Abbott, "Vanquishing Banquo's Ghost: The Anwar Ibrahim Affair and Its Impact on Malaysian Politics," *Asian Studies Review* 25, no. 3 (2001): 285–308.

15. "The Greening of Malaysia," *The Economist*, April 5, 2003, https://www.economist.com/special-report/2003/04/05/the-greening-of-malaysia.

16. Pamela Sodhy, "U.S.-Malaysian Relations During the Bush Administration: The Political, Economic, and Security Aspects," *Contemporary Southeast Asia* 25, no. 3 (2003): 363–71.

17. On Mahathir's anti-West tirades and positioning in foreign policy issues such as Asian regionalism, Third World empowerment, the Israeli-Palestinian conflict, and the Bosnian War, see Johan Saravanamuttu, *Malaysia's Foreign Policy, the First Fifty Years* (Institute of Southeast Asian Studies, 2010), 189–97.

18. Barak Mendelsohn, "Sovereignty Under Attack: The International Society Meets the Al Qaeda Network," *Review of International Studies* 31, no. 1 (2005): 45–68.

19. Speech by Mahathir Mohamad at the Extraordinary Session of the Islamic Conference of Foreign Ministers on Terrorism, Palace of the Golden Horses, Selangor, Malaysia, April 1, 2002.

20. Pınar Kemerli, "The Islamist Terrorist as the New Universal Enemy: Discourses on Terror at the United Nations," in *The Oxford Handbook of the History of Terrorism*, ed. Carola Dietze and Claudia Verhoeven (Oxford University Press, 2014).

21. "US Visa Ban a 'Price to Pay' for Being Islamic: Mahathir," *Agence France-Presse*, September 19, 2002.

22. Eileen Ng, "Malaysia Mounts Media Offensive to Assure Investors of Safe Haven," *Agence France-Presse*, February 6, 2002; "Malaysia: A Good Place to Lie Low," *Newsweek*, February 3, 2002, https://www.newsweek.com/malaysia-good-place-lie-low-147779; "US, not Malaysia the Launch Pad for Attack, says PM," *The Sun*, January 29, 2002.

23. On the Hamburg contingent, see National Commission on Terrorist Attacks upon the United States, *The 9/11 Commission Report: Final Report of the National Commission on Terrorist Attacks upon the United States* (2004), 160–69, https://govinfo.library.unt.edu/911/report/911Report.pdf.

24. "Malaysian PM Mahathir Gives Bush Advice on Fighting Terrorism," *Agence France-Presse*, October 7, 2001.

25. *US Congressional Budget Justification: Foreign Operations*, Fiscal Year 2007, 363–64. One should take care to not overstate the "improvement" in US-Malaysia security ties, which were already considerably close prior to September 11 in matters of security. For example, as mentioned above, despite the 9/11 Commission Report calling Malaysian security as "lax when it came to Islamist jihadists," the Malaysian Special Branch acceded to the US request for surveillance on a meeting in Kuala Lumpur involving several of the September 11 hijackers in January 2000. See *National Commission on Terrorist Attacks*, 158.

26. JI was founded in Malaysia in 1993 by Abdullah Sungkar and Abu Bakar Basyir. Both were Indonesian exiles who broke away from Darul Islam, a militant movement that had struggled against the Indonesian state since its inception to establish the

negara Islam Indonesia (Islamic state of Indonesia). On how Darul Islam should be understood more as a "collective identity," or a "nation" of radical Muslims, see Quinton Temby, "Imagining an Islamic State in Indonesia: From Darul Islam to Jemaah Islamiyah," *Indonesia* 89 (2010): 1–32. On suspicions that the Malaysian political elites offered protection to the JI exiles, see Quinton Temby, "Jihadists Assemble: The Rise of Militant Islamism in Southeast Asia" (PhD diss., Australian National University, 2017), 130.

27. Najib Razak, "U.S.-Malaysia Defense Cooperation: A Solid Success Story," *The Heritage Foundation*, May 3, 2002, https://www.heritage.org/asia/report/us-malaysia-defense-cooperation-solid-success-story.

28. Tong Yee Siong, "US Thanks Mahathir for Support, Understands Malaysia's Dilemma," *Malaysiakini*, October 15, 2001, https://www.malaysiakini.com/news/5124.

29. *New Sunday* Times, April 16, 2002, cited in Sodhy, "US-Malaysia Relations," 367.

30. Sidney Jones, "Indonesian Government Approaches to Radical Islam Since 1998," in *Democracy and Islam in Indonesia*, ed. Mirjam Künkler and Alfred Stepan (Columbia University Press, 2013), 109–25.

31. Liow, *Piety and Politics*, 82.

32. The announcement is considered a landmark moment (or according to Liow, the "apex" process in a game of "piety-trumping") for many because, despite the extensive Islamization programs undertaken, politicians from UMNO had hitherto refrained from calling Malaysia an "Islamic state" due to sensitivities from the non-Muslim populace. Mahathir's announcement probably cleared the way for many from the UMNO side, or those linked to the Islamic bureaucracy, to be more upfront in their "Islamic" posturing in the upcoming years. See Liow, *Piety and Politics*, 13–14.

33. Kevin Tan, "Malaysia a Fundamentalist Islamic Country, says PM," *Malaysiakini*, June 17, 2002, https://www.malaysiakini.com/news/11804.

34. Joseph Chinyong Liow, "Political Islam in Malaysia: Problematising Discourse and Practice in the UMNO-PAS 'Islamisation Race,'" *Commonwealth & Comparative Politics* 42, no. 2 (2004): 184–205.

35. Liow, "Political Islam in Malaysia," 198.

36. *Hudud* in Islamic jurisprudence refers to a set of penal codes that is instituted in the Quran and Sunnah and understood as directly ordained by God, thus eliminating any room for human interpretation. This explains the term's original meaning in Arabic: "limits." Characteristically favored by many Islamist movements, the code often attracted a lot of controversy, as the prescribed punishments included stoning and amputation. On *hudud*'s increasing salience in Malaysian politics, see Ahmad Fauzi Abdul Hamid, "The Hudud Controversy in Malaysia: Religious Probity or Political Expediency?" *Southeast Asian Affairs* (2005): 205–19.

37. Nicholas Chan, "Rethinking the Causes of Islamisation: Ontological (In)security, Postcoloniality, and Islam in Malaysia," *Journal of Southeast Asian Studies* 54, no. 3

(2023): 438; Patricia Sloane-White. *Corporate Islam: Sharia and the Modern Workplace* (Cambridge University Press, 2017), 188–94.

38. Wael Hallaq, *The Impossible State: Islam, Politics, and Modernity's Moral Predicament* (Columbia University Press, 2014).

39. Speech by Mahathir Mohamad at the Conference on Terrorism, Putrajaya World Trade Centre, Kuala Lumpur, November 16, 2001.

40. Speech by Mahathir Mohamad, November 16, 2001. Note that the term "counter-terrorism" was used by Mahathir to describe the anti-Communist operations. This is unsurprising, given that the militants were called Communist terrorists in official communications during the Emergency. In fact, Malaysia's first legal definition of a terrorist was crafted in the image of the Communist terrorists. See Nicholas Chan, "The Malaysian 'Islamic' State Versus the Islamic State (IS): Evolving Definitions of 'Terror' in an 'Islamising' Nation-State," *Critical Studies on Terrorism* 11, no. 3 (2018): 415–37.

41. Speech by Mahathir Mohamad, November 16, 2001.

42. Speech by Mahathir Mohamad, April 1, 2002. It is interesting to note that the Organisation of Islamic Cooperation delegates did not accept Mahathir's definition because, despite its intended indictment of Israel, Hamas would have been indicted by the definition as well.

43. Shanti Nair, *Islam in Malaysian Foreign Policy* (Routledge, 1997), 223.

44. Speech by Mahathir Mohamad at the Meeting and Dialogue Session with Moroccan Islamic Intellectuals, Think Tanks and Parliamentarians, Rabat, Morocco, April 16, 2002.

45. Speech by Mahathir Mohamad, April 16, 2002.

46. Speaking to Organisation of Islamic Cooperation leaders, Mahathir said, "We [Muslim state leaders] must build up our strength in every field, not just in armed might. Our countries must be stable and well administered, must be economically and financially strong, industrially competent and technologically advanced." See speech by Mahathir Mohamad at the Opening of the Tenth Session of the Islamic Summit Conference, October 16, 2003.

47. Speech by Mahathir Mohamad, April 16, 2002.

48. See Speech by Mahathir Mohamad, October 16, 2003. Bakar calls this "perhaps the most important" speech by Mahathir, as the premier was only about two weeks from his (first) retirement from his two-decade rule of Malaysia. Given his impending retirement, the speech perhaps encapsulates Mahathir's most honest assessment of the Muslim world, and how he, as did many Muslim elites, continued to process the issue of terrorism in civilizational terms. See Osman Bakar, "The Impact of the American War on Terror on Malaysian Islam," *Islam and Christian–Muslim Relations* 16, no. 2 (2005): 107–27.

49. Both Badawi's paternal grandfather Haji Abdullah Fahim (1870–1961) and his father Haji Ahmad Badawi (1907–1978) were prominent Islamic scholars. Abdullah Fahim was the first mufti of Penang, whereas Ahmad Badawi once served as

a state assemblyman for UMNO in Penang. Interestingly, both of them, as members of UMNO's religious bureau, were involved in the founding of PAS before the party broke ranks with UMNO. See Ahmad Fauzi Abdul Hamid and Muhamad Takiyuddin Ismail, "Islamist Conservatism and the Demise of Islam Hadhari in Malaysia," *Islam and Christian–Muslim Relations* 25, no. 2 (2014): 174; Farish A. Noor, *The Malaysian Islamic Party PAS 1951–2013: Islamism in a Mottled Nation* (Amsterdam University Press, 2014), 41–43.

50. *Mahazalim* is a portmanteau combining Mahathir's name and the Malay term of *zalim*, which means "tyranny". See Farish A. Noor, "How Mahathir Became 'Mahazalim,'" September 24, 2006, https://kuntakinte.wordpress.com/2007/04/10/how-mahathir-became-mahazalim/.

51. Liow, *Piety and Politics*, 86.

52. Mahathir Mohamad, 'Malaysia: The Way Forward (Vision 2020)," paper presented to the Malaysian Business Council, February 28, 1991, https://policy.asiapacificenergy.org/sites/default/files/vision%202020.pdf.

53. *Bangsa* can be loosely translated to "race," but in this context Mahathir's Bangsa Malaysia was meant to transcend the ethnic identities of the Malaysian people. It hews closer to the idea of "nation," as the official Malay translation of "nation-state" is *negara bangsa*.

54. Liow, *Piety and Politics*, 95.

55. On critical appraisals of Badawi's Islam Hadhari and its pragmatic framing as a developmentalist state ideology, see Gerhard Hoffstaeder, "Islam Hadhari: A Malaysian Islamic Multiculturalism or Another Blank Banner?" *Contemporary Islam* 3 (2009): 121–41; Terence Chong, "The Emerging Politics of Islam Hadhari," in *Malaysia: Recent Trends and Challenges*, ed. Saw Swee-Hock and K. Kesavapany (Institute of Southeast Asian Studies, 2005), 26–46; Terence Chong, "The Construction of the Malaysian Malay Middle Class: The Histories, Intricacies and Futures of the Melayu Baru," *Social Identities* 11, no. 6 (2005): 573–87.

56. Terence Chong, "Malay Capitalists: Ambassadors for Moderate Islam," *The Straits Times*, September 27, 2004.

57. Badawi led the BN to one of the greatest victories in Malaysia's electoral history in 2004, winning 198 out of the 219 seats in the parliament.

58. Abdul Hamid and Ismail, "Demise of Islam Hadhari," 171. The ten principles are faith and piety in Allah, a just and trustworthy government, a free and independent people, a vigorous pursuit and mastery of knowledge, a balanced and comprehensive economic development, a good quality of life, protection of the rights of minority groups and women, cultural and morality integrity, the safeguarding of the environment, and strong defense capabilities.

59. On Islam Hadhari's eclecticism, see Muhamad Ali, "Eclecticism of Modern Islam: Islam Hadhari in Malaysia," *Studia Islamika* 18, no. 1 (2011): 1–32.

60. Ali, "Eclecticism of Modern Islam," 172; Hoffstaeder, "Islam Hadhari."

61. Norshahril Saat, *The State, Ulama and Islam in Malaysia and Indonesia* (ISEAS-Yusof Ishak Institute, 2018), 193–94.

62. Speech by Abdullah Badawi at UMNO General Assembly 2004, September 23, 2004.

63. Speech by Abdullah Badawi, September 23, 2004.

64. Speech by Abdullah Badawi at the Informal Summit on Inter-Religious, Inter-Cultural and Inter-Civilisational Dialogue and Cooperation, United Nations, New York, September 13, 2005.

65. Speech by Abdullah Badawi, "Islam Hadhari in A Multi-Racial Society," in Sydney, Australia, April 8, 2005.

66. As Anthony Giddens puts it, "Modernity is universalising not only in terms of its global impact, but in terms of the reflexive knowledge fundamental to its dynamic character. Is modernity distinctively Western in *this* respect? This question has to be answered affirmatively, although with certain definite qualifications. The radical turn from tradition intrinsic to modernity's reflexivity makes a break, not only with preceding era, but with other cultures. See Anthony Giddens, *The Consequences of Modernity* (Polity, 1990), 174.

67. Speech by Abdullah Badawi, April 8, 2005. My point here is not about making any normative claims about Islam's compatibility with liberal democracy, which is an overdetermined question by itself. Rather, it is to highlight the pressures Muslim interlocutors faced when they speak about Islam, especially to a Western audience.

68. Speech by Abdullah Badawi, April 8, 2005.

69. Speech by Abdullah Badawi, April 8, 2005.

70. Speech by Abdullah Badawi, April 8, 2005.

71. The ruling Barisan Nasional saw its parliamentary seats dropped from 198 to 140 in the 2008 elections, effectively losing its two-thirds majority for the first time since 1969. The opposition managed to form the government in five state governments, which is also unprecedented in Malaysian history. For an analysis of the 2008 elections, see Thomas B. Pepinsky, "The 2008 Malaysian Elections: An End to Ethnic Politics?" *Journal of East Asian Studies* 9, no. 1 (2009): 87–120.

72. Edmund T. Gomez, "State–Business Linkages in Southeast Asia: The Developmental State, Neo-liberalism, and Enterprise Development," in *East Asian Capitalism: Diversity, Continuity, and Change*, ed. Andrew Walter and Xiaoke Zhang (Oxford University Press, 2012), 80; Cassey Lee and Lee Chew-Ging, "The Evolution of Development Planning in Malaysia," *Journal of Southeast Asian Economies* 34, no. 3 (2017): 452–54.

73. Michael O'Shannassy, "More Talk than Walk? UMNO, 'New Politics' and Legitimation in Contemporary Malaysia," *Journal of Contemporary Asia* 43, no. 3 (2013): 428–51.

74. *Wasatiyyah,* which can be broadly translated to "Islamic moderation," comes from the Quranic terms *wasaṭ* and *wusṭa* that also carry the meaning of "perfect,"

"superior," and "just." The use of the term *wasatiyyah* in Islamic scholarship is a fairly recent phenomenon that can be traced to the "early twentieth century in the works of Muhammad Rashid Rida, Hasan al-Banna, and Muhammad al-Madani." See Mohammad Hashim Kamali, *The Middle Path of Moderation in Islam: The Qur'ānic Principle of Wasaṭiyyah* (Oxford University Press, 2015), 10.

75. "One real and symbolic cause looming large as a rallying cry for global extremism is the unresolved Middle East problem, the plight of the Palestinian people." "The Coalition of the Moderates and Intercivilisational Understanding," speech by Najib Razak at the Oxford Islamic Centre, United Kingdom, May 16, 2011.

76. Dr. Abdullah was the chairman of the IWM from its inception in 2012 to its disbanding in 2018 following the collapse of the Najib government after an electoral defeat.

77. Hishan Harun, "A Balanced Approach that Is Islam Hadhari," *New Straits Times*, August 1, 2004.

78. Saifuddin Abdullah was the chief executive of GMMF from 2013 to 2015 until he left UMNO to join the People's Justice Party led by Anwar Ibrahim. Back then, the move was not seen as surprising given that Saifuddin's "liberal" leanings tended to clash with UMNO's ethnoreligious conservatism. Saifuddin would later surprise many when he left the People's Justice Party and became a member of UMNO's splinter party, the ethnonationalist Malaysian United Indigenous Party (Bersatu).

79. Selecting figures that are deemed "liberal," or at least friendly to the liberal internationalist circuit is not unique to Malaysia. See the case of Morocco's selection of Dr. Ahmed Abbadi as the secretary general of the Mohammedan League of Religious Scholars "for his ability to represent the institution abroad" in Wainscott, *Bureaucratizing Islam*, 122–23. Unlike in Morocco where the king himself led these campaigns, the deep ties Malaysia's conservative religious establishment have with the Malay royalty arguably impeded unorthodox appointments like these.

80. Razak Ahmad and Oh Chin Eng, "Langkawi Declaration Among Three Documents Endorsed by Asean Leaders," *The Star Online*, April 27, 2005, https://www.thestar.com.my/news/nation/2015/04/27/asean-adopts-three-documents-at-close-of-summit/; "United Nations Adopts Malaysia's Resolution of Moderation," *New Straits Times*, December 9, 2017, https://www.nst.com.my/news/nation/2017/12/312589/united-nations-adopts-malaysias-resolution-moderation.

81. A critic calls the GMMF a failure for being "neither global, a movement, nor moderate." See Athena Angel, "Najib's 'Global Movement of Moderates' is a Failure," *The Malaysian Insight*, July 24, 2017, https://www.themalaysianinsight.com/s/8500.

82. See "Malaysian Prime Minister's Speech on Moderation," May 20, 2011. Emails leaked on Wikileaks at https://wikileaks.org/clinton-emails/emailid/27882; "Joint Statement by President Obama and Prime Minister Najib of Malaysia," April 27, 2014, https://obamawhitehouse.archives.gov/the-press-office/2014/04/27/joint-statement-president-obama-and-prime-minister-najib-malaysia-0.

83. On IS, notable references include Fawaz A. Gerges, *ISIS: A History* (Princeton University Press, 2016); Graeme Wood, *The Way of the Strangers: Encounters with the Islamic State* (Random House, 2017); William McCants, *The ISIS Apocalypse: The History, Strategy, and Doomsday Vision of the Islamic State* (St. Martin's, 2015).

84. Scott Shane and Ben Hubbard, "ISIS Displaying a Deft Command of Varied Media," *The New York Times*, August 30, 2014, https://www.nytimes.com/2014/08/31/world/middleeast/isis-displaying-a-deft-command-of-varied-media.html.

85. Barack Obama, "Statement by the President," August 7 2014, https://obamawhitehouse.archives.gov/the-press-office/2014/08/07/statement-president.

86. Simone Molin Friis, "'Behead, Burn, Crucify, Crush': Theorizing the Islamic State's Public Displays of Violence," *European Journal of International Relations* 24, no. 2 (2018): 258.

87. Anthony H. Cordesman, "Islam and the Patterns in Terrorism and Violent Extremism," *CSIS*, October 17, 2017, https://www.csis.org/analysis/islam-and-patterns-terrorism-and-violent-extremism; Ayaan Hirsi Ali, 'Islam Is a Religion of Violence', *Foreign Policy*, November 9, 2015, https://foreignpolicy.com/2015/11/09/islam-is-a-religion-of-violence-ayaan-hirsi-ali-debate-islamic-state/.

88. Alireza Doostdar, "How Not to Understand ISIS," *Sightings*, October 2, 2014, https://divinity.uchicago.edu/sightings/articles/how-not-understand-isis-alireza-doostdar.

89. Zarakol alluded to this fear of being seen as barbaric and uncivil in her exploration of Japan's and Türkiye's state denial of World War II atrocities and the Armenian Genocide respectively. See Ayşe Zarakol, "Ontological (In)security and State Denial of Historical Crimes: Turkey and Japan," *International Relations* 24, no. 1 (2010): 3–23.

90. Saudi Arabia reportedly "ranked second after the United States of America in the number of air strikes carried out within the Global Coalition in (Syria)," https://web.archive.org/web/20190508134438/https://theglobalcoalition.org/en/partner/saudi-arabia/. Given Saudi Arabia's unique status as the Custodian of the Two Holy Mosques, its self-conception as the "leader of the Sunni world" (a claim made by IS as well), and IS's "claim to the Wahhabi heritage," its animosity toward IS can arguably be understood as stemming from an ontological insecurity of identity similarity. See May Darwich, "The Ontological (In)security of Similarity: Wahhabism versus Islamism in Saudi Foreign Policy," *Foreign Policy Analysis* 12, no. 3 (2016): 471. On IS and Wahhabism, see Cole Bunzel, *The Kingdom and The Caliphate: Duel of the Islamic States* (Carnegie Endowment for International Peace, 2016).

91. The signatories of the letter include scholars like Abdallah bin Bayyah, Hamza Yusuf, and then–Grand Mufti of Egypt Shawqi Allam. The signatories from Malaysia are Osman Bakar, Islamic studies scholar, and Wan Zahidi Wan Teh, former mufti of the Federal Territories of Malaysia. See letter at http://www.lettertobaghdadi.com/pdf/Booklet-English.pdf.

92. David Wasserstein, *Black Banners of ISIS: The Roots of the New Caliphate* (Yale University Press, 2017), 207.

93. Malaysia is the only Muslim-majority state in Southeast Asia to be a member of both coalitions. Indonesia participated in neither, while Brunei is only a member of the IMCTC.

94. Prasanth Parameswaran, "Where Is the New Malaysia–Saudi Arabia Counter-terrorism Center?," *The Diplomat*, April 18, 2017, https://thediplomat.com/2017/04/where-is-the-new-malaysia-saudi-arabia-counterterrorism-center/.

95. Interview with Saifuddin Abdullah, former chief executive officer of GMMF, Putrajaya, February 19, 2019.

96. Abdullah Muhammad Zin, *Pendekatan Wasatiyyah Dalam Menangani Keganasan: Pengalaman Malaysia* [Malaysia's experience in countering violent extremism through the *Wasatiyyah* approach] (Institut Wasatiyyah Malaysia, 2015).

97. Zin, *Pendekatan Wasatiyyah Dalam Menangani Keganasan*, 50.

98. Zin, *Pendekatan Wasatiyyah Dalam Menangani Keganasan*, 50.

99. As stated in the Introduction, Malaysia only suffered from one ISIS-related attack in that period when a grenade was thrown into a bar in Puchong in 2016, injuring eight.

100. Speech by Najib Razak at the 70th United Nations General Assembly, October 1, 2015.

101. On the two declarations, see Stacey Gutkowski, "We Are the Very Model of a Moderate Muslim State: The Amman Messages and Jordan's Foreign Policy," *International Relations* 30, no. 2 (2016): 206–26; Vebjørn L. Horsfjord, "The Marrakesh Declaration on Rights of Religious Minorities: Opportunity or Dead End?," *Nordic Journal of Human Rights* 36, no. 2 (2018): 151–66.

102. Speech by Najib Razak at the 69th United Nations General Assembly, September 26, 2014.

103. Nasharudin Mat Isa is a former PAS politician who was sacked from the party for disagreeing with the party's (now defunct) political cooperation with the secularist Democratic Action Party. After that partnership ended, PAS moved closer to UMNO, with Nasharudin credited as the go-betweens between Najib and PAS President Hadi Awang. Nasharudin later faced trial on charges of corruption and criminal breach of trust for, among others, the misuse of GMMF's funds. See Syed Jamal Zahid, "As Nasharudin Stands Trial for Corruption, Pundits see PAS Unscathed by Scandal," *The Malay Mail Online*, October 28, 2019, https://www.malaymail.com/news/malaysia/2019/10/28/as-nasharudin-stands-trial-for-corruption-pundits-see-pas-unscathed-by-scan/1804351.

104. Interview with former GMMF staff, February 19, 2019.

105. "Jihadist Groups 'Invented' to Put a Dent on Islam, GMM Chief Suggests," *The Malay Mail Online*, December 6, 2015, https://www.malaymail.com/news/malaysia/

2015/12/06/jihadist-groups-invented-to-put-a-dent-on-islam-gmm-chief-suggests/1018105.

106. Speech by Najib Razak, October 1, 2015. This is admittedly an odd move on the part of Najib, given that Mahathir had declared that Malaysia is an Islamic state a decade prior. However, the continuous efforts to justify the "Islamic state" identity, both to an internal and external audience, does signify the sense of insecurity associated with it.

107. "Bukit PAS tidak Sama Taliban, Bukan Pengganas" [Evidence that PAS is not like the Taliban and the Terrorist], *Harakah Daily*, March 24, 2019 https://harakahdaily.net/index.php/2019/03/24/bukti-pas-tidak-sama-taliban-bukan-pengganas/.

108. Ayşe Zarakol, "Revisiting Second Image Reversed: Lessons from Turkey and Thailand," *International Studies Quarterly* 57, no. 1 (2013): 150–62.

109. On the legacy of the Bandung conference as one of the earliest efforts to mobilize an Afro-Asian consensus, see Amitav Acharya, "Studying the Bandung Conference from a Global IR Perspective," *Australian Journal of International Affairs* 70, no. 4 (2016): 342–57; Vijay Prashad, *The Darker Nations: A People's History of the Third World* (New Press, 2007), 31–50.

110. Malaysia came the closest to shunning the West in Mahathir's effort to foster a kind of "Asian subregionalism" through his idea of the East Asia Economic Grouping, which was later called the East Asia Economic Caucus. Proposed within two years of the formation of the Asia-Pacific Economic Cooperation with its clear exclusion of the "Western" members (including Australia and New Zealand), the project was abandoned, however, due to Mahathir's combative attitude and the reticence of Japan to lead the effort. See Saravanamuttu, *Malaysia's Foreign Policy*, 190–93; Glenn Hook: The East Asian Economic Caucus: A Case of Reactive Subregionalism?" in *Subregionalism and World Order*, ed. Glenn Hook and Ian Kearns (Palgrave Macmillan, 1999).

111. For a discussion of Malaysia's policy of nonalignment—adopted since the 1970s—which underpinned its push for neutrality in Southeast Asia, its diplomatic recognition of China in 1974, and its iconoclastic championing of Third Worldism within a "neo-mercantilist" framework during the 1980s and 1990s, see Saravanamuttu, *Malaysia's Foreign Policy.*

112. Iza Hussin, "'The New Global Politics of Religion': Religious Harmony, Public Order, and Securitisation in the Post-Colony," *Journal of Religious and Political Practice* 4, no. 1 (2018): 93–106.

Chapter 5

1. I chose 2018 as the end of my study because it coincided with the ousting of the Najib government in Malaysia's fourteenth General Elections in 2018, which marked Malaysia's first power transition since its independence in 1957. Also, by 2018, IS had lost most of its territories in Syria and Iraq, resulting in the group's loss of appeal. In Malaysia, the number of arrests had dropped from 105 in 2017 to the double digits in 2018. By 2019, only twenty-six Malaysians were arrested for terrorism-related offenses. See

Farik Zolkepli, "Bukit Aman: Cops Have Nabbed 533 Suspected Militants Nationwide Since 2013," *The Star Online*, January 13, 2020, https://www.thestar.com.my/news/nation/2020/01/13/bukit-aman-cops-have-nabbed-533-suspected-militants-nationwide-since-2013; "Islamic State Remains the Top Terror Threat for Malaysia in 2018: Police," *Channel News Asia*, December 30, 2017.

2. For example, as of January 1, 2023, there were 246 individuals charged for IS-related terrorism offenses in the United States. See "GW Extremism Tracker: The Islamic State in America," https://extremism.gwu.edu/sites/g/files/zaxdzs5746/files/Dec2022-4.pdf.

3. Limor Samimian-Darash and Meg Stalcup, "Anthropology of Security and Security in Anthropology: Cases of Counterterrorism in the United States," *Anthropological Theory* 17, no. 1 (2017): 61.

4. Lisa Stampnitzky, *Disciplining Terror: How Experts Invented "Terrorism"* (Cambridge University Press, 2013).

5. For a nuanced discussion of Islamic reformism and its utility in P/CVE, see Georges Fahmi, "Why Reforming Islam to Fight Violent Extremism Is a Bad Idea," *Chatham House*, November 24, 2020, https://www.chathamhouse.org/2020/11/why-reforming-islam-fight-violent-extremism-bad-idea.

6. Interview with Ayob Khan Mydin Pitchay, Head of E8, Special Branch, July 18, 2019, Kuala Lumpur. After spending most of his policing career in counter-terrorism, Ayob Khan was later promoted to the position of chief police officer of the state of Johor in March 2020, head of the Federal Narcotics Division in December 2021, and the head of the Federal Crime Investigation Division in March 2023. Continuing his meteoric rise, by June 2023, Ayob Khan was appointed the deputy inspector general of police, the no. 2 position in the police force.

7. Andrew Humphreys, "A Total Approach: The Malaysian Security Model and Political Development" (PhD diss., University of Wollongong, 2009).

8. Jef Huysmans, "What's in an Act? On Security Speech Acts and Little Security Nothings," *Security Dialogue* 42, no. 4–5 (2011): 371–83; Gavin Sullivan, *The Law of the List: UN Counterterrorism Sanctions and the Politics of Global Security Law* (Cambridge University Press, 2020).

9. Sullivan, *The Law of the List*, 30.

10. E8's predecessor was a Special Task Force (Operations/Counterterror) that operated from 2009 to 2014. Interview with Ayob Khan, July 18, 2019. In any case, the Special Branch in Malaysia has been involved in counter-terror operations since the period of the Communist Insurgency. On the Special Branch's history, see Leon Comber, *Malaya's Secret Police 1945–60: The Role of the Special Branch in the Malayan Emergency* (ISEAS, 2008).

11. Under SOSMA, a person can be detained without trial up to twenty-eight days under suspicion of being involved in "security offenses." Even as the law specifically prohibits against politically motivated detentions, such instances still occurred. Under

POTA, a person can be detained up to two years for terrorism offences, which can be extended indefinitely based on the decision of the Prevention of Terrorism Board.

12. Video recording of a seminar entitled "The Threat of the Islamic State," given by Ayob Khan Mydin Pitchay, Head of E8, in Masjid Bukit Antarabangsa, Kuala Lumpur, February 22, 2016. Video obtained from social media, but has since been deleted.

13. A fatwa is a legal opinion or ruling, usually issued by an Islamic scholar or religious authority, on a particular issue, question, or dilemma posed by the Muslim community, based on their interpretation of the sharia. Notwithstanding its symbolic authority, the effective exercise of fatwas as a means of governance in Malaysia is complicated by Malaysia's dual legal system, where the sharia courts only have limited jurisdiction.

14. On the membership of JKF, see "Jawatankuasa Muzakarah Majlis Kebangsaan Bagi Hal Ehwal Ugama Islam Malaysia," https://i-fiqh.islam.gov.my/index.php?ef=d2VifCRONGszIQ==&id=NDl8JE40azMh.

15. See JKF, "Isu Umat Islam Yang Terlibat Dengan Perjuangan Islamic State" [The issue of Muslim's involvement with the Islamic State], 2015, https://web.archive.org/web/20220615195459/http://e-smaf.islam.gov.my/e-smaf/index.php/main/mainv1/fatwa/pr/10340.

16. The importance of gazetting fatwas lies in the fact that, in Malaysia, sharia penal codes explicitly make going against a fatwa a punishable crime. For example, under Section 4 of the Syariah Criminal Offenses (State of Penang) Enactment 1996, any religious doctrine "that is contrary to Islamic Law or any *fatwa* for the time being in force in the State of Penang" is liable to punishment of a fine up to MYR 5,000, imprisonment up to three years, and up to six strokes of whipping, or a combination thereof.

17. Fatwa Gerakan Militan Al-Dawla Al-Islamiya Fi Iraq Wa Al-Sham (Daesh), Atau Militan Islamic State in Iraq and Syams (ISIS), Atau Islamic State of Iraq and the Levant (ISILl) Atau Militan Islamic State (IS) [Fatwa on IS], *Government of Selangor Gazette* 69 (2), February 3, 2016.

18. The constitution imposes a sentencing limit on the sharia courts at MYR 5,000 fine, three years' jail imprisonment, and six lashes at a maximum. This limit became a contentious issue in what Abdul Hamid calls the "shariaization" of Malay-Muslim politics, as it is seen by many Islamists as the stumbling block toward enacting *hudud* laws in Malaysia. See Ahmad Fauzi Abdul Hamid, "Shariaization of Malay-Muslim Identity in Contemporary Malaysia," *Journal of the Malaysian Branch of the Royal Asiatic Society* 91, no. 2 (2018): 49–78.

In late 2024, the news reported that the Anwar Ibrahim government is planning to table a controversial amendment that would increase the limits to MYR 100,000 fine, imprisonment up to thirty years, and one hundred strokes of caning. It is also noteworthy that in February 2021, the Federal Court of Malaysia, the highest court in the federation, has ruled that only the civil courts have jurisdiction over criminal matters when it presided over a case about the constitutionality of the Selangor sharia court punishing one Muslim man for "unnatural" sexual relations with another man.

19. Part II of the Syariah Criminal Offenses (Selangor) Enactment 1995 is categorized as "Offences related to Aqidah," see https://web.archive.org/web/20240613065528/http://www2.esyariah.gov.my/esyariah/mal/portalv1/enakmen2011/Eng_enactment_Ori_lib.nsf/f831ccddd195843f48256fc600141e84/48907f4adb469cf84825760a0040fe64?OpenDocument.

20. Azura Abas and Fairuz Mohd Shahar, "Religious Institutions Must Play Role to Combat Extremist Ideologies," *New Straits Times*, January 6, 2018, https://www.nst.com.my/news/nation/2018/01/322190/religious-institutions-must-play-role-combat-extremist-ideologies.

21. Hariati Azizan, "JAKIM in All-Out War Against IS," *The Star Online*, April 19, 2015, https://www.thestar.com.my/news/nation/2015/04/19/jakim-in-allout-war-against-is-dept-reaches-out-to-youths-to-battle-spread-of-terrorist-ideology/.

22. "Hard to Defeat Isis on Internet, Says Jakim," *The Edge*, January 15, 2016, https://www.theedgemarkets.com/article/hard-defeat-isis-internet-says-jakim.

23. The six agencies were the Home Ministry's Malaysian Civil Defence Department, Prime Minister Department's National Security Council, the police force, Institute of Islamic Understanding Malaysia (IKIM), Al-Hijrah Media Corp and the Institute of Islamic Strategic Research Malaysia (IKSIM). The latter three were part of Malaysia's Islamic bureaucracy. Al-Hijrah and the now-defunct IKSIM was linked to JAKIM as its media and research arm respectively, while IKIM is a research institution established in 1992 by Mahathir to "correct the wrong interpretation of Islam without the use of force." See Azizan, "All-Out War"; Norshahril Saat, *The State, Ulama and Islam in Malaysia and Indonesia* (ISEAS Yusof Ishak Institute, 2018), 85–86.

24. "Malaysia to Expand Data Analytics Use in Public Sector," *GovInsider*, April 3, 2016, https://govinsider.asia/smart-gov/malaysia-to-expand-data-analytics-use-in-public-sector/.

25. Under the Printing Presses and Publications Act 1984, the power to ban a publication comes under MOHA. Nevertheless, according to ministerial guidelines, all publications have to comply with JAKIM's guideline that prohibits publications from going against the orthodoxies prescribed by the religious authorities and their fatwas. See *Garis Panduan Penerbitan Di Bawah Akta Mesin Cetak Dan Penerbitan 1984 (Akta 301)* [Guidelines for publications under the Printing Presses and Publications Act], https://www.moha.gov.my/utama/images/Perkhidmatan%20KDN/PQ/Garis_Panduan_Penerbitan_2017.pdf.

26. JAKIM, *Laporan Tahunan 2017* [Annual report 2017] (JAKIM, n.d.), 26. On cases where *Tarbiyah Jihadiyah* was raised as a terrorism-related possession, see *Public Prosecutor v Siti Noor Aishah Atam*, Written Judgement of Kuala Lumpur High Court, September 29, 2016; Hafizah Abdul Hamid, "Jailed for Possessing Subversive Books," *The Borneo Post*, May 9, 2019, https://www.theborneopost.com/2019/05/09/jailed-for-possessing-subversive-books/; Bernama, "Prosecution Fails in Appeal to Increase

Barista's Jail Term for Possession of IS Books," *New Straits Times*, October 4, 2019, https://www.nst.com.my/news/crime-courts/2019/10/527132/prosecution-fails-appeal-increase-baristas-jail-term-possession; "Clerk Jailed Two Years for Supporting Terror Groups," *The Star Online*, October 21, 2016, https://www.thestar.com.my/news/nation/2016/10/21/clerk-jailed-two-years-for-supporting-terror-groups.

27. In 2016, JAKIM was allocated a budget of MYR 724 million. The largest portion of that budget (MYR 486 million) was allocated to the policy sector, which mentioned "controlling faith perversions by deviant groups that threaten national security" as one of its major portfolios. The budget document claims that more than two thousand research and monitoring activities were conducted, although it is uncertain if they were all related to P/CVE work. "Johor Sultan: Why Does JAKIM Need RM1b Budget?," *The Malay Mail Online*, December 27, 2015, https://www.malaymail.com/news/malaysia/2015/12/27/johor-sultan-why-does-jakim-need-rm1b-budget/1030189; "Budgetary Details of the Prime Minister's Department for 2016," https://www1.treasury.gov.my/pdf/bajet/maklumat_bajet_kerajaan/2016/b6_1.pdf (page no longer available).

28. Stampnitzky, *Discipling Terror*, 13.

29. See examples of such publications at ICG, *Jemaah Islamiyah in South East Asia: Damaged but Still Dangerous*, ICG Asia Report no. 63 (2003); ICG, *Terrorism in Indonesia: Noordin's Networks*, ICG Asia Report no. 114 (2006); Institute for Policy Analysis of Conflict, *The Evolution of ISIS in Indonesia*, IPAC Report no. 13 (2014); Institute for Policy Analysis of Conflict, *Marawi, the "East Asia Wilayah" and Indonesia*, IPAC Report no. 38 (2017).

30. See discussion of the "Singapore School" at See Seng Tan, "The 'Singapore School' and the Contested Enterprise of Terrorism," in *Assembling Exclusive Expertise: Knowledge, Ignorance and Conflict Resolution in the Global South*, ed. Anna Leander and Ole Wæver (Routledge, 2019).

31. On details of the database, see Nur Azlin Mohamed Yasin, Tuty Raihanah Bte Mostarom, Nur Aziemah Binte Azman, and Nur Irfani Binte Saripi, "Terrorist Manuals and Tradecraft Online: Indicators of Higher Risk?," *Counter Terrorist Trends and Analyses* 3, no. 2 (2011): 7.

32. Tan, "Singapore School," 115.

33. I have ventured to provide an analysis of the IS phenomenon in Malaysia here, but even that is bounded by the constraints of having to work with publicly accessible information that varies in depth from case to case. See Nicholas Chan, "From Jemaah Islamiyah to Islamic State in Malaysia," in *Global Jihad in Southeast Asia: Examining the Expansion of the Islamic State and Al-Qaeda*, ed. M. K. Sheikh (Danish Institute of International Studies, 2019), 64–69. Two other works about IS in Malaysia were published after the first draft of this manuscript is finished, but, tellingly, none were written by scholars based in Malaysia. See Rueben Dass and Jasminder Singh, "Pathways to the Caliphate: Mapping Malaysian Foreign Fighter Networks in Iraq and Syria from 2012–2019," *Terrorism and Political Violence* 35, no.

7 (2023): 1502–35; Amira Jadoon, Nakissa Jahanbani, Elina Noor, Marley Carroll, and William Frangia, *Risks, Recruits, and Plots: Understanding and Mitigating the Influence of the Islamic State in Malaysia* (Combatting Terrorism Center, US Military Academy, 2022).

34. Lydia Wilson, "Gone to Waste: The 'CVE' Industry After 9/11', *New Lines Magazine*, September 10, 2021, https://newlinesmag.com/argument/understanding-the-lure-of-islamism-is-more-complex-than-the-experts-would-have-you-believe/.

35. Saiful Edris Zainuddin, "Social-Media Combating Terrorism and Terrorism-Related Crimes: Has the Current Legal Framework Been Effective?" Presentation Slides for the 8th Event of the Attorney General's Chambers of Brunei Darussalam, Malaysia and Singapore.

36. For a review of the field of terrorism, or rather radicalization studies, see Alex P. Schmid, "Radicalisation, De-Radicalisation, Counter-Radicalisation: A Conceptual Discussion and Literature Review," *The International Centre for Counter-Terrorism—The Hague* 4, no. 2 (2013), https://icct.nl/publication/radicalisation-de-radicalisation-counter-radicalisation-conceptual-discussion-and.

37. Malaysian Prison Department, Ministry of Home Affairs, "Taklimat dan Penyampaian Watikah Ahli Panel Deradikalisasi [Briefing and presentation of letters of appointment for Deradicalisation Panel members]," June 1, 2017, https://www.prison.gov.my/ms/artickle/48366-Taklimat-Dan-Penyampaian-Watikah-Ahli-Panel-Deradikalisasi. There is no indication that all those appointed to the panel were actively involved in deradicalization work within prisons. In practice, many served only as consultants. The names mentioned in this book belong to those most actively involved in counter-terror practices and have received the most publicity for it.

38. Mohd Mizan Aslam, "A Model of Deradicalisation in Malaysia," in *International Case Studies of Terrorist Rehabilitation*, ed. Rohan Gunaratna and Sabariah Husin (Routledge, 2018), 95. I am well aware that the term *deradicalization* has its problematic implications and some scholars would prefer the terms *rehabilitation* and *disengagement*. The problematization of "deradicalization" will be done in the next chapter.

39. That certainly is not the case for the many scholars who study jihadist violence as anthropologists, political scientists, political theorists, psychologists, and sociologists.

40. *Ustaz* is a popular designation given to the ulamas in Malaysia. It basically means "teacher."

41. The thesis is entitled *Doktrin "Salfiyyah Wahabiyyah" Dan Respon Umat Islam Di Malaysia: Kajian Dalam Kalangan Penjawat Awam Di Putrajaya Dan Kuala Lumpur* [The response of Malaysians toward the Salafi-Wahhabi doctrine: A study of the civil servants in Putrajaya and Kuala Lumpur]. Public Facebook Post under Ustaz Zamihan Al-Ghari, August 21, 2016.

42. On the ulama as a vocation and its social standing in the Malay world, see Saat, *The State, Ulama and Islam*, 55–59.

43. Interview with Ustaz Zamihan Mat Zin Al-Ghari, February 21, 2019, Kuala Lumpur; Institute for Policy Analysis of Conflict, *Puritan Political Engagement: The Evolution of Salafism in Malaysia*, Policy Report no. 52 (2018), 13.

44. One reason for Ahmad's prominence as compared to the other practitioners is his fluent command of English, making him the resource person for many Western/English-speaking journalists interested in writing about terrorism in Malaysia. See, for example, "Are Terrorists Beyond Reform? Malaysia Is Gambling They Aren't," *Apolitical*, November 6, 2018, https://apolitical.co/solution-articles/en/are-terrorists-beyond-reform-malaysia-is-gambling-they-arent.

45. The full thesis title is "The Ideological Formulation of Jama'ah Islamiyyah and Malaysia's Rehabilitative Approach in Negotiating Jama'ah Islamiyyah Discourse, 1993–2012."

46. The *pondok* system refers to a network of religious boarding schools that began as centers of informal Islamic education in Malay villages. It was centered on a local teacher in their own home (hence the name, *pondok*, which means "huts"). Nonetheless, in the present day, the *pondok* system is integrated into the national or state-level education system with very few left as independent institutions. See Azmil Tayeb, *Islamic Education in Indonesia and Malaysia: Shaping Minds, Saving Souls* (Routledge, 2018), 63.

47. "Mustaza bin Abdul Rahman v Public Prosecutor," *Malayan Law Journal* 11 (2020): 240.

48. For a chronicle of Ustaz Uthman's life, see Mohd Ammryul Ashraf Sairan and Shukri Ahmad, "Jejak Intelektual dan Pemikiran Akidah Muhammad Uthman El-Muhammady [Tracing the intellectual and Aqidah teachings of Muhammad Uthman El-Muhammady]," *Journal of Contemporary Islamic Studies* (JCIS) 4, no. 2 (2018): 99–118; Shameem Abdul Jali, "The Nation Has Lost a Great Scholar," *New Straits Times*, April 3, 2013.

49. Farik Zolkepli, "Facing Down Terror," *The Star Online*, April 23, 2017, https://www.thestar.com.my/news/nation/2017/04/23/facing-down-terror-the-man-who-leads-a-bukit-aman-division-in-fighting-terrorism-has-many-tales-to-s/.

50. See, for example, Singapore's Religious Rehabilitation Group (RRG) that hosts a group of Islamic scholars who participate in the deradicalization programs for detainees suspected of Islamist militancy. The cofounder and former cochairman, Ustaz Ali Haji Mohamed (d. 2023), was the father of another RRG member, Ustaz Mohamed Ali. Mohamed Ali took over his father's cochairmanship in 2022. Earning a doctorate in Islamic studies from the University of Exeter, Ustaz Dr Mohamed Ali is also a senior fellow at the S. Rajaratnam School of International Studies where the aforementioned "Singapore School" of terrorism studies is located.

51. Interview with Ahmad El-Muhammady, February 22, 2019, Kuala Lumpur.

52. "Lapan Pakar Deradikalisasi Bendung Ideologi Pengganas" [Eight deradicalization experts to stem terrorist ideology]," *Harian Metro*, May 22, 2018.

53. Interview with Mohd Mizan Aslam, January 28, 2019, Perlis.

54. Interview with Mohd Mizan Aslam, January 28, 2019.

55. Mohd Mizan Aslam, "A Critical Study of Kumpulan Militant Malaysia, Its Wider Connections in the Region and the Implications of Radical Islam for the Stability of Southeast Asia" (PhD diss., Victoria University of Wellington, 2009).Yet, despite writing what is considerably the most empirically rich study of Islamist militancy in Malaysia, Mizan, according to his Google Scholar profile, has not published anything related to the topic since 2009. That hiatus ended in 2017, which saw a slew of publications related to the IS phenomenon.

56. According to his biodata for a professorial lecture, Ahmad Fauzi received his religious training through self-learning, family ties, and a famous cleric in Perak by the name of Haji Muhammad Saman Kati (1922–1995). Trained at Oxford University and Leeds, Ahmad Fauzi wrote his dissertation at the University of Newcastle Upon Tyne on Darul Arqam. He also authored a book that was banned for allegedly showing sympathy to the sect, which was deemed a "deviant" movement by the government (see chapter 3). See Ahmad Fauzi Abdul Hamid, "Islamisme Dan Bahananya: Cabaran Besar Politik Malaysia Abad Ke-21" [Islamism and its consequences: The challenges to Malaysian politics in the 21st century], *Siri Syarahan Umum Pelantikan Professor 2014/ Bil. 8* (University Sains Malaysia, 2018), v–xi.

57. Interview with Ahmad Fauzi Abdul Hamid, March 7, 2019, Penang.

58. In our interview, Hizam admitted being self-taught in the study of radicalization and was involved in the deradicalization program through his connection with Zamihan. The two also coauthored a book on IS. See Interview with Mohd Hizam Hanafiah, May 9, 2019, Bangi; Mohd Hizam Hanafiah and Zamihan Mat Zin al-Ghari, *Bahaya ISIS (Daesh)* [The dangers of ISIS (Daesh)] (AlHimna Enterprise, 2017).

59. Aslam, "Model of Deradicalisation," 90.

60. "Zahid: Deradicalisation Programme has 97.5pct Success Rate," *Malaysiakini*, February 20, 2017, https:/www.malaysiakini.com/news/373066.

61. That was the case for Ahmad. Zamihan intended to earn a second PhD by writing about deradicalization too, though his status is listed at "inactive" when I last checked.

62. Interview with Mohammed Saiful Alam Shah, member of the RRG, April 22, 2019, Singapore.

63. "Peguam Cabar Zamihan Dedah Kelayakan Sebagai Pakar Keganasan" [Lawyer challenged Zamihan to reveal his credentials as a terrorism expert], *Free Malaysia Today*, June 13, 2018, https://www.freemalaysiatoday.com/category/bahasa/2018/06/13/peguam-cabar-zamihan-dedah-kelayakan-sebagai-pakar-keganasan/.

64. "Zamihan Has a History of Targeting Christians, Moderate Muslims," *The Star Online*, October 11, 2017, https://www.thestar.com.my/news/nation/2017/10/11/zamihan-has-a-history-of-targeting-christians-and-moderate-muslims/.

65. Interview with deputy public prosecutor of Serious Crimes Unit, July 7, 2019, Putrajaya.

66. Expert reports provided by a defense attorney for a terrorism trial involving a religious teacher. Names of experts anonymized. All translations from Malay are mine.

67. *Tarbyiah Jihadiyah* refers to one of Abdullah Azzam's posthumously distributed books, which has the original title of *al-tarbiya al-jihadiyya wa'l-bina'* [Jihadi education and edification]. It is a compendium that collects up to sixteen volumes of Azzam's writings and lectures, most of which is about his experience in the Soviet-Afghan War. The book was translated into Indonesian as three volumes, each consisting of about seven hundred pages, and was cited as "the favourite *jihad* manual" by terrorism analysts interested in Malaysia and Indonesia. See references to the book's influence in studies of Southeast Asian Islamist militancy at Zulkaranain Haron and Nordin Hussin, "A Study of the Salafi Jihadist Doctrine and the Interpretation of Jihad by Al Jama'ah Al Islamiyah," *Kemanusiaan* 20, no. 2 (2013): 30; Ahmad Fauzi Abdul Hamid, "Islamist Violence in Malaysia: Reflections from the Pre-GWOT Era with Special Reference to the Memali and Al-Mau'nah Cases," in *SEARCCT Selection of Articles 2020* (Southeast Asia Regional Centre for Counter-Terrorism, 2020), 16; Kumar Ramakrishna, "Reflections of a Reformed Jihadist: The Story of Wan Min Wan Mat," *Contemporary Southeast Asia* 38, no. 3 (2016): 504.

68. Report by Expert A (political scientist) on *Tarbiyah Jihadiyah*, May 2, 2018, 1.

69. Report by Expert B (lecturer in Islamic Studies) on *Tarbiyah Jihadiyah*, May 3, 2018, 3.

70. This is a contestable claim, given that Abdullah Azzam was assassinated in 1989, almost twenty-five years before the emergence of IS in its so-called caliphate form. Thomas Hegghammer, who wrote an authoritative biography of Abdullah Azzam, claims ambivalence as to how Azzam would hypothetically react to IS's claim to a territorial Islamic caliphate if he is alive today. For Hegghammer, the only thing he can be certain of is that Azzam would be "very critical of IS's brutality and the youthful arrogance of its members." See Thomas Hegghammer, *The Caravan: Abdallah Azzam and the Rise of Global Jihad* (Cambridge University Press, 2020), 491.

71. Report by Expert C (lecturer in Islamic Studies) on *Tarbiyah Jihadiyah*, August 14, 2018, 5.

72. Sullivan, *The Law of the List*, 61.

73. The National Security Council is the highest coordinating body for security matters concerning Malaysia. It was formed after the Emergency declaration following the 1969 racial riots and is kept as a coordinating body under the Prime Minister's Department.

74. JAKIM, *Jihad dan Konsepnya* [Jihad and its concepts] (JAKIM, 2015), https://www.islam.gov.my/images/ePenerbitan/jihad_dan_konsepnya.pdf. All page numbers cited are based on the online version.

75. Both Hasan al-Banna (1906–1949) and Ustaz al-Qaradawi (1926–2022) were prominent figures within the Muslim Brotherhood, or Ikhwan. Banna founded the movement in Egypt in 1929, while Qaradawi, a prolific writer, served as one of its most

prominent ideologues. Qaradawi founded the International Union of Muslim Scholars and stepped down as its president in 2018. He was sentenced to life in prison in absentia by the al-Sisi government in 2018 for "alleged involvement in acts of violence in 2015," although the charge was widely disputed. See "Yusuf al-Qaradawi Sentenced to Life in Prison in Egypt," *Al Jazeera*, January 18, 2018, https://www.aljazeera.com/news/2018/01/yusuf-al-qaradawi-sentenced-life-prison-egypt-180118065805129.html.

76. On the ideology of IS, see Cole Bunzel, "From Paper State to Caliphate: The Ideology of the Islamic State," Analysis Paper no. 19 (Brookings Institution, Center for Middle East Policy, 2015); William McCants, *The ISIS Apocalypse: The History, Strategy, and Doomsday Vision of the Islamic State* (St Martin's, 2015).

77. This claim is a direct challenge to Abdullah Azzam who preached that armed jihad is an individual obligation (*fardhu 'ain*) instead of a collective one (*fardhu kifayah*). As Li argues, the image of a "foreign fighter" is rather menacing to the nation-state due to their defiance of the principle of violence as a state monopoly, and of the declaration of war as a state prerogative. See Darryl Li, *The Universal Enemy: Jihad, Empire, and the Challenge of Solidarity* (Stanford University Press, 2020), 82.

78. See Saudi debates on the threat of IS in Raihan Ismail, "Reclaiming Saudi Salafism: The Saudi Religious Circles and the Threat of ISIS," *Journal of Arabian Studies* 9, no. 2 (2019): 164–81. See Al-Qaeda's denouncement of IS as Kharijites for their extremist attitudes in Cole Bunzel, "Jihadism on its Own Terms," Hoover Institution, https://www.hoover.org/sites/default/files/research/docs/jihadism_on_its_own_terms_pdf.pdf, 10.

79. Jeffrey T. Kenney, *Muslim Rebels: Kharijites and the Politics of Extremism in Egypt* (Oxford University Press, 2006), 9.

80. In discussing the *khawarij*, the booklet cites one hadith (12–13): "In the last days of this world there will appear some young foolish people who will use (in their claim) the best speech of all people (i.e., the Qur'an) and they will abandon Islam as an arrow going through the game. Their belief will not go beyond their throats (i.e., they will have practically no belief), so wherever you meet them, kill them, for he who kills them shall get a reward on the Day of Resurrection." *Sahih al-Bukhari* 3611, translation taken from https://sunnah.com/bukhari/61/118.

81. Kamarulnizam Abdullah, "National Security and Malay Unity: The Issue of Radical Religious Elements in Malaysia," *Contemporary Southeast Asia* 21, no. 2 (1999): 261–82.

82. "The US, IS and the Conspiracy Theory Sweeping Lebanon," *BBC*, August 12, 2014, https://www.bbc.com/news/world-middle-east-28745990.

83. Ayob Khan also went on to detail how the US and its Arab allies were once funders of Al-Qaeda. On IS, he used the fact that Abu Bakar al-Baghdadi, the first "caliph" of IS, was once a detainee at an American-run prison camp, and that in 2015 IS attacked the Al-Yarmouk camp that housed a lot of Palestinian refugees instead of Israel as evidence that "behind IS are the enemies of Islam." The crisis discourse

of how Muslim nations fell one by one into chaos was invoked as well, using examples of Iraq, Syria, and Libya. See video recording of a seminar entitled *Ancaman Daesh & Istilah Kafir Harbi* (The threat of Daesh and the term Kafir Harbi) given by Ayob Khan Mydin Pitchay in Saloma Bistro, Kuala Lumpur, August 13, 2016. Video obtained from YouTube, https://www.youtube.com/watch?v=5L3iJ3fcsyc.

84. The *fiqh al-awlawiyyat*, or the *fiqh* of priorities, refers to Qaradawi's advice to Islamist movements that they need to reconcile questions of doctrine with complex social, economic, and political realities. Qaradawi preaches that "what should be postponed must not be hastened, nor is what should be hastened be postponed. This is what we have called 'understanding priorities.'" He used that principle to advise the Taliban to at least postpone the destruction of the Bamiyan Buddha statutes because "Afghanistan had more pressing problems," such as poverty, low living standards, and violence. See Sagi Polka, *Shaykh Yūsuf Al-Qaradāwī: Spiritual Mentor of Wasatī Salafism* (Syracuse University Press, 2019), 201 and 333.

85. On discussions of the jihad on more anthropological grounds, see Li, *Universal Enemy*; Engseng Ho, "Empire through Diasporic Eyes: A View from the Other Boat," *Comparative Studies in History and Society* 46, no. 2 (2004): 210–46. On the atomized nature of Malaysia's IS phenomenon, see Chan, "From Jemaah Islamiyah to Islamic State," 67.

86. I have discussed the *kaum tua/kaum muda* rivalry in chapter 2.

87. For an excellent review of this evolving theological divide, see Maszlee Malik, "Theology in Malaysia: Between Mainstream and the Periphery," *hikma: Journal of Islamic Theology and Religious Education* 6 (2013): 51–65; Maszlee Malik, "Salafism in Malaysia: Historical Account on Its Emergence and Motivations," *Sociology of Islam* 5 (2017): 303–33.

88. On the surface, the term *Ahlus Sunnah Wal Jamaah* carries the generic meaning of Sunni Islam. In reality, however, the traditionalists seized the term to label themselves as representing "true" Islam in opposition to what they call the Salafi/Wahhabi camp. This "seizure" was made literal when a nongovernmental organization that calls itself the Pertubuhan Ahlus Sunnah Wal Jamaah (Aswaja) was formed in 2013, with Zamihan as its president. Aswaja's formation is about pushing back against the Salafis that are gaining popularity through its popular preachers, especially among the middle classes. On the history of the struggle to define what constitutes the ASWJ, see Maznah Mohamad, *The Divine Bureaucracy and Disenchantment of Social Life: A Study of Bureaucratic Islam in Malaysia* (Palgrave Macmillan, 2020), 123–33.

89. On the Salafi-oriented camp and their entanglement with Malaysian politics, see Institute for Policy Analysis of Conflict, *Puritan Political Engagement*; Mohamed Nawab Mohamed Osman, "Salafi Ulama in UMNO: Political Convergence or Expediency?," *Contemporary Southeast Asia* 36, no. 2 (2014): 206–31; Ahmad Fauzi Abdul Hamid, "The Extensive Salafization of Malaysian Islam," *Trends in Southeast Asia* no. 9 (ISEAS–Yusof Ishak Institute, 2016).

90. Maznah Mohamad, "Religion and Politics on Malaysian Nation-Building: A 'Double-Movement' of Hegemonic and Plural Islam," *Inter-Asia Cultural Studies* 18, no. 3 (2017): 449.

91. Institute for Policy Analysis of Conflict, *Puritan Political Engagement*, 13.

92. Institute for Policy Analysis of Conflict, *Puritan Political Engagement*, 13; Interview with Ayob Khan, July 18, 2019.

93. Presentation slides by Abdullaah Jalil, "Perkongsian Tentang Daesh" [Sharing about Daesh] for the "Terrorism Has No Religion" seminar, National Mosque of Malaysia, May 18, 2017.

94. The Salafists' concept of Tauhid 3 is seen as contradicting the traditionalists' Tauhid Sifat 20 (Twenty Attributes of God) that follows from their Ashaarite-Maturidite tradition. Accompanying the theological struggle between traditionalists and modernists (who were seen as influenced by Salafi and Wahhabi teachings) is a contest for influence within Malaysia's religious and political institutions, with stakes involving broader issues such as Islamic education and practices. See Abdul Hamid, "Extensive Salafization."

95. Fathul Bari was one of the very few pro-Salafi figures who got appointed into the counter-terror regime, albeit not as an expert witness or a deradicalization practitioner as those mentioned above. An Islamic Studies doctorate graduate from the International Islamic University of Malaysia who was also educated in Jordan and Saudi Arabia, Fathul Bari was an active member of the youth wing of UMNO and was instrumental in securing close ties between the Najib administration and the Saudi administration, see Institute for Policy Analysis of Conflict, *Puritan Political Engagement*, 13. The irony is that, despite this appointment, Fathul Bari was banned from preaching in certain states in Malaysia, such as Johor and Selangor, because of his Salafi-leanings.

96. "ISIS Khawarji Modern" [IS as modern-day *khawarij*]; "Fiqh Jihad menurut Maqasid Syariah" [The fiqh of Jihad according to the principles of sharia]; presentation slides shared by Fathul Bari in 2019.

97. According to a published paper, Maszlee's research lasted around a year when he was engaged as a participant in the rehabilitation sessions by virtue of the invitation of the director of the Sungai Buloh prison. See Maszlee Malik and Mohd Yazid Zul Kepli, "ISIS in Malaysia: Understanding Their Logics," *Islamiyyat* 40, no. 1 (2018): 16. My informants told me that Maszlee's access to the detainees was later blocked by Zamihan.

98. Maszlee Malik was a lecturer at the International Islamic University of Malaysia who earned his bachelor's degree in al-Bayt University, Jordan, in the field of *fiqh* and *usul fiqh*. He got his master's degree from the University of Malaya in the same field and got his PhD from Durham University with a thesis on Islamic governance in 2011. Maszlee joined the UMNO splinter party, Bersatu, in 2018 and was made the minister of education briefly (2018–2020) when the party's coalition won the election in 2018. He later quit the party and joined Anwar's People's Justice Party in early 2022. Maszlee is a member of the Islamist NGO Pertubuhan IKRAM Malaysia, and was labeled as

Salafi-leaning with alleged close ties to the Perlis Mufti Asri, who was seen by many as the most prominent figure of the Salafi camp in Malaysia. See "Former Associate Not Surprised by Protests over Maszlee as Education Minister," *Free Malaysia Today*, May 20, 2018, https://www.freemalaysiatoday.com/category/nation/2018/05/20/former-associate-not-surprised-by-protests-over-maszlee-as-education-minister/; "As Dr M Takes Over MoE, Claims Abound of Maszlee's Men in Key Positions," *Free Malaysia Today*, January 19, 2020, https://www.freemalaysiatoday.com/category/nation/2020/01/19/as-dr-m-takes-over-moe-claims-abound-of-maszlees-men-in-key-positions/.

99. Malik and Zul Kepli, "ISIS in Malaysia," 18–19; Maszlee Malik, "ISIS in Malaysia: A Case Study," ISEAS Yusok Ishak Insitute Regional Forum Discussion Papers (2016), 3.

100. Zamihan Mat Zin Al-Ghari, *Bahaya Doktrin Salafiyyah Wahhabiyyah* [The dangers of the Salafi-Wahhabi doctrine] (Al-Himna Enterprise, 2018).

101. Al-Ghari, *Bahaya Doktrin Salafiyyah Wahhabiyyah*, 158–76. This claim of IS bearing the Wahhabi heritage is also made in a recent book by a renowned scholar on Wahhabism and Salafism, see Cole Bunzel, *Wahhābism: The History of a Militant Islamic Movement* (Princeton University Press, 2023), 339–41.

102. Anthony Milner, *The Invention of Politics in Colonial Malaya* (Cambridge University Press, 2002), 151–63; Michael Christopher Low, "Empire and the Hajj: Pilgrims, Plagues, and Pan-Islam under British Surveillance, 1865–1908," *International Journal of Middle East Studies* 40, no. 2 (2008): 269–90; A. J. Stockwell, "Imperial Security and Moslem Militancy, with Special Reference to the Hertogh Riots in Singapore (December 1950)," *Journal of Southeast Asian Studies* 17, no. 2 (1986): 322–35.

103. Al-Ghari, *Doktrin Salafiyyah*, 167–68.

104. "Cops: Stamp Out Radicalism," *The Star Online*, August 21, 2016, https://www.thestar.com.my/news/nation/2016/08/21/cops-stamp-out-radicalism-the-message-from-the-police-on-is-militants-is-chilling-the-threat-to-thi/.

105. For an example of such technical writing on the topic of the dangers and deviances of Wahhabism, see Zamihan Mat Zin Al-Ghari, *Aswaja Menjawab 70 Penyelewengan Wahhabi* [Aswaja answers the 70 deviancies of the Wahhabis] (AlHimna Enterprise, 2018).

106. Interview with Zamihan, February 21, 2019; Malik, "ISIS in Malaysia," 5.

107. While my writing thus far has largely focused on the lack of discretion from the ASWJ camp in their demonization of the Salafis, that is not to say that the Salafi-leaning figures were more discerning in their animus either. For instance, due to the Salafis' purported anti-Shia attitudes, Perlis Mufti Asri was accused of involvement in the enforced disappearance of one alleged Shia activist last seen in his state in 2016, a claim he denied. In 2019, pro-Salafi figures also embarked on a social media campaign to associate certain Hindu members of the Democratic Action Party with the now-defunct Liberation Tigers of Tamil Eelam through tenuous connections, which eventually led to a few individuals getting charged for supporting terrorism. See Institute for

Policy Analysis of Conflict, *Puritan Political Engagement*, 14; Hew Wai Weng, "The Politics of Muslim Majoritarianism," *Asialink*, April 6, 2020, https://web.archive.org/web/20221128005052/https://asialink.unimelb.edu.au/insights/the-politics-of-muslim-majoritarianism2.

108. Hazlin Hassan, "8 Held in Malaysia for Suspected Terror Links," *The Straits Times*, October 6, 2018. The *madrasah* was said to be linked to Yemeni cleric Sheikh Muqbil bin Hadi al-Wadi'i (1993–2001), who was expelled from Saudi Arabia due to his close ties to Juhayman al-'Utaybi who led the siege of the Grand Mosque in 1979. Muqbil was highly influential in developing "Yemeni Salafism" and was known to hold extremely conservative social attitudes. His death in 2001 meant any postulation of his support for the violent extremism of IS can only be speculative, but his movement has been characterized by scholars as "apolitical." See Laurent Bonnefoy, "How Salafism Came to Yemen: An Unknown Legacy of Juhayman al-'Utaybi 30 Years On," *Middle East Institute*, October 1, 2009, https://www.mei.edu/publications/how-salafism-came-yemen-unknown-legacy-juhayman-al-utaybi-30-years; Laurent Bonnefoy, "Deconstructing Salafism in Yemen," CTC Sentinel January Special Issue (2010): 16–18.

109. *The Straits Times*, October 6, 2018.

110. Zamihan, *Aswaja*, 22.

111. In interviews with pro-ASWJ figures, it was hinted to me that Asri's political connections was the reason why Salafi-Wahhabism was never officially identified as the key contributor to violent extremism, despite that was the view held by senior counter-terror practitioners such as Ayob Khan and Zamihan.

112. The madrasah Dar al-Quran Wal Hadeeth, was listed as one of the nine *tahfiz* (Quran memorization) schools that had received an official permit to operate in Perlis. See "Hanya 9 Tahfiz Di Perlis Beroperasi Secara Sah" [Only nine Tahfiz were operating legally in Perlis], *Mynewshub*, October 2, 2017, https://www.mynewshub.tv/terkini/hanya-9-maahad-tahfiz-di-perlis-beroperasi-secara-sah/. On the donation, see Facebook post by ASWJ-linked Pusat Kajian Ancaman Ekstremis Agama, October 9, 2018, https://www.facebook.com/share/p/1NMPK74H8Q/.

113. The arrest involved eight detainees, seven of whom were non-Malaysians. The Malaysian that was arrested was released soon after, while the rest were deported. One of the detainees, a French national, was killed in a road traffic accident while they were transported to Kuala Lumpur. See Asri's response at Shakira Buang, "Asri: Sebut Ayob Khan terbayang muka Zamihan" [Asri: Uttering the name of Ayob Khan reminds me of Zamihan], *Malaysiakini*, February 9, 2019, https://www.malaysiakini.com/news/463317.

114. Interview with Academic A, May 9, 2019. I have taken the discretion to not reveal the identity of this academic who is still teaching in a public university.

115. On the Dabiq prophecy in IS's ideology, see McCants, *The ISIS Apocalypse*, 97–101.

Chapter 6

1. Michael Dillon, "Governing Terror: The State of Emergency of Biopolitical Emergence," *International Political Sociology* 1, no. 1 (2007): 11.

2. Gavin Sullivan, *The Law of the List: UN Counterterrorism Sanctions and the Politics of Global Security Law* (Cambridge University Press, 2020), 41.

3. Jef Huysmans, "Security! What Do You Mean? From Concept to Thick Signifier," *European Journal of International Relations* 4, no. 2 (1998): 226–55.

4. Lisa Stampnitzky, *Disciplining Terror: How Experts Invented "Terrorism"* (Cambridge University Press, 2013), 203.

5. Sullivan, *The Law of the List*; Marieke de Goede, "The Politics of Preemption and the War on Terror in Europe," *European Journal of International Relations* 14, no. 1 (2008): 161–85.

6. Joseph Chinyong Liow, *Piety and Politics: Islamism in Contemporary Malaysia* (Oxford University Press, 2009); Patricia Sloane-White, *Corporate Islam: Sharia and the Modern Workplace* (Cambridge University Press, 2017).

7. ML deRaismes Combes, "Encountering the Stranger: Ontological Security and the Boston Marathon Bombing," *Cooperation and Conflict* 52, no. 1 (2017): 127.

8. Nicholas Chan, "The Malaysian 'Islamic' State Versus the Islamic State (IS): Evolving Definitions of 'Terror' in an 'Islamising' Nation-State," *Critical Studies on Terrorism* 11, no. 3 (2018): 417–18.

9. Ayşe Zarakol, "What Makes Terrorism Modern? Terrorism, Legitimacy, and the International System," *Review of International Studies* 37, no. 5 (2011): 2315.

10. Helen Irving, "The Concept of Allegiance in Citizenship Law and Revocation: An Australian Study," *Citizenship Studies* 23, no. 4 (2019): 372–87.

11. Patrick Sykes, "Denaturalisation and Conceptions of Citizenship in the 'War on Terror,'" *Citizenship Studies* 20, no. 6–7 (2016): 749–63; Christian Joppke, "Terror and the Loss of Citizenship," *Citizenship Studies* 20, no. 6–7 (2016): 728–48. For an exception, see Nicholas Chan, "In Moderation of 'Strangers': Terrorism, Ontological (In)Security and Counter-Narratives in Malaysia," *Critical Studies on Security* 8, no. 1 (2020): 28–45.

12. Claire Lyness, "Governing the Suicide Bomber: Reading Terrorism Studies as Governmentality," *Critical Studies on Terrorism* 7, no. 1 (2014): 79–96; Sullivan, *The Law of the List.*

13. Mohd Azizuddin Mohd Sani, "ISIS Recruitment of Malaysian Youth: Challenge and Response," *Middle East Institute*, May 3, 2016, https://www.mei.edu/publications/isis-recruitment-malaysian-youth-challenge-and-response. Similar trends can be seen in other places. Leaked documents from IS have shown that 87 percent of the Saudi foreign fighters were under the age of twenty-nine, with most of them in their early twenties. See Khaled Al-Saud, *Saudi Foreign Fighters: Analysis of Leaked Islamic State Entry Documents* (International Centre for Studies of Radicalisation, King's College London, 2019), 11.

14. "Malaysian Police Detain 14-Year-Old Girl Trying to Join ISIS," *The Straits Times*, February 19, 2015, https://www.straitstimes.com/asia/se-asia/malaysian-police-detain-14-year-old-girl-trying-to-join-isis; "'Brainwashed' Teenager Holds Woman at Knifepoint in Malaysian Supermarket to Prove ISIS Membership," *The Straits Times*, January 12, 2016, https://www.straitstimes.com/asia/se-asia/brainwashed-teenager-holds-woman-at-knifepoint-in-malaysian-supermarket-to-prove-isis; "Malaysian Teen in Beer Fest Terror Plot Exposed to ISIS Ideology When He Was 15 Years Old," *The Straits Times*, October 23, 2017, https://www.straitstimes.com/asia/se-asia/malaysian-teen-in-beer-fest-terror-plot-exposed-to-isis-ideology-when-he-was-15-years.

15. *Hansard*, Senate of Malaysia, December 20, 2016, 10.

16. The phenomenon of army personnel or veterans being radicalized is not a feature exclusive to Malaysia or Islamist extremism. In the United States, radicalization happened among veterans but more importantly, in the name of the veterans, as a blowback to the Vietnam War. See Kathleen Belew, *Bring the War Home: The White Power Movement and Paramilitary America* (Harvard University Press, 2018).

17. Stuart Croft, *Securitizing Islam: Identity and the Search for Security* (Cambridge University Press, 2012).

18. *Kami Warga ATM Menolak Daesh (ISIS): Garis Panduan Pencegahan Fahaman Ekstremisme & Radikalisme Dalam Angkatan Tentera Malaysia* [The Malaysian Army rejects Daesh (IS): Guidelines to counter extremist and radical thinking in the Malaysian Army] (Task Force Perisai Wira ATM, Bahagian Staf Perisikan Pertahanan [Heroes' Shield Special Taskforce of Malaysian Army, Defense Intelligence Unit], 2017).

19. "MAF Perisai Wira Task Force Roadshow," *Malaysia Military Times*, November 13, 2019, https://mymilitarytimes.com/index.php/2019/11/13/maf-perisai-wira-task-force-roadshow/.

20. Sabah stood out as a risk factor because it is a famous transit zone for militants to move in and out of Malaysia, especially for the purposes of joining the struggle in Mindanao as well as Indonesia. See Institute for Policy Analysis of Conflict, *Pro-Isis Groups in Mindanao and Their Links to Indonesia and Malaysia*, Policy Report no. 33 (2016).

21. Thomas Martin, "Governing an Unknowable Future: The Politics of Britain's Prevent Policy," *Critical Studies on Terrorism* 7, no. 1 (2014): 72, 75.

22. *Channel Duty Guidance: Protecting Vulnerable People from Being Drawn into Terrorism-Statutory Guidance for Channel Panel Members and Partners of Local Panels* (HM Government, 2015), 12.

23. These alleged *bid'ah* practices include *Yassin and tahlil* ceremonies, prayer rituals such as reading the *Qunut* and *talkin*, and *maulid* Nabi S.A.W (the celebration of the Prophet's birthday). Actors from the pro-ASWJ camp who claim to represent traditionalist Islam in Malaysia have long taken issue with the pro-Salafi camp for their denouncement of these local and more syncretic practices of Islam. See chapter 5.

24. Report uploaded in a Facebook post by Alwi Al-Bakaniyy, May 19, 2019.

25. Scott Atran, "ISIS Is a Revolution," *Aeon*, December 15, 2015, https://aeon.co/essays/why-isis-has-the-potential-to-be-a-world-altering-revolution.

26. IYRES, *Garis Panduan Pencegahan Fahaman Radikalisme dan Ekstremisme dalam Kalangan Belia dan Masyarakat* [Guidelines on preventing radicalism and extremism among youths in Malaysia] (IYRES, 2018).

27. IYRES, *Laporan Akhir Kajian Profil Belia Dalam Kegiatan Ekstremisme* [Final report for the study of youth profiles in extremist activities] (IYRES, 2016), 11–16.

28. IYRES and Universiti Malaysia Kelantan, *Kajian Pembangunan Kesejahteraan: Pendidikan Agama Islam dan Penglibatan dalam Gerakan Islam Radikal di Kalangan Belia'* [Development of well-being: Islamic education and the involvement of youths in radical Islamic movements] (IYRES, 2015), 81.

29. IYRES and Universiti Malaysia Kelantan, *Kajian Pembangunan Kesejahteraan*, 84.

30. The misinterpretation is defined as "wrong interpretation of the Quran, misunderstanding concepts such as *jihad*, *hudud*, Islamic state, *hijrah*, and loyalty to rulers," see IYRES, *Laporan Akhir*, 20.

31. IYRES, *Laporan Akhir*, 25.

32. IYRES, *Laporan Akhir*, 26. My point is not that these beliefs concerning *tauhid* are inconsequential or even unproblematic in its practical manifestations. Rather, it is extremely difficult to extrapolate one's political beliefs and convictions from their interpretation of *tauhid* alone, let alone extremist tendencies. Even if personal connections to Salafi thinking can be identified, one's political attitudes are hardly predetermined. For example, electoral Salafi parties have emerged in Egypt and Tunisia. Even if these parties are "free riding" on democracy, this still represents a deviation from the Salafis' earlier stances that democracy is haram. See Emmanuel Karagiannis, "The Rise of Electoral Salafism in Egypt and Tunisia: The Use of Democracy as a Master Frame," *The Journal of North African Studies* 24, no. 2 (2019): 220.

33. Dillon, "Governing Terror, 16."

34. Dillon, "Governing Terror," 24.

35. Dillon, "Governing Terror," 22.

36. The panic was partly stoked by one of the studies commissioned by IYRES, which reported that 20 percent of university students were "Daesh sympathizers." That figure came from a research paper that shows that close to 20 percent of the students surveyed said that they agreed with the statement that "they respect the political ideology of ISIS." The paper then went on to claim that "low understanding" of ISIS's ideology and the success of its propaganda were the reasons behind this, but the evidence for those claims was not offered. The paper only measures understanding of IS's ideology by asking respondents what kind of organization ISIS is (religious, political, terrorist, and others) and what is their religious orientation (Syiah, Sunni, Salafi, and Sufi). See "20% Varsity Students Daesh 'Sympathisers,'" *The Sun Daily*, August 24, 2016, https://www.thesundaily.my/archive/1946908-FSARCH389789; Che Mohd Aziz Yaacob,

Bakri Mat, Fakhrorazi Ahmad, Mohd Azizuddin Modh Sani, Rusdi Omar, and Kamarul Zaman Haji Yusoff, "Kefahaman dan Penerimaan Mahasiswa University Awam terhadap Gerakan ISIS" [Understanding and acceptance of IS among local university students], *Malaysian Journal of Youth Studies* 15 (2016): 89–106.

37. Two high-profile cases have sustained this myth of supposedly "highly educated" individuals being radicalized by IS. One is a former Islamic studies lecturer by the name of Mahmud Ahmad, who reportedly trained in an Al-Qaeda camp in Afghanistan in the late 1990s and was a pivotal figure in the Marawi siege in 2017. He was later killed by the Filipino army in late 2017. The other is Siti Noor Aishah Atam, a postgraduate student in Islamic studies who was a student of Mahmud's, a case I will return to later. To be sure, they were pretty much the exception and not the norm. On Mahmud's involvement in the Marawi siege, see Institute for Policy Analysis of Conflict, "Marawi, The 'East Asia Wilayah' and Indonesia," *IPAC Report* no. 38 (2017).

38. Until 2012, the ISA was the key legislation underpinning Malaysia's counter-terror operations, including the hundreds of arrests of JI-related militants after September 11. The law was instituted during the Communist Insurgency and could be used to detain someone for up to two years under the orders of the home minister, which could be renewed indefinitely. Its history of use against political dissidents eventually led to its replacement by SOSMA that contains the provision, "No person shall be arrested and detained under this section solely for his political belief or political activity." See Section 4(3), SOSMA Act 2012. On a detailed reporting of the ISA's secrecy and alleged abuses, see Human Rights Watch, "In the Name of Security: Counterterrorism and Human Rights Abuses Under Malaysia's Internal Security Act," *Human Rights Watch* 16, no. 7 (2004): 1–57.

39. Data given by SAC Azman Omar of the E8 Division in Roundtable Discussion on "Islam, Radicalism and Extremism in the Age of Pandemic." Zoom seminar organized by the International Institute of Advanced Islamic Studies, Malaysia, March 25, 2021.

40. Only when the son of an opposition leader was caught in one of the raids did counter-terrorism receive scrutiny in the early 2000s. Mark Landler, "War on Terror Fuels Political Feuds in Malaysia," *The New York Times*, October 19, 2001, https://www.nytimes.com/2001/10/19/world/war-on-terror-fuels-political-feuds-in-malaysia.html.

41. See Nicholas Chan, "From Jemaah Islamiyah to Islamic State in Malaysia," in *Global Jihad in Southeast Asia: Examining the Expansion of the Islamic State and Al-Qaeda*, ed. M. K. Sheikh (Danish Institute of International Studies, 2019), 67; Sulastri Osman, "Jemaah Islamiyah: Of Kin and Kind," *Journal of Current Southeast Asian Affairs* 29, no. 2 (2010): 157–75.

42. Chan, "Evolving Definitions,." Also see Kent Roach, "Comparative Counter-Terrorism Law Comes of Age," in *Comparative Counter-Terrorism Law*, ed. Kent Roach (Cambridge University Press, 2015), 25.

43. Section 130B of the Malaysian Penal Code.

44. For example, the definition of terrorism in Malaysia excludes "advocacy, protest, dissent or industrial action" that is not intended to cause serious harm. See Section 130B of the Malaysian Penal Code.

45. Section 13 of POTA; Section 19A of POCA.

46. Interviews with deradicalization officers A and B, February 21, 2019, and July 5, 2019.

47. In official government data released, between 2014 and 2019, 487 IS-related arrests were made under SOSMA, while 47 and 36 were made under POCA and POTA, respectively. Data downloaded from data.gov.my.

48. "Siti Noor Aishah Jailed Five Years for Possession of IS Books," *The Sun Daily*, April 26, 2017, https://www.thesundaily.my/archive/siti-noor-aishah-jailed-five-years-possession-books-ITARCH441618. In this case, the accused was rearrested under POCA after her acquittal was overturned, resulting in her conviction.

49. Other than detention, both POTA and POCA allow for forced relocation, the installation of electronic monitoring devices, and movement controls of individuals. In other words, the person would have to live with the consequences and legal incrimination of being a terrorist despite not convicted as one.

50. According to a former public prosecutor turned academic who specializes in antiterrorism law, "90 percent" of the accused pleaded guilty. Interview with Mukhriz Mat Rus, January 22, 2019, Perlis.

51. There are no official statistics as to how many individuals charged under terrorism offenses were acquitted at the end, but interviews as well as my own case tracking have suggested almost none. The only case where an individual was successfully acquitted at the end of the legal process was a police officer accused of concealing "terrorism-related information from the authorities." Even that was based on a technicality. On the case, see Hidir Redhuan, "Terrorism—Top Court Acquits Ex-Cop of Withholding Info," *Malaysiakini*, March 11, 2019, https://www.malaysiakini.com/news/467439.

52. Interview with Farida Mohammad, defense counsel in several terrorism cases, September 12, 2019, Kuala Lumpur.

53. Sections 4, 13, and 17–26 of SOSMA Act 2012.

54. Radzi Razak, "Malaysian Court Sentences 3 Suspects to Jail in IS-linked Terror Plot," *BenarNews*, April 15, 2019, https://www.benarnews.org/english/news/malaysian/suspects-sentence-04152019154517.html.

55. Adam Abu Bakar, "Ibu 8 Anak Fobia Menderma Selepas Suami Dituduh Bantu Pengganas" [Mother of 8 is scared of donations after her husband is accused of supporting terrorism], *Free Malaysia Today*, December 25, 2019, https://www.freemalaysiatoday.com/category/bahasa/2019/12/25/ibu-8-anak-fobia-menderma-selepas-suami-dituduh-bantu-pengganas/.

56. See Sections 17, 18A, 18B, 19 and 26 of SOSMA Act 2012. Also see Human Rights Watch, "Malaysia: Repeal Abusive Security Law," October 31, 2019, https://www.hrw.org/news/2019/10/31/malaysia-repeal-abusive-security-law.

57. Interviews with lawyers A and B, July 17 and 18, 2019; former SOSMA detainee, August 6, 2019.

58. Interview with Farida Mohammad, July 18, 2019; Interview with family member of SOSMA detainee, July 22, 2019.

59. "Movida Attackers Jailed 25 Years Each," *The Star Online*, March 30, 2017, https://www.thestar.com.my/news/nation/2017/03/30/movida-attackers-jailed-25-years-each-duo-also-accused-of-supporting-is-group.

60. Section 130B of the Malaysian Penal Code.

61. The excerpts were taken from *Murad Halimuddin bin Hassan and Others v Public Prosecutor*, Written Judgement of the Court of Appeal, July 23, 2018; *Public Prosecutor v Kadir bin Uyong and Others*, Written Judgement by the Court of Appeal, November 8, 2017. The latter refers to the Lahad Datu incursion that happened in 2013 when a group of Sulu militants launched an attack on the titular location while claiming the state of Sabah as their own. It is interesting to note that the militants were charged not only with waging war against the head of state of Malaysia, the Yang di-Pertuan Agong, but also with being members of a terrorist group under Section 130KA of the Malaysian Penal Code, which carries a maximum penalty of life imprisonment. The second charge proved contentious, as the Sulu militants were not known to be affiliated with any recognized terrorist organization in the region, such as Abu Sayyaf. In fact, the defense argued that the militants identified themselves as the Royal Sulu Force, which was not listed as a terrorist organization. Nevertheless, the court concluded that because their actions amounted to terrorism, their status as a terrorist group was unquestionable.

62. Sullivan, *The Law of the List.*

63. Sullivan, *The Law of the List*, 76–77.

64. Sullivan, *The Law of the List*, 28.

65. Sullivan, *The Law of the List*, 77.

66. Section 130B of the Malaysian Penal Code.

67. As Section 66C of AMLA puts it, "Where the Security Council of the United Nations decides, in pursuance of Article 41 of the Charter of the United Nations, on the measures to be employed to give effect to any of its decisions and calls upon the Government of Malaysia to apply those measures, the Minister of Home Affairs may, by order published in the *Gazette*, make such provision as may appear to him to be necessary or expedient to enable those measures to be effectively applied."

68. See Sections 130J, 130JB, 130K, 130KA, 130N and 130Q in the Malaysian Penal Code. There are up to twenty-five statutes within the terrorism offences section of the penal code.

69. "Malaysian Soldier Gets Seven Months' Jail for ISIS Image on Mobile Phone," *The Straits Times*, October 20, 2015, https://www.straitstimes.com/asia/se-asia/malaysian-soldier-gets-seven-months-jail-for-isis-image-on-mobile-phone; "Lelaki Dipenjara 6 Tahun Miliki Item Berkaitan Pengganas" [Man jailed for 6 years for possession related to terrorism], *Malaysiakini*, July 13, 2018.

70. One exception to the usual lineup of Islamic scholars summoned to the Malaysian court is Rohan Gunaratna, a terrorism studies professor at the Nanyang Technological University, Singapore. However, as someone who made his name as the "go-to" Al-Qaeda expert in the early days of the GWOT, Gunaratna has a checkered reputation due to his ties to the military-industrial complex and his tendency to make sweeping, "apocalyptic," and, at times, dubious, claims on matters of terrorism. For example, in his book on Al-Qaeda, he made the claim that both PAS and the Malaysian Islamic Youth Movement (ABIM) were part of Al-Qaeda's terror network, none of which was substantiated at all. See David Miller and Tom Mills, "The Terror Experts and the Mainstream Media: The Expert Nexus and Its Dominance in the News Media," *Critical Studies on Terrorism* 2, no. 3 (2009): 427; Gary Hughes, "Analyse This," *The Age*, July 20, 2003, https://www.theage.com.au/world/analyse-this-20030720-gdw2tg.html. On a serious critique of Gunaratna's book on Al-Qaeda, see Farish A. Noor, "Fighting Their Own Demons," *Malaysiakini*, July 5, 2002, https://www.malaysiakini.com/columns/20547.

71. This is the case of Siti Noor Aishah Atam, a postgraduate drop-out in Islamic Studies in the University of Malaya, making her, notwithstanding the public panic surrounding the matter, one of the rare cases involving a university student. On the case of Siti Noor Aishah, see Nicholas Chan, "Reflecting on the Curious Case of Siti Aishah," *Iman Research*, January 3, 2018, https://www.imanresearch.com/2018/01/03/reflecting-on-the-curious-case-of-siti-aishah/.

72. *Public Prosecutor v Siti Noor Aishah Atam*, Written Judgement of the Kuala Lumpur High Court, September 29, 2016. It is interesting to note that out of the three experts consulted, two of them were Islamic scholars: Zamihan, whom we discussed in chapter 5, and Wan Adli bin Wan Ramli, who is an Islamic Studies lecturer in the University of Malaya. Wan Adli does not specialize in the study of terrorism, as far as my research suggests. The third is Rohan Gunaratna (see above), whose testimony was rejected by the court because he admitted he could not read Malay (the language in which the books were written) and had made his assessments of the books based on translations and a database hosted in Singapore, both of which the court could not cross-examine.

73. Expert reports by Zamihan Mat Zin for the case *Public Prosecutor v Yazid Sufaat and Others* shared by Farida Mohammad. Zamihan had testified in court claiming that the accused had "spread misguided religious teachings and had manipulated the meaning of jihad and the Quran." See "*Saksi Dakwa Yazid Semai Salafi Jihadi*" [Witness claims Yazid spreads Salafi Jihadism], *Harian Metro*, October 6, 2015, https://www.hmetro.com.my/mutakhir/2015/10/82680/saksi-dakwa-yazid-semai-salafi-jihadi.

74. *Public Prosecutor v Siti Noor Aishah Atam*, Written Judgement of the Kuala Lumpur High Court, September 29, 2016.

75. *Public Prosecutor v Aszroy Achoi*, Written Judgement of the Kota Kinabalu High Court, March 26, 2018.

76. "Judge Gives IS Trainer a Lecture on Religion Before Handing Out Sentence," *The Sun Daily*, February 4, 2016, https://www.thesundaily.my/archive/1686468-ISARCH349142.

77. Despite significant effort spent locating this case in public records, I was unable to find any terrorism cases involving an academic charged in court. However, given the judge's vivid memory of the incident, this anecdote feels too important to omit.

78. Interview with High Court Judge, July 16, 2019.

79. In my interviews thus far, I have not come across a case where human rights activists and lawyers believe an outrightly innocent person has been wrongly convicted. The major complaint they have is with the laws and how the process is vulnerable to abuse.

80. The virtual aspect is particularly important in IS-related cases in Malaysia, as many involve records of online activity submitted as evidence, such as the *ba'iah* (pledge of allegiance) given to IS. Police crackdowns often targeted entire chat groups. For example, one group called Gagak Hitam (Black Crows), led by a high-profile Malaysian militant in Syria named Muhammad Wanndy Mohamed Jedi, resulted in at least a dozen individuals being prosecuted for terrorism-related crimes.

81. One of the major critiques of viewing terrorism through network theory is that it may support the expansion of the surveillance state, while overlooking the root causes of individual radicalization. See Patrick Radden Keefe, "Can Network Theory Thwart Terrorists?," *The New York Times*, March 12, 2006, https://www.nytimes.com/2006/03/12/magazine/can-network-theory-thwart-terrorists.html; Mari Cecilie Tolfsen Reinskou, "Is Network Theory the Most Suitable for Understanding Terrorist Radicalisation?," *Security Forum* 1, no. 1 (2017): 39–47.

82. Ahmad Fauzi Abdul Hamid, "ISIS in Southeast Asia: Internalized Wahhabism Is a Major Factor," *ISEAS Perspective* no. 24 (2016).

83. John Horgan, "Deradicalization or Disengagement?: A Process in Need of Clarity and a Counterterrorism Initiative in Need of Evaluation," *Perspectives on Terrorism* 2, no. 4 (2008): 3–8; M. S. Elshimi, *De-Radicalisation in the UK Prevent Strategy: Security, Identity and Religion* (Routledge, 2017); Alex P. Schmid, "Radicalisation, De-Radicalisation, Counter-Radicalisation: A Conceptual Discussion and Literature Review," *ICCT Research Paper* (2013), https://icct.nl/publication/radicalisation-de-radicalisation-counter-radicalisation-conceptual-discussion-and.

84. On the gardening state, see Zygmunt Bauman, *Modernity and Ambivalence* (Polity, 1991), 20–35. On high modernism, see James C. Scott, *Seeing Like a State: How Certain Schemes to Improve the Human Condition Have Failed* (Yale University Press, 1998).

85. Section 4(1) of POTA.

86. On the foreign fighter phenomenon as a subset of Muslim militancy and political violence in general, see Thomas Hegghammer, "The Rise of Muslim Foreign Fighters:

Islam and the Globalization of Jihad," *International Security* 35, no. 3 (2010): 53–94; David Malet, "Why Foreign Fighters? Historical Perspectives and Solutions," *Orbis* 54, no. 1 (2010): 97–114.

87. See note 47 for POTA figures.

88. The 97 percent figure is unverifiable, nor is it immediately clear if the success is measured in terms of actual deradicalization or mere disengagement. In any case, it is still too early to tell if the IS-related detainees will refrain from recidivism. It is known that at least five individuals who made up the earliest batch of Malaysian foreign fighters in Syria (important to note that they did not join IS at the first instance) were former detainees under the ISA. See "Five Former ISA Detainees Fighting for Isis Militants, Report Says," *The Edge*, September 11, 2014, https://www.theedgemarkets.com/article/five-former-isa-detainees-fighting-isis-militants-report-says.

89. "Malaysia Offers to Help Europe Reform Terrorists," *The Star Online*, November 2, 2016, https://www.thestar.com.my/news/nation/2016/11/02/kl-offers-to-help-europe-with-is-malaysia-offers-to-help-europe-reform-terrorists/.

90. BBC News, "Deradicalisation in Malaysia," YouTube, February 19, 2020, https://www.youtube.com/watch?v=poTDSEQwoZA.

91. Dipanjan Roy Chaudhury, "India Approaches Malaysia For an Anti-Radicalisation Islamic Education System," *The Economic Times*, July 26, 2016, https://economictimes.indiatimes.com/industry/services/education/india-approaches-malaysia-for-an-anti-radicalisation-islamic-education-system/articleshow/53388777.cms; "New Zealand Seeks Help on Deradicalisation of Terrorists," *The Star Online*, May 2, 2017, https://www.thestar.com.my/news/nation/2017/03/02/nz-seeks-help-on-deradicalisation-of-terrorists/.

92. See UN Security Council Counter-Terrorism Committee Executive Directorate, *Implementation of Security Council Resolution 2178 (2014) by States Affected by Foreign Terrorist Fighters: A Compilation of Three Reports* (S/2015/338; S/2015/683; S/2015/975), 79.

93. Ministry of Home Affairs, *Integrated Deradicalisation Module for Terrorists* (UPM Press, 2016); Ahmad Zahid Hamidi, "Malaysia's Policy on Counter-Terrorism and Deradicalisation Strategy," *Journal of Public Security and Safety* 6, no. 2 (2016): 1–19.

94. Whereas there is a team in MOHA dedicated to only POTA detainees, the police still bring in experts such as Ahmad El-Muhammady, who worked with not just POTA detainees but also other terrorism detainees. Interview with MOHA officer, September 4, 2019, Penang; Interview with Ahmad El-Muhammady, February 22, 2019.

95. I was not able to access the prisons department or the POTA detainees, most of whom were still under detention during my fieldwork in 2019. See discussion of fieldwork methodology in Introduction.

96. Michel Foucault, "Governmentality," in *The Foucault Effect: Studies in Governmentality*, ed. Graham Burchell, Colin Gordon, and Peter Miller (University of Chicago Press, 1991), 102.

97. Ministry of Home Affairs, *Integrated Deradicalisation Module*, 59–60.

98. To paraphrase a MOHA officer involved in the POTA program, they would not force detainees to participate. But if they did not participate, they would not be released anyway. Interview with MOHA officer, September 4, 2019.

99. Ministry of Home Affairs, *Integrated Deradicalisation Module*, xxii.

100. Section 19 of the POTA Act.

101. Section 8 of POTA.

102. "Ahli Lembaga POTA Perlu Dilantik Secara Terbuka—Gerakan [POTA members should be elected openly—Gerakan]," *Gerakan*, April 9, 2015, https://www.gerakan.my/news-media/gallery/states-gallery/item/8111-ahli-lembaga-pota-perlu-dilantik-secara-terbuka-gerakan#.YGjm52hKhPY (page no longer available).

103. For example, the program has a Phase Four that is not mentioned in the manual, which consists of community service, such as visiting elder care homes, "to remind the detainees of their responsibilities to their family." Interview with MOHA officer, September 4, 2019. See also "Program Khidmat Masyarakat Bagi Tahanan Fasa Iv Di Bawah Akta Pencegahan Keganasan (Pota) 2015" [Community service program for POTA Phase 4 detainees], *Prisons Department of Malaysia*, March 23, 2018, https://www.prison.gov.my/ms/artickle/49382-Program-Khidmat-Masyarakat-Bagi-Tahanan-Fasa-Iv-Di-Bawah-Akta-Pencegahan-Keganasan-(Pota)-2015.

104. Ministry of Home Affairs, *Integrated Deradicalisation Module*, xvi.

105. Hamidi, "Malaysia's Policy," 13.

106. According to one lecturer who was also involved in the deradicalization programs, the police and MOHA brought in experts of their own because the religious officers in the JPN were found to be "less competent" as they were only used to giving basic classes on religion and were ill equipped to discuss in-depth concepts such as *kafir* (disbelief), *negara* (state), and jihad that were pivotal to disarming the ideology of the detainees. Interview with Academic B, August 5, 2019.

107. All terrorism-related detainees, be it POTA or SOSMA, were isolated from other prisoners due to the risk of them radicalizing others. Even prison wardens were reportedly radicalized by the terrorism detainees. See "7 Malaysian Wardens Radicalised by Detainees," *The Straits Times*, July 29, 2016, https://www.straitstimes.com/asia/se-asia/7-malaysian-wardens-radicalised-by-detainees. Nevertheless, the "special" treatment afforded to all the detainees may risk stereotyping them as charming ideologues when only a very tiny minority of them could play that role. For example, only one name kept coming up when I spoke to counter-terror practitioners about this archetypical "charismatic" radicalizer, which is Yazid Sufaat, who caused a lot of issues for the prison officers for his unrepentant ways. Interview with Special Branch Officers A and B, September 17, 2019. Yazid, known as Bin Laden's anthrax scientist, was a former captain in the Malaysian army and a biochemistry graduate from the California State University–Sacramento. He is a veteran of jihadist militancy due to his involvement with Al-Qaeda since the early 1990s. Nonetheless, his is not a résumé typical of the average IS detainee,

nor had Yazid ever pledged his allegiance to IS. On Yazid's biography, see Alexandra Pocek Joosse and H. Brinton Milward, "Organizational Versus Individual Attribution: A Case Study of Jemaah Islamiyah and the Anthrax Plot," *Studies in Conflict & Terrorism* 37, no. 3 (2014): 242.

108. Ministry of Home Affairs, *Integrated Deradicalisation Module*, 187 and 189.

109. Michel Foucault, *The History of Sexuality. Volume I: An Introduction* (Pantheon Books, 1978), 61–62.

110. Mohammed Elshimi, "De-Radicalisation Interventions as Technologies of the Self: A Foucauldian Analysis," *Critical Studies on Terrorism* 8, no. 1 (2015): 123.

111. Ministry of Home Affairs, *Integrated Deradicalisation Module*, 13–14. 19–20.

112. Ministry of Home Affairs, *Integrated Deradicalisation Module*, 186.

113. Elshimi. "De-Radicalisation Interventions," 122.

114. As the detainee progressed through difference phases of the module, they were granted more privileges, including visitation rights and contact with their family members. Interview with MOHA officer, September 4, 2019.

115. Ministry of Home Affairs, *Integrated Deradicalisation Module*, 72. The only "technical" measurement used in the module for detainee evaluation is a method called "digital stress voice analysis," a method used to measure deception from a person's voice (xxii). Nevertheless, research has found the method "not promising." See Kelly R. Damphousse, Laura Pointon, Deidra Upchurch, and Rebecca K. Moore, *Assessing the Validity of Voice Stress Analysis Tools in a Jail Setting* (Research report submitted to the US Department of Justice, 2007), 88, https://www.ncjrs.gov/pdffiles1/nij/grants/219031.pdf.

116. Michel Foucault, *Wrong-Doing, Truth-Telling: The Function of Avowal in Justice* (University of Chicago Press, 2014).

117. The ability of the state to maintain close contact with former detainees and militants can be seen in an iftar (breaking fast during Ramadhan) event hosted in 2019, during which 122 individuals who were former detainees or prisoners convicted under terrorism offenses attended with their families. See Muzlia Mustafa and Ali Nufael, "Di Malaysia, Iftar adalah Masa untuk Jalin Semula Silaturahim dengan Bekas Militan" [In Malaysia, Iftar is the time to rekindle with former militants], *BenarNews*, May 21, 2019, https://www.benarnews.org/malay/berita/special-iftar-05212019162035.html.

118. "Are Terrorists Beyond Reform? Malaysia Is Gambling They Aren't,'" *Apolitical*, November 6, 2018, https://apolitical.co/en/solution_article/are-terrorists-beyond-reform-malaysia-is-gambling-they-arent.

119. Ulu Tiram is a notable spot for JI because it was where JI founders Abu Bakar Bashir and Abdullah Sungkar started a religious school, the Luqmanul Hakim Islamic School. As a result, Ulu Tiram became a node for JI activities in Malaysia in which many of its militants have stayed and even taught in the school. Abdul Matin was one of the JI operatives who harbored Mas Selamat Kastari, another JI operative who famously escaped from the custody of the Singapore police in 2008 until he was recaptured a year

later in a village in Malaysia. Ulu Tiram was also the location of perhaps Malaysia's second IS-inspired attack in 2024, undertaken by a family that used to identify with JI. On the JI network, see Mohd Mizan Mohammad Aslam, "A Critical Study of Kumpulan Militant Malaysia, Its Wider Connections in the Region and the Implications of Radical Islam for the Stability of Southeast Asia," PhD diss., Victoria University of Wellington, 2009.

120. Paraphrase from interview of Ayob Khan Mydin Pitchay with *Malaysia Gazette*, July 10, 2020, https://www.youtube.com/watch?v=MBSlObccqOo. It is worth noting that despite each of them calling the other *Pak* (uncle), Ayob Khan was only in his early fifties but Pak Abu was in his seventies already.

121. Ministry of Home Affairs, *Integrated Deradicalisation Module*, 175.

122. Ministry of Home Affairs, *Integrated Deradicalisation Module*, 195–98.

123. Ministry of Home Affairs, *Integrated Deradicalisation Module*, 205.

124. Interview with MOHA officer, September 4, 2019; Interview with Ayob Khan, July 18, 2019.

125. Ministry of Home Affairs, *Integrated Deradicalisation Module*, 111–12, 126–27.

126. Terence Chong, "The Construction of the Malaysian Malay Middle Class: The Histories, Intricacies and Futures of the Melayu Baru," *Social Identities* 11, no. 6 (2005): 573–87.

127. On the bureaucratization of Islam as a hybrid phenomenon, see Dominik M. Müller and Kerstin Steiner, "The Bureaucratisation of Islam in Southeast Asia: Transdisciplinary Perspectives," *Journal of Current Southeast Asian Affairs* 37, no. 1 (2018): 3–26.

Conclusion

1. Mahathir Mohamad, "Respect Others," October 29, 2020, http://serambichedet.com/respect-others/ (page no longer available).

2. Mohamad, "Respect Others."

3. Lucy Williamson, "Samuel Paty: Beheading of Teacher Deepens Divisions over France's Secular Identity," *BBC*, October 20, 2020, https://www.bbc.co.uk/news/world-europe-54602171.

4. Conrad Duncan, "Muslims Have a Right to 'Kill Millions of French People' Over Past Actions, Former Malaysian PM Suggests," *The Independent*, October 29, 2019, https://www.independent.co.uk/news/world/europe/muslims-france-malaysian-pm-mahathir-mohamad-macron-charlie-hebdo-b1424838.html.

5. Mohamad, "Respect Others."

6. Garett M. Graft, "After 9/11, the U.S. Got Almost Everything Wrong," *The Atlantic*, September 8, 2021, https://www.theatlantic.com/ideas/archive/2021/09/after-911-everything-wrong-war-terror/620008/.

7. Without underplaying the symbolic significance of the idea, one should note that this notion of a united Muslim world generally does not play out in international relations. If anything, continued fragmentations in Middle Eastern geopolitics would

signal that the *ummah* probably has less saliency than the idea of Europe as a political unifier.

8. "Anwar Discusses Madani Governance, Islamophobia During Friday Sermon in New York Mosque," *New Straits Times*, September 23, 2023, https://www.nst.com.my/news/nation/2023/09/958570/anwar-discusses-madani-governance-islamophobia-during-friday-sermon-new. Important to note that this appeal was made before the October 7 attacks by Hamas and the Gaza crisis that followed.

9. Sarah Logan, *Hold Your Friends Close: Countering Radicalization in Britain and America* (Oxford University Press, 2023), 6.

10. William T. Cavanaugh, *The Myth of Religious Violence: Secular Ideology and the Roots of Modern Conflict* (Oxford University Press, 2009), 205.

11. Arun Kundnani and Ben Hayes, *The Globalisation of Countering Violent Extremism Policies: Undermining Human Rights, Instrumentalising Civil Society* (Societal Security Network, 2018).

12. See, for example, Peter Mandaville and Melissa Nozell, "Engaging Religion and Religious Actors in Countering Violent Extremism," *United States Institute of Peace Special Report* 413 (2017): 9–11.

13. Mark Danner, "Taking Stock of the Forever War," *The New York Times*, September 11, 2005, https://www.nytimes.com/2005/09/11/magazine/taking-stock-of-the-forever-war.html.

14. Peter Mandaville and Shadi Hamid, *Islam as Statecraft: How Governments Use Religion in Foreign Policy* (Brookings Institution, 2018), 25; Ann Marie Wainscott, *Bureaucratizing Islam: Morocco and the War on Terror* (Cambridge University Press, 2017).

15. Wainscott, *Bureaucratizing Islam*, chap. 8; Yahia Hatim, "France to Start Training Native Imams," *Morocco World News*, February 18, 2020, https://www.moroccoworldnews.com/public/2020/02/293914/france-to-start-training-native-imams; Safaa Kasraoui, "Morocco to Resume Imam Training Program in January 2021," *Morocco World News*, November 24, 2020, https://www.moroccoworldnews.com/public/2020/11/326921/morocco-to-resume-imam-training-program-in-january-2021.

16. Wainscott, *Bureaucratizing Islam*, 223.

17. On the need to integrate local politics into the understanding of jihadist movements, including those claiming a "global" goal, see Alexander Thurston, *Jihadists of North Africa and the Sahel: Local Politics and Rebel Groups* (Cambridge University Press, 2020); Darryl Li, "A Jihadism Anti-Primer," *Middle East Report* 276 (2015): 12–17.

18. Stefano Bonino, "Policing Strategies Against Islamic Terrorism in the UK After 9/11: The Socio-Political Realities for British Muslims," *Journal of Muslim Minority Affairs* 32, no. 1 (2012): 5–31.

19. James D. Fearon and David D. Laitin, "Does Contemporary Armed Conflict Have 'Deep Historical Roots'?" paper prepared for delivery at the 2014 Annual Meeting of the American Political Science Association, August 28–31, 2014.

20. Kikue Hamayotsu, "Moderate-Radical Coalition in the Name of Islam: Conservative Islamism in Indonesia and Malaysia," *Kyoto Review of Southeast Asia* 23 (2018), https://kyotoreview.org/issue-23/conservative-islamism-indonesia-malaysia/; Hew Wai Weng, "The Politics of Muslim Majoritarianism," *Asialink*, April 6, 2020, https://web.archive.org/web/20221128005052/https://asialink.unimelb.edu.au/insights/the-politics-of-muslim-majoritarianism2.

21. Roxanne Euben, *Enemy in the Mirror: Islamic Fundamentalism and the Limits of Modern Rationalism* (Princeton University Press, 1999); T. K. Wilson, *Killing Strangers: How Political Violence Became Modern* (Oxford University Press, 2020).

22. Li, "Anti-Primer," 16.

23. "Cops: Stamp Out Radicalism," *The Star Online*, August 21, 2016, https://www.thestar.com.my/news/nation/2016/08/21/cops-stamp-out-radicalism-the-message-from-the-police-on-is-militants-is-chilling-the-threat-to-thi.

24. Interview with Mustaza Abdul Rahman, family member to one of the detainees and activist, July 22, 2019, Kuala Lumpur.

25. "Saya Bekas Ekstremis! (Ep 3—Tiga Sekawan) " [I am a former extremist! Episode 3: Three friends], YouTube, November 23, 2020, https://www.youtube.com/watch?v=TDHHTUXAm7I&list=PL1d-NZ0GhtnsafW1M49LtzgnCZdGq4Yvr&index=4.

26. Ingrid van Biezen, Peter Mair, and Thomas Poguntke, "Going, Going . . . Gone? The Decline of Party Membership in Contemporary Europe," *European Journal of Political Research* 51, no. 1 (2012): 24–56;Tim Bale, Paul Webb, and Monica Poletti, *Footsoldiers: Political Party Membership in the 21st Century* (Routledge, 2020).

27. Darryl Li, *The Universal Enemy: Jihad, Empire, and the Challenge of Solidarity* (Stanford University Press, 2020); Thomas Hegghammer, *Jihad in Saudi Arabia: Violence and Pan-Islamism since 1979* (Cambridge University Press, 2010), chap. 9.

28. Li, "Anti-Primer," 16.

29. See Appendix for a detailed discussion of the sources behind this dataset and the methodology used to classify the occupational classes of the detainees. Jadoon et al. also performed a profiling of Malaysia's IS landscape, but it does not involve an analysis of the occupational status. See Amira Jadoon, Nakissa Jahanbani, Elina Noor, Marley Carroll, and William Frangia, *Risks, Recruits, and Plots: Understanding and Mitigating the Influence of the Islamic State in Malaysia* (Combatting Terrorism Center, US Military Academy, 2022).

30. Hegghammer offers a sophisticated take between the link of economics and terrorism: "*The bottom line for me is that there is enough evidence to take socioeconomics a bit more seriously than we have thus far. We can no longer dismiss it by pointing to*

anecdotes of rich jihadis or evidence from the Middle East. We have [to] get away from the notion that to invoke socioeconomics is somehow exonerating jihadis, or that if socioeconomics matter, then ideology and other factors do not matter. We must also get away from the notion that jihadis need to be destitute for economics to be a credible explanation" (emphasis mine). See Thomas Hegghammer, "Revisiting the Poverty-Terrorism Link in European Jihadism," paper presented at the Society for Terrorism Research Annual Conference, Leiden, November 8, 2016.

31. By occupational classes, I refer to my socioeconomic grouping of occupations (low, medium, high) that is extrapolated from the government's categorization of low-skilled, semiskilled, and high-skilled jobs. How this extrapolation is done is addressed in the Appendix.

32. :"Malaysia Unemployment Rate 1998–2021 Data," Trading Economics, https://tradingeconomics.com/malaysia/unemployment-rate.

33. "School Enrollment, Tertiary (% Gross)—Malaysia," *The World Bank*, https://data.worldbank.org/indicator/SE.TER.ENRR?locations=MY.

34. Olivier Roy, *Globalized Islam: The Search for a New Ummah* (Columbia University Press, 2004)

35. Hew Wai Weng, "Middle Class Competition and Islamic Populism," *New Mandala*, May 25, 2017, https://www.newmandala.org/competitions-among-middle-classes/; Patricia Sloane-White, "The Shifting Status of Middle-Class Malay Girlhood: From 'Sisters' to 'Sinners' in One Generation," in *Girlhood: A Global History*, ed. Jennifer Helgren and Colleen A. Vasconcellos (Rutgers University Press, 2010); Patricia Sloane-White, *Corporate Islam: Sharia and the Modern Workplace* (Cambridge University Press, 2017).

36. For an example of a study that seeks to analytically connect observations of middle-class female religiosity with IS-type violent activism, see Serina Rahman, "Hand that Rocks the Cradle: Nurturing Exclusivist Interpretations of Islam in the Malaysian Home," *Trends in Southeast Asia Issue 2/2020* (ISEAS Yusof- Ishak Institute, 2020).

37. See, for example, some of the pathologies of middle-class majoritarian activism in Malaysia in Nicholas Chan, "'Human Rights . . . but for the Majority': The Appropriation and Subversion of the Human Rights Agenda by Right-Wing NGOs in Malaysia," *Trans-Regional and -National Studies of Southeast Asia* 12, no. 1 (2024): 1–26.

38. Although overlooked by the Eurocentric literature, the weaponization of the phobia rhetoric (using leftist language) by non-Western authoritarian actors against liberal opponents and progressive critics is nothing special, as seen in trends in Türkiye as well as India. See Ihsan Yilmaz and Mustafa Demir, "Manufacturing the Ummah: Turkey's Transnational Populism and Construction of the People Globally," *Third World Quarterly* 44, no. 2 (2022): 320–36; Kira Huju, "How 'Decolonial Hindutva' Marries Nativist Politics with Left-Wing Vocabulary," *Scroll*, April 8, 2024, https://scroll.in/article/1065727/how-decolonial-hindutva-marries-nativist-politics-with-left-wing-vocabulary.

39. Diego Gambetta and Steffen Hertog, *Engineers of Jihad: The Curious Connection Between Violent Extremism and Education* (Princeton University Press, 2016), 60–66; Gary Lafree, Michael Jensen, Patrick James, and Aaron Safer-Lichtenstein, "Correlates of Violent Political Extremism in the United States," *Criminology* 56, no. 2 (2018): 233–68; Michael Jensen, Elizabeth Yates, and Sheehan Kane, "Profiles of Individual Radicalization in the United States (PIRUS)," *START Research Brief* (University of Maryland, 2020).

40. Abdullah bin Khaled Al-Saud, *Saudi Foreign Fighters: Analysis of Leaked Islamic State Entry Documents* (International Centre for the Study of Radicalisation, 2019), 20.

41. Gambetta and Hertog, *Engineers of Jihad*; Richard A. Nielsen, *Deadly Clerics: Blocked Ambition and the Paths to Jihad* (Cambridge University Press, 2017).

42. Institute of Policy Analysis for Conflict, "The Evolution of ISIS in Indonesia," *IPAC Report* no. 13 (2014); Zubair, "Wahhabi's Influence on ISIS Ideology in Indonesia: A Study on Aman Abdurrahman's Theological Thoughts," *Advances in Social Science, Education and Humanities Research* 302 (2018): 79–82. Malaysia had one such figure in Mahmud Ahmad, who was an Islamic studies lecturer and had recruited several Malaysians to join the Maute brother's siege of Marawi in 2017. However, he did not emerge as a leadership figure for the Malaysians who traveled to Syria, or for the cells pledging allegiance to IS within the country. As being a lecturer at a public university is, by all means, a comfortable position of employment, Mahmud's case also contradicts the "blocked ambition" thesis. On Mahmud, see chapter 6, note 37.

43. The same socioeconomic marginality in terms of job status and education level is observed among far-right extremists in the United States, although their mean age of exposure (37.6) is far higher than the IS supporters/militants in Malaysia, who tend to be in their twenties or early thirties. See Jensen et al., "Profiles of Individual Radicalization," 1.

44. Olivier Roy, *Jihad and Death: The Global Appeal of Islamic State* (Oxford University Press, 2017); Olivier Roy, "Who Are the New Jihadis?" *The Guardian*, April 13, 2017, https://www.theguardian.com/news/2017/apr/13/who-are-the-new-jihadis.

45. Roy, *Jihad and Death*, 6, 22, 33.

46. This trio was directly involved in the attack, although the entire Telegram chat group was busted by the police. My examination of the case files suggests that most of those in the chat group were not involved in the attacks, even if some were supportive of it. See *Public Prosecutor v Mustaza Abdul Rahman*, Written Judgment of the Kuala Lumpur High Court, 2017.

47. Rohan Gunaratna, "Commentary: The Life and Death of Wanndy, Malaysia's Top IS Recruiter," *BenarNews*, May 16, 2017, https://www.benarnews.org/english/commentaries/asia-pacific-threat-update/Rohan-Gunaratna-05162017180047.html.

48. Gunaratna, "Commentary."

49. The alleged targets of IS cells in Malaysia, which included a prominent Hindu temple at Batu Caves, entertainment outlets, and a brewery, also mimicked that of Al-Maunah, which had its members attack a Carlsberg brewery and Batu Caves. See Ray Sherman, "Malaysia: IS-Linked Movida Nightclub Attackers Sentenced to 25 Years," *BenarNews*, March 29, 2017, https://www.benarnews.org/english/news/malaysian/movida-sentence-03292017150449.html.

50. Another interesting observation is that neither Wanndy's, Wahyudin's, nor Jonius's name was a conventional Malay-Muslim name. Wanndy's father name, Mohamed Jedi, prompts one to wonder if that is a Star Wars–inspired name. Wanndy's brother, Mohamed Danny Mohamed Jedi, who was charged for terrorism financing for transferring money to him, appears to have also inherited an atypical name that is not religiously inspired. Wahyudin's name suggests Indonesian parentage, while Jonius is likely from one of Sabah's many non-Malay indigenous communities. There is a chance that Wahyudin and Jonius are first- or second-generation immigrants to West Malaysia, meaning that the social alienation they felt as members of the lower rungs of society mirrored, or even exceeded, that of the second-generation radicals in Europe observed by Olivier Roy. See Roy, *Jihad and Death*, 32.

51. This is most likely referring to the eleven years of primary and secondary schooling, which is mandatory for all Malaysians.

52. *Public Prosecutor v Imam Wahyudin bin Karjono and Jonius Ondie @ Jahali*, written judgment by the Kuala Lumpur High Court, 5.

53. Mohamed Nawab Mohamed Osman and Aida Arosoaie, "Jihad in the Bastion of 'Moderation': Understanding the Threat of ISIS in Malaysia," *Asian Security* 16, no. 1 (2020): 7.

54. Nicholas Chan, "From Jemaah Islamiyah to Islamic State in Malaysia," in *Global Jihad in Southeast Asia: Examining the Expansion of the Islamic State and Al-Qaeda*, ed. M. K. Sheikh (Danish Institute of International Studies, 2019), 67–69.

55. For example, almost every sitting parliamentarian in Malaysia has a university education, which is also the case for most civil society activists. By contrast, according to 2020 data, only 35 percent of the Malaysian labor force has a tertiary education, 55 percent having completed secondary education, and the rest having only primary or no education at all. Ironically, the IS dataset I referenced above is more representative of the population than parliament itself.

56. If anything, contemporary Malaysian politics is characterized by a weak, socially marginal, and demonized presence of leftist movements and parties. See Meredith L. Weiss, "Legacies of the Cold War in Malaysia: Anything but Communism," *Journal of Contemporary Asia* 50, no. 4 (2020): 511–29.

57. John T. Sidel, *Riots, Pogroms, and Jihad: Religious Violence in Indonesia* (Cornell University Press, 2006), 16.

58. David Kloos, *Becoming Better Muslims: Religious Authority and Ethical Improvement in Aceh, Indonesia* (Princeton University Press, 2018); Daan Beekers and David

Kloos, eds., *Straying from the Straight Path: How Senses of Failure Invigorate Lived Religion* (Berghahn Books, 2017).

59. In my interviews, it was suggested to me that the police in Malaysia, as in the US, were likely to have resorted to sting operations that may raise concerns of entrapment. See Antony Field, "Ethics and Entrapment: Understanding Counterterrorism Stings," *Terrorism and Political Violence* 31, no. 2 (2019): 260–76.

60. Fatemah Alzubairi, *Colonialism, Neo-Colonialism, and Anti-Terrorism Law in the Arab World* (Cambridge University Press, 2019); Arjun Appadurai, *Fear of Small Numbers: An Essay on the Geography of Anger* (Duke University Press, 2006); Caterina Kinnvall, *Globalization and Religious Nationalism in India: The Search for Ontological Security* (Routledge, 2006); Stanley Jeyaraja Tambiah, *Buddhism Betrayed?: Religion, Politics, and Violence in Sri Lanka* (University of Chicago Press, 1992).

61. Iza Hussin, *The Politics of Islamic Law: Local Elites, Colonial Authority, and the Making of the Muslim State* (University of Chicago Press, 2016); Tamir Moustafa, *Constituting Religion: Islam, Liberal Rights, and the Malaysian State* (Cambridge University Press, 2018).

62. Ayşe Zarakol, ed., *Hierarchies in World Politics* (Cambridge University Press, 2017).

63. S. Sayyid, *A Fundamental Fear: Eurocentrism and the Emergence of Islamism* (Zed Books, 1997); Ahmet T. Kuru, *Secularism and State Policies Toward Religion: The United States, France, and Turkey* (Cambridge University Press, 2009).

64. Ayşe Zarakol, *After Defeat: How the East Learned to Live with the West* (Cambridge University Press, 2011).

65. Mandaville and Hamid, "Islam as Statecraft,"; Ahmad Rizky Mardhatillah Umar, "A Genealogy of Moderate Islam: Governmentality and Discourses of Islam in Indonesia's Foreign Policy," *Studia Islamika* 23, no. 3 (2016): 399–433; Ahmet Erdi Ozturk, "Islam and Foreign Policy: Turkey's Ambivalent Religious Soft Power in the Authoritarian Turn," *Religions* 12, no. 1 (2021): 38, https://doi.org/10.3390/rel12010038.

66. Ayşe Zarakol, "Theorising Hierarchies: An Introduction," in *Hierarchies in World Politics*, ed. Ayşe Zarakol (Cambridge University Press, 2017), 1–14; John M. Hobson and J. C. Sharman, "The Enduring Place of Hierarchy in World Politics: Tracing the Social Logics of Hierarchy and Political Change," *European Journal of International Relations* 11, no. 1 (2005): 63–98; Jelena Subotic and Srdjan Vucetic, "Performing Solidarity: Whiteness and Status-Seeking in the Non-Aligned World," *Journal of International Relations and Development* 22, no. 3 (2017): 722–43.

67. There are long utterings of such cultural dominance eroding, of course, especially under the nativist stewardship of the Trump administration. See Robert O. Keohane and Joseph S. Nye Jr., "The End of the Long American Century: Trump and the Sources of U.S. Power," *Foreign Affairs* 104, no. 4 (2025): 68–79.

68. Maznah Mohamad, *The Divine Bureaucracy and Disenchantment of Social Life: A Study of Bureaucratic Islam in Malaysia* (Palgrave Macmillan, 2020); Joseph

Chinyong Liow, *Piety and Politics: Islamism in Contemporary Malaysia* (Oxford University Press, 2009); Ahmad Fauzi Abdul Hamid, "Religious Diversity in Malaysia: Between Islamic Orthodoxy, Unorthodoxy and Deviancy," in *Islam and Peacebuilding in the Asia-Pacific*, ed. Mohamed Nawab Mohamed Osman (World Scientific, 2018), 179–211.

69. Luca Mavelli, "Between Normalisation and Exception: The Securitisation of Islam and the Construction of the Secular Subject," *Millennium: Journal of International Studies* 41, no. 2 (2013): 163. On India and China, see, for example, Sheena Chestnut Greitens, Myunghee Lee, and Emir Yazici, "Counterterrorism and Preventive Repression: China's Changing Strategy in Xinjiang," *International Security* 44, no. 3 (2020): 9–47; Eviane Leidig, "Hindutva as a Variant of Right-Wing Extremism," *Patterns of Prejudice* 54, no. 3 (2020): 215–37.

70. Kuru, *Secularism*; Alzubairi, *Colonialism*; Robert W. Hefner, *Civil Islam: Muslims and Democratization in Indonesia* (Princeton University Press, 2000).

71. Tobias Müller, "Engaging 'Moderates' Against 'Extremists' in German Politics on Islam," *The Review of Faith & International Affairs* 15, no. 2 (2017): 64.

72. Carsten Bagge Laustsen and Ole Wæver, "In Defence of Religion: Sacred Referent Objects for Securitization," *Millennium: Journal of International Studies* 29, no. 3 (2000): 708.

73. Laustsen and Wæver, "In Defence of Religion," 726.

74. Speech by Mahathir Mohamad at the opening of the Third International Seminar on Islamic Thoughts, Asia Pacific Development Centre, Kuala Lumpur, July 26, 1984.

75. On how religion's securitization can be conceptualized through religion's multiple dimensions and/or its doctrines, see Mona Kanwal Sheikh, "Religious Challenge to Securitisation Theory," *Millennium: Journal of International Studies* 43, no. 1 (2014): 252–72.

76. Rohan Mukherjee, *Ascending Order: Rising Powers and the Politics of Status in International Institutions* (Cambridge University Press, 2022); Steven Ward, *Status and the Challenge of Rising Powers* (Cambridge University Press, 2017); Michelle Murray, *The Struggle for Recognition in International Relations: Status, Revisionism, and Rising Powers* (Oxford University Press, 2019).

77. Coral Davenport and Eric Lipton, "How G.O.P. Leaders Came to View Climate Change as Fake Science," *The New York Times*, June 3, 2017, https://www.nytimes.com/2017/06/03/us/politics/republican-leaders-climate-change.html.

78. Human Rights Watch, "China: Muslim-Majority States Whitewash Abuses," *Human Rights Watch*, July 17, 2019, https://www.hrw.org/news/2019/07/17/china-muslim-majority-states-whitewash-abuses.

79. Greg Barton, Ihsan Yilmaz, and Nicholas Morieson, "Religious and Pro-Violence Populism in Indonesia: The Rise and Fall of a Far-Right Islamist Civilisationist Movement," *Religions* 12, no. 6 (2021): 397, https://doi.org/10.3390/rel12060397; Ahmet

T. Kuru, "Secularism, Islamism, and the Future of Turkey," *Journal of Democracy* 36, no. 3 (2025): 92–105.

80. Zarakol, *After Defeat*: Andrew Linklater, "The 'Standard of Civilisation' in World Politics," *Human Figurations* 5, no. 2 (2016), http://hdl.handle.net/2027/spo.11217607.0005.205.

81. Damian Radcliffe, "Egypt's Building a New Capital: Inside the Smart City in the Desert," *ZDNET*, January 28, 2020, https://www.zdnet.com/article/egypts-building-a-new-capital-inside-the-smart-city-in-the-desert/; Damian Radcliffe, "Guide to Smart Cities in the Arabian Gulf: Why This Is a Region to Watch," *ZDNET*, September 18, 2017, https://www.zdnet.com/article/guide-to-smart-cities-in-the-arabian-gulf-why-this-is-a-region-to-watch/.

82. Justin Scheck, Rory Jones, and Summer Said, "A Prince's $500 Billion Desert Dream: Flying Cars, Robot Dinosaurs and a Giant Artificial Moon," *The Wall Street Journal*, July 25, 2019, https://www.wsj.com/articles/a-princes-500-billion-desert-dream-flying-cars-robot-dinosaurs-and-a-giant-artificial-moon-11564097568.

83. Calvert Jones, *Bedouins Into Bourgeois: Remaking Citizens for Globalization* (Cambridge University Press, 2017), 69, 120.

84. The Middle Eastern and North African (MENA) region, despite all the attention it received, is by no means the only region that faced the brunt of Islamist militancy. According to this source, between 2013 and 2019, the five countries most affected by Islamist terrorism are Afghanistan, Iraq, Somalia, Nigeria, and Syria (in that order). See "Islamist Terrorist Attacks in the World 1979–2019," Fondation pour l'innovation politique, November 2019, https://www.fondapol.org/app/uploads/2020/06/enquete-terrorisme-gb-2019-11-18versionfinale-3.pdf, 24.

85. "Neom," e-flux Directory, https://www.e-flux.com/directory/533851/neom.

86. Muhizam Mustafa, "Public Art in the Federal Territory of Putrajaya: Questions of Value and Role," *Wacana Seni: Journal of Arts Discourse* 8 (2009): 73.

Appendix

1. *Jusninawati Abdul Ghani v Public Prosecutor*, Written Judgment of the Court of Appeal, July 31, 2018, 2.

2. The category of "security forces" is separated out because unless the rank of the accused is given, it is difficult to ascertain their income. My observation is that most of them should belong to either the low or medium socioeconomic grouping. The police officer I mentioned above was only a corporal, one of the lowest ranks within the police. Another high-profile case involving a police officer concerns a lance corporal, which is one rank lower than corporal. So far, I have not come across anyone accused of terrorism offences in the security forces that can be considered as high ranking (inspector and above for the police). See "'Lance Corporal' Charged with Three Counts of Terror-Related Activities," *New Straits Times*, December 9, 2016, https://www.nst.com.my/news/2016/12/195698/lance-corporal-charged-three-counts-terror-related-activities.

3. I use the year 2016 as my point of reference as most of these individuals were active between 2013 to 2018, making 2016 a good median point for reference. All data on salaries is based on the *Salaries & Wages Survey Report 2016* released by the Department of Statistics of Malaysia (DOSM). See Department of Statistics Malaysia (DOSM), *Salaries & Wages Survey Report 2016* (Department of Statistics Malaysia, 2017).

4. DOSM, *Salaries*, 17.

Index

Papier | Fördert gute Waldnutzung
FSC® C083411

Zeitfracht Medien GmbH
Ferdinand-Jühlke-Straße 7
99095 Erfurt, Deutschland
produktsicherheit@kolibri360.de